Fundamentals of
Public Relations

Fundamentals of Public Relations

Professional Guidelines,
Concepts and Integrations

Second Edition

Lawrence W. Nolte, APR
Public Relations Consultant
San Francisco, California

Consulting Editor
Dennis L. Wilcox Ph.D., APR
Coordinator, PR Degree Program
Department of Journalism and Advertising
San Jose State University

EMERSON COLLEGE LIBRARY

EMERSON COLLEGE LIBRARY

Pergamon Press
New York Oxford Toronto Sydney Frankfurt Paris

Pergamon Press Offices:

U.S.A.   Pergamon Press Inc., Maxwell House, Fairview Park,
                        Elmsford, New York 10523, U.S.A.

U.K.   Pergamon Press Ltd., Headington Hill Hall,
                        Oxford OX3 0BW, England

CANADA   Pergamon of Canada, Ltd., 150 Consumers Road,
                        Willowdale, Ontario M2J 1P9, Canada

AUSTRALIA   Pergamon Press (Aust) Pty. Ltd., P O Box 544,
                        Potts Point, NSW 2011, Australia

FRANCE   Pergamon Press SARL, 24 rue des Ecoles,
                        75240 Paris, Cedex 05, France

FEDERAL REPUBLIC   Pergamon Press GmbH, 6242 Kronberg/Taunus,
OF GERMANY   Pferdstrasse 1, Federal Republic of Germany

Copyright © 1979 Pergamon Press Inc.

Library of Congress Cataloging in Publication Data

Nolte, Lawrence W.
    Fundamentals of Public Relations, Second Edition

    1. Public relations. I. Title.
HM263.N64 1974   659.2   79-156902
ISBN 0-08-022470-9

*All Rights reserved. No part of this publication may be reproduced,
stored in a retrieval system or transmitted in any form or by any means:
electronic, electrostatic, magnetic tape, mechanical, photocopying,
recording or otherwise, without permission in writing from the
publishers.*

*Printed in the United States of America
Second Printing 1980*

"PUBLIC SENTIMENT is everything . . .
With public sentiment nothing can fail;
Without it, nothing can succeed.
He who moulds public sentiment
goes deeper than he who executes
statutes or pronounces decisions.
He makes statutes or decisions
possible or impossible to execute."

ABRAHAM LINCOLN

About the Author

Lawrence W. Nolte is a San Francisco public relations consultant who is both a practitioner and a teacher. His background has enabled Mr. Nolte to present in this book a unique combination of theory and practice — a synthesis of academic and commercial viewpoints.

As a practitioner Mr. Nolte has had more than 30 years of experience in a wide variety of public relations activities. Among the organizations he has served are: the American Dry Milk Institute, Batten, Barton, Durstine & Osborn, California Canners & Growers, California Milk Producers Advisory Board, Carnation Company, Cling Peach Advisory Board, Cunningham & Walsh, Daniel J. Edelman, Inc., Johns-Manville, National Federation of Independent Business, Pendleton Woolen Mills, and White King Soap Co.

As a teacher he has served on the faculties of Northwestern University and College of San Mateo. He has also been a guest lecturer at many colleges and universities.

He is an accredited member (APR) of the Public Relations Society of America and serves on its national task force on Continuing Education. In the San Francisco Bay Area Chapter he has been a member of the board of directors, delegate to the national assembly, and chairman of the education committee.

Contents

Every major topic in the book is identified by a **PRIMARY** subhead which is indexed here by page number. Within the book secondary and tertiary topics are identified by **Secondary** and *Tertiary* subheads. Using this index enables the reader to find almost any topic rapidly, and with a minimum of confusion.

Contents

Foreword

Since the first edition of this book was published there have been many changes in the field of public relations and in the problems which it must help to solve. Accordingly there are substantial changes in this edition.

Among the most important are a new way of describing how public relations functions in adapting an organization to its social, political, and economic environment and a comprehensive review of that environment as it exists at the present time.

There are five new dialogues which emphasize critical problems affecting the practice of public relations. One covers the role of the chief executive officer in public relations. Another deals with corporate social responsibility. A third shows the attitudes of labor on the question of jobs versus the environment. A fourth reports on current problems of protecting the environment. The fifth takes a searching look at the energy crisis.

Major changes will be found in the chapters dealing with public opinion, employees, owners, customers, educators, government, outbound communication, house organs, annual reports, and publicity. All other chapters are improved, updated, and in some cases expanded to include important new material. In total, over a third of this edition is completely new. As may be expected, suggested readings list numerous new references. On the other hand, some references of substantial age are still given because nothing better or newer has been found. And some references are so significant that they are really ageless. One example of the latter is *Silent Spring,* which was published in 1962 and is still noteworthy as the book which ignited the fires of environmental concern.

Despite changes, the basic objectives of this book remain the same. The first is to show the function of public relations in our social, political, and economic environment. The second is to explain the basic theories and principles involved in the practice of public relations. The third is to supply the practical information needed to implement public relations activities.

This book is designed to serve as a basic text for college classes in public relations. The exercises are planned for use in oral questions or in written papers. (Answers and interpretations will be found in the instructor's manual, which is available to any teacher of public relations.) It can also serve as a guide to those who are not students, but who are in need of a refresher or even an introduction to the subject of public relations. In spite of the growing numbers who study public relations in college there are still many people who are given responsibilities in this area without adequate academic preparation. There are also many specialists who might gain greater professional breadth through reading this book.

In writing *Fundamentals of Public Relations*, one of the biggest problems has been deciding what to include and what to omit. If all of the desirable information were included this book could run to 30 volumes instead of 30 chapters. So, to keep it down to a reasonable size, it has been necessary to cut, condense, and trim wherever possible.

Some books in this field give considerable attention to public relations for specific types of organizations. We find books, chapters, or substantial segments dealing with large business, small business, health care, associations, police, schools, and so on. That treatment has been deliberately avoided here for two reasons. First, it is highly repetitious. Second, many years of personal experience with large and small, public and private, commercial and noncommercial organizations have led me to conclude that the practice of public relations is essentially the same in all organizations. The problems may be different, but they are all solved in the same way. This conclusion is confirmed by the ease and frequency with which public relations practitioners move between organizations. It is further confirmed by the organizational structure of counseling firms. They are organized to solve certain kinds of problems, not to fit certain kinds of clients.

Public relations is becoming more professional. Those in the field who cherish this concept are trying to advance the quality of work done by all practitioners. It is hoped that this book will contribute to the attainment of that goal.

Acknowledgments

This second edition has been changed significantly from the first edition of this book. Making these changes has been materially aided by many people who have contributed ideas and materials. To all these contributors I am most grateful. Specifically, I want to thank:

The numerous reviewers who, by their comments on the first edition, have instigated a number of significant improvements.

The five men who participated in the dialogues: James F. Langton, APR — *Bank of America*, John M. Black, Jr. — *Pacific Telephone & Telegraph Co.*, John F. Henning — *California Labor Federation AFL-CIO*, Michael McCloskey — *The Sierra Club*, and Jon B. Riffel — *Southern California Gas Co.*

Those who provided information and exhibits: Ernest L. Arms — *Sears Roebuck & Co.*, Leone Baxter — *Whitaker & Baxter, International*, William Braznell — *Del Monte Corporation*, George Cozard — *Pacific Gas & Electric Co.*, Richard Farana — *National Federation of Independent Business*, Denny Griswold — *Public Relations News*, R.V. Guelich — *Montgomery Ward & Co.*, Dr. Earl Jandron — *San Jose State University*, Bruce Johnson — *Pacific Gas & Electric Co.*, Arnold Lerner — *International Business Machines Corp.*, Richard L. McGrath — *Chevron USA, Inc.*, Ralph Miller — *Pacific Gas & Electric Co.*, Henry Ortiz — *Southern Pacific Co.*, James C. Schwaninger — *J. C. Penney Co.*, Elena Smith — *General Foods Corporation*, Ronald Thompson — *Associated Press*, and F. Bryan Williams, APR — *Public Relations Society of America*.

Some very special thanks go to Dr. Rex F. Harlow, APR, not only for permission to quote his comprehensive definition of public relations, but also for his detailed evaluation of the first edition. His comments have been most helpful.

Finally, and most important, is an expression of gratitude to the Consulting Editor, Dr. Dennis L. Wilcox, APR. Dr. Wilcox's contribution includes a very comprehensive critique of the first edition, many suggestions for upgrading and professionalizing the content of the book, and active involvement in the planning of this edition. In addition, he has supplied much of the new material, has participated in numerous conferences as the work progressed, and has read and reread every word. If this edition is materially better than the first edition — and I think that it is — a large share of the credit should go to Dr. Wilcox.

LAWRENCE W. NOLTE

I
The Nature of Public Relations

Public relations is a familiar but often misunderstood subject. Few people can define it and even the dictionaries disagree materially as to the meaning of these two words, beyond a general acceptance of the idea that public relations means activity that affects public opinion.

Public relations is as old as civilization and as new as tomorrow's newspaper. Its utilization has increased constantly. At first, its use was spasmodic and infrequent but, as population grew and means of communication improved, efforts to influence public opinion also grew. With this growth has come increased skill and increased awareness of the importance of good public relations.

Today it is not possible to function in our complex and crowded society without attention to public relations. Appreciation of this fact is almost universal. The time and money expended on improving relations with the public are ample proof that a public relations program is a necessity, not a luxury.

The ensuing four chapters will tell what public relations means, highlight its history, and show why it is so important.

Definitions | 1

Most people are familiar with the words public relations, but few can agree on their meaning. In simplest terms, these words mean "relations with the public," but that is still confusing because the words are used to describe both a condition and an activity.

PUBLIC RELATIONS AS A CONDITION

When describing the condition, we can say that an organization has good public relations. By this we mean that public attitudes toward, and opinions about, the organization are favorable. Conversely, we can say that an organization has bad public relations. By this we mean that public attitudes toward and opinions about the organization are unfavorable.

The public opinion polls of Gallup, Harris, etc. that are periodically reported in newspapers are a measurement of the public relations of the institutions that are the polls' subjects. We can read that the public has much, some, little, or no confidence in politicians, doctors, lawyers, used-car salesmen, television, newspapers, and so on. If the public has little or no confidence in an institution we can be sure that its public relations are poor. If confidence is high we can be certain that its public relations are good.

Most people don't think much about, or talk about, public relations as a *condition*. They do think and talk about the *activity*, and that is what this book is about — the *activity* called public relations.

PUBLIC RELATIONS AS AN ACTIVITY

When we talk about public relations as an activity, we mean an activity whose purpose is to affect the attitudes and opinions of the public. This activity may take many forms.

We see television commercials which explain that there is only two cents of profit in a gallon of gasoline. We read advertisements urging us to save energy. We read news items reporting on the speeches of labor leaders urging Congress to save American jobs by restricting imports of foreign goods. We read statements by conservationists opposing offshore oil drilling. We read about or see people demonstrating against a nuclear power plant. All these ads, speeches, statements, and demonstrations are designed to affect public attitudes and opinions. All are public relations activities. There is much ignorance about these activities. It is based to a considerable degree on misconceptions.

MISCONCEPTIONS ABOUT PUBLIC RELATIONS

One of the most common misconceptions is to think that public relations means propaganda. If we used the word propaganda in its denotive sense of distributing information about one's views and beliefs, there could be some tie-in. The word is used that way in Europe. In the United States we commonly use the word propaganda in its connotative sense, which implies the manipulation of minds by shady characters who make people believe what isn't so. Public relations is not an effort to make people believe what is not true.

Propagandists use several techniques to accomplish their purposes, techniques which are anathema to honest public relations practitioners. Among the techniques of propaganda are:

the "Big Lie" — distortion of truth, exaggeration and omission of facts,

appeal to prejudice — stating an issue so that it appeals to bias,

name calling — applying unfavorable names to issues or people,

association — tying opponents to others without justification,

provocation — causing emotional response by outrageous action,

delaying — stalling action while pretending to support it,

card stacking — presenting only favorable facts,

straw men — setting up phony arguments on behalf of opponents,

red herrings — creating diversions to confuse the issue.

"...and you call yourself a public relations man!"

Fig. 1.1

To repeat: these are *not* public relations.

A second, and widely believed, misconception is that public relations means publicity, that it consists solely of getting items or stories into news media. A third activity which is often confused with public relations is press agentry. This is a variety of publicity devoted almost entirely to the world of entertainment. Many a press agent uses the words public relations to describe his activities, but this is a misuse.

A fourth activity which is often described as public relations is lobbying — the systematic and continuing contacts made with governmental bodies in order to procure favorable laws and regulations or to block unfavorable laws and regulations. A fifth misconception is the personification of public relations as an individual — a personable, fast-talking man or woman who has connections in the right places and the ability to fix almost anything by pulling strings.

Among these misconceptions there are a few facts. Public relations people do use publicity as a channel of communication, they may be involved in lobbying at some times, and many of them are personable and do have friends.

At this point it is in order to answer a question which is often asked by students. The question is "What is the difference between advertising and public relations?" The question should really be: "What is the difference between advertising and publicity?" The answer is "Both are channels of mass communication. Advertising is paid for, publicity is free. With advertising the sponsor controls every word that is said, he decides where it is to go and how much there will be. With publicity there is no control of the words or the distribution or the amount.

This question undoubtedly arises from confusion about the nature of public relations and the misconception that it is only publicity. To put this into better perspective, it should be remembered that "Public relations tries to promote favorable opinion about an organization and its policies. Among the communication channels used are advertising and publicity. Marketing tries to promote sales of products and services. Among the communication channels used are advertising and publicity."

DEFINING PUBLIC RELATIONS

Now that some of the misconceptions have been eliminated, it is timely to state what public relations really is. This is not an easy task because public relations is not easy to define. Many people have tried. Some early practitioners, notably E. L. Bernays, defined it as "the engineering of consent" or "social engineering," but social scientists have since found that opinions can't be engineered. Another definition is "PR means performance plus recognition." Still another is "managing reputation." Most of these statements are not really definitions in the dictionary sense.

Dictionary Definition

Unfortunately, dictionaries do not help much because they define the term narrowly. Webster says public relations means:

1. The promotion of rapport and goodwill between a person, firm, or institution and other persons, special publics, or the community at large through the distribution of interpretative material, the development of neighborly interchange, and the assessment of public reaction.

2. The degree of understanding and goodwill achieved between an individual, organization, or institution and the public.
3. The art or science of developing reciprocal understanding and goodwill.*

Number 1 describes an activity but it overlooks the possibility that an organization could have a policy which would completely destroy any rapport and goodwill. Number 2 describes a condition but it does not recognize the fact that there may be no understanding and that the "will" may all be "ill." Number 3 describes an occupation but it is so vague that it does not begin to explain what it involves.

When we turn to other sources, we find some definitions that come closer to describing this very complex subject.

Robinson Definition

E. J. Robinson (1966) says:

Public relations as an applied social and behavioral science is that function which:
1. measures, evaluates and interprets the attitudes of the various relevant publics.
2. assists management in defining objectives for increasing public understanding and acceptance of the organization's products, plans, policies and personnel.
3. equates these objectives with the interests, needs and goals of the various relevant publics, and
4. develops, executes and evaluates a program to earn public understanding and acceptance.

PR News Definition

Public Relations News says:

Public relations is the management function which evaluates public attitudes, identifies the policies and procedures of an individual or an organization with the public interest and plans and executes a program of action to earn public understanding and acceptance.

Harlow Definition

Dr. Rex F. Harlow, APR, Professor Emeritus of Stanford University and a pioneer in public relations education, spent many months developing the following definition. The study was made possible by a grant from the Foundation for Public Relations Research and Education. It is the most comprehensive definition available. The definition is printed here

*From *Webster's Third New International Dictionary* © 1966 by G. & C. Merriam Co., Publishers of the Merriam-Webster Dictionaries. By permission.

with the permission of Dr. Harlow. (For details on the study, see *Public Relations Review*, Winter 1976 and Spring 1977.)

A Working Definition

Public relations is a distinctive management function which helps establish and maintain mutual lines of communication, understanding, acceptance and cooperation between an organization and its publics; involves the management of problems or issues; helps management to keep informed on and responsive to public opinion; defines and emphasizes the responsibility of management to serve the public interest; helps management keep abreast of and effectively utilize change, serving as an early warning system to help anticipate trends; and uses research and sound and ethical communication techniques as its principal tools.

A Description-Definition

1. Public relations is a specialized body of knowledge, skills and methods.

2. It is a management function which deals with the relations between two or more organizations or publics, both national and international, producing the kind of relations desired or used by those organizations or publics.

3. Public relations activities are carried on by practitioners, who serve many types of organizations and publics, such as business, government, finance, labor, education, scientific, trade and professional organizations, special interest groups, racial and sex groups, customers, stockholders, employees, suppliers, opinion leaders, cultural groups and others.

4. The public relations practitioner, seeking to serve the public interest, is aware of the influence of public opinion on decision-making and decisions, and counsels and communicates in the following ways:

a) Serves as a two-way conduit between an organization and the public.

b) Makes an effort to project not only what the organization is but also what it has been and is becoming, by interpreting it to the public in terms that people can understand and interpreting the public to members of the organization in terms they can understand.

c) Researches the organization's relations needs, as well as the attitudes held by its publics, recommends a policy and a program to meet them, and measures the effectiveness of the policy and program.

d) Seeks to build and maintain favorable recognition of the organization by establishing an interchange of information between the organization and its publics on the social, political, economic and other important forces in our society, depending on feedback from the public for guidance.

e) Suggests adjustment of the organization's behavior to meet the social, political and economic responsibility and the needs created by shifting human standards and attitudes, as research indicates.

f) Strives to anticipate and correct false impressions and respond appropriately to criticisms of the organization.

g) Sees that meaningful relations are maintained with the government and that legislation and regulations affecting the organization are reported to management and suggestions are made for dealing with them.

h) Conducts research on the public's attitudes, especially of audiences that are important to the organization, and informs management of the attitudes found.

i) Tries to help the organization demonstrate a keen sense of social responsibility along with profit responsibility.

j) Assists members of the organization to speak clearly and forthrightly in all public contacts when presenting facts and viewpoints.

k) Helps management read the signs of the times correctly, apply them construc-
tively, and think in terms of change.

l) Uses as important tools public opinion and other forms of research, the principles, methods and research findings of the social sciences, visual, written and spoken
presentations in the press, the radio, TV and film tape.

m) Serves as a part of management, either as an internal staff member or officer or
as an external professional counselor or consultant.

World Assembly Definition

The World Assembly of Public Relations Associations has adopted this
definition:

"Public relations practice is the art and social science of analyzing trends, predicting
their consequences, counseling organization leaders, and implementing planned
programs of action which will serve both the organizations' and the public interest."

The preceding definitions cover many points, but thorough study will
reveal the fact that there is a common thread running through them.
Each definition includes these basic ideas:

1. *Planning* — public relations is organized and directed toward
   specific objectives.
2. *Social responsibility* — public relations is not self-centered.
3. *Two-way communication* — public relations involves listening as
   well as talking.
4. *Honesty* — there must be no deceit.
5. *Performance* — the organization must earn public approval by its
   policies and actions.

THE ECOLOGICAL CONCEPT OF PUBLIC RELATIONS

During recent years we have heard much about ecology — the relationships of organisms to their environment. In simple terms ecology means
what the environment does to an organism and what the organism does to
its environment. A deer, for example, is at the mercy of its environment.
It lives if the environment is favorable. It dies if the environment is
unfavorable. The deer cannot alter the environment in its own interest.

Primitive man was largely at the mercy of the environment. He, too,
lived if the environment was favorable and died if it was unfavorable. But
there was a difference between the deer and the man. Man learned how to
alter the environment in his own interest, and he has been doing it ever

since he first rolled rocks in front of the entrance to his cave in order to exclude predatory animals.

For thousands of years, we have altered and abused the environment without any thought of the future and with an impact so great that some people fear an ultimate catastrophe which might put a few survivors back into the caves where it all started.

Fortunately we are becoming aware of the problem and there is hope that we can attain a balance between our desires and the limitations of our planet. Instead of continuing to alter the environment to fit our needs, we are now trying to alter our needs to fit the environment. We are at last thinking in terms of ecology.

The physical environment is indeed important, but there is another environment which is also important, especially to those in public relations. That is the social, political, and economic environment. Every organization is affected by this environment and every organization has some effect on it. Perhaps we should go further and say "every person," but since most public relations activity involves organizations we shall talk in terms of groups rather than individuals.

During the early years of public relations most attention was given to modifying the social, political, and economic environment in the interests of the organizations in that environment. Practitioners concentrated their efforts on the public and paid relatively little attention to the organizations for which they were trying to build public favor. In other words they tried to adapt the environment to the organization.

All that has changed. No longer can a public relations program be based entirely on adapting the environment to the organization. Now it must give equal attention to adapting the organization to the environment. Under this ecological concept we might say:

> Public relations is the management function which adapts an organization to its social, political, and economic environment and which adapts that environment to the organization, for the benefit of both.

This implies two types of activity. First, the public relations practitioner must persuade management to do the things to the organization that will make it worthy of public approval. Second, the public relations practitioner must convince the public that the organization deserves its approval.

Here is a theoretical example of how this works. Factory X has polluted the air for many years. The public hates Factory X. In response to this hostile environment, the public relations department persuades the management of Factory X to install a smoke scrubber. This greatly reduces air pollution. This is adapting the organization to its environment. Then Factory X, through its public relations department, informs the public that it is no longer polluting the air. Public opinion about Factory X is greatly improved. This is adapting the environment to the organization.

There could be other possible outcomes in this sort of case. Management might refuse to believe that pollution is a problem. Management might agree that it is a problem but decide to live with public disapproval. Management might direct the public relations department to try to convince the public that the pollution is unimportant. Management might direct the public relations department to tell the public that it can't afford to stop the smoke — that if forced to stop the pollution, it will have to close the factory. These alternate solutions aren't very satisfactory, but they do occur.

A real example of the ecological concept in action is a problem of one of our largest companies. General Foods uses certain additives in the products it makes. Some consumer groups are hostile to additives. In response to this attitude, General Foods has discontinued the use of some additives which were once approved by the Food and Drug Administration but are now questioned by some authorities. This is adapting the organization to the environment.

But there are other additives which are harmless and which General Foods considers necessary and desirable. General Foods uses advertising, booklets, and other materials to tell the public why the additives are necessary and desirable. This is adapting the environment to the organization. The effort seems to be successful. It is improving public opinion about additives in general and General Foods in particular.

POLICY

As the practice of public relations devotes more and more attention to adapting the organization to its social, political, and economic environment the policies of the organization become ever more important. Policy is determined by management. In a public relations context, it can have three meanings:

1. What management does (or does not do) without consideration of

the public. This is often the result of ignorance or inertia. "We've always done it" or "We never thought it was important" are typical excuses. Obviously there has been no public relations input in situations of this sort.

2. What management decides to do (or not to do) after consideration of possible public reaction. This usually reflects input from public relations people.

3. A definite publicized statement as to what management will do (or not do). This is often written by public relations people.

Participation of public relations practitioners in policy determination has grown materially in recent years. At one time only the most prestigious practitioners dared to make suggestions regarding organization policies. As time went on it became customary for the practitioner to advise management and to make recommendations.

Today many public relations directors and counselors actively partici-pate in policy decisions. It seems reasonable to state that no organization should make a policy decision affecting any of its publics without the concurrence of public relations professionals.

Public relations policies must be made known to the public and to the organization involved. The actual form that statements of these policies may take is quite variable. A policy may be contained in one statement or several. General Foods uses a booklet that has two sections: the "Creed" of General Foods and "Basic Policies" concerning various publics. Follow-ing is an extract from the "Creed":

We must strive — through sound, progressive management — to discharge our obligation to our stockholders by increasing the long-term value of their investment.

Our operations must be based on faith in our employees and the courage to give them heavy responsibility and commensurate support. In so doing, we must foster consultative management, which solicits and considers employees' views on matters affecting their jobs and leads to job satisfaction. Our organization must be efficient and purposeful. We must provide appropriate incentives and rewards for demonstra-tive ability, initiative, and results.

We must build and maintain consumers' confidence by providing products and services of consistent quality and recognized value. We must also earn their respect for our brands as leaders in the marketplace.

We must earn and hold customer respect by being honest and dependable in all our dealings, and by adhering to firm, fair, consistent trade policies.

We must demonstrate responsible corporate citizenship by our active, knowledge-able participation in local, state and national affairs. We do this to contribute to the continued strength of a free society and the promise of better living which it holds.

We must be actively dissatisfied with every General Foods product and service in the firm belief that better ones can be developed. We must be equally dissatisfied with our methods, processes and practices, with the stubborn conviction that there is a better way to do practically everything we are doing.

ACTION

What the organization really does is just as important as policy. A policy may be excellent, but if it is not supported it will fail. If a firm says, "We are an equal opportunity employer," but never hires people from the minorities its inaction destroys the value of the policy. Worse, this leads to complete mistrust. Public opinion polls repeatedly point out the problems created by lack of public confidence. It is imperative that an organization live up to what it says about itself.

UNPLANNED ACTIONS

Public opinion can be materially affected by an individual who is not classed as a public relations specialist. Sometime in the nineteenth century, someone told Commodore Vanderbilt, the head of the New York Central Railroad, that he should consider the public. Vanderbilt is credited with the rejoinder: "The public be damned."

Ford cars were all black for years after other manufacturers were offering a choice of colors. To a suggestion that he should offer a similar choice, Henry Ford replied, "They can have any color they want as long as it's black." Needless to say, this was widely quoted and undoubtedly helped Ford's competition.

In the spring of 1968, George Romney was a candidate for the Republican presidential nomination, and a "dove." In trying to explain why he had been so "hawkish" after a trip to Vietnam, he stated that he had been "brainwashed" by the Army. That one word killed his campaign.

These words and phrases were clear; they were pungent; they had a profound effect on public opinion. *And, whether good or bad, they were remembered.*

THE PUBLIC RELATIONS FIELD

If you will look in the Yellow Pages of the telephone directory of any major city, you will find a sizable number of listings under the heading of

13

public relations. Most of them undoubtedly do work in the field, but there is a considerable difference in the way they work. Some are press agents, some are product publicists, some are journeymen, some are fund raisers, some are political election specialists, some are specialists in financial problems, some are public relations counselors.

Many of these specialists are engaged in press agentry. Their job is to publicize individuals, to make their names, faces, or bodies known to the public. They also publicize entertainment events.

Others are in the area of product publicity. Their job is to make the public aware of a product or service and to make them want to buy that product or service. This activity might well be classed as a function of marketing because its purpose is to sell a specific item, but it is generally listed as a PR activity.

Still others perform various functions on an "as-ordered" basis. They publish house organs, prepare publicity, write speeches, booklets or reports. These are the journeymen — they know how to use tools and will apply their skills at the direction of the individual or organization employing them.

The fund raisers are experts in getting financial contributions for organizations.

The political specialists work on election campaigns and, in some cases, plan the entire campaign — even deciding what their candidate will say and where and when he will say it.

The financial specialists work on mergers, on proxy fights, and on problems with the financial community.

Finally, there is a group of people who can and do perform the complete public relations function. They collect and interpret facts, they analyze problems, they recommend PR policy, and they conduct public relations programs. They prepare plans, they execute plans through use of public relations tools and techniques, and they evaluate the results. These are "public relations professionals" in the best sense of the words.

All of these people are independent operators, but they don't comprise the whole field. Many more public relations people work for business, for government agencies, for nonprofit organizations.

EXERCISES

1. Ask three people (separately) to define "public relations."
   (a) How do their definitions compare with those in the text?
   (b) Do they indicate a general understanding of the term?

2. From current news, find examples of policies affecting public opinion
   (a) favorably,
   (b) unfavorably.
3. Are these policies the result of
   (a) action?
   (b) inaction?
4. From current news, find items affecting public opinion which give to the same or different subjects
   (a) highly favorable treatment,
   (b) highly unfavorable treatment.

The Function of Public Relations

2

For many years, political, economic, social, and management decisions were made with "tunnel vision." Problems were solved without consideration of the effect that the solution would have on the total system. Often, the solution was good for the immediate problem but created additional and larger problems by its success.

SYSTEMS

The Aswan Dam in Egypt is a good example. As an engineering and irrigation system, it is a success. It has added thousands of acres of farmland to the food-producing potential of the country. But its total effect on Egypt has been little short of disastrous. By stopping the annual flooding of the Nile basin, it has stopped the annual deposit of fertile topsoil on the lower river valley and thus reduced crop production. By reducing river flow in the delta, it has caused the silting of the river's channels and the intrusion of salt water into once-productive delta farms.

By reducing the flow of nutrients into the Mediterranean, it has reduced the fish population and cut the food supplies from that source. The lower reaches of the river have become infected with snails which carry disease to the population and drastically injure the nation's health.

In the reservoir itself, millions of acre-feet of water have evaporated and the growth of aquatic plants has created further problems by plugging the canals with vegetation and speeding the silting of the reservoir.

Closer to home we have other examples: the demise of passenger trains caused by the growth of air and private automobile travel; the eutrophication of lakes — with much of the blame now assigned to the phosphates

17

used in laundry detergents; the garbage and litter problems which have been so magnified by disposable merchandise packages.

On a smaller scale, we see that no organization lives unto itself. Putting up buildings in central cities adds to traffic problems. Moving businesses to suburbs creates housing problems. Introduction of new products causes the death of old products with far-reaching effects on those whose incomes have been derived from them.

In all of these situations, public relations can have an important function; but, before we attempt to integrate PR into the system, let us examine another basic concept.

A large amount of research has been done on the problem of management and, from this research, managers have learned how to manage groups more efficiently.

Managers have discovered that any result is the product of many interacting forces which cannot be classified as *good* or *bad* but only as *natural*. They have also discovered that they must face management problems not on the basis of how people *should be* but of how they *are*.

By analyzing all the factors in group performance, managers have found that many intangibles, once disregarded, can have a profound effect on overall accomplishment. They must look at more than numbers and machines if they are to achieve maximum results, and they must recognize that the function of any activity is only a part of the total activity.

From these studies, it is possible to postulate some basic factors. In any situation where something is to be accomplished, there must be consideration of the activities of the people, their reaction to others, the ideas, beliefs, and sentiments that people have, the beliefs they must have if they are to work effectively, and the emergent sentiment as to what is reasonably attainable (Lawrence and Seiler, 1965).

Within an organization, these concepts can provide fundamental guidelines for solving work problems. They give managers a foundation for more effective management of groups and departments — or of the whole organization. And, since management is in a position to dictate action, it can induce better performance by applying these concepts to the problems it faces.

So too with an organization that is part of a larger system. Its activities cannot be considered without reference to the effect on the larger system. This larger system is the social, political, and economic environment described in Chapter 1.

PUBLIC RELATIONS AND THE SYSTEM

The larger system is not controlled by the organization; yet it is affected by and can profoundly affect the organization. Since management cannot dictate to the larger system, it must have some means of integrating its own organization into that larger system. It will thus attain its maximum possible performance not only in economic terms but in acceptance as a valuable part of the whole.

The means with which management can accomplish this is public relations. To see how this applies, let us go back to a small group performing some production job. By studying the job — the materials, the machines, and the people (particularly the people) — it is possible to increase production. At some point, management makes decisions, puts them into effect, and gets results.

This is relatively easy because management controls everything. But, in the larger system, management does not control — it must persuade. And that is the task of public relations.

In a work group, management can shift jobs, realign production lines, hire and fire, praise and admonish, install new machines, or move the whole installation. In the larger system (of which the organization is a part), the only controllable element is the organization itself. It is analogous to a working group where one man has a considerable stake in the results and must get the cooperation of others by convincing them that he is helping them and deserves their help. In a small group this might be accomplished by personal contact. In the larger system the members of the group are themselves groups — the owners, the employees, the customers, the community, the educators, the government, the suppliers, the dealers, the competitors, and all the special interest groups and unorganized publics.

Opposition or obstruction by any one can be harmful. Only if all these forces are benign can an organization attain its full potential. And, occasionally, an organization may need not just benign tolerance but active help.

Because all the groups or publics mentioned consist of many individuals, often at a considerable distance from each other, it is not possible to reach them by personal contact. Their ideas and beliefs are not always evident. Their interests and values may be hard to discover. Many of them have only a slight awareness of an organization and its problems.

HOW PUBLIC RELATIONS FUNCTIONS

To understand the functioning of public relations, please note the flow from block to block as you read the description of each block in the chart.

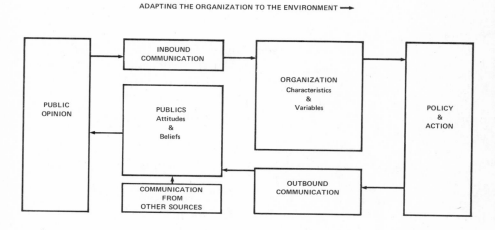

Public Opinion

This is the beginning and end of the chart. It is also the beginning and the end of public relations. Essentially it is what the public feels, thinks, says, and does about an organization. It may be strong or weak, vocal or silent, widespread or limited, favorable or unfavorable. Favorable public opinion is essential to any organization. (See Chapter 7.)

Inbound Communication

Inbound communication involves learning the opinion of the public, determining its validity and significance, and recommending action. For example, it may be found that policy is faulty. This calls for a recommendation to change policy and inform the public about the change. Conversely, it may be found that policy is good but unknown or misunderstood. This calls for a recommendation to give the public the facts. (See Chapter 19.)

The Organization

What management does with the recommendation depends on the characteristics and intervening variables of the organization. All of these factors can influence the decisions of management.

The philosophy of management may be important. For many years one of the country's biggest manufacturers encouraged cutthroat competition among its executives because the founder had decided that in this way the ablest would reach the top.

Organization values influence management decisions. This was expressed by the president of a public utility who, on a national TV network, justified a dam on the Snake River because it would enable him to provide more and more electricity at very low cost in an area where per capita electric consumption was already about twice the national average.

Objectives are important factors. An organization that is trying for a "fast buck" will act quite differently from one that considers itself a long-time entity.

The nature of the organization will influence its decisions and actions. A telephone company may be especially sensitive to public opinion, while a manufacturer of heavy machinery may be unconcerned.

Conditions can be a critical factor. A firm that is prospering will act differently from one that is failing. A company in a growing industry may see things through rose-colored glasses, while its counterpart in a declining field may have a radically different viewpoint.

Management is a particularly important influence. It may be flexible or rigid. It may be progressive or conservative. It may be on firm ground or in jeopardy from the stockholders or trustees. All these factors and many more will affect management decisions.

The attitude of the organization toward the public is possibly the most significant characteristic affecting its public relations. At one extreme, there can be a "public-be-damned" attitude. At the other extreme, there can be an actual fear of the public which inhibits constructive action that could improve public opinion. Most commonly, the range will be from less extreme positions, with lip service at one end and enthusiastic support at the other.

The status of the public relations function within the organization has much to do with the acceptance and execution of its recommendations. Here too there can be extremes — from direct access to, and wholehearted support from the chief executive, to a subordinated position with reluctant haggling over every activity and every cent.

Finally, there is the quality of the PR performance. This depends on the ability of the people who practice public relations for the organization. If they know their business and do their work well, the organization will be much more likely to approve their recommendations and support the program. And, of course, the actual outflow will be more effective.

Policy and Action

If an organization has an enlightened management it will establish policies which adapt it to its environment. Through inbound communication it learns which policies it should adopt or change. This must be a continuing process because the social, political, and economic environment is constantly changing. What is good policy today may be bad policy tomorrow. The policy must be supported by action. (See Chapter 1.)

Outbound Communication

The policies and actions of the organization are made known to the public through outbound communication. Outbound communication may be directed to one or several or many publics depending on the need. (See Chapter 21.)

Publics

This includes every group or public whose attitudes and opinions can affect the organization or be affected by the organization. It includes the general public as well as specific publics such as constituents, employees, owners, customers, the community, educators, government, suppliers, dealers, and competitors. This also includes special publics, unorganized publics, and special-interest groups. (See Part III.)

Communication From Other Sources

The process of adapting the environment to the organization would be easier and simpler if it were possible to omit this element. But this block has to be included because the publics are reached by a large volume of communication from other sources. This may reach the public through television, radio, newspapers, magazines, mail, books, booklets, pictures, word of mouth, or any other medium which conveys messages. This communication includes almost anything the public can see, read, or hear. It may be rumor or fact. It may be true or untrue. It may be old or new. It may be planned or unplanned. There may be much or little. It may come from any source. All of it has a chance to affect the attitudes and opinions of the public.

This requires public relations people to be keenly aware of the kind and volume of information reaching the public in this manner. It is impossible to keep track of everything, but it is imperative to keep track of the major topics.

Public Opinion

At this point the cycle is complete. If the outbound communication is successful (and if the communication from other sources does not negate the activity), public opinion of the organization will be favorable. The social, political, and economic environment will be adapted to the organization.

Please remember — Fig. 2-1 is a highly simplified chart of a very complex activity. No organization suddenly and easily becomes adapted to its environment. No environment suddenly and easily becomes adapted to an organization. It is a long, slow process involving many elements. Success usually comes slowly and one step at a time.

THE CASE OF THE HYPOTHETICAL PAPER COMPANY

To show how this works, we will create a fictional situation. Any resemblance to organizations or people, living or dead, is purely coincidental. The incidents *could* happen and the problems *could* exist.

The Scene

The Hypothetical Paper Company is a large manufacturer of paper products. Its major markets are in California. Its stock is traded on the American Exchange and stockholders — while mainly in the West — are scattered throughout the country.

Hypothetical Paper Company is profitable. Its facilities are in reasonably good condition. Its research is excellent and so are its products.

Headquarters is in Portland, Oregon, and there are two mills — one in Oregon and one in Washington. The largest mill is in River City, Oregon, a city of 40,000 people located on a small river that flows into the Willamette River a few miles above Salem, the state capital. The payroll of the mill (3,800 employees) is the economic backbone of the city.

Everything about the operation of The Hypothetical Paper Company is excellent, with one exception. Its Oregon mill pollutes the air and water. Some things have been done to reduce the volume of pollutants but the reduction is only partial. Sulfurous fumes still pour from the stack and solid and chemical wastes still flow into the river.

The key executives of the company are all competent and cooperative. John A. Peters, the president, has been with the company 32 years, having climbed the production ladder. The directors include the president, manufacturing vice-president, marketing vice-president, financial vice-president, plus several noncompany people including bankers, lawyers, and industrialists.

The public relations department is headed by Pete Ryan, who will be referred to hereafter as PR. He reports directly to the president.

The Problem

As pollution of the environment became more and more of a public issue, PR periodically reported to Peters about the growing concern and warned that, ultimately, Hypothetical would have to do something drastic to stop pollution. Peters listened, agreed in principle, but always ended the discussion with comments such as: "It would cost us a lot of money and I see no reason why we should be the only firm to act when our competitors are also polluting."

During the spring of 19--, PR (being a good "sensor" of public opinion) became convinced that the pollution issue was growing in importance. Verbal and written criticisms of the pollution grew more numerous and more vehement. Most centered on the River City mill. Concurrent with these unorganized criticisms, PR became aware of an active environmentalist named Joe Clark who headed a slimly financed group called SPN (Stop Pollution Now!). Clark was a voluble lawyer who, recognizing that long hair and wild clothing were antagonizing many people, was the epitome of good grooming and of cogent persuasion.

More and more bumper stickers appeared bearing the slogan "Stop Pollution Now," and Clark surfaced more frequently in the news. In meeting after meeting, Clark told his listeners: "The only way to reduce pollution is to stop it now!"

PR started some informal research and found that many people agreed with Clark. So many that PR recognized the need for an accurate appraisal of public opinion. He recommended to Peters that Hypothetical conduct a statewide survey to determine the strength of feeling about pollution.

Since the survey would cost thousands of dollars, PR had to convince Peters that the expenditure was necessary, to prepare a formal recommendation and present it to the directors. It took considerable persuasion; there were heated arguments and some blind opposition, but finally the research was approved.

PR got the fieldwork started immediately and began thinking about what to recommend if the research proved that the problem was indeed as serious as he suspected. A week later Joe Clark announced his candidacy for the state senate as an independent on a three-word platform "Stop Pollution Now."

PR had just finished reading the newspaper report of this announcement when Peters called him into the office and said, "I've just had a call from Sam White [President of the White Paper Company] and he thinks we had better stop this nut Clark right now. What do you know about him?"

PR reported that Clark was not a nut, that he was extremely able, that his cause had merit, that he had a substantial following, and that opposition would strengthen him. After some discussion, Peters agreed. He called White and relayed PR's advice, which White finally accepted.

The public opinion survey was completed in seven weeks and it showed two very significant factors:

1. 62% of the people surveyed would favor legislation forcing paper mills to cease operation until they had installed equipment that would stop pollution.
2. 88% of the people in River City would oppose such legislation. (Quite obviously because their incomes depended on the mill.)

PR gave a complete report of the findings to the Executive Committee and said, "This situation is very serious. I don't know how much time we have but Hypothetical is going to have to clean up or close up, and we'd better act immediately."

After considerable argument and discussion, Peters ordered a study of the problem of ending all pollution. It would include facilities needed, costs involved, effect on products and personnel, and the time needed to make physical changes. He decided on a two-month time limit for the preliminary report and set December 1 as the date for the final report. At this point PR suggested a special letter to stockholders apprising them of the growing environmental problem and telling them that the whole subject of eliminating pollution was being investigated. Peters approved and PR, working with the corporate secretary, drafted the letter, which was sent out over Peters' signature two days later.

Meanwhile, Clark's campaign for the senate gained momentum. Public opinion polls showed him gaining on the incumbent Democrat and well ahead of the rival Republican.

When Peters received the preliminary report on the clean-up plan, he was shocked. It would cost several millions of dollars, it would take two years to complete, it would require shifting some operations from one plant to another, and it would change the quality of some of the papers — notably newsprint, which would be grayer. Peters took no action at this point. Election day came and Clark won with 58% of the votes in his district.

On December 1, Peters received the complete report on the pollution project but he decided to wait until the first of the year before presenting it to the directors.

The legislature convened on January 2 and, on January 4, PR got a telephone call from Bill Montgomery, the legislative lobbyist for the paper industry. "Well, he's done it," said Bill. "What's who done?" asked PR. "Clark! He's introduced a bill giving paper mills six months to stop pollution or stop production," replied Bill. "I tried to reach Peters but he's not in. So pass the word, will you?"

When Peters came into the office, PR told him of the call and reported that he had asked Montgomery for a copy of the bill, a rundown on the members of the committee on pollution (to which the bill had been referred) and a quick informal poll of the legislature to see what chance the bill had. Peters then called a special meeting of the board of directors and also arranged for a meeting with the heads of all the other paper mills in the state — to discuss the problem and to arrive at policy decisions.

While this was going on, PR did some of the hardest thinking of his life. The Hypothetical Paper Company had a big problem and PR had to solve it. As he studied the situation, he concluded that it could be confronted piecemeal. First, the proposed law had to be stopped — or at least delayed until Hypothetical could make decisions. Second, Hypothetical had to make a major policy decision. Third, once the decision was made, Hypothetical had to convince all interested publics that it was working on the problem. And fourth, when the changes were completed, Hypothetical must reap some large benefits in goodwill.

A report from Bill Montgomery was not reassuring. The Pollution Committee was largely in favor of the Clark bill. It had set hearings for February 5 and a good many legislators had indicated an intention to vote "yes." One favorable fact was present: one member of the Pollution Committee represented the district in which River City was located.

The directors' meeting on January 9 approved all actions and expenditures necessary to stop pollution. PR's presentation of the facts laid the foundation for the decision but the costs of eliminating pollution caused consternation. As one director put it, "We can't afford to do it but it's better to have no dividends for four years than to abandon the business."

When the construction started, PR found many problems needing his talents. Working with all the members of the Executive Committee, he prepared a special report to stockholders informing them of the directors' decision and its effect on dividends. Then he went to work on his plans.

The Holding Action

The objective was to block Clark's bill — or have it amended to take effect at a date that would give the paper mills enough time to make the necessary changes. PR drove to the state capital, picked up Montgomery and called on the senator from River City. They arranged for the appearance of numerous witnesses at the hearing. Next, PR talked to his colleagues at the other paper mills and arranged for a meeting two days later to plan the presentation. At this meeting, PR was elected chairman; he assigned to each interested mill the job of producing witnesses and gathering facts.

PR had four witnesses: Peters, the president of the River City Chamber of Commerce, the head of the Hypothetical Union, and a professor from Oregon State University who was an expert on paper chemistry. Each was to present certain facts. Peters was to relate how large the problem was — how long it would take and how much it would cost to solve. The Chamber of Commerce president was to tell how a shutdown of the mill would bankrupt River City and its people. The union president was to add that many families would have to go on relief. And the professor would confirm the technical problems.

On February 5, the Pollution Committee started its hearings. Clark brought many witnesses and much evidence of the environmental damage caused by paper mills. As the hearings went on, the capitol was circled by hundreds of demonstrators chanting "Stop pollution now!"

The witnesses against the bill were well-coached and highly effective. For a time, there was hope that the bill might be killed. Then, on the fourth day, all hope went up in smoke — thick, stinking, yellow smoke. By some freak of wind, the smoke from Hypothetical's River City mill was held close to the ground and blown into Salem. Coughing and weeping, the committee recessed the hearing. As witnesses and committee went out the door, Clark shouted: "If you think this is bad, just go down to the river and look at the garbage coming from that Hypothetical Stink Bomb."

When the committee reconvened the next day, it unanimously recommended passage of the bill — but with one amendment sponsored by the senator from River City. The mills were given two years, instead of six months, to clean up or close up. Both houses of the legislature passed the bill overwhelmingly and the governor signed it into law.

The Continuing Action

During the time of construction, there were many public relations problems and activities. Most important were the transfer of some employees to the Washington mill, the question of assessment and taxation of the pollution-suppressing facilities, the gray newsprint, the establishment of rapport with the SPN group, and the continuing information to the public about progress. All of these were conducted simultaneously but for clarity's sake, we will describe them separately — and briefly.

The transfer of employees   People do not like to be uprooted from a familiar environment, especially women. Yet PR had to try to sell 103 families on the idea of moving from River City, Oregon, to Paperton, Washington. Hypothetical had agreed to pay all moving expenses, to aid in finding new housing, and to spend a substantial sum of money to sell the employees on the move. (It did not want to lose the employees or have to train replacements.) In a conference with the union leaders, the superintendent and the foremen of the department being transferred, PR and the production vice-president explained the necessity for the transfer and what the company would do to ease it.

PR prepared and distributed a leaflet explaining the whole idea to all employees eligible for transfer. He published a detailed explanation in the Hypothetical House Organ so that all employees would understand. From the Chamber of Commerce in Paperton, PR obtained numerous leaflets and booklets describing the virtues of Paperton. He visited Paperton, talked to the Chamber of Commerce, and enlisted its support in a project to find housing for the Hypothetical families. He called on the *Paperton Tribune* and provided detailed information about Hypothetical's plans. He then set himself the task of sending a steady flow of press releases to the paper so that Paperton would maintain interest in the newcomers.

Back in River City, PR arranged for a meeting of all the families involved in the transfer. One of the speakers was the secretary of the Paperton Chamber of Commerce. Another was a PTA president who told of the excellent schools in Paperton. A delegation of six wives was selected to go to Paperton and see for themselves — at Hypothetical's expense. There they were met by six of their counterparts who showed them around the city and entertained them at a luncheon. Their generally favorable reports were presented at another meeting in River City.

Through a combination of hard work and luck, it soon was learned that all families who wanted to transfer could find adequate housing. In the end, 81 families moved while only 22 refused.

The assessment and tax problem   With construction costs approaching $4 million, it was immediately evident to the county tax assessor that this could be a new source of taxes. It was also evident to Hypothetical that this did not add one cent to the productive value of the River City plant. It would be a more costly plant but no more productive and hence no more valuable. PR and the legal vice-president had repeated conferences with the assessor, but they made little progress. Through contacts with the *River City Clarion*, PR kept Hypothetical's story before the people. He coined a key phrase, which was repeatedly published and quoted: "Why tax people for stopping pollution? Why not tax the pollution?" The pressures increased but the assessor quoted the law, which gave him no alternative but to increase Hypothetical's assessment.

The next move was to try to change the law. Conferences were held with the senator and assemblyman from the River City districts. After prolonged discussion and much soul-searching, it was agreed that the assemblyman would introduce a bill providing for reduced assessments on antipollution installations and that the senator would support it in the senate. The bill finally was passed by a very narrow margin and became law.

The gray newsprint   With most of Hypothetical's income at River City coming from newsprint, an apparent reduction in quality could result in a loss of its contracts with the Los Angeles newspaper that was its largest customer as well as with smaller papers in other cities. As soon as it was learned how gray the paper would be, the production vice-president, the marketing vice-president, and PR took some samples to the Los Angeles newspaper. A conference was arranged with the publisher, the editor, the production manager, and the advertising director. There was stiff resistance to the gray paper but the sale was finally made when someone (destined to remain anonymous) said: "Grayer paper means bluer skies." The advertising director liked the thought and persuaded the rest of his team to use the phrase in introducing the new paper. The line was used as the heading of a front-page editorial on pollution, in which it was pointed out that everyone had to give up something if we were not to lose the very quality of life itself.

The SPN group   One of PR's most difficult problems during this period was Clark. Clark did not accept the two-year moratorium graciously and he continued his campaign to "Stop Pollution Now!" PR made many efforts to meet Clark and finally succeeded after six months. The first meeting was frosty and unproductive but another one two months later broke the ice and achieved some slight mutual understanding. PR worked hard to convince Clark that he and Hypothetical were concerned about the environment and that they were trying to do their part. With Peters' approval, PR addressed a meeting of SPN and considered it a triumph when he was able to finish his speech. He answered many questions, some difficult and some impossible, but on the whole he accomplished some good.

PR continued to cultivate Clark and, as the months went by, earned his respect, if not his friendship. Recognizing the power of Clark's ideas, PR fed some of them back to his own management and to other paper companies and gradually became a "clear channel" of communication between the paper industry and the leader of the environmentalists. PR's relation with Clark paid off overwhelmingly when Clark vigorously supported the bill to reduce assessments on antipollution installations.

Informing the public   Throughout the construction period, PR kept progress reports flowing to the news media and to all the publics concerned. He prepared a series of leaflets describing what was going on as each step was started. These were distributed to employees, to visitors, to stockholders, and to numerous environmental groups. A series of special stockholder letters was distributed. Plant tours were arranged for business, labor, and student groups. Large signs near the plant told how Hypothetical was spending $4 million to stop pollution.

Customers, dealers, and competitors were informed, as were members of the legislature. PR arranged for a plant tour and seminar of college professors interested in the prevention of pollution. River City was, of course, the object of much attention. PR arranged for speeches to local and statewide organizations. With Hypothetical firmly committed to stopping pollution, PR made sure that everyone within reach knew about Hypothetical's attitude, policy, and action.

The finale At long last, and five days short of the two-year time limit, Hypothetical went "on-stream" with the new facilities. But it did not do it quietly. For months PR had been planning a grand opening ceremony and plant tour. There was a parade up the main street of River City and there were speeches by the governor, the chairmen of the senate and assembly committees on pollution, and the mayor. The starting button was pressed by Joe Clark. The plant tour drew the biggest crowd in the history of River City. The events were covered by all the newspapers in the area, by the wire services, and by two TV networks. Of all the speakers, Clark got the most attention; it was his very brief speech that made the headlines and it was his face that appeared on TV as he said, "These people have shown that we *can* stop pollution. If Hypothetical can do it, so can all the rest of you."

EXERCISES

1. What other things could PR have done in the situation of the Hypothetical Paper Company?
2. From current news, find items that indicate an environmental problem of some organization. What do you think should be done?

Historical Highlights

To understand and appreciate the public relations of today, it is most helpful to know something about the beginnings of the art of influencing public opinion. The subject is worthy of a book, or several, but in this particular volume it must be condensed to a few highlights.

IN THE BEGINNING

Public relations began as soon as there was a public because as soon as there was a public, someone undoubtedly wanted to influence its opinion. It is quite possible that PR goes back to the Stone Age. Perhaps a caveman persuaded his clan to join in a hunt or in a migration to another locality.

We know very definitely that public relations was being practiced nearly 4,000 years ago. The evidence is a cuneiform tablet found in Iraq. It is a bulletin telling farmers how to grow better crops — a direct forerunner of the bulletins being released today by the U.S. Department of Agriculture.

When Julius Caesar wrote his commentaries, he was writing history. He was also doing a skillful job of public relations with the citizens of Rome. The *Commentaries on the Gallic Wars* convinced the readers that Caesar was a great and able leader and helped to pave the way for Caesar's eventual seizure of Rome.

One of the earliest public relations organizations was the Society for the Propagation of the Faith (Congregatio de Propaganda Fide). Its purpose was and is obvious — to influence public opinion and thus increase membership in the Roman Catholic Church. From this name, we get our common word "propaganda," which we use with a considerably different meaning.

THE AMERICAN REVOLUTION

Most of us think of the American Revolution as the spontaneous uprising of the people of the 13 colonies. We admit that a few Tories stayed loyal to the Crown, but the general visualization is of a people united in opposition to a tyrannical king — all equally desirous of independence.

The facts are quite different. There were lots of Tories — and lots of Whigs, too. For these were the two political parties of the Colonies and of England. Most people, whether Whig or Tory, did not really feel like fighting over such things as molasses, stamp and tea taxes, taxation without representation, or even the Writs of Assistance. Most people wanted to go on about their business. Even if they were inconvenienced or annoyed by some of the laws passed by Parliament, they could have a good life regardless of what Parliament and George III did.

There were, however, a few people who did feel deeply and bitterly about what Parliament and King George were doing. These were the makers of the American Revolution. They changed indifference into anger and anger into revolution (Davidson, 1941). The molasses tax affected only a few rum distillers. The stamp tax was just a minor item. It did not add much cost to the recording of a deed. The tea tax did not make a cup of tea terribly expensive. But Sam Adams and a flock of others felt very strongly about these things (Harlow, 1923; Miller, 1960). Through skillful use of publicity and other techniques, they made many hitherto indifferent people feel the same way — and the Revolution was on. (See *Public Relations Review*, Winter 1976.)

Committees of Correspondence

One of the first moves was the establishment of Committees of Correspondence—small groups throughout the Colonies who wrote letters to each other exchanging information, discussing problems, and planning action. Through these committees, the citizens of the entire country were kept informed of and annoyed about the actions of the Royal government.

The Colonial Press

With only four cities (Boston, New York, Philadelphia, and Charleston, S.C.) and few towns big enough to support a newspaper, there were very few papers. But practically every one of them was on the side of the colonists and against the Crown. Their pages carried the stories of repression and the reaction of the American people. Their editorials clamored for action.

The Boston Massacre

The cold facts about this event are that a bunch of Boston roughnecks attacked some British troops with epithets and with bricks and stones. The British officer called "Don't fire," but somebody misunderstood and fired. Several of the Americans were killed. In a trial where John Adams defended the British officer, the latter was found not guilty.

This was too good an opportunity to be passed over by Samuel Adams, John's cousin. Within hours after the shooting, messengers were on the way to all the Colonies with lurid accounts of the "Boston Massacre." "Brutal British soldiers had killed several peaceful Americans." The victims were turned into martyrs by the force of publicity, and colonial support of British rule took another blow.

The Boston Tea Party

Everyone, or almost everyone, knows how the Sons of Liberty, dressed as Indians, threw 342 cases of tea into Boston Harbor. The purpose was not so much to destroy the tea as to dramatize colonial opposition to England's tax on tea. Again the story went through the Colonies and again the resentment against the Crown increased.

The Battle of Bunker Hill

After the Battle of Lexington, it might have been possible to avoid the Revolution. But after Bunker Hill, there was no choice. It is true that when the colonists ran out of ammunition, the British drove them off the hill — so it was technically a defeat for the Americans. But as long as the ammunition lasted, the Americans were more than a match for the British. Three times the loosely organized militia withstood the attacks of the best troops on earth. The amateurs proved that they could lick the professionals. The Battle of Bunker Hill was not planned as a public relations activity, but it achieved a tremendous PR goal — the mobilization of public opinion in support of a revolution against the established government.

"When in the Course of Human Events . . ."

The Declaration of Independence was a public relations document — a statement issued to the world out of a "decent respect to the opinions of mankind." The words declaring the Colonies free and independent were quite brief. Most of the document is a statement of grievances against King George III and the British Parliament, and a listing of the rights that had been violated.

It was written with great care, and much rewriting was done in order to make the best possible case for the action that had been taken. In current language, it was a "white paper." But, because it was brilliantly written and because the Revolution succeeded, the "white paper" became a great historic document.

THE CONSTITUTION

The Constitution of the United States was drafted with considerable attention to public opinion. Article after article was planned to appease public sentiment or cash in on public grievances. The 13 colonies were fearful of a strong government, so the Constitution was filled with restrictions on the power of the proposed national government. But even this was not enough. Jay, Madison, and Hamilton took on the job of selling the Colonies on the desirability of adhering to the Union and its Constitution. They did it with . . .

The Federalist Papers

This series of papers sold the American people on the Constitution and the necessity for a union of the 13 sovereign states.

These papers collectively were one of the greatest examples of the art of public relations. A series of articles, distributed throughout the states, explained the Constitution, discussed the advantages and disadvantages, and pointed out clearly the inevitable conclusion: survival depended upon the formation of a nation.

The papers explained in great detail the protection of the people that had been built into the document. And they sold the various states — conditionally, because even with all the assurances of men whose integrity was trusted, there were still many people who were fearful of the powers of government. It was only on the assurance of all concerned with the new Constitution that further safeguards would be incorporated that the people assented to the Constitution.

The Bill of Rights

The first ten amendments to the Constitution were drafted in response to public fears — fears of an all-powerful centralized government that would take the place of King and Parliament. All ten amendments restrict the powers of the national government. All counter the large or small tyrannies imposed by Britain on the 13 Colonies, and all are designed to protect the freedom of the people and of the States. All reflect the public opinion of the times. They were added to the Constitution in order to create favorable public opinion about the national government established by the Constitution.

THE NEW REPUBLIC

As the new nation emerged in the last years of the eighteenth century, there were several significant developments. Washington had hardly settled his feet under the presidential desk before political differences became apparent. The struggle for power through public support grew strong and noisy. Washington himself was attacked by opponents. The voting franchise, once limited to taxpayers, was extended; more people went to school; more papers were published; more opinions were expressed; more people tried to persuade others to their point of view.

THE NINETEENTH CENTURY

With the death of Washington in 1799, the tide turned completely. And with no sacrosanct figure to hold emotions even slightly in check, the political struggles became all-out efforts to attain power and to demolish the opposition.

Jackson and Amos Kendall

Andrew Jackson came into the White House as a war hero and as a champion of the common man — a sure-fire formula for success in a country founded on the thesis that all men are equal.

Jackson was aided by a unique man. Amos Kendall was his name. Kendall was a newspaperman — one of the first men in America to perform a true public relations function. He analyzed public opinion and recommended policy; he advised Jackson on what to say and how to say it; and he wrote newspaper articles and ghosted speeches. The Jacksonian program was successful due in no small degree to an acute awareness of public opinion and how to sway it.

"There's a Sucker Born Every Minute"

P. T. Barnum was a great nineteenth century press agent. True, his official occupation was owning a circus, and there were many circus owners, but only Barnum mastered the art of press agentry to the fullest degree. He took an unknown singer named Jenny Lind and soon had people throughout the country standing in line to hear "The Swedish Nightingale." He found a personable midget and made him "General Tom Thumb." He bought an African elephant, named him "Jumbo," and made the name a synonym for enormous size. All of these names are still current in the American language after more than a century.

Barnum coined the phrase at the head of this section. He understood people, he knew what aroused public interest, and he blazed the trail for generations of press agents.

Temperance and Abolition

Two causes of the early nineteenth century utilized public relations extensively. Advocates of temperance published magazines, pamphlets, and books; temperance societies were organized; speeches, poems, and songs were aimed at "Demon Rum." Meetings and conventions dramatized the opposition to liquor. Restrictive legislation was passed. Maine enacted a statewide prohibition law but eventually the movement ran out of steam and it was not revived until the early twentieth century.

Abolition of slavery was another storm. The antislavery forces published magazines and books; they organized societies; they wrote and spoke; they boycotted the products of slave labor; and they forced politicians to support the cause. The South fought back with the same tools and techniques. The controversy grew so great that it finally ended on the battlefields of the Civil War.

The Civil War

Abraham Lincoln had a real understanding of public relations. (See quotation in preliminary pages.) He actively sought the support of the press. He sent agents to Europe to muster support for the North (Jefferson Davis did the same thing for the South). He was the first Republican president, yet he appointed many Democrats to high office in order to broaden his base of support.

An important trend in PR was started during the war — the use of public relations to raise money, both through the sale of government bonds and through gifts to the "Sanitary Commission," the predecessor of the Red Cross. These tools, techniques, and organization were highly effective, and they have been used ever since by both government and private fund raisers.

Politics Makes Strange Bedfellows

In the early years of the nineteenth century, political campaigns featured free whiskey, stump speeches, torchlight parades, and campaign songs. But these relatively simple efforts were soon outmoded. By 1880, both major parties were using large quantities of campaign literature extolling the virtues of their platform and their candidate and warning the public of the catastrophe that would ensue if the opposition party came to power.

The 1896 presidential campaign of McKinley vs. Bryan set the pattern that still applies to national election campaigns. Campaign literature, speeches in various parts of the country, newspaper and outdoor advertising, fund-raising dinners, whistle-stop talks — all were there. The only real change since then has been the use of radio and television.

The Public Be Damned: 1865—1900

The last third of the nineteenth century was the era of the Robber Barons, businessmen who were interested in only one thing — money (Josephson, 1934). They built the railroads and rigged freight rates; they manipulated the stock market; they looted the forests and the mines; they adulterated foods; and they preyed upon labor, consumers and small stockholders. The times are epitomized by the statement attributed to Commodore Vanderbilt, owner of the New York Central, "The public be damned."

True, there were few laws against what they were doing except possibly the Golden Rule, which has no enforcement provision. But even though there were few law violations, there were a lot of sore toes. A few people were getting very, very rich and millions were being victimized.

Although the "robber barons" were only a small minority, the entire business world received a black eye from which it has not yet fully recovered. The times were ripe for a public reaction — and there was one. It began as the nineteenth century came to an end.

A NEW ERA

With so many bad policies, it was only natural that the public would react. It did so with such vehemence that it made modern public relations, both policy and practice, an absolute necessity.

The Muckrakers: 1901—1912

Novelists, newspapers, and politicians shared in the attack on the people who were at fault and the policies that permitted them to plunder and pillage without restraint. Ida M. Tarbell, Lincoln Steffens, Charles G. Norris, Upton Sinclair and others wrote magazine exposes and novels about big businessmen and their ruthless battles for power and money. They told in vivid detail how these plutocrats were making their money by cheating or defrauding the public (Regier, 1932).

Newspapers of that time flourished on sensationalism. The name for it was "yellow journalism," and it reported on the power struggles and money-grabbing of the "robber barons."

Politicians, typified by President Theodore Roosevelt and Senator Robert M. LaFollette of Wisconsin, seized the opportunity and succeeded in passing numerous laws restricting the pillage.

LaFollette led in securing legislation protecting the public as individuals, and Roosevelt led in breaking up trusts and conserving the natural wealth of the country. Roosevelt was so successful in his assaults on big business that he became known as the "Trust Buster."

Legal Reactions

The results of these activities were a number of far-reaching laws.

The Interstate Commerce Commission was established to control the railroads. The Packers and Stockyards Act was the means of regulating the meat packers. The Food and Drug Act required food processors to produce and sell only clean wholesome foods. The Anti-Trust laws broke up the great Standard Oil Co. and other trusts. Laws were passed regulating stock sales. The U.S. Forest Service was made the guardian of the nation's forests.

All of these laws (and there were others than those listed) came about because the policies of business were bad and because the public was told that the policies were bad.

Positive Steps Forward

While most businessmen were unaware of the importance of public opinion until the storm burst upon them, a few far-sighted individuals and organizations existed.

In 1883, the American Telephone Co., which is now AT&T, made definite efforts to improve relations with its customers. In 1885, the American Medical Association formally resolved to aid the press in reporting the transactions of the association. In the late 1880s, the Mutual Life Insurance Co. hired a "literary agent." In the 1890s, Harry Payne

Whitney and Thomas Fortune Ryan, two well-known financial leaders, hired a newspaperman to help improve their public relations.

Counterattack

With novelists, newspapermen, and politicians in full cry, business reacted predictably. The first efforts were largely "whitewashing." If reporters were digging up dirt, business would try to keep the reporters away from the dirt. If the reporters found dirt, the owners hired other reporters to refute the charges or to discredit the reporters who found the dirt. But this was unsound, of course, and businessmen began to learn that good public relations were a necessity. One of the first constructive moves in this direction was made when the railroads established a press bureau. But the most important development in modern public relations policy and practice was due largely to one man.

Ivy Lee

Ivy Lee was probably the first true public relations counselor. The basic structure of twentieth century public relations rests on the foundation he established (Hiebert, 1966).

Lee placed great emphasis on policy and management's responsibilities for that policy. Lee established the necessity for two-way communication with the public. He taught his clients that listening was as important as talking. He startled them with his advice to be completely honest and frank with the press. While handling public relations for a coal-mine operation during a strike, he induced the owners to issue a "statement of policy," the first one ever to be published. When his client, the Pennsylvania Railroad, had a bad accident, Lee induced the railroad to help reporters get the story. Today these things sound so reasonable and logical that we would be surprised at any other attitude. But they were revolutionary when Lee did them.

One of his most unusual accomplishments was for a personal rather than corporate client — the Rockefeller family. When Lee took on the responsibility of improving its public image, he faced a tremendous problem. John D. Rockefeller, Sr. was supposedly the richest man in the world, and possibly the most hated because he was also the head of the Standard Oil Trust, a monopoly that was a juicy target for the brickbats of reporters and politicians.

But John D. Rockefeller had many virtues. He had a natural inclination to build public monuments and to support socially desirable action. The

41

Rockefeller Foundation is an expression of this attitude. Lee made Rockefeller's virtues known and thus improved public opinion so much that today the name of Rockefeller is almost a synonym for enlightened public service. One of his grandsons was governor of New York and later became vice-president of the United States. Another Rockefeller grandson was elected governor of Arkansas and a great-grandson has been elected governor of West Virginia.

While Lee is often called the "father" of modern public relations, there were many others engaged in the same sort of work. During the years before World War I, they established public relations as a necessary function for business, for government and for nonprofit organizations. Especially important in this group was Theodore N. Vail, President of the American Telephone & Telegraph Company, a true pioneer in building good corporate public relations.

WORLD WAR I

Three significant public relations landmarks came out of this war: the success of British practice, the failure of German policy, and the establishment of public relations as an arm of our Federal Government.

British Successes and German Failures

While we spoke the same language and most of our population had come from the British Isles, we had fought two wars against Britain and Independence Day orators still delighted in "twisting the Lion's tail." The United States did not really like Britain, but the British did a masterful job of swinging American public opinion to their side. And the Germans made mistake after mistake in policy that no amount of practice could have overcome, even if there had been no language barrier.

The British made their case early and often. A steady stream of news stories came over the cables telling of the fight of little Belgium against the German juggernaut, of the last-ditch stands of British troops against the militaristic Prussians, of German atrocities.

There was the sinking of the Lusitania, a British ship torpedoed by a German submarine off the coast of Ireland. The Germans had published advertisements in New York newspapers warning Americans not to travel on British ships because they might be sunk without warning. But many Americans ignored the admonition, and a lot of them went down with the Lusitania.

The British did not have to exploit this; the American press did it for them. American attitudes toward Britain grew warmer and warmer and their opinion of Germany sank lower and lower.

The greatest public relations coup of the war was the case of the Zimmerman Papers. Zimmerman was the German foreign minister. Somehow, the British acquired and decoded a copy of a message he sent to the German Ambassador in Mexico. The papers instructed the Ambassador to try to persuade the Mexican government to make war on the United States and to offer Mexico the states of Texas, New Mexico, and Arizona as their reward in case of victory. When this was publicized, American entry into the war against Germany was inevitable.

The Committee on Public Information

Soon after the Declaration of War on April 6, 1917, it became evident that while the people were in favor of fighting and winning, their sentiments needed to be steered into effective channels in order to accomplish all that had to be done.

Headed by George Creel, a committee was staffed with a group of able communicators, many of whom later became famous as public relations counselors.* The committee steered and implemented complete acceptance of the draft, which in Civil War days had been violently opposed. Through a succession of "drives," they sold "Liberty Bonds," raising money in quantities that had seemed almost impossible. Gifts to the Red Cross reached levels that had previously been considered astronomical. Meatless days and wheatless days conserved food. Home gardens were planted everywhere. Peach pits were saved to make charcoal for gas masks. Restaurants posted signs reading "Only one spoonful of sugar and stir like hell — we don't mind the noise." In every city and town, in every factory and on every farm, public opinion was mobilized in support of policies that were believed necessary for success in the war (Creel, 1920; Mock and Larson, 1939).

The whole project was highly successful — so successful that those involved in the program became convinced that they had discovered a new law of nature, a new way to control the public, a means by which the public mind could be steered in whatever direction the practitioners chose. It was a gross overestimation of the power of public relations and led to many disappointments when PR failed to accomplish miracles.

---

*Among them were Edward L. Bernays, Carl Byoir, and John Price Jones. The first two became counselors; Jones became a specialist in fund raising.

POSTWAR DEVELOPMENTS

The years immediately following World War I saw a rapid expansion in public relations. Organizations that had seen the possibilities of swaying public opinion decided to do some swaying in their own favor.

Corporations and associations hastened to establish public relations departments or retain public relations counselors. Continuing appropriations for public relations programs showed up in more and more budgets. Before the war, an organization that had a public relations department or counselor was a rarity. By 1929, it was not at all unusual.

The success of the Liberty Bond drives during World War I led some of the people involved into the field of fund raising. Applying the same techniques of emotional appeal and graphic goals, the business moved from the haphazard and feeble efforts of amateurs to a polished and effective art, which increased the endowments of universities and gifts to charities in a spectacular manner.

Collegiate public relations took a long step forward at this time. Stimulated by the growing popularity of intercollegiate football, college after college expanded its output of publicity. In many cases what started as a press agency for the football team turned into a full-fledged department serving the entire school. And, during this period, PR entered college curricula; Edward L. Bernays taught the first PR class in 1923 at New York University.

The Depression: 1929-1940

The late 1920s saw no unusual developments in public relations. Even when the Depression started in 1929 there was little news in the field. But the political campaign of 1932 changed things decisively. Herbert Hoover, a Republican, had been elected president in 1928 at the crest of a wave of prosperity. By 1932, we were at the bottom of the trough and the Democratic Party conducted an extremely successful campaign that blamed every ill on Hoover and the Republicans — "The Party of Big Business" — a tag that still handicaps both the Party and business. Franklin D. Roosevelt was elected and reelected three times on the basic premise that he was "for the people" and against the "malefactors of great wealth," although he was a very wealthy man himself.

Roosevelt, aided by his Brain Trust and guided by Louis Howe, swayed public opinion as had never been done before. Roosevelt introduced the "fireside chat," a nationwide radio broadcast to all the people that enabled him to gain overwhelming public support in spite of the nation's press, which was almost totally against him.

Roosevelt's administration demonstrated the power of the masses and the fact that it is easier to sway the masses "against" rather than "for," as was further demonstrated in the presidential election of 1964 when millions of people voted "against" Goldwater rather than "for" Johnson (White, 1965).

The continuous attacks of the Democratic Party on "Big Business" were reminiscent of the earlier muckraking days and they had a similar effect. Business had to put up a defense. It had to sell itself as well as its products. And businessmen knew that if they failed, the entire economic system might be changed. So they took a hard look at the problem. They recognized that private business must be in the public interest and that public interest changes. They also learned that business as an institution had to be sold to the public and, most significantly to PR people, they learned that public relations tools and techniques could help solve the problem. These realizations were not universal then, and still are not wholly accepted, but they were broad enough to result in a great expansion of the whole field of public relations.

WORLD WAR II

The Japanese bombing of Pearl Harbor brought the United States into World War II, which had been going on for two years. The Japanese attacked on December 7, 1941, and the United States declared war on December 8. We did not declare war on Germany until they declared war on us several days later.

The United States did not want to go to war. In fact, President Roosevelt won reelection in 1940 by a campaign in which he repeatedly promised to keep us out of war. Germany tried desperately to keep us out of the war and Britain tried just as strongly to get us in on her side.

German and British Propaganda

Germany was supported by many Americans. The "America First" group, while not pro-German, was a leader in the fight for neutrality. The "German American Bund" mobilized Americans of German ancestry to support Germany. United States subsidiaries of German firms gave financial support to German intelligence agents and to pro-German propaganda. John L. Lewis, head of the United Mine Workers, was violently anti-British until Hitler attacked Russia, whereupon Lewis changed his position. United States Senator Burton K. Wheeler was very anti-British. Twenty-four members of Congress franked 1,173,000 pieces of mail in support of Germany. President Roosevelt spoke of "Americans in high places . . . supporting the Nazis."

Britain sponsored the "Fight for Freedom" Committee. It stacked public opinion polls. It hired an astrologer who released faked predictions of bad luck for the Germans. False information was constantly fed to the news media (Stevenson, 1976).

The propaganda did have an effect, but there was undoubtedly a basic distaste for Hitler and his methods. Also there was latent sympathy for the peoples whose ideals and systems of government were so much like ours. Two men were major factors in the battle for America's minds and hearts.

"This . . . Is London"

Night after night, while German bombs rained on London, Edward R. Murrow, an American radio newscaster, opened his report with those words and then went on to describe the horrors of the "Blitz" and the indomitable spirit of the British people. A host of other able reporters, through radio or newspapers, brought the war into the living rooms of America and moved American public opinion to a warm sympathy for the suffering of their cousins.

"Blood and Sweat and Tears"

The list of Sir Winston Churchill's accomplishments and honors is probably the largest in *Who's Who*. Most Britons and Americans think of him as the greatest man of the twentieth century. Nowhere do we find a listing of Churchill as a public relations man; yet, in terms of swaying public opinion, he undoubtedly accomplished more than any other man.

Becoming prime minister when Britain was on her knees, Churchill electrified millions with the speech in which he offered his compatriots "nothing but blood and sweat and tears," and his promise to fight on until final victory.

Churchill was a great writer, a great speaker, and a great practitioner of the art of influencing public opinion. He kept Britain fighting when she was licked. He made America's alliance with Britain inevitable.

The Office of War Information

Headed by Elmer Davis, the World War II public relations arm of the government smoothly and effectively mobilized public opinion and aided in the attainment of numerous specific objectives.

The munitions needs of this war required construction of entire new industries. Ships, trucks, tanks, planes, ammunition, fuel, food, uniforms, and a host of other needs had to be provided. Recruiting labor for these industries was a task for the OWI. Millions of people were found for millions of jobs.

The drive for production was stimulated by the awards to munition plants of "E" (for efficiency) pennants.

War bonds were sold in quantities many times larger than in World War I. Conservation of scarce materials became universal. Tin cans with their bottoms cut out were flattened and recycled.

Although the OWI was not involved directly, employee publications—house organs—blossomed in every large plant to provide a means of telling the employees what they were making, why it was important, and why the work must be good. They also helped the newcomers to find homes and gave them a sense of belonging.

Public relations played a large part in the conduct of the war. It became firmly established as a desirable and necessary function. Its techniques were polished and its capabilities came to be properly understood. The art had come of age.

Psychological Warfare

Both sides used radio broadcasts aimed at listeners in the armed forces of their opponents. The messages included entertainment, usually music, to attract listeners and propaganda telling the listeners that they were fighting for the wrong cause, that they were sure to lose, that their wives or girl friends were untrue, that their leaders were incompetent, that they would be well-treated if they surrendered, and so on.

Extensive use was also made of leaflets which were dropped from aircraft or delivered in artillery projectiles which scattered the leaflets when they exploded.

There is some doubt about the effectiveness of these efforts. Social scientists question the power of propaganda to change opinions. The efforts of Germany and Japan produced no discernible results among the troops facing them. There is no publicly available information about success of the psychological warfare of the Allies, yet there must have been some favorable results because psychological warfare units have become a permanent part of the military establishment.

Suggested Reading

"Public Relations in American History," *Public Relations Review*, Fall, 1978.

NEW DEVELOPMENTS

Since the end of World War II public relations has grown in size and importance. According to *PR News*, between 1945 and 1975, the number of PR departments in American business organizations increased by 382%.

This growth has undoubtedly come because of increased awareness of the importance of public opinion and because of the increased complexity of our society. Organizations of all kinds have realized that they must adapt to the social, political, and economic environment and that they must make a continuing effort to inform the various publics about their policies and actions.

EXERCISES

1. From current news, find an item that has modified your opinion about a subject. Why did it modify your opinion?
2. How would you have tried to swing U.S. public opinion from support of Israel to support of the Arab nations?

Public Relations Today 4

Public relations today is an established and accepted institution. We all talk about public relations, we are all involved in and affected by it. Most organizations and many individuals devote considerable time and money to the "things that affect public opinion."

Expenditures on public relations amount to several billion dollars a year. There are at least 100,000 practitioners in the business. There are probably 1,500 public relations counseling firms. Most large U.S. companies have a public relations department, often headed by a vice-president, and many of the others have public relations counselors. The utilization of public relations programs goes far beyond large corporations. Small companies also have programs, to say nothing of trade associations, labor unions, educational institutions, professional groups, politicians, agricultural organizations, pressure groups, and various governmental bodies — national, state, and local.

IT WORKS

Today public relations is a mature but still imperfect art. Fortunately, it is not a science. If it were, we would all be at the mercy of the string-pullers. If human attitudes and opinions were all reasonable and rational, it would be possible to sway those attitudes and opinions in a predictable manner.

But human beings are not reasonable and rational — they are emotional. They will be violently opposed to a law and in favor of all its provisions. They will hate a corporation and buy its products, or love its advertising but refuse to buy the product advertised.

In spite of all the uncertainties, there are some things that can be counted on. We do know how people act and react in general. We know that certain things offend most people and that certain things please most people. We still cannot accurately measure the degree of offense or pleasure.

Public relations practitioners know how to get along with most people most of the time. They know how to present facts in a way most likely to get a favorable public reaction. In one sense the public relations man is akin to the weatherman who says "there is a 60% chance of rain." These odds are not at all unreasonable.

THE GENERAL ENVIRONMENT

The widespread acceptance of public relations as an indispensable function of management has been brought about by growing efficiency in the practice of public relations and by major changes in our society.

Bigger But Not Better

Organizations have grown larger. For example, A.T. & T. has about 1 million employees, 3 million stockholders, and more than 60 million customers. As organizations grow larger, the individuals concerned become less important to the organization without becoming less important to themselves. Two-way communication becomes more difficult. Sheer size makes organizations impersonal. And while people like and use the products and services of big organizations they don't like their "bigness." To many people, a big organization is a bad organization.

Complexity

As our society becomes more complex, we become more helpless in dealing with it and more dependent on the performance of others. New York City was virtually paralyzed by a bolt of lightning which hit an electric power plant. Thousands of people can be thrown out of work by a labor dispute in a small factory. We are subject to many forces beyond our individual control.

Social Responsibility

Accompanying our growth in population we have had a growth in social conscience. The nineteenth century climate of "laissez faire" has gone forever. Today every organization must consider what society will think of its actions. (See Dialogue I. Also see "How Far Toward a Social Audit," *Public Relations Review,* Summer 1975.)

Mobility

The mobility of our population has created a rootlessness which makes problems for every institution. People change jobs and move to other towns. Companies transfer employees. Rural people move to the cities. City people move to the suburbs. Factories move to new locations. Every year one family in five moves to a new location. There was a time when people had attachments to specific locations but now such ties have weakened and this means that the relationships of people to the institutions of society are transient.

THE CURRENT ENVIRONMENT

In addition to the previously cited factors, which are relatively permanent, there are others which are more subject to change. If the general environment is the theater, the current environment is the stage on which public relations must carry out its role of adapting the organization to its social, political, and economic environment — and adapting that same environment to the organization.

Economic Ignorance

Public knowledge of economics is pitifully inadequate. Corporate profits are vastly overestimated. People frequently guess that profits are 25% to 50% of sales, say that 10% would be fair, and are amazed to learn that few firms make more than 5%. People question *how* profits are made and how they relate to social good.

The economic effect of taxes is a mystery to nearly everyone. People vote on economic issues without understanding them. Efforts are being made to remedy this situation but the task is enormous. (See "Public Relations and Economic Literacy," *Public Relations Review,* Summer 1975. Also see "Why Economic Education IS Working," *Public Relations Journal,* June 1977.)

The Intellectual Elite

Strongly affecting both public and private sectors of the economy are those who believe that everything can be managed from above. These are the people who try to convince the public that the average citizen can't buy a can of soup without being told how by government agencies.

The resistance to the Food and Drug Administration's attempts to limit the use of saccharin and the state laws legalizing laetrile reflect public dislike for this concept. Daniel Yankelovich, a nationally known public-opinion pollster, has criticized the arrogance which presumes that people don't know what is good for them and therefore should be protected from their own folly.

The Activists

Public opinion and the power leaders of the country are being strongly influenced by special-interest groups such as labor unions, consumerists, environmentalists, pro- and antiabortionists, and many others. These people have learned how to exploit television and, by sensational statements and actions, give their ideas a large volume of publicity. The temperate rebuttal of these ideas usually gets little attention from the average citizen (Lesly, 1974).

Terrorism

Bombings and sabotage have become so common that many organizations have had to set up extreme security measures. Access to buildings is restricted. Packages and cases are searched. Guards keep wary eyes on visitors. Identification badges have become routine. All of this tends to isolate the organization from the public and increases the problem of building frindly relations with people. (See "The Radicals are Coming," *Public Relations Journal,* December 1976.)

Consumerism

Not all consumers are convinced that business is cheating them, but there are many who believe this and their voices are loud and persuasive. Consumer groups were once considered to be extremist. Now they are being listened to.

Militancy

Because the proponents of various causes have a crusading attitude, and because the wheels of government and business and labor turn slowly, there has been much frustration among those who intensely believe that they are right and that the "Establishment" is not paying attention. The result has ranged from peaceful picketing to riots. In many situations there is an emotional powder keg that can explode with very little provocation. No one should attempt to ignore this condition.

Morality

There is a strange dichotomy on this subject. On one side there is a demand for the freedom of individuals to do whatever they choose, to not conform to established mores. On the other side there is a demand for the most rigidly moral conduct by our institutions. The same person who cheats an insurance company with faked claims may loudly criticize that same company for illegal political contributions.

Law and Order

The activists who defied segregation laws because they claimed the laws were unjust have spawned a host of others who wish to obey only the laws which *they* consider just. Public employees defy laws prohibiting strikes, unions refuse to obey court orders, motorists violate the 55 miles per hour speed limit.

Privacy vs. Freedom of Information

In two rather contradictory laws, Congress has decreed that an individual's privacy must be protected but that most public records must be open. This has sharply reduced the questions that may be asked of prospective employees. It makes references practically worthless because people are afraid that their comments will be made known to the person commented on. College instructors are afraid to say anything critical about students. People in government are afraid to express their opinions because the opinions may be publicized.

A classic example of the extremes to which this can lead is the case of a moving company which was sued for damages because an employee had raped a customer. The company, because of limitations on questioning, had been unable to learn that the man involved had a long record of similar crimes.

The "Rights" Explosion

American society is being splintered into many groups demanding special privileges based on race, sex, sexual orientation, socioeconomic status, physical handicaps, national origin, age, weight, height, and even left-handedness. These demands are based on a belief that these groups have been at a disadvantage and must now be compensated.

Today any organization may be sued by anyone who feels that he or she can make a case of adverse discrimination. This places all personnel policies under threat and requires extreme care in hiring, firing and promotion. Peter Sanchez-Novarro, formerly with the Equal Employment Opportunity Commission, has said that so many suits have been filed that judges now insist on "very good" cases.

Inflated Expectations

Some observers have stated that we now have a maximum of dissatisfaction and a minimum of willingness to work for the desired goals. Things which were once considered privileges are now considered rights. People are demanding many things without any thought of the costs and who pays the costs. (See Schumacher, 1973.)

Exaggerated Promises

Both politicians and advertisers have promised the public far more than they deliver. The result is a surfeit of skepticism which makes it ever more difficult to get the public to believe what they are told, even if it is true. Elliot Richardson, former Secretary of Health, Education and Welfare, says "What Congress authorizes — and what it actually appropriates — is a 'shell-game.' "

The Illusion of Perfection

Basic confidence in the system, plus success in many achievements has led to a general belief that anything can be fixed. "If they can put a man on the moon why can't they _____?" is a widely heard phrase. The result is public demand for the total elimination of manufacturing defects, of pollution, of sickness, of accidents, of unemployment, of crime, of racial and sexual discrimination — of every real or imagined fault in society.

Guilt by Accusation

It has been said that the indictment is always published on page one, while the dismissal is buried on page nineteen. There is truth in this statement and those who want to attack an institution rely on it. In many cases, unwarranted accusations are publicized — and the public too often believes the accusation and never sees the refutation.

Guilt by Association

A class-action lawsuit presumes that if one person is injured all others in that class are injured. In a reversal of that thesis, we now find many efforts to attribute guilt to all who are in the same class as the organization which was the source of the injury. "If one corporation is guilty, all corporations are guilty." A prize example is the bombing of public utility installations in Califormia because of the actions of a public utility in Ohio.

Blaming the System

This problem may have started with social scientists who blamed society for the failures of individuals. Now we have a situation where every shortcoming or failure may be blamed on society. People in ever increasing numbers are refusing to accept personal responsibility for their actions (Strumpel, 1975).

Loss of Faith in Institutions

For several years, opinion polls have shown a steady decline in public faith in our institutions. The tide seems to be turning but it will undoubtedly take years to restore a climate in which there is widespread confidence. Meanwhile public relations must operate in a skeptical atmosphere and for organizations which the public doesn't quite trust. (See "The Changing American" in Chapter 7.)

The Effect of Television

There has been much discussion of television violence. President Carter has said "There's too much violence on TV." This may be an important problem, but even more important is the general effect of this electronic monster. Television offers quick and easy solutions to hard problems.

In one hour, a detective solves a complicated crime. In one hour, a doctor cures a near-hopeless illness. Many doctors have said that Dr. Marcus Welby has created huge problems for the medical profession because patients expect to get the same highly personalized treatment and easy cures that Welby gives his patients. The result of all this is to lead the public to believe that they are being cheated if their problems aren't also solved in jig time.

Most people get their news from TV, and TV news is headline news. It seldom attempts in-depth coverage and when it does, it frequently fails. This leaves the public with only the sketchiest knowledge about important subjects.

Three networks supply nearly all the national and international news. What the public gets is decided by a handful of people — people who are not infallible and who are very conscious of "ratings."

TV news is often biased. The American Security Council Educational Foundation analyzed the CBS news coverage of national defense budgets for one year. It found 79 sentences in favor of higher spending; 774 sentences indicating that defense budgets were adequate and 1382 sentences favoring reduced expenditures. The Foundation filed a complaint with the Federal Communications Commission charging massive violation of the fairness doctrine. The Grocery Manufacturers of America and the American Meat Institute have filed a similar complaint against NBC because of an NBC documentary on food.

Michael Robinson of Catholic University of America has written an essay entitled: "American Political Legitimacy in an Era of Electronic Journalism — Reflections on the Evening News." In this essay, he indicates that hostility toward our institutions is due to impressions received from network journalism. He also indicates that people who rely solely on TV news have more negative opinions than those who rely on newspapers and magazines.

TV Guide has published many articles accusing the networks of biased and inaccurate reporting. Peter Braestrup, a Vietnam correspondent for the *New York Times* and later for the *Washington Post,* has published the book *Big Story* in which he details the falsity of network coverage of the famous Tet offensive.

The Computer Problem

We need computers to handle the information needed by our complex society, but computers are inhuman. They reduce people to coded numbers. Most important, from the standpoint of public relations, computers can contain vast amounts of information about people. By pushing the right buttons, the operator may learn much more about an individual than that person wants anyone to know.

Politicians use computers to produce what purport to be personalized letters to their constituents. Fund raisers, mail order firms, and others use computerized mailing lists to single out the most likely prospects. Even lawyers use computers to appraise jurors on the basis of how the juror may be expected to vote.

Special-interest groups use computers to generate letters to Congress, to state legislatures, and to executive departments. Often these groups represent only a small part of the populace, but a few thousand letters can be very persuasive — especially if there are few or none in opposition.

Government agencies exchange information with other agencies. The social security number is the key identifier used, and many people object to this usage. Objections have grown so strong that there is even great resistance to centralizing information about criminals.

Computers can make mistakes, they can permit massive thefts and they can be tapped by unauthorized people. We must learn to live with them, but we must also recognize the fact they they can create enormous public relations problems.

Suggested Readings

The foregoing is just a sampling of the current environment. A more comprehensive analysis can be found in a book which is recommended without reservation. Every public relations practitioner should read it, and make his chief executive officer or client read it. The book is:

Lesly, Philip. *The People Factor*. Homewood, Ill.: Dow-Jones, Irwin, 1974.

Other books which bear on the current environment are:

Alexander, Yonah, and Finger, Seymour M. (Eds.) *Terrorism: Interdisciplinary Perspectives.* New York: John Jay Press, 1977.
Bell, D. *Toward the Year 2000.* Boston, Mass.: Beacon Press, 1969.
Carson, R. *Silent Spring.* Boston, Mass.: Houghton Mifflin, 1962.
DeBell, G. *The Environmental Handbook.* New York: Ballantine, 1969.
Drucker, P. F. *The Age of Discontinuity.* New York: Harper & Row, 1968.
Dunstan, M. J., and Garlan, P. W. *Worlds in the Making.* Englewood Cliffs, N.J.: Prentice-Hall, 1970.
Ehrlich, P. R. *The Population Bomb.* New York: Ballantine, 1968.
Ehrlich, Paul R., and Anne H. *The End of Affluence.* New York: Ballantine, 1974.
Fabun, D. (Ed.) *The Dynamics of Change.* Englewood Cliffs, N.J.: Prentice-Hall, 1969.
Hill & Knowlton Executives. *Critical Issues in Public Relations.* New York: Parker, 1976.
Hirsch, Fred. *Social Limits to Growth.* Cambridge, Mass.: Harvard University Press, 1976.
McLuhan, M. *Understanding Media: The Extension of Man.* New York: McGraw-Hill, 1965.
Meadows, Donella H. et al. *The Limits to Growth.* Washington, D.C.: Potomac, 1974.
Reich, C. A. *The Greening of America.* New York: Random House, 1970.
Schumacher, E. F. *Small is Beautiful.* New York: Harper & Row, 1973.
Silberman, C. E. *Crisis in the Classroom.* New York: Random House, 1970.
Strumpel, Burkhard (Ed.). *Economic Needs for Human Needs.* Ann Arbor, Mich.: University of Michigan Press, 1975.
Toffler, A. *Future Shock.* New York: Random House, 1970.

PROBLEMS OF PUBLIC RELATIONS

Many would like to call public relations a profession, but it has not yet reached that status. For the present, it has to be called an art or craft, or even an occupation. Regardless of the designation, public relations has problems in and of itself.

The Image of Public Relations

Public opinion of public relations seems to be improving. Few describe practitioners as "slick" or "dishonest." Many people think that they perform a useful purpose in society, but most people still think that publicity is the chief function. Few, if any, are aware of the practitioner's role in formulating policy which can assure good relations with the public. All of this proves that the people in the field must do a public relations job for their craft.

Incompetents

Unfortunately, there are incompetent people practicing public relations. Some are outright frauds without any real knowledge of the meaning of PR. Others are just misfits. The author knows intimately one person who was given the top public relations job in a major department of the federal government. The person had not one day of education, training or experience in PR, but got the job through political influence.

Other examples of untrained and unqualified people in public relations jobs can be found easily, sometimes in quite large organizations. If the president chooses to appoint an incompetent with no training and no experience, there is nothing that competent professionals can do about it.

Professionalism

The goal of the Public Relations Society of America is to establish the professional practice of public relations as an essential function in the American democratic system. It has made substantial progress toward that objective. Many practitioners are truly professional, but public relations is still not a profession in the traditional or legal sense.

A profession has some control over its membership. It sets standards for admission and can prevent untrained and incompetent people from practicing. Usually this involves some form of licensing and legal penalties for practicing without a license. So far, no one has come up with a definition of what a practitioner should do, or be able to do, as qualification for professional status or a license. There is considerable controversy and many diverging opinions about this among even the most highly regarded practitioners in the Society.

Accreditation

The closest approach to establishing public relations as a profession is the accreditation program of the Public Relations Society of America. Practitioners with at least five years of experience take exhaustive oral and written examinations. These cover the history of PR, the basic principles and techniques, the personal history of the applicant, and the solution of specific public relations problems.

Those who pass—and not all pass—are given a Certificate of Accreditation and the right to use behind their names the initials APR, which mean "Accredited (in) Public Relations." This program is growing, and more and more organizations are requiring accreditation as a qualification for advancement or even employment.

Euphemisms

There are thousands of people practicing public relations for the federal government, but not one can admit it. The reason is that several laws forbid spending government money for "public relations." These laws are an attempt to keep government agencies from trying to influence Congress. So we have "public information," or "public affairs," or "information," or other words used to describe this function.

The same situation exists in private business. The misconceptions about public relations described in Chapter 1, plus the misuse of the words in connection with the Watergate affair have caused many to adopt euphemisms such as "communications," "public affairs," "public information," and so on. These euphemisms may serve in some cases, but they don't adequately describe the PR function.

The leaders of the public relations field generally agree that there is only one correct name and that it should be used, even though it is often used by the uninformed as an epithet.

Ethics

The conduct of public relations practitioners has a big effect on public opinion about the practice. Anyone can practice, or try to practice, public relations. There is no profession to enter, no license to acquire. No one can be restricted or deprived of a license. The closest approach to control or guidance of conduct is through the PRSA. The Society has established a code of professional standards which is quoted below.

PUBLIC RELATIONS SOCIETY OF AMERICA

This Code, adopted by the PRSA Assembly, replaces a similar Code of Professional Standards for the Practice of Public Relations previously in force since 1954 and strengthened by revisions in 1959, 1963 and 1977.

DECLARATION OF PRINCIPLES

Members of the Public Relations Society of America base their professional principles on the fundamental value and dignity of the individual, holding that the free exercise of human rights, especially freedom of speech, freedom of assembly and freedom of the press, is essential to the practice of public relations.

In serving the interests of clients and employers, we dedicate ourselves to the goals of better communication, understanding and cooperation among the diverse individuals, groups and institutions of society.

We pledge:

To conduct ourselves professionally, with truth, accuracy, fairness and responsibility to the public;

To improve our individual competence and advance the knowledge and proficiency of the profession through continuing research and education;

And to adhere to the articles of the Code of Professional Standards for the Practice of Public Relations as adopted by the governing Assembly of the Society.

CODE OF PROFESSIONAL STANDARDS FOR THE PRACTICE OF PUBLIC RELATIONS

These articles have been adopted by the Public Relations Society of America to promote and maintain high standards of public service and ethical conduct among its members.

1. A member shall deal fairly with clients or employers, past and present, with fellow practitioners and the general public.

2. A member shall conduct his or her professional life in accord with the public interest.

3. A member shall adhere to truth and accuracy and to generally accepted standards of good taste.

4. A member shall not represent conflicting or competing interests without the express consent of those involved, given after a full disclosure of the facts; nor place himself or herself in a position where the member's interest is or may be in conflict with a duty to a client, or others, without a full disclosure of such interests to all involved.

5. A member shall safeguard the confidences of both present and former clients or employers and shall not accept retainers or employment which may involve the disclosure or use of these confidences to the disadvantage or prejudice of such clients or employers.

6. A member shall not engage in any practice which tends to corrupt the integrity of channels of communication or the processes of government.

7. A member shall not intentionally communicate false or misleading information and is obligated to use care to avoid communication of false or misleading information.

8. A member shall be prepared to identify publicly the name of the client or employer on whose behalf any public communication is made.

9. A member shall not make use of any individual or organization purporting to serve or represent an announced case, or purporting to be independent or unbiased, but actually serving an undisclosed special or private interest of a member, client or employer.

10. A member shall not intentionally injure the professional reputation or practice of another practitioner. However, if a member has evidence that another member has been guilty of unethical, illegal or unfair practices, including those in violation of this Code, the member shall present the information promptly to the proper authorities of the Society for action in accordance with the procedure set forth in Article XIII of the Bylaws.

11. A member called as a witness in a proceeding for the enforcement of this Code shall be bound to appear, unless excused for sufficient reason by the Judicial Panel.

12. A member, in performing services for a client or employer, shall not accept fees, commissions or any other valuable consideration from anyone other than the client or employer in connection with those services without the express consent of the client or employer, given after a full disclosure of the facts.

13. A member shall not guarantee the achievement of specified results beyond the member's direct control.

14. A member shall, as soon as possible, sever relations with any organization or individual if such relationship requires conduct contrary to the articles of this Code.

OFFICIAL INTERPRETATIONS OF THE CODE OF PROFESSIONAL STANDARDS FOR THE PRACTICE OF PUBLIC RELATIONS

Interpretation of Code Paragraph 2 which reads, "A member shall conduct his or her professional life in accord with the public interest."

The public interest is here defined primarily as comprising respect for and enforcement of the rights guaranteed by the Constitution of the United States of America.

Interpretation of Code Paragraph 5 which reads, "A member shall safeguard the confidences of both present and former clients or employers and shall not accept retainers or employment which may involve the disclosure or use of these confidences to the disadvantage or prejudice of such clients or employers."

This article does not prohibit a member who has knowledge of client or employee activities which are illegal from making such disclosures to the proper authorities as he or she believes are legally required.

Interpretation of Code Paragraph 6 which reads, "A member shall not engage in any practice which tends to corrupt the integrity of channels of communication or the processes of government."

1. Practices prohibited by this paragraph are those which tend to place representatives of media or government under an obligation to the member, or the member's employer or client, which is in conflict with their obligations to media or government, such as:
   a. the giving of gifts of more than nominal value;
   b. any form of payment or compensation to a member of the media in order to obtain preferential or

guaranteed news or editorial coverage in the medium;

c. any retainer or fee to a media employee or use of such employee if retained by a client or employer, where the circumstances are not fully disclosed to and accepted by the media employer;

d. providing trips for media representatives which are unrelated to legitimate news interest;

e. the use by a member of an investment or loan or advertising commitment made by the member, or the member's client or employer, to obtain preferential or guaranteed coverage in the medium.

2. This Code paragraph does not prohibit hosting media or government representatives at meals, cocktails, or news functions or special events which are occasions for the exchange of news information or views, or the furtherance of understanding which is part of the public relations function. Nor does it prohibit the bonafide press event or tour when media or government representatives are given an opportunity for on-the-spot viewing of a newsworthy product, process or event in which the media or government representatives have a legitimate interest. What is customary or reasonable hospitality has to be a

matter of particular judgement in specific situations. In all of these cases, however, it is or should be understood that no preferential treatment or guarantees are expected or implied and that complete independence always is left to the media or government representative.

3. This paragraph does not prohibit the reasonable giving or lending of sample products or services to media representatives who have a legitimate interest in the products or services.

Interpretation of Code Paragraph 13 which reads, "A member shall not guarantee the achievement of specified results beyond the member's direct control."

This Code paragraph, in effect, prohibits misleading a client or employer as to what professional public relations can accomplish. It does not prohibit guarantees of quality or service. But it does prohibit guaranteeing specific results which, by their very nature, cannot be guaranteed because they are not subject to the member's control. As an example, a guarantee that a news release will appear specifically in a particular publication would be prohibited. This paragraph should not be interpreted as prohibiting contingent fees.

The code should be followed by members and nonmembers alike. Members of PRSA who are found guilty of violating the code may be expelled from the society.

In the general area of ethics, it seems the biggest question is this: Is the practitioner solely an advocate for his principal or client? Lawyers provide their services to people regardless of their character. They justify this by saying that everyone is entitled to legal representation. So we find lawyers fighting to save the most hardened criminals from a fate which many onlookers think is richly deserved.

Some public relations practitioners use the same justification, others say that we should not use our talents to advocate something that is not socially desirable. This raises the question of what is or is not socially desirable. Often there are two sides to a question with both proponents and opponents convinced that their side is the one that is socially desirable.

Perhaps the best solution is for the practitioner to work only for what he or she sincerely believes in. It will result in better work and free the practitioner from feeling like a charlatan. Recently the author worked in a campaign to defeat a statewide ballot initiative. He worked for half price because he was opposed in principle to the measure. No conceivable sum of money could have induced him to work for the other side. Yet, the people on the other side were just as firm in the opinion that theirs was the right side.

Impersonal Managers

Lack of public confidence is probably the biggest problem facing the institutions of our society. Yet in many institutions, the top executives are still running their organizations without really thinking about the public. Books on management often totally disregard the public factor. Our colleges of business administration graduate M.B.A.s who have no exposure to the idea that public attitudes and opinions are vital to the success of any organization. More and more of these deficiently educated people are progressing into top levels of management.

Public relations practitioners repeatedly state that one of their biggest problems is to get top management to really *think* about the public and to *do* what is necessary to build public confidence. True, the status of public relations is improving, but there are still too many chief executive officers who treat the activity as of secondary importance. (See Dialogue II.)

In contrast to this, Justin Dart, Chairman of Dart Industries, has said that any chief executive officer who doesn't devote at least a third of his time to public affairs should be fired.

Silent and Invisible Executives

Another great problem of public relations is the inability or refusal of top executives to talk to the public. This point is discussed at length in Dialogue II.

PROBLEMS OF OUR SOCIETY

Some of these problems may be solved in a few years; others may take many years; still others may never be completely solved. All of these problems are crucial and all will necessitate the employment of public relations to a degree and at a level of performance far above what has been done in the past. This list of problems is not necessarily complete, but it does show the things that are most conspicuous at present.

Urban Problems

Inadequate housing, inadequate transportation, the exodus of businesses and the jobs they create, the flight to the suburbs, the physical and moral decay of our inner cities all contribute to an urban problem which affects the entire country. The national Mayors' Conference has made impassioned pleas for federal help on this problem.

The Population Explosion

Ever-increasing numbers of people are putting ever-growing burdens on all of our resources. Dr. Paul Ehrlich of Stanford University estimates that the world's population will double in 37 years and predicts that millions will starve before the year 2000 (Ehrlich, 1968).

Limited Resources

James Schlesinger, President Carter's first Secretary of Energy, has said that world supplies of oil and natural gas will be exhausted in 40 years. The Environmental Protection Agency predicts that there will be drastic water shortages in most of the United States by the year 2000. Shortages of minerals, timber, and farmland are also anticipated. All this suggests that future generations will be less affluent (Ehrlich, 1974).

Employment

Large numbers of people have no usable skills, particularly young members of the minorities. Fifty years ago, there was work for the un-skilled; today there is practically none. The National Urban League estimates that 50% of all black teenagers have no jobs. Even the employ-ment of skilled workers is affected by environmental restraints and by imports of goods made by low-cost labor.

Inflation

No one accepts responsibility, but continuing inflation is eroding sav-ings and reducing incomes for millions of people, especially the elderly.

Dr. Robert J. Gordon of Northwestern University says the outlook is "grim."

Minorities

Integration, civil rights, and opportunities for employment and promotion are continuing problems. Much progress has been made, but there is still a long way to go.

The Environment

Air pollution, water pollution, waste disposal, urban sprawl, mining, lumbering, and thousands of construction projects all damage the physical environment. The cost of preserving and protecting the environment will be enormous. Explanation of the costs and benefits will be a great problem for public relations practitioners.

Immigration

Estimates of illegal Mexican aliens in the U.S. range from 6 to 12 million. There is one estimate that the next generation will have to cope with 60 million illegal Mexicans. Mexico is only one of several countries having more people than they can employ or feed.

Distaste for Hard Work

Thousands, or perhaps millions, of Americans won't take jobs that are hot, cold, dirty, or sweaty. Attempts to reduce welfare rolls by offering jobs in this category have met great resistance. Increasingly, illegal aliens are filling these jobs. Restoration of some form of the old "bracero" plan, which admitted foreign laborers on a temporary work permit, is being advocated.

Aid Programs

Health care, welfare, unemployment compensation, social security, and several smaller programs are performing poorly, yet at ever-increasing costs. President Carter has set welfare reform as a major objective of his administration. Radical changes seem necessary in some of these areas. Getting the changes made will be another problem for public relations. Senator Lawton Chiles of Florida says that welfare is "out of control" and must be harnessed quickly.

Crime

With millions of people living in fear of violent crime, there must be some solution which will reduce this threat. There is no agreement on the causes of crime, nor on the methods of prevention. Yet, there is wide public demand for safety in our homes, at work, at play, and wherever we choose to go.

The Cost of Government

With the costs of government approaching half of the gross national product, many economists fear that it is becoming impossible for the economy to support this imbalance. Predictions range from a taxpayers' strike to governmental bankruptcy.

The Burden of Government

This may be one of the biggest problems of all. Laws, regulations and red tape have become so complicated that it is extremely difficult to accomplish anything. With an estimated 150,000 new laws every year, even lawyers can't keep up with the flood.

The problems don't apply to business alone. States and cities are hampered by federal laws. The federal government is restricted by state laws. Colleges are loaded with restrictions. Churches and hospitals are burdened. Contractors report that it now takes from 18 to 27 months to clear developments which once could be cleared in 9 months. The list could go on for pages. Chapter 15 will elaborate on this problem.

OPPORTUNITIES

At first glance, the preceding list of problems may seem appalling. There are indeed many serious problems, but they should be looked at as challenges rather than difficulties, as opportunities rather than barriers. Every one of these problems involves the public. In every problem, there is a need for the services of public relations professionals. The social, political, and economic environment is indeed turbulent but it shouldn't be discouraging.

EXERCISES

1. Get a copy of the latest daily newspaper. Mark all items that presumably will *not* affect public opinion.
2. What is the subject on which public opinion is most intense at this time?
3. Find a news item that you think was originated by a public relations practitioner.

Case Problem

In order to reduce airplane and airport congestion it is proposed to ban air travel between New York and Boston. Travelers would have to use railroads, buses, or private cars.

Who would favor this ruling? What organizations, groups, and individuals would support it?

Who would oppose this ruling? What organizations, groups, and individuals would help?

What ideas would you try to convey in order to get support for or against this proposal?

How would you get your ideas to the interested parties?

Dialogue I

Dialogue with Mr. James F. Langton, APR, Senior Vice-President for Social Policy, Bank of America.

This dialogue pinpoints many of the problems of public relations at the present time, showing how one of America's largest business organizations is coping with these problems.

Q. Why does Bank of America devote so much attention to social policy?
A. For some years, this was handled as a part of the general public relations activity of the bank. However, the problems became so important that the bank decided to establish this program as a separate major entity, parallel to and cooperating with the public relations department.
Q. Then the bank must consider social policy a very important factor in its operation?
A. It certainly does. No corporation can survive in a hostile environment. We must be aware of and respond to public needs. In an era of consumerism, we must look at our ethics and attitudes. In an era of changing value systems, we must conform to those systems.
Q. What is the bank's policy on social responsibility?
A. To see that all of the bank's policies and practices are in reasonable consonance with the values and expectations of the society in which we operate.
Q. In other words, the bank feels that it must adapt to its social, political, and economic environment?
A. Yes, emphatically yes!
Q. Public attitudes and opinions change. How do you keep up with them?

A. By constantly studying them. We must be aware of what people are thinking and saying. Some of that awareness comes from professional intuition, sensitivity to what is going on. When we spot a potential problem, we investigate. Sometimes we do our own research. We rely heavily on the surveys of emerging public issues conducted by Yankelovich, Skelly and White, and other pollsters.

Q. What do you do with this information?

A. The first step is to find out how it impacts on the bank.

Q. Can you give me an example?

A. Let's take the question of discrimination against women. This may involve many different phases of our operation. To name just three, it affects employment, promotion, and credit policies. All are separate but interrelated functions.

Q. When you determine that a social problem does affect the bank, what do you do?

A. When relevance to the bank is clear, we prepare a report and recommend action to the social policy committee.

Q. What is this committee?

A. It is a top-level committee which is responsible for identifying problems and issues and changing bank policy and practice when appropriate. The ten-member committee is made up of senior executive officers who operate many of our major divisions.

Q. Can this committee act?

A. Yes, the people on the committee can make a decision and carry it out. They do this regularly.

Q. Who does this committee report to?

A. To the chief executive officer — the president.

Q. You also have a committee of the board of directors?

A. Yes, the public policy committee consists of six directors. They meet monthly to review the bank's performance in social, political and (physical) environmental areas.

Q. Where do you fit into this program?

A. I am chairman of the social policy committee and secretary of the public policy committee. I report to an executive vice-president who is responsible for this and other areas.

Q. Do you publicize the decisions on social policy?

A. If it is of general interest, we inform the public relations department and they make the announcement. For example, the bank decided it would not support memberships in private clubs which discriminated against women or racial minorities. This was publicized. On the other hand, some policies may be changed without any general publicity.

Q. I have been reading much about "red-lining," the designation of areas which are believed unsuitable for real estate loans.

A. We don't "red-line." Strangely, that activity really started with a federal agency, the Federal Housing Authority, which set up areas where it would not guarantee loans. Naturally no financial institution can lend its depositors' money without a good chance of getting it back, but the individual loan is the important thing. We have about a dozen different programs to put money into areas where special problems exist.

Q. Can you give me some examples of actions the bank is taking to implement its social policies?

A. Our annual report on social policy activities fills a 26-page booklet. Among the general topics are: community, urban restoration, consumers, environment, education, employment, agriculture, the arts, and volunteer activities. In just one area, education, we offer student loans, loans to medical students, achievement awards, community college awards, career symposiums, English as a second language, and the Fromm Institute for Lifelong Learning.

Q. What is the bank's record in employing minorities?

A. 26.5% of California's population are minorities. 28.3% of our staff in California are from the minorities. More than 75% of our staff are women.

Q. I frequently see complaints that there are relatively few women in higher office in your bank and in other companies.

A. Higher officers attain their positions through experience, not through arbitrary quotas. As our women employees progress, they are moving into higher positions and we are helping them through our management-training program. In the lower levels of management, about 55% of the officers are women. In the upper grades, the percentage is rising every year.

Q. What about racial minority executives?

A. The situation is similar — progress upward as experience is gained and capability is proved.

Q. What problems do you see ahead?

A. There are such problems as urban decay, the elderly, energy, the physical environment, and many others — but there are two which are especially important in public relations.

Q. What are they?

A. First is the public questioning of how large corporations are governed. Corporate government is the "in" term. The people are saying in effect, "What assurance do we have that the giant corporations are being run in a manner beneficial to us?" Second the people are demanding openness in corporate operations. The Securities and Exchange Commission demands "full and timely disclosure," but this goes beyond that. Corporations must get out from behind their veils of secrecy. This is an open society and our institutions must be open.

▌▌
Public Relations People

The public relations specialist has a dual role. He is both advisor and practitioner. As an advisor, he makes public relations policy recommendations to
management. As a practitioner, he does all the specialized work of public
relations, which includes recommending public relations programs to management and carrying them out when they are approved. Public relations is
one of the most versatile occupations known. No two jobs are identical, no two
days are alike, and no two problems can be solved in the same way. Among the
activities that might be considered "normal" are:

> advising top management on policy
> participating in policy decisions
> planning PR programs
> selling programs to top management
> getting cooperation of middle management
> getting cooperation of other employees
> listening to speeches
> making speeches
> writing speeches for others
> getting speakers for organization meetings
> providing speakers for outside organizations
> attending meetings
> planning and conducting meetings
> attending conventions
> planning and managing conventions
> preparing publicity items
> talking to editors and reporters
> holding press conferences
> writing feature articles
> doing research on public opinion
> planning and managing events

conducting tours
writing letters — both form and individual
planning, writing, and producing booklets, leaflets, reports, and bulletins
editing house organs
supervising bulletin boards
designing posters
planning and, sometimes, directing films or videotapes
planning and preparing slide presentations and film strips
planning and producing exhibits and demonstrations
taking pictures or supervising photographers
planning and managing PR advertising
making awards
greeting visitors
screening charity requests
and almost anything else that involves contact with the public.

The following two chapters discuss the ways in which the public relations function is performed and the qualifications that are necessary for successful individual accomplishment in this field.

Organization for Public Relations 5

Effective public relations programs do not just happen. They require a lot of time and effort. Everyone in an organization should be concerned with public relations, but someone must be specifically responsible if anything is to be accomplished.

In small organizations the PR function may be handled by the head of the organization or it may be assigned as a part-time duty to someone else. In larger organizations the use of specialists becomes a necessity because the nature and volume of the work to be done requires the employment of someone who is especially skilled in the techniques of public relations. When the head of a small organization handles public relations, he has a dual role. He not only determines policy, but he also practices public relations.

In organizations where there is a public relations director or counselor, that individual advises management on public relations policy and recommends public relations programs. When the recommendation is approved, the PR director or counselor carries out the program.

A good parallel can be found in an army division. The division engineer is the advisor on engineering problems. He is also commander of the engineer battalion of the division. In his dual role he may "advise" the commanding general to cross a certain river today because heavy rains will make it impassable tomorrow. He may recommend that certain bridges be built in certain locations. When the advice is accepted and the recommendation approved, the engineer must then use his battalion to build those bridges.

There are three principal ways in which the practice of public relations is carried out: through the use of an internal PR department, through the employment of an external PR counselor, or through the use of both. Each of these methods has advantages and disadvantages. There is no *best* way.

The practice of public relations is substantially the same regardless of whether it is done by one man or by a large number of people, by an internal department, an external counselor, or both.

THE INTERNAL PUBLIC RELATIONS DEPARTMENT

The internal PR department may be simply the few hours a month that the head of the organization devotes to the subject. It may be the part-time responsibility of some specially designated individual. It may be one man working exclusively on public relations. Or it may be hundreds of people working in offices scattered throughout the country. Regardless of size or numbers, the function is basically the same.

Pros . . .

The internal public relations department has some very definite advantages. One of the first is that it *is* internal. The PR director is part of the team. His complete loyalty to the organization is automatically assumed. He is close, psychologically, to the other members of the team. He belongs.

Another advantage is that the public relations director can know the organization and its problems in great detail. Spending all his time with one group, he is bound to get the feel of it. He can learn the underlying causes of problems. He can become familiar with the foibles and failings, the strengths and abilities of the people who run the show. And his management can know him better.

Because the internal PR department is normally in the same building with top management, it is readily available. Conversely, this makes top management more accessible to the public relations director. Appointments are easier to schedule. In some cases they may not even be needed.

Contacts can be informal. Quick decisions can be made. Rush jobs can be done more quickly. This constant presence makes others think more about public relations. It increases the frequency of informal contacts and conversations with others. It gives the PR director many more opportunities to get information and many more opportunities to "sell" his program and himself to others in the group.

. . . and Cons

A disadvantage of the internal department is that it may lose objectivity. Being within the organization, it is possible to become so close to what is going on that there is no understanding of its significance. The PR director may become deeply involved in some activity and completely overlook a problem that requires immediate action. He may get so busy on execution that he neglects planning, or he may concentrate too much on planning and fail to do an adequate job of advising top management.

A further danger is that enthusiasm for what is being done may lead to self-delusion. Public relations is a business of enthusiasts and, with no professional critics to judge the nature of the performance, it is possible to get off the track.

Any workman worth hiring should be proud of his work. PR people are almost certain to be proud of their work, but an objective evaluation by professionals in the same field has some very definite advantages.

Accessibility has its disadvantages as well. By the mere fact that it is there, the PR department is all too often involved in unimportant activities. The "daily crisis" can become routine and the PR director can spend far too much time struggling with minor problems and going to unnecessary meetings; he may even run errands for top management.

THE PUBLIC RELATIONS COUNSELOR

The public relations counselor may be one man devoting most or all of his time to a specific organization. He may be one man with several clients or a nationwide firm with hundreds of employees and scores of clients. The counselor may also be a department of an advertising agency.

Pros . . .

Objectivity is one great advantage of the PR counselor. Detached from the effects of the problems, he can look at them more calmly and more professionally than those directly involved. Doctors always get another doctor to operate on members of their families because they want calm professionalism completely free from personal involvement. In the same way, the outside counselor can look at his client with detachment and make recommendations that are based on cold reason and logic.

Serving a number of clients gives the external counselor the benefit of very broad experience with a wide variety of problems. No two organizations have identical problems, but often there are similarities, and experience in handling one may be invaluable in another like situation.

Thus, the counselor may be better prepared for the new or unexpected than the internal PR man. His experience may not be so deep with one particular organization, but what he loses in depth he gains in breadth.

The external counselor provides the exact amount and caliber of talent needed — and that is possibly his greatest service. It may be preferable to employ a $30,000-a-year man one-third of the time than a $10,000-a-year man full-time, since many public relations functions can often be performed by less costly talent.

Another advantage of the external counselor is that a number of experts can be made available as needed by the clients who could not afford to hire them all individually. If Company A needs guidance in one area today and another area tomorrow it can draw on its counselors for what is needed. The following week, Company B may be relying on those same people for help with similar problems.

Last, but by no means least, we should recognize that the outside counselor often has more prestige than the internal department. The chairman of the board of a large PR firm may be better able to impress the chairman of the board of the client.

. . . and Cons

The external counselor is always external. In many cases he is not given a chance to become familiar with the organization he is serving. True, he gets answers to his questions, but he may not get the full truth. If he does, he can do a much better job than he can with incomplete information. But some organizations find it difficult to be completely frank with an outsider. This condition is not universal; many organizations do trust the PR counselor completely, but the fact that he is an outsider remains a disadvantage.

Another handicap burdening the external public relations counselor is the possibility that his work may occasionally be superficial, or that there may be friction with the internal department.

PAYING THE PIPER

If public relations counsel is retained on a continuing basis, it may charge for services in one of these ways:

1. a fixed retainer fee (monthly or annual),

2. a retainer fee plus monthly charges for actual staff time on an hourly or per diem basis, or

3. a basic fee plus added charges for additional services performed beyond the retainer.

Out-of-pocket charges for things like travel, printing, mailing, etc. are also billed to the client. Sometimes they are billed at cost, but often there is a surcharge ranging from 5% to 17.65% to cover overhead expenses of buying and billing. Sometimes PR counselors are retained on a job basis — so much to handle a convention, so much to produce a booklet, etc. These jobs are usually paid for by a fee plus expenses.

The most widely used system is the fee plus costs. It has the advantage of putting all the counselor's income on a fee basis agreed upon in advance.*

Fees for public relations counselors depend on who the clients are, who the counselor is, and how big the problem is. A small factory might pay a few hundred dollars a month to a local counselor. A nationwide firm in the billion-dollar class or a large trade association might pay $500,000 a year to one of the larger counselors.

GIVE 'EM BOTH BARRELS

Many large organizations have both a sizable internal department and an external counselor. This tends to minimize the disadvantages and maximize the advantages of each. The use of an external counselor enables the department to get extra help to even out the work load and to provide special talent that may be needed for a short time only. Also, the combination of department and counselor permits each to benefit by the other's experience and judgment and gives each the test of criticism by professionals.

WHERE DOES THE PUBLIC RELATIONS DEPARTMENT BELONG?

No two company organization charts are alike and no two public relations problems are alike, so the placement of the PR department varies widely. Ideally, the director of public relations should report directly to the president or chief executive. This is an important function and, since

*For more complete information, *see Fees, Charges, and Overhead in the Practice of Public Relations,* Public Relations Society of America, 1972 and *Public Relations and Public Relations Counseling,* Public Relations Society of America, 1966.

it affects the entire organization, it should be supervised by the man who runs the organization. Unfortunately, this is not always the case. Sometimes PR is under the advertising director, sometimes under the sales director, sometimes under the treasurer or even the legal department. All of these are unsatisfactory situations. Most organizations that recognize the need for a PR department also recognize its importance and give it a direct line of communication to the head man.

BRANCH OFFICES AND BRANCH DEPARTMENTS

In many organizations, the public relations department is centralized at the principal place of business. There are a few cases, however, where branch departments exist. A large manufacturer may have a centralized PR department and PR offices in various manufacturing plants. The most elaborate organization is probably in the telephone business. AT&T has a large PR department; each of its operating divisions (such as Pacific Telephone Co.) has a PR department, and there are PR departments at regional or area offices.

Many large organizations with numerous branches, plants, or offices but with a centralized PR department provide the local managers with detailed manuals on public relations. These usully foresee close liaison with the central PR department, but do instruct the manager specifically in a wide variety of situations.

WHAT DEPARTMENTS ARE INVOLVED?

The PR department (or counselor) is at one time or another involved with almost every department in the organization. It may work with Personnel in preparing a booklet to explain the training system; with Industrial Relations in explaining the terms of a union contract; with Advertising in telling employees about a new campaign; with Sales in publicizing an improved product; with Operations in preparing a statement for a government regulatory body; with Engineering in publicizing the reasons behind the choice of a site; with Manufacturing in designing a safety poster; with Accounting in developing the annual report; with Legal in preparing a press release about the effects of a proposed law.

Because all departments can affect the public relations of the company, it is most important that they cooperate with the PR department. Here

MONTGOMERY WARD & CO.

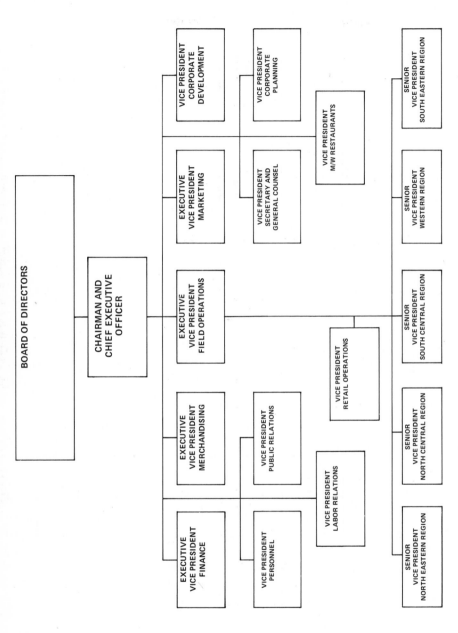

Fig. 5.1 Status of public relations in a large company.

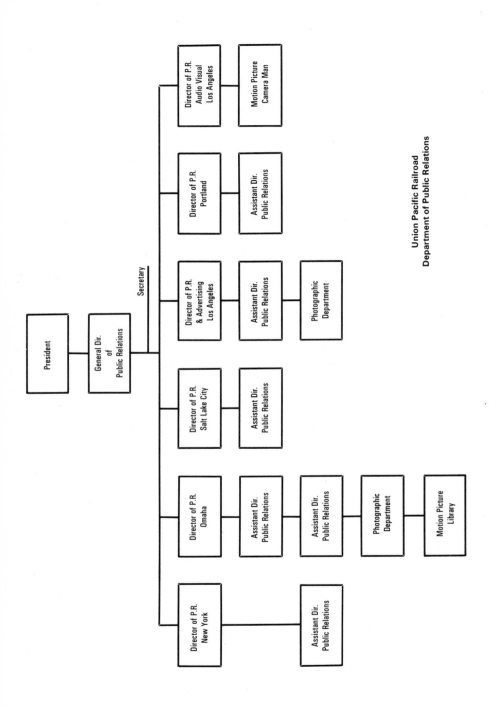

Fig. 5.2 Organization chart of a multioffice public relations department.

the burden is on PR. It must win that cooperation by conducting an internal and informal public relations program with them.

One principle to be followed rigidly is "don't encroach on anyone's authority." The PR function is a staff function. It cannot order anyone outside the PR department to do anything. It is, of course, possible to get the head of the organization to order cooperation but, if that is done, it will probably be grudgingly given and when that order is complied with the next job will be even more difficult. The only way to get enthusiastic cooperation is by friendly persuasion and by involving the other departments in the program.

If a department head has helped to formulate a plan, he will be much more enthusiastic than if he learns about it through a bulletin.

With all departments involved in public relations, it is obvious that the PR department must get a lot of its work done by others. This requires not only cooperation, but also coordination. Group discussions involving all departments can often be helpful.

In many organizations there is a joint committee on public relations. This has the advantage of continuous participation by other departments, but it has several drawbacks. It tends to downgrade the importance of the PR department by making it the organization that carries out the plans of the committee rather than the organization that really handles the function. If the committee is used as a consultative or advisory body, it can be very helpful. But if it assumes too much authority, it can soon hamstring the whole program. Nevertheless, a PR committee can be an asset when it functions properly in an advisory role.

SELLING THE PUBLIC RELATIONS FUNCTION

If an organization has a PR department or counselor, it is reasonable to assume that someone has sold the organization on the idea. But that is only the beginning, because public relations must be resold constantly.

Top management has to be continually persuaded because public relations activities cost money and there are many demands for that money. Middle management, too, must be sold. At the upper levels, it is often a matter of convincing the various departments that PR is a necessary function and that they should not look at it as an expense cutting into their share of the budget. Even more important, however, is the help that middle management can give in carrying out a program.

HOW TO SELL PUBLIC RELATIONS TO THE ORGANIZATION

Above all, the PR practitioner must know his own business. If the PR director is competent, it will be evident to those he contacts. In addition, he must know the business of his organization. He should know something about every department. That is a tall order but a good one because he has to work with all parts of the organization. The more he knows about the organization, the better will be his understanding of its problems.

There are a number of things the PR director should do to learn about his organization.

First, he should read everything he can find about his own organization and the area in which it functions. Books, bulletins, reports, house organs, magazine and newspaper articles — anything that is written should be included in this study. Trade publications deserve special attention because they are loaded with information about their particular field of interest. And there is hardly a business without its own special trade journal.

Second, the practitioner should get away from the desk and talk with people in the organization — department heads, assistants, junior executives, and run-of-the-mill employees. All can contribute to the process of education. Communicating with people is a two-way process that involves both talking and listening. A very large part of the talking should be asking questions. People are always flattered when someone asks a question. When a question is asked it not only gets some information but also pleases the person asked.

Most of the questions will be about the how's and why's of the operation of the business. "When did we start this?" "Where do we get the raw material?" "Why do we do such and such?" Inevitably, there will be some coverage of items affecting public relations, but it should be considered secondary in this context.

The PR director asks questions for two purposes: first, to thoroughly understand the organization; second, to learn about the public relations of the organization so that they can be improved. In a later chapter we will devote considerable attention to the questions bearing directly on public relations.

A bonus gained from talking with others is acquaintance with the people in the organization — and this is the first step toward selling the organization on the PR function and its personnel.

Public relations people must do their homework. Without proper un-

Hill and Knowlton...Administrative Organization

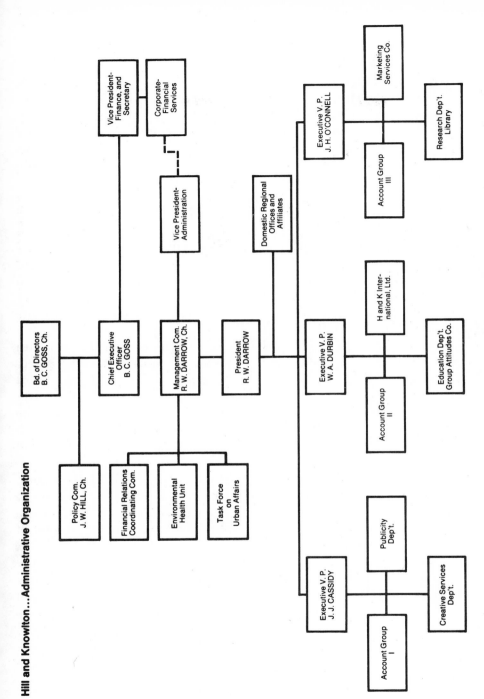

Fig. 5.3 Organization chart of a large public relations counselor.

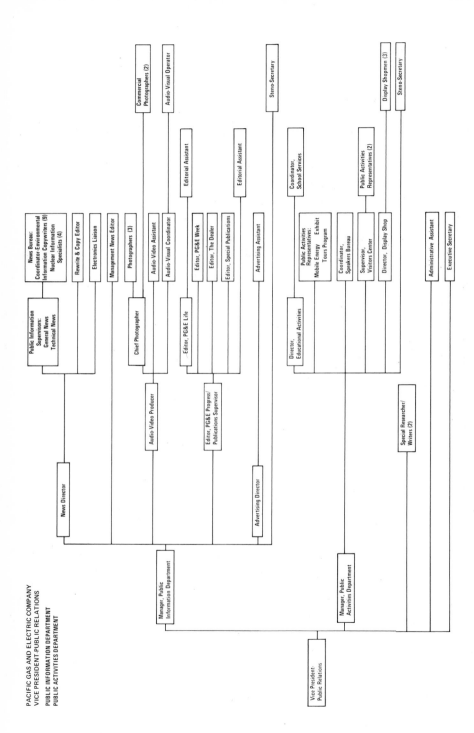

PACIFIC GAS AND ELECTRIC COMPANY
VICE PRESIDENT-PUBLIC RELATIONS

PUBLIC INFORMATION DEPARTMENT
PUBLIC ACTIVITIES DEPARTMENT

Fig. 5.4 Organization chart of a large public relations department.

derstanding of the organization, they may make recommendations that are either impractical or so far out of keeping with the spirit of the organization that they are unacceptable. Any PR recommendation must be both practical and palatable. To be sure of both points requires a thorough knowledge of the organization and its people.

If a PR program is to succeed, it must be backed by the entire organization. People must believe in it and they must participate. This means that the first step in any PR activity is an internal program — to sell the associates on the importance of public relations and on the character of the people who are responsible.

EXERCISES

1. How many public relations firms are listed in the classified section of the telephone directory of the nearest city?
2. You are the president of a manufacturing concern with 500 employees. You have decided that you need to start a public relations program.
   (a) Would you engage a counselor or start a department?
   (b) Why?
   (c) How would you start to locate a counselor or director?
   (d) What qualifications would you seek?

Case Problem

You are the president of a telephone company. You are spending $1 million a year on advertising designed to create favorable public opinion about your company. A group of telephone users are trying to get the public utilities commission to forbid expenditures for this advertising, claiming that you are spending "their" money unnecessarily.

What arguments would you use to defend this expenditure? What groups or organizations would you try to reach?

The Public Relations Practitioner | **6**

There are two fundamental requirements for success in the field of public relations. First, the practitioner must be sensitive to, and aware of, public attitudes and opinions. Prominent practitioners have said that many people in public relations shouldn't be there because they lack sensitivity. Second, the practitioner must be a skilled communicator. He or she must be able to learn what the public thinks and must be able to transmit ideas to the public by writing and speaking clearly and effectively.

PERSONALITY

A listing of all the characteristics desirable in a PR practitioner would be a listing of all desirable human characteristics. This may sound extreme, but since the purpose of public relations is to affect public opinion, the more characteristics that will favorably impress others, the better chance there is for affecting their opinion. Whether any PR practitioner has all the following desirable features may never be known, but most successful practitioners have most of them.

Curiosity

There must be a lively desire to know what, why, how, when, where, and who. Without this, he or she will not get the facts nor be able to interpret them.

Diplomacy

Success depends on affecting the thinking of other people. A roughshod approach always breeds resentment. A considerate and tactful approach can gain understanding and cooperation.

Poise

Public relations work involves contacts with many people (sometimes individually, sometimes in masses) and with all sorts of people. Making a good impression is an essential part of these contacts — and poise is essential in making that impression.

Interest in Others

A self-centered person cannot succeed in public relations because the whole practice of PR is based on appealing to the self-interest of others. To discover that self-interest, one must know the people who are to be influenced.

Objectivity

The ability to take a detached look at oneself, one's problems, one's recommendations, and one's performance is a necessity.

Enthusiasm

If faith will move mountains, certainly enthusiasm will sell them. The practice of public relations is a constant series of sales — to the people who pay for it, to the people who help with the program, to the people at whom it is directed.

Persuasiveness

Affecting the thinking of others often involves changing their minds. The practitioner must be a skillful persuader who is able to analyze existing viewpoints and their weaknesses and then present ideas in a convincing way.

Integrity

There is no room for the charlatan in public relations. The practitioner must be honest, decent, sincere, and loyal. Success depends on trust.

Common Sense

When dealing with intangibles and working through people's emotions, it is all too easy to get carried off into the wild blue yonder. The brake of plain old-fashioned common sense is a necessity.

Imagination

Public relations is a creative occupation. New ideas and new methods are necessary to break through the resistance of established patterns of thinking. The practitioner should constantly ask himself or herself "What would happen if . . .?"

Courage

It takes courage to tell the boss that he is wrong or to recommend a large expenditure, the value of which may be difficult to prove. But no PR program gets very far unless the PR director has the courage of his or her convictions.

Energy

Sitting in a fancy office at a clean desk may look glamorous, but that is not public relations. Public relations is work — and lots of work — which means that the PR practitioner must be a worker, not a coaster.

Responsibility

In the armed services, the commanding officer of every unit is completely responsible for its success. If it performs well, he gets credit; if it performs badly, he gets relieved of command. In public relations, the same rule applies. The only successful PR men or women are those who really feel complete responsibility for whatever public relations tasks they may be charged with.

Discretion

Dealing with the public is a sensitive activity. PR people must be very careful about what they do and say. A slip of the tongue can be disastrous.

ABILITY

The primary ability requirement in public relations is skill in communication — two-way communication. This means skill in getting information — by reading, questioning, and listening. It also means skill in giving information to others — by writing and by speaking. A secondary but vital requirement is managerial ability.

Why Johnny Has to Read

Reading skill is necessary for two reasons. First, the public relations practitioner must acquire a great deal of information from printed or typewritten sources. If he has to labor through books, booklets, and memoranda, he will not be able to do enough reading to keep himself informed. Second, he must know the language so thoroughly that he will be able to use the exact words and phrases needed to express any idea he may wish to convey. The only way to acquire an adequate vocabulary and learn the proper usage of the language is by reading extensively.

Listening Is an Art

Listening requires more than just a pair of functioning ears. It involves attention, comprehension, and the ability to ask the right questions (Barbera, 1965). In fact, we might stretch the meaning a bit and include the whole process of research, which is basically the art of asking questions and getting answers.

The tone of voice and the choice of words can be as significant as the primary message. There are many ways to say yes: enthusiastically, hesitantly, doubtfully, tenderly, emphatically, firmly, loudly, softly, whispered, shouted, and so on. Every one of these variations places a slightly different meaning on the word. The PR man must be able to recognize the significance of these variations.

Also, there are many synonyms for our common words. For example, several hundred words or phrases can be used to indicate that something is bad, yet each of these has a slightly different meaning. The exact word used may indicate quite a bit about how the user feels.

The manner of expressing an idea is just as significant as the idea itself. Lest there be any doubt, it should be remembered that there once was an actor who could recite the alphabet and, depending on his choice, leave his audience in either tears or laughter by the time he got to Z.

A public relations man must be able to recognize the differences in words and tones and interpret their meaning. A good PR man is a good listener. He should also be a good observer. People often reveal themselves with gestures and postures (Fast, 1970).

Writing and Writing and Writing

Writing is the primary occupation of people in public relations. Most people in the field got started by demonstrating the ability to write — and no one can get very far in PR without this particular talent. The writing does not have to be literature, but it must be literate. It must be clear, direct, and convincing. It must be good readable English. It must avoid tricks and obscurities and be free of jargon, gobbledygook, and little-known words.

Every business or trade has its own vocabulary, but this should be used only to communicate with people in that business or trade, not to show off one's own special knowledge. Governmental, professional, and academic writing is filled with these obscurities. They may impress the writer, but they do not impress the reader. Writing has only one purpose — to convey ideas. Anything that hinders that communication is wrong.

The following is a verbatim copy of a newspaper item. It is reprinted here with permission of the Associated Press.

Houston.
The parent of a Houston high school pupil received a message from the principal about a special meeting on a proposed educational program. It read:
"Our school's cross-graded, multiethnic individualized learning program is designed to enhance the concept of an open-ended learning program with emphasis on a continuum of multiethnic, academically enriched learning using the identified intellectually gifted child as the agent or director of his own learning.
"Major emphasis is on cross-graded, multiethnic learning with the main objective being to learn respect for the uniqueness of a person." The parent wrote the principal:
"I have a college degree, speak two foreign languages and four Indian dialects, have been to a number of county fairs and three goat ropings, but I haven't the faintest idea as to what the hell you are talking about. Do you?"

To aid one's writing, there are two skills that are invaluable — the ability to operate a typewriter and the ability to spell. A beginner will have a very difficult time if he or she cannot type. (In some cases this skill is an absolute requirement for employment.) At the higher levels, it is usually possible to get the services of a stenographer, but frequently the PR practitioner must rely on his own fingers. As for spelling, so many people do it poorly that the PR practitioner cannot depend on others to catch the errors; he had better be able to prevent their occurrence.

"Friends, Romans, Countrymen, Lend Me Your Ears"

Among the qualifications of the public relations practitioner, public speaking is almost as important as writing. While few PR people get started in the business because of their speaking ability, it is impossible to succeed without it. It does not have to be oratory, but it must be clear and direct. Sometimes the speech will be directed to a large audience, sometimes to a small group, and sometimes to an individual. In every case it must convey the thoughts of the speaker and affect the opinions of the listeners. The speaker must know what he is trying to accomplish. He must have his ideas organized in logical sequence and express himself in language that will be understood.

Often the practitioner is called on to write a speech for someone else. This gives him the opportunity to put his ideas into someone else's mouth. It also gives him the responsibility of using the kind of language — the words and phraseology that the speaker would normally use.

Managing Public Relations

A public relations program has to be managed. Someone has to study the facts, make the plan, sell it to top management, and then execute it. Someone has to be sure that everything in the plan is done, done on schedule, and done properly. Even the smallest public relations operation normally involves more than just the one person carrying the title of PR director or counselor. There will be secretaries, assistants, photographers, printers, binders, delivery personnel, and numerous others all having some part in the operation and all needing supervision.

Not the least of managerial problems is management of himself. There are usually dozens of demands for the time of the PR practitioner. If he does not organize himself, he will not use his time properly or be effective. A public relations practitioner must be a good manager.

EDUCATION FOR PUBLIC RELATIONS

More than 300 colleges now offer at least one course in public relations. There are 16 degree programs accredited by the American Council on Education for Journalism (ACEJ) and about 90 major sequences. Most of these are centered in journalism or communications departments. General emphasis is on the liberal arts. A typical major might involve 6 academic units in public relations, 30 to 35 in journalism or communications, and 55 or 60 in social sciences and humanities out of a 124-semester-unit degree program (Walker, 1975).

Many practitioners have questioned the journalistic orientation of public relations education. Some have suggested that it belongs in the department of business administration or public administration. Others have suggested creation of separate schools of public relations. In general, however, practitioners seem to concur with the emphasis on the liberal arts.

One subject which is not given much prominence in these discussions is English. Perhaps it is implied by the emphasis on journalism and communications. Certainly public relations practitioners *must* be able to write and speak good English. If the would-be practitioner cannot use good English, he or she had better learn how.

English

English grammar has taken a beating in recent years at the hands of numerous educators. Some of them have stated that all rules should be abolished and that the speaker or writer should do as he pleases. This certainly makes it easy for the user, but one is bound to wind up with a situation like the scene in *Through the Looking Glass* where Humpty Dumpty tells Alice, "When I use a word it means just what I choose it to mean, neither more nor less." Without a common acceptance of the meaning of words and phrases, there can be no understanding. An ungrammatical sentence, paragraph, or speech will not only fail in purpose but will also brand the user as incompetent. Good grammar is essential to good writing and speaking.

English composition, the purposeful putting together of words and sentences and paragraphs in order to convey ideas, is a badly neglected subject in our schools and colleges. *Editor and Publisher* has harshly criticized journalism graduates who can't write understandably. In every walk of life, the recurring complaint is that communications have failed. To communicate well, one must know English composition. The purpose of this study should be not only to attain understanding but, more importantly, to prevent misunderstanding.

Sir Winston Churchill has been recognized as one of the greatest writers and speakers of the twentieth century. He was also one of the greatest public relations men, if that judgment is based on his ability to affect public opinion. Churchill was a student of English literature. Many of his ideas, phrases and expressions that resounded around the world were extracted or paraphrased from the writings of others. Also, his writing style could not have developed without extensive exposure to the writings of his predecessors. Churchill was effective because he borrowed from all the resources of the language. Incidentally, he had considerable experience as a reporter.

Public Speaking

Very few people are good public speakers without training. The need for speaking ability is so obvious in so many fields that courses are offered by many high schools, practically all colleges, and numerous nonacademic institutions. At least one course in public speaking is a must for anyone who hopes to practice public relations; more would be better.

Journalism

Because a large part of public relations writing is newswriting and because a PR practitioner must know what is news and what is not news, he or she needs to know quite a bit about the whole process of newsmaking, newsgathering, and newswriting. Study of journalism is the quickest way to learn the fundamentals of this art. It will not make a polished newsperson out of the student, but it will introduce the basic principles and, depending on the extent of study, give actual practice in reporting and editing.

Writing

Many colleges offer courses in writing. The nature of these courses varies so widely that a thorough investigation should be made before registration. The courses worth taking are those whose purpose is to teach people to write effectively and understandably.

Psychology

Some courses in psychology can be very useful. They will give the student some basic knowledge and teach him or her to think about how people act and react. Among courses to be considered are social psychology, group dynamics, and persuasion.

Economics

Study of economics is most desirable. The practitioner's work is often judged on the basis of how much good it does for the money expended. Management has many places to spend its funds and public relations will not get very far unless the expenditure is economically sound.

Another, and possibly more important, reason for studying economics is to gain an understanding of the broad effects of economics in our society. The importance of the subject has increased tremendously in recent years as public attention has focused on such subjects as pollution, integration, minority employment, consumer protection, the population explosion, the housing shortage, and many others. Solving these problems will cost many billions of dollars, and that money cannot be obtained out of thin air; somebody will have to pay. The public relations practitioner who understands economics will be bettter able to perform his or her tasks.

Sociology

A basic course in this social science is highly desirable, and several more could be beneficial. The broader the scope the better, because intense specialization may have limited applicability in the public relations field.

Anthropology

Human nature, how people live and what they do, is a subject that can well be included in education for public relations. Obviously, courses should be selected on the basis of relevance. Knowledge of the customs of the Trobriand Islanders may not be very useful to a public relations practitioner dealing with a problem in Harlem.

History

An understanding of history, particularly American history, is invaluable. At least one course in American history is essential. A good supplement would be a course in American government.

Semantics

Because public relations deals largely with words, the meaning conveyed by those words to the listener or reader is especially important. The study of semantics will not only add to the student's knowledge, but will also create a lively awareness of the importance of using the right words and phrases. A course in semantics is, if not indispensable, at least highly desirable. And, if it is not possible to study semantics, it is easy to do some reading on the subject.

Suggested Readings

Evans, Garth, and McDowell, H. John (Eds.). *Essays in Semantics.* Oxford: Oxford University Press, 1976.
Fillmore, Charles J., and Langendoen, D. *Studies in Linguistic Semantics.* New York: Irvington, 1977.
Hayakawa, S. I. *Through the Communication Barrier.* New York: Harper & Row, 1978.
Miller, George A. *Communication, Language and Meaning.* New York: Basic Books, 1977.

Management

Public relations is a business. An internal department or an external counselor must be managed like a business. In addition, the organization served is usually either a business or an entity operated on business principles. An understanding of these principles is invaluable and a course in business organization and management can provide that understanding.

Extracurricular Activities

The education of a prospective public relations practitioner does not stop at the door of the classroom. There are numerous activities that can be directly helpful in preparing for PR work. Debating, dramatics, even oratory, will help to develop and polish verbal skills and, at the same time, reduce or eliminate the fear of public speaking. Work on school publications such as newspapers, magazines, and yearbooks will give familiarity with writing, editing, and the production of printed matter. And, if the student is working, the most desirable kind of work is selling — because a large part of PR work is selling.

EXPERIENCE BENEFICIAL IN PUBLIC RELATIONS

Experience in journalism is most useful in public relations. Investigating, reporting, writing, and editing of newspapers or magazines is excellent preparation for work in PR. Most people in the field have had experience in this area.

Other experience that can be beneficial is work in advertising, in selling, and in opinion research. In each case, the more directly the work is involved with influencing people, the more helpful it will be. Copywriting or account management is more useful than media work. Door-to-door selling is better than compiling orders and issuing shipping instructions. Interviewing respondents is more beneficial than tabulating questionnaires.

Last, but far from least, is experience with a public relations department or counselor. This, of course, is always desirable.

SELF EDUCATION

The academic courses cited in the preceding pages are most desirable but it is possible to learn the subjects informally. Even if the courses have been taken, their impact weakens with the passage of time. The education of the public relations man should never stop, so this section is addressed equally to those who have formally studied and to those who have not.

A fairly good education in many of the skills needed in public relations can be obtained by reading and by personal inquiry.

Reading

To improve one's knowledge of the language, there are two categories of books worth considering. First are the classics or semiclassics: The King James Bible and the writings of authors and poets like Shakespeare, Chaucer, Twain, Longfellow, Whitman, Stevenson, Conrad, Pepys, Whittier, Lincoln, Dickens, the Brontës, Poe, Emerson, Holmes, Bunyan, Milton, Goldsmith, Coleridge, Irving, Cooper, Tennyson, Sandburg, Churchill, Steinbeck, Hemingway, Faulkner, and many others.

Reading books by these writers is no chore because most of them are highly interesting. More important, they familiarize the reader with good English usage and with the thoughts and ideas that are the basis of our thinking and speaking. Our everyday writing and conversation is liberally sprinkled with phrases from these classics. The PR practitioner's education will be vastly improved if he meets these thoughts in their original context.

Reading about the language itself is also beneficial. Both the origin and history of the English language are covered by such authors as Barret and Pei. For correct and effective usage, there are many sources. Some of the best are listed below.

Suggested Readings

Barret, L. *The Treasure of our Tongue.* New York: Knopf, 1962.
Flesch, R. *How to Write, Speak and Think More Effectively.* New York: Harper & Row, 1964.
Flesch, R. *Say What You Mean.* New York: Harper & Row, 1972.
Flesch, R. *The Art of Readable Writing.* New York: Harper & Row, 1974.
Mambert, W. A. *Effective Presentation.* Somerset, N.J.: Wiley Interscience, 1976.
Newman, Edwin. *A Civil Tongue.* Indianapolis, Ind.: Bobbs-Merrill, 1976.
Newman, Edwin. *Strictly Speaking.* Indianapolis, Ind.: Bobbs-Merrill, 1974.
Pei, Mario. *The Story of the English Language.* New York: Simon & Schuster, 1972.
Pickens, J. et al. *Without Bias.* San Francisco: IABC, 1977.
Strunk, W., Jr., and White, E. B. *The Elements of Style.* New York: Macmillan, 1972.

To attain knowledge of current conditions and familiarity with current newswriting style, there should be regular reading of newspapers, magazines, and trade journals. Any public relations practitioner who does not read these publications is not going to last very long; he will be completely out of touch with the public.

Another area of reading worth attention is the books that the general public is reading. Frequently, bestsellers have a great effect on public opinion. *Silent Spring* was the spark that aroused public concern for the environment. In the nineteenth century, *Uncle Tom's Cabin* had enormous effects on the public. Whenever a book attains great popularity, it should be read by the public relations practitioner so that he or she will be aware of this opinion influencer.

No one in public relations knows all the answers. Knowledge is never complete. To attain and maintain competence it is essential to read about public relations. Among the most important periodicals are: *IABC News, Public Opinion Quarterly, Public Relations Journal, Public Relations News, Public Relations Quarterly, Public Relations Review, P.R. Reporter,* and *Practical Public Relations.* The addresses of these publications are shown on page 514 of this book. For books on public relations, see the Selected Bibliography.

Personal Inquiry

Much information can be acquired by asking questions. Regardless of the nature of the question, in many cases someone knows the answer. The problem is to know what question to ask and to find the person who knows the answer. When information is needed and a source is not readily at hand, the only solution is to start asking the question, "Who might know something about the subject?" Eventually someone will point in the right direction. The best sources, of course, are the people in the business. If the question is about transportation, someone in transportation will know the answer. If it is about public relations, someone in PR will know the answer.

Organization Membership

Membership and active participation in the activities of organizations is one of the best ways to develop contacts and sources of information. Theodore Roosevelt once said that every man should devote some time to the advancement of the business or trade in which he is employed. He did not mention the benefits to the individual that result from this participation, but they will more than pay for the effort involved.

Membership in the Public Relations Society of America can be very helpful to a PR practitioner.

The All-Purpose Rule for PR People

Because public relations work has only one purpose — to affect the opinions of other people — there is one overall rule that should always be remembered:

"PUT YOURSELF IN THE OTHER MAN'S SHOES!"

A CAREER IN PUBLIC RELATIONS

The readers of this book who hope for a career in public relations probably have two major questions in mind. First, "What preparation is needed?" and second, "How do I get started?" Here are some answers.

Preparation

It is likely that each prospective employer will have specific requirements, but some general requirements seem to be rather widely accepted. In a survey on the West Coast conducted by Dr. Dennis L. Wilcox at San Jose State University, 90 top-level employers were asked about the traits, qualities, and educational background that were desirable. Sixty-five replied. Highlights of the answers indicate that the ideal applicant will have: (1) a four-year undergraduate degree, (2) courses in news writing, business, and the social sciences, (3) an outstanding personality and a willingness to work, (4) the ability to write well, (5) work experience in a related field.

Of the respondents, 80% said a bachelor's degree is a minimum. Several noted that a master's degree is helpful. Courses in news and feature writing were important to 86%. Courses in the principles of public relations were called assets by 65%. Publicity techniques were endorsed by 35%; editing and layout skills were checked by 24%. Other courses favored were speech communication (15%), radio and television (12%), advertising (11%), and photography (3%). About 40% of the employers said courses in the social sciences were valuable, while 36% valued finance and accounting. Business administration and economics were both listed by 28%.

In the area of personal traits, 77% said a likeable personality was important. Ambition got a 71% vote and appearance was important to 62%. Desire to work for the specific firm was endorsed by 35% of those questioned.

Of the employers, 62% gave considerable weight to related part-time or full-time work. Experience on a newspaper (other than a college paper) received a 57% vote. Related campus activities got 20% and the grade point average was given "a lot" of consideration by 17%. Unsolicited letters of recommendation were unimportant, but if the employer does the soliciting, references were considered important by 55%.

Attitude of the applicant was important to 97% of the employers and writing ability got a 95% vote. Other traits which weighed heavily in appraising applicants were growth potential (88%), poise (71%), cooperativeness (69%), speaking ability (65%), and knowledge of the media (58%).

Getting Started

The first step is to prepare a resume which tells who you are and what you can do. Remember that there will be many other resumes with which yours will be compared. Make it neat, complete, and convincing. Stress your writing ability because that is the most important ability an employer will be looking for. A printed resume is worth the cost.

Select some organizations you would like to work for. Learn as much as you can about these organizations.

Send your resumes with cover letters asking for interviews. Don't send a badly mimeographed letter with a hand-printed fill-in of the name of the addressee and numerous corrections in the letter made in the same way. The author once received such a letter from a Phi Beta Kappa graduating senior of a major university. Don't make mistakes. On one application for a top-level job, the author counted fifteen errors in spelling, grammar, or punctuation. Needless to say, it went into the wastebasket in spite of the impressive facts in the resume.

Whenever you are turned down — and this will probably happen frequently — always ask where else you might try. This is the way to get hooked into the "grapevine." In the survey quoted above, it was reported that "grapevine referrals" were used by about 65% of the employers. Resumes received were used by 35%.

One more suggestion. Don't confine your thinking to PR firms or departments. Ask about communications, consumer affairs, community relations, publications, information. There is a great need in many organizations, both profit and nonprofit, for people who can explain things in writing. Both laws and public demand are forcing all organizations who communicate with the public to do so in clear simple language.

One example is the insurance field, where companies are now starting to tell their customers what the policies mean in layman's language. There are many other areas where there are opportunities. The organization may have no public relations department or counselor. It may even be afraid of the words "public relations," but if you can get your foot in the door by writing you may be able to move forward to a full-fledged public relations operation. (That is the way the author got started.)

In the early days a job on a newspaper was commonly recommended as the first step into the field. There is still agreement that such experience can be helpful, but it is not essential.

Suggested Reading

Bolles, Richard H. *What Color is Your Parachute?* Berkeley: Ten Speed Press, 1976.

EXERCISES

1. What other qualifications would you think desirable in a public relations practitioner?
2. What additional subjects for college courses or for self-education would you suggest for PR education?
3. Find some "Help Wanted" ads for public relations people.
   a. What type of person is the employer looking for?
   b. Select one ad and write a covering letter and resume for the job.

Case Problem

You are the public relations director of a large department store. Shoplifters have become such a problem that management has decided on a policy of prosecuting all offenders and publicizing their arrests.

How would you publicize this policy? To whom?
The first person apprehended after the policy was made public is the wife of the mayor.
What action would you recommend?
Why?

Dialogue II

Dialogue with Mr. John M. Black, Jr., Assistant Vice-President for Public Affairs, Pacific Telephone and Telegraph Company.

> This dialogue focuses sharply on a major problem of public relations practitioners — their relationships with top management. It also points out what may be a trend for the future, the possibility that practitioners may be spending more time on advising and counseling and less time on the "nuts-and-bolts" of communication.

Q. What is the biggest problem in public relations today?

A. It's getting top management to really communicate with the public — to meet with and talk to the people.

Q. Why is this a problem?

A. There are three reasons. First, most CEO's have so many problems on their hands that it's very hard to get them to devote adequate time to this particular problem. Second, many of them just don't see the benefits which could be gained. Third, most members of top management aren't equipped to do it. In fact, I've heard the statement that there are only about four corporation presidents in the country who are really competent to do this well on the national level. To do it well, the executive must be adequately informed and, even more important, taught how to handle the problems of communication with the public.

Q. Is this the fault of management or is it the fault of the public relations people?

A. I think some of this can be blamed on the public relations people. Rather than help the CEO tell the story, we try to do too much ourselves. We field the complaints, fend off the detractors, and try to tell the story of management. The result is that the organization does not pay enough attention to the outside criticism — and since top management does not speak out, the statements made by the public relations people lack credibility.

Q. That sounds as though you believe public relations people should devote more attention to informing, advising, and coaching top management and less attention to the role of spokesman for the organization.

A. Yes, I do believe that. The guts of the business credibility problem is that the public wants to hear from the people who run the operation. The public is saying, "We don't understand why the President of General Motors or A.T. & T. has the right to manipulate all those resources and all those lives." They are questioning whether anyone should have such power. It's essential for those who do have the power to reach out to the people — to listen, to explain, to tell their side of the controversy, to answer the critics like Ralph Nader.

Q. Why is Nader so effective?

A. Because he finds the problems that concern the public and voices their concerns. Top management has not yet discovered this.

Q. Why doesn't management learn these things?

A. Because they don't pay attention to the information provided by their public relations people. All too often, they look at research as a sort of PR "Show and Tell." In many cases management has been warned of potential troubles but has done nothing until the roof has fallen in.

Q. You mentioned that CEO's were generally not equipped to answer the questions of the public. Can this weakness be overcome?

A. Yes. For example, we have been working through the California Round Table (a group of top executives) and have developed a training course. We have recommended that all company presidents take the course.

Q. What do the courses cover?

A. We cover four major areas:
   1. Platform speaking. In this we try to build credibility.
   2. TV talk shows. Here we show how to get the key points across.
   3. Confrontation with a hostile audience. Here we teach methods of dealing with adverse and unfair arguments.
   4. TV press conferences. These are complete surprises to the "student." The reporters are unfriendly and supercritical.
      All these sessions are videotaped so that the "student" can see just what was good or bad. We make these as realistic as possible.

Q. I frequently see a TV news story in which a charge has been made against some organization. The charge is fully stated and then the reporter says, "We have been unable to get a statement from the _____ Company." What do you have to say about this?

A. Most companies are not organized to respond. It requires trained people and a system to get quick answers. Most of all it requires a commitment on the part of top management and the willingness to accept the risk as well as the benefit.

Q. What happens when top management does not speak out?

A. Here's a sample. Some time ago, the *Washington Post* acquired a supposedly secret list of "problem banks." The *Los Angeles Times* considered publishing the story but in order to check the accuracy of the information, the financial editor of the *Times* called each of the banks on the list. No one would comment. The *Times* ran the story, and then the banks raised hell with the newspaper for publishing the story.

Q. Aside from answering criticisms, what else can management do to tell its story to the public?

A. Management should actively hunt opportunities to talk to people.

Q. How does the telephone company do this?

A. Our chairman and president make many speeches every year. In addition, we try to get them into all the principal cities of the state at least once a year. We set up conferences with the editorial boards of the major newspapers and broadcasters. We get good news coverage and good editorial support.

Q. What about public reaction?

A. It is good. On the national scale, we have an excellent example. Mr. John DeButts, Chairman of A.T. & T., has been making numerous speeches — and because he has been speaking out on public issues, he has become a very credible spokesman for the company and for the entire business world.

Q. What kind of audience should be sought for the CEO?

A. It doesn't do much good to talk to our friends. They are already sold. We can accomplish much more by talking to the skeptics, the critics, the enemies. Recently Mr. DeButts talked to the National Consumer Congress, an organization which can hardly be classified as a dear friend of big business.

Q. All our institutions, both commercial and noncommercial, are criticized from time to time by a wide variety of individuals and organizations. What should be done about those critics?

107

A. They may be abrasive, but they aren't necessarily "kooks." They should be given serious answers. The people who wrote off Nader made a big mistake. He isn't a "kook," he is a power.

Q. What is the most important message the CEO should try to put across?

A. That goes back to the question of power. Most people have a vast misconception about the operation of business. Too many think that a corporation is a small bunch of people with great wealth. They have no idea as to who owns American business. Most stock is owned by pension trusts, mutual funds, and insurance companies. These account for nearly all big stock holdings. The typical individual stockholder has a thousand or two thousand dollars worth of stock. Most corporations are really owned by tens of thousands of little people. If the public really understood that, we would have a very different situation.

Q. You have told me that the members of top management should speak out to the public. You have also told me that they should tell the people that big business isn't the creature of a few wealthy individuals — that it is the savings of millions of little people. How can we in public relations get our bosses to speak out?

A. Most of the CEO's with whom I have discussed this problem agree that they should speak out. Their principal barrier is time and some lack of confidence. We in public relations can build confidence by organizing training programs and then scheduling opportunities to meet with various publics.

III
Public Opinion and Publics

Public opinion is the reason for public relations. If public opinion was not important, there would be no public relations activity. But because favorable public opinion is necessary for the success of any organization, it is imperative to consider it at all times.

Public opinion is the sum of individual opinions. Understanding how people arrive at their opinions is therefore the key to understanding how groups arrive at their opinions.

There are many publics and they are not mutually exclusive. Any individual may belong to several different publics and any organization may be involved with numerous publics, each of which must be recognized and dealt with as a separate entity.

The following 12 chapters discuss the importance of public opinion, its origins in individual opinion, and the principle publics with which public relations must be concerned.

Public 7
Opinion

The power of public opinion is almost limitless. No king or dictator ever succeeded without public support. Even though all power was theoretically vested in him, he had to consider the people he ruled. Even the cruelest controls fail when the people refuse to obey. Soviet Russia is a twentieth century dictatorship. The ruling oligarchy controls everything, yet it continually cultivates favorable public opinion with a never-ending barrage of propaganda. Thomas Jefferson confirmed the power of public opinion when, in the Declaration of Independence, he wrote of governments "deriving their just powers from the consent of the governed." Abraham Lincoln was also much aware of public opinion, although he called it "public sentiment."

Public opinion affects every person and every organization. No one, other than a hermit, can succeed without public support.

Public opinion is well-named and easily defined. A good general definition is:

Public opinion is the sum of individual opinions on an issue affecting those individuals.

In short, public opinion is the sum of individual opinions. When enough individuals have the same opinion, we can speak of public opinion. Until there is some agreement, there is only individual opinion. If 95% of the people favor some idea and 5% oppose it, we can say that public opinion favors the idea. If 5% favor it, 5% oppose it and 90% are undecided, we can say that there is no public opinion on the subject. If 50% are for and 50% against, we have to say that public opinion is divided. Public opinion can be added up in different ways. For example, in one company it may be found that 90% of the stockholders are in favor of something and 90% of the employees are against it.

Since public opinion is the sum of individual opinions, the only way to sway public opinion is to sway individuals. To influence the opinion of individuals, it is necessary to know something about opinions.

An opinion is an expression of attitude. Sometimes the expression is spoken or written. Sometimes it is expressed by action and sometimes by inaction on the part of individuals whose attitudes are weak — or who think it will do no good to express an opinion.

An attitude is a predisposition to act or speak or think in a favorable or unfavorable way about a particular subject (Costello and Zalkind, 1963).

To understand the effect of attitude on opinion, let us look at the opinions expressed about a speech given by the President of the United States. Most members of his party will praise the speech and most members of the opposition will criticize it. The reason for the differing opinions is that the attitudes are different. Members of the President's party have a generally favorable attitude toward him — and members of the other party have a generally unfavorable attitude.

Note that we say "most" members and "generally." On any given subject the President may, and often does, find some members of his own party who disagree and some members of the other party who agree — *on that specific topic*. The reason for this is that we all have many attitudes. Some of these attitudes are strong and some are weak. When one of the strong attitudes is touched, the reaction tends to overcome weaker attitudes. Thus, we see individual congressmen supporting the President on almost every issue but opposing him on one or two — and vice versa.

In public relations we talk a lot about public opinion and do not say much about attitudes. We speak of changing or influencing opinion yet, since opinion is merely an expression of attitude, often we are really trying to influence attitudes so that those improved attitudes will be expressed in favorable opinion. We try to change antagonistic attitudes and to mobilize favorable attitudes.

Some attitudes are hard to change and some are easy. When an attitude is tied in strongly with other attitudes, beliefs, and values, it is much more difficult to change than an attitude that stands all by itself.

No one is born with an attitude. They are all learned. Our attitudes are determined by many factors — our human nature, culture, nationality, sex, family, class, and the various groups with which we associate (Morgan, 1961).

Attitude has a great influence on belief. People tend to believe those with whom they agree and to disbelieve those with whom they disagree.

In the Oklahoma election to repeal the state prohibition law, it was found that both sides rated opposition statements close to "very false" while statements with which people agreed were rated close to "very true" (Sherif and Jackman, 1966).

There are many theories about how attitudes are changed. The functional theory is that people's attitudes change as they tend to serve the interests of the individual. Thus, people who have lost their jobs will be more receptive to radical political and economic ideas. The learning theory is that it is possible to "educate" people to a desired attitude — by application of basic principles of learning — thus, in theory, any attitude can be changed if enough effort is made (Wagner and Sherwood, 1969).

Suggested Readings

Carlson, Robert O. (Ed.). *Communications and Public Opinion*. New York: Praeger, 1975.
Oskamp, S. *Attitudes and Opinions*. Englewood Cliffs, N.J.: Prentice-Hall, 1977.
Sherif, Carolyn W. *Attitude, Ego Involvement and Change*. Westport, Conn.: Greenwood, 1976.

THE NATURE OF PUBLIC OPINION

People have studied public opinion for centuries. More than 2,000 years ago Thucydides, in his *History of the Peloponnesian War*, covered the distribution of public opinion, how public opinion is formed, and the effect of public opinion on government.

Jay, Madison, and Hamilton in *The Federalist Papers* stated that governments must be supported by public opinion but warned against relying too heavily on something that might be transitory. In modern language they might have said, "Governments must have public support but they shouldn't operate on the basis of public opinion polls."

In the twentieth century, public opinion has been heavily researched and sampled. There have been many attempts to determine how it is formed and what is involved. Numerous researchers have worked on this problem with considerable variation in their conclusions and the way they are stated. Nevertheless there is some agreement and consistency in their findings. Following are a few of the more important points:

1. Public opinion is not necessarily mass opinion. Frequently it is the opinion of specific publics about specific subjects.
2. Public opinion changes, sometimes rapidly and violently. Stability comes only when people have had time to appraise the situation.
3. Public opinion is very hard to measure.
4. A widely known issue is always involved. Unless people are aware, they are not likely to be concerned.

5. Events are the motivation. Something significant must happen in order to arouse interest.
6. Demands for action must be made. People have to express their opinions in positive terms.
7. Action must be possible. There must be a belief that something can be accomplished and that there are others who are ready for action.
8. Verbalization is essential. People must talk about the subject.
9. Means must exist. Whether it is the ballot box or an ad hoc committee, there has to be an evident way in which to make the opinion felt.
10. Public opinion does not anticipate events, it reacts to them.
11. Public opinion is much more definite on goals than on the means of attaining them.
12. Opinions are commonly group opinions formed by small groups with common interests.

THE OPINION GROUP

Small groups are a key factor in public opinion. People seek as companions other people of similar attitudes and interests. The result is informal groupings which interact on the members in development of their opinions.

Any person may belong to several groups, each based on a different attitude or interest. Thus one individual might be a member of a work group at the place of employment, a completely different group in a church, and a still different group at a golf course or a bowling alley. The possible groupings might go into several more fields such as age, sex, race, political party, place of residence, income, occupation, presence of children in the family, organization membership, etc.

In general, people tend to associate with others who are like themselves. From this group membership comes reassurance to the individual and some degree of uniformity of opinion. People in a group try to conform to group norms — even when their own reason indicates that the group is wrong. In a controlled test, it was found that when all but one of the members of a group purposefully gave an incorrect answer, the one member who had given the right answer changed his answer in order to conform to the group's opinion (Asch, 1952).

The functioning of a group in developing public opinion depends on several factors:

1. There must be frequent and continued association. A casual assemblage of strangers at a baseball game may loudly express their opinion that the umpire is blind, but that isn't the kind of public opinion with which we are concerned. The public opinion group is relatively permanent, and its members talk to each other frequently.
2. The group must have shared norms and standards. Group membership induces uniformity. A maverick is expelled or finds things so uncomfortable that he or she withdraws. Those who do adhere to the norms discuss topics of interest and by this verbalization adjust each other's opinions to a common ground.
3. The group must have its own human communications system. This is centered in an opinion leader, one person who, more than any other, is listened to by the members of the group. The opinion leader is normally more exposed to and interested in messages from outside the group. This is the person who comments on the news or the directive from management. Presumably the opinion leader is better informed, or more interested or more persuasive than other group members, so his opinions seem to carry more weight and thus move others to like opinions.

PUBLIC OPINION POLLS

Several organizations use sophisticated polling techniques to predict election results and periodically assess public opinion on various topics.

Election predictions are usually quite accurate. Pollsters have developed methods which, based on a small but carefully designed sample, are dependable when it comes to determining which one of a few candidates will get the most votes.

However, when the pollsters get into the area of public opinion their reports are not as consistent. "Who do you intend to vote for?" is much easier to answer than a question which asks for opinion on some issue.

To assess opinion may require several different questions. The kinds of questions asked may strongly warp the answers. For example, both Gallup and Harris have studied and restudied the degree of public confidence in the major institutions of our society. Often these polls cover an extensive list of institutions or occupations. For each, the respondent is asked to give a rating.

Harris asks: "How much confidence do you have in _____?"
　　　　　　　_____A great deal
　　　　　　　_____Only some
　　　　　　　_____Not any
Gallup asks: "How much confidence do you have in _____?"
　　　　　　　_____A great deal
　　　　　　　_____Quite a lot
　　　　　　　_____Some
　　　　　　　_____Very little
　　　　　　　_____None

The result is that the Harris polls consistently show a lower rating for all institutions than the Gallup polls. Apparently there are many people whose opinions are not so enthusiastic as to indicate "a great deal" of confidence, but who do have "quite a lot" of confidence. At the lower levels, it would appear that "some" is more favorable than "only some," and "very little" is still better than "not any" or "none."

The lesson here for public relations practitioners is to be very careful when attempting to determine what the public thinks. This will be discussed at length in Chapter 19.

KNOW THE PUBLIC

The PR practitioner must know human nature. He or she must understand attitudes and beliefs — why people have certain attitudes and how strong these attitudes are.

If the PR practitioner knows the attitudes of the various publics, he or she can tailor communications accordingly and thus be more effective in influencing opinions. A message to ghetto residents will be quite different from a message to suburban dwellers. A message to members of a labor union will be unlike a message to stockholders. Knowing the public is the first step in affecting public opinion.

THE NATURE OF THE BEAST

Anthropologists, sociologists, and psychologists have studied human beings for centuries. They have written books by the thousands and have stated countless theories and "laws" about how and why people act as they do. In spite of all the time, money, and brainpower devoted to this subject, there is still no agreement, no universally-accepted conclusion as to the true nature of man. Sometimes we behave like human beings and sometimes we behave like animals. At our best, we occasionally show a spark of the divine. At our worst, there is no animal that cannot look down on us.

Virgil, Rousseau, Jefferson, and Marx had one major idea in common. They all believed that man was innately good and that all his faults of conduct were due to civilization. Each in his own way believed that most of the evils of the earth could be eliminated if man were somehow returned to his original primitive state. This idealistic appraisal of human nature has profoundly affected the whole world, but the cold pages of history show that man is just not living up to these specifications.

Some writers, in an attempt to show how good and gentle man is when unspoiled by civilization, cite various small isolated tribes as examples of the true nature of man. But these are not typical of the human species. They are cultural failures. To understand human nature, we must look at the mainstream (Morris, 1967). There are very few gentle and generous people and there are billions of tough and selfish people. In spite of all that is said about how man ought to be, man often continues to be fearful, aggressive, greedy, cruel, combative, and selfish. Note, particularly, the word "selfish," because that characteristic is one that is very important in public relations.

Self-Interest

The purpose of any public relations program is to affect public opinion, which means to affect many individual opinions. The easiest way to affect individual opinion is to appeal to the self-interest of the individual.

Self-interest has several facets, all of which are so deeply ingrained in human nature that attempts to ignore them or defy them can lead only to failure. These instincts transcend reason and argument. It is not possible to talk people out of them.

Self-Preservation

Self-preservation is the first law of nature. Without this instinct, no living thing could survive. The survival instinct is stronger in man than in any other animal because it is reinforced by man's ability to look into the future, to consider the consequences of action, and to imagine possible events. Man fears not only real dangers, but also the unknown, the strange, the new, the different. Today we deplore resistance to change, we criticize racial antagonisms, we dislike blind adherence to old ways. But we must realize that those attitudes are all based on fear and that they are so deeply ingrained as to be almost instinctive. Changing them is not easy.

With man, self-preservation covers more than physical life; in our complex society it also includes economic life. So man is fearful of disease or injury or age which will make him unable to work. He fears change in business or industry which will make his skills obsolete. He fears others who will deprive him of his job by working for less money or with greater ability.

With this powerful instinct planted firmly in every member of the public, it is imperative that it be considered in any attempt to influence the public. Any threat to physical or economic survival will arouse the most violent possible reaction.

Territoriality

The instinct of territoriality is almost as strong as that of self-preservation. It is found in many animals and birds. It reaches tremendous heights in man. It is a more powerful instinct than sex because there are countless examples wherein defense of territory supersedes defense of the mate. In its simplest form, territoriality is largely concerned with the hunting or feeding territory and the home, nest, or resting place. In human society it applies to personal property as well as to real property.

Territoriality in animals is most commonly manifested by the male who tries to eject all other males of the same species from his territory. Among humans, the female also manifests the instinct by her defense of her home and her other possessions, against the intrusion or violence of others.

Territoriality is the instinct that leads to ownership. It is manifested in our common-law statement that a man's home is his castle. It is included in the provision of the U.S. Constitution that forbids unreasonable search and seizure. It applies to real property and to personal property, to intangibles as well as to tangibles. It is a part of man and it cannot be ignored in dealing with man (Ardrey, 1966).

Public relations programs must recognize this primeval instinct. Any idea or project that threatens the individual's territory or property is certain to be opposed with every available weapon.

Family Protection

The protective instinct is especially strong in man. The long years of infancy and childhood require that the young be guarded, trained, and cared for to a far greater degree in man than in the lower animals.

Without this protective instinct, the human race could not have survived. The instinct is probably stronger in the female than in the male. In addition to protection of the young, this instinct also leads to protection of the mate. The man cares for the woman, and vice versa, all in the interest of maintaining an intact and functioning family group. Even the young protect each other from outsiders of whatever nature.

Primitive man survived because the family unit clung together. The better the family ties, the greater were the chances for the individual members. Those who did not help and protect each other did not live and reproduce themselves.

Sex

Freud and a host of his followers taught that almost everything man does is rooted in sex. For a long time, sex and sexual problems were seen as the beginning and the end of human behavior. In recent years, some more realistic study has begun to put sex into its proper position as a powerful instinct but not *the* most powerful. There are many examples in nature to prove that the instinct of self-preservation or of territoriality is much stronger than sex.

Group Formation

Most animals group together with others of their kind. A school of fish, a flock of birds, or a herd of caribou all show the instinct to draw near to and stay with those that are alike. Parallel to this is the instinct to stay away from those that are different. No one ever saw a mixed flock of sparrows and robins. Salmon and tuna do not swim together and elk and moose do not associate with each other. The key to all grouping is inward amity and outward enmity.

The grouping instinct is especially strong in man. As a weak, clawless, fangless being, the only way primitive man could hold his own against more powerful and better armed adversaries was by joining a group. One man was no match for a bear or a wild boar, but a group of men could rout or kill amost any animal (Tiger, 1969).

The grouping instinct leads to the formation of clans, tribes, and nations. It also leads to the formation of golf clubs, lodges, veterans' organizations, trade associations, and many thousands of other gatherings of people with a common interest.

This instinct is a tremendous aid to the practice of public relations.

Through groups, it is possible to communicate with people who are actively concerned with some problem or project or interest.

Grouping made man's survival possible. It accounts for many of his nobler attributes. Deep within all of us is an instinct that makes us sacrifice much individual advantage for the common good. Self-sacrifice, cooperation, compassion, help for others, restraint of personal desires, in fact most of the good things about human nature, are the result of this basic instinct.

On the other hand, grouping can be blamed for some of man's worst characteristics. Arthur Koestler, in a talk to the fourteenth Nobel Symposium in 1969, pointed out how membership in a group reduced man's critical faculties and increased his emotional potential. This leads to uncritical devotion to the group, to mass aggression, and to war — an aberration unique to the human species.

BASIC NEEDS OF MAN

There are several ways of describing man's needs. Essentially, most authorities agree on those needs, but they arrange them in different ways and describe them in different words. Some of the needs are biological and some are psychological. Public relations is little concerned with biological needs, but very much concerned with psychological needs. The subject is worthy of considerable study, because a thorough understanding of people and how they act and react is a necessity in public relations. At this point, anthropology, sociology, and psychology all apply.

One way of listing man's needs is to group them under three headings, identity, security, and stimulus (Ardrey, 1961).

Identity

We are all egotistical and we are all individualists. We belong to groups but we jealously guard our status or position within the group. We like personalized checks and hate the electronically-coded accounting that reduces us to numbers. We buy mass-produced automobiles but individualize them with a myriad of optional accessories. We live in mass-produced houses but make our own house different from all the others. We wear individualized clothing.

Within every animal group there is rank, status, and order. In a flock of chickens, every hen has her own position. There is always a boss who can peck every other. There is always a number two and so on down the line to the lowliest, who is pecked by every other but dares not retaliate. This situation, described as a "henpeck hierarchy," is not limited to the chickenyard. In every group there is a boss. In every group there is relative rank and status. There must also be order. And in every group the price of acceptance is conformity.

Rank and status among human beings is not as sharply defined as among chickens. We have a great deal of egalitarianism in our makeup but still we do have hierarchy.

As population increases, the individual actually becomes less important, yet this very situation makes people more anxious to be individuals and to maintain their identity against the pressures of the sheer mass of humanity. Identity is a vital need and public relations programs must recognize this.

Security

Security has always been a need, but in recent years it has assumed much more conscious importance. The various government welfare projects such as Social Security and Medicare are a reflection of the increased public concern about security. It is also possible that the greater ease of obtaining security has been a factor. In any event man needs security and he increasingly strives to attain it. In the primitive state, security was a strong man, a good cave, and possibly some food. Today, security may be life insurance, a labor agreement about layoffs, a teacher's tenure, hospital insurance, money in the bank, or a score of other economic protections.

Security can also be psychological. It can be an employer who really knows his employees and to whom they can turn for advice or help. It can be friends or neighbors. It can be an efficient police department or a good school system. All of these and dozens of others can contribute to the individual's feeling that he is not alone and helpless. A threat to a man's security is a threat to his survival. In public relations anything that makes a person feel secure is desirable. Anything that makes him feel insecure should be avoided.

Stimulus

For a good many years, psychologists overlooked the need for stimulus. In fact, in many ways we have tried to eliminate this element from human life. Yet, as we make life more secure, we find that people rebel against the humdrum monotony of life without challenge. Some of man's survival in this world is due to his response to outside stimuli. Primitive man lived a stimulating life and his descendants still retain the characteristics that respond to stimuli. When there is no stimulus, man gets bored, unhappy, and resentful. Winning an argument or making a sale is stimulating. So is climbing a mountain or winning a fight.

Civilized work and civilized home life are monotonous in many ways. There is nothing very exciting about work on an assembly line but there is stimulus in a strike. This does not mean that strikes are desirable; it merely means that they are different, exciting, and challenging.

Sweden has succeeded in providing everyone with security. No one fears unemployment, poverty, stricken old age, or disability. Yet there are reports that many young Swedes are bored and unhappy because there is little stimulus in their lives. Recent elections in Sweden indicate dissatisfaction with the heavily regulated monotony.

A Hierarchy of Needs

Another way of describing man's needs is to place them in a hierarchy ranging from the most basic biological needs to the highest and most self-actualizing needs (Maslow, 1959; McGregor, 1960).

The assumption is that higher needs cannot be fulfilled until the lower needs are reasonably satisfied. The needs are defined as: physiological, safety, social, ego, and self-fulfillment.

Physiological needs include air, water, food, exercise, rest, and shelter.

Safety needs are protection against threats, danger, and deprivation. They have been described as an assurance of a fair break — not an absolute guarantee.

Social needs mean acceptance, belonging, association, the giving and receiving of friendship, and love.

Ego needs are internal and external. The internal needs are for self-esteem, self-respect, self-confidence, independence, achievement, skill, and knowledge. The external needs are for reputation, status, recognition, appreciation, and the respect of others.

Self-fulfillment needs are those that let the individual reach his or her full potential for continuous development and creativity.

Overlapping Needs

Still another way of looking at needs is to consider them as interdependent variables. When one is threatened, all are threatened. On a base of physiological needs, there is a higher need level that includes self-esteem, the esteem of others, belonging, autonomy, opportunity for interaction and influence. Self-esteem is gratified by autonomy and belonging is gratified by opportunities for interaction (Barnes, 1960).

Application

In most cases public relations activity must be directed to the lower or more basic needs, because these are most important to most people. However, we must never forget the higher needs, because public opinion is strongly affected by individuals trying to satisfy ego needs and self-fulfillment needs. Cesar Chavez, leader of the United Farm Workers Organizing Committee, is a good example.

His campaign to organize farm workers and gain recognition for the union was a masterpiece of public relations. It was highly successful because he rallied public opinion behind his cause.

To his followers, he offered physiological, safety, and social benefits, but, in so doing, he undoubtedly gained much for himself in ego and self-fulfillment.

OTHER NEEDS

These needs may, in large degree, be parts of the basic needs previously cited. In fact, they might all be included under one of the preceding headings, yet in the interest of emphasis it seems advisable to list them as separate entities.

Self-Respect

People must have self-respect if they are to achieve. Experiments with children have shown that most of those who think they will succeed do succeed. Most of those who think they will fail do fail. A person constantly criticized and belittled loses his self-respect and hates the source of that loss. A person who is encouraged to take pride in himself and his work gains in self-respect and in efficiency. Public relations programs must encourage the self-respect of those to whom the programs are directed.

Acceptance

With all human society based on groupings, acceptance by the group is absolutely indispensable to a successful adjustment to life.

Few people want to be hermits and live by themselves. Most people want to be accepted by those they like, admire, and respect, and they are willing to pay the price of conformity to the customs and standards of those others.

Trust

In spite of all that is said about embezzlement, cheating, shoplifting, the "crime wave," and "goofing off," most people are honest and worthy of trust. Nearly all employees deliver a fair day's work for a fair day's pay. Nothing breeds more resentment than oversupervision and rigid rules over petty procedures. Suspicious people usually encourage the very thing they suspect. Trusting people usually encourage trustworthiness. It is indeed difficult to strike the right balance between complete trust and adequate control, but, whenever it is possible to convey the feeling of trust, it results in big rewards in the area of public opinion.

Accomplishment

Man exists today because he accomplished the task of standing upright — and making weapons and tools, building fires, and inventing the wheel. Man's whole time on earth has been a succession of accomplishments, and accomplishment has been so long established in man's life that it might almost be called an instinct. Man *has* to accomplish things. Pride in what one has done is a major foundation of self-respect.

One of the greatest faults of modern manufacturing techniques is that the sense of individual accomplishment is lost. It is hard to be proud of bolt No. 87. It is easy to be proud of a homemade table. Restoration of a sense of accomplishment is one of the biggest PR problems in industry today; if a man does not feel that he is accomplishing something, he cannot be very proud of or happy in his work.

Recognition

The Congressional Medal of Honor is a bronze star hung on a ribbon. Its cost is just a few dollars. Yet, it is the highest military honor an American can attain, because it is his country's recognition of the recipient's heroism in defense of his country. Usually it is presented with considerable ceremony by the President. This is recognition. No one can buy it.

There are many other forms of recognition. They include titles and

promotions, plaques and letters, public acclaim and private compliments
— but all are essentially the same. They single out an individual and say to
him, "You have done well and we appreciate it." Recognition contributes
to the individual's identity. It lifts him out of the uniform mass and makes
him something unique and different. Organized plans for recognition of
individuals and groups are essential in public relations.

Suggested Readings

Ardrey, R. *African Genesis*. New York: Atheneum, 1961.
Ardrey, R. *The Territorial Imperative*. New York: Atheneum, 1966.
Ardrey, R. *The Social Contract*. New York: Atheneum, 1970.
Ember, C., and Ember, M. *Anthropology*. Englewood Cliffs, N.J.: Prentice-Hall, 1977.
Greenwood, Davydd, and Stini, William A. *Nature, Culture and Human History*. New York:
   Harper & Row, 1977.
Hardesty, Donald L. *Ecological Anthropology*. New York: Wiley, 1977.
Maslow, A. H. *Motivation and Personality*. New York: Harper & Row, 1954.
Maslow, A. H. *New Knowledge in Human Values*. New York: Harper & Row, 1959.
Maslow, A. H. *Toward a Psychology of Being*. New York: Van Nostrand Reinhold, 1968.
Morris, D. *The Naked Ape*. New York: McGraw-Hill, 1967.
Morris, D. *The Human Zoo*. New York: McGraw-Hill, 1969.
Tiger, L. *Men in Groups*. New York: Random House, 1969.

THE UNIQUE AMERICAN

Practitioners of international public relations put great emphasis on
understanding the people of the countries where they conduct their
programs. Leone Baxter, President of Whitaker & Baxter, International
says that every country has its own special customs, attitudes, and values
— and that public relations activity which does not consider these factors
is doomed to fail.

The same thing might be said about public relations activity in the
United States. Americans too have special customs, attitudes, and values.
Knowing these factors would seem to be essential for the practice of
public relations here.

American differences were identified by S. J. de Crevecoeur as early as
1782. They have been repeatedly noted by such observers as Alexis de
Tocqueville, Harriet Martineau, Frederick Jackson Turner, Charles Dickens, and Rudyard Kipling.

Dr. Alex Inkeles of Stanford University has compared these early
observations with current psychological test results and public opinion
data. He found that most of the early observations were indeed accurate.
Many of these unique American characteristics are unchanged after

some two hundred years. A few seem to be changing. The characteristics confirmed by Dr. Inkeles are:

National Pride

Americans believe that the United States is the best country on earth and that it has the best system of government. They are proud that they are Americans.

Self-Reliance

There is a strong conviction that the individual is responsible for his or her own success, that persistence, hard work, and initiative are important. There is little belief that fate or luck controls the destiny of the individual.

Voluntarism

Americans are conspicuous for their willingness to cooperate with others, to join organizations, to work together for a common cause.

Trust

Americans are basically unsuspicious of others; they are willing to take people at face value; they expect to be trusted by others.

Efficacy

Americans believe that almost any problem can be solved if the effort is made. "The difficult we do immediately, the impossible takes a little more time."

Optimism

There is a deep-rooted confidence that if we try we will succeed, that things will get better, that the future is bright.

Innovativeness

Americans are notably willing to try new things and new ideas. We don't cling to the old just because it is familiar.

Antiauthoritarianism

Americans dislike direction from above; they persist in asserting individual rights and resisting governmental controls.

Equality

Americans believe that "all men are created equal," that none should have unearned privileges, that everyone has the same rights.

Other Differences

Some other American characteristics which may be significant are individualism, restless energy, pragmatism, this-worldliness, brashness, boastfulness, a preference for the concrete rather than the abstract, and discomfort with esthetic and emotional expression.

THE CHANGING AMERICAN

Most American characteristics have been long established and seem resistant to change. A few, however, are apparently being modified. These changes have shown up in the last twenty-five or thirty years and may or may not be permanent.

Tolerance

Early observers noted little tolerance of diversity. Bigotry and prejudice were all too common. At the present time there is considerable evidence that tolerance is steadily increasing.

The Puritan Ethic

Hard work, temperance, and frugality were widely accepted precepts in the early days of this country. Commonly attributed to the Puritans, these ideals were praised by many others. Now these virtues are questioned and many of our citizens aren't willing to work hard, live temperately, and save for the future.

Political Confidence

Americans seem to have lost much of their political confidence. There is an apparent conviction that the functions of government are not being properly performed and that the individual has little, if any, effect on the political system.

Suggested Readings

Boorstin, Daniel J. *The Americans*. New York: Random House, 1974.

Chase, Stuart. *American Credos*. New York: Harper & Row, 1975.

Commager, Henry S. *The Empire of Reason*. New York: Doubleday, 1977.

Commager, Henry S. et al. *American Heritage and Horizons*. Memphis, Tenn.: Memphis State University Press, 1977.

Kristol, Irving, and Weaver, Paul H. *Americans 1976*. Lexington, Mass.: Lexington Press, 1976.

Steinbeck, J. et al. *America and Americans*. New York: Viking, 1966.

THE ROOTS OF INDIVIDUAL ATTITUDES

There are many factors that influence individuals and affect their attitudes and opinions. Among them are family, religion, education, economic status, occupation, political affiliation, union membership, race, residence, national origin, organization membership, social class, individual experience, age, and physical condition.

Family

The family is the strongest influence on individual attitudes. Most people acquire religious affiliation and political conviction from their families (Hyman, 1959). Manner of speech comes from the family. Food tastes are rooted in family habits. If a father does not think much of advanced education, it is probable that none of the children will go to college. If he is ambitious, it is likely that his children will set high goals. The reason for all this is very simple. Children are impressionable. Their first impression normally comes from their own families, so they tend to conform to family attitudes and customs (Hennesey, 1965).

Religion

Religion has a profound effect on individual attitudes. Most church members conform to most of the rules of their church. Whenever an issue runs contrary to church dogma, it is to be expected that the members will oppose that issue. Not many will support a proposal opposed by their church (Hennesey, 1965).

Education

The amount and kind of education received by an individual has considerable effect on his attitudes. Public opinion surveys show that the more education people have, the more "liberal" they become.* Part of this may be due to the sheer volume of learning and part may be due to the influence of "liberal" teachers. The subjects studied have a marked influence on the individual. Those who studied engineering will think differently from those who studied English. Those who majored in business will be quite different from those who majored in archaeology (Hennesey, 1965).

Economic Status

The financial condition of the individual has a powerful effect on his thinking. Many a radical has turned conservative as soon as he had anything to conserve. People with little or no money are usually in favor of higher governmental expenditures. They are always ready to support tax increases if they are aimed at the well-to-do.

In a study on welfare conducted by CBS and the *New York Times*, a question was asked about government-provided minimum income. A full 60% of respondents whose annual income was under $8,000 favored the idea, 35% opposed it. Of respondents whose annual income was over $20,000, only 34% favored the idea while 62% were opposed.

People who have money want to keep it, so they want less government activity and lower taxes. Employees want bigger paychecks and lower corporate profits. Stockholders want the opposite. On almost every economic issue, people's attitudes can be predicted from their economic status. They vote with their pocketbooks. Self-interest hits its highest peak when money is involved (Hennesey, 1965).

Residence

Where a person lives has considerable bearing on his attitudes. People who live in the country differ from urban dwellers. Suburbanites have different attitudes from those who live in the cities. Labor union officials are much concerned about the nonmilitancy of their prosperous members who have moved out of the tenements and into individual houses in

*One Gallup Opinion Index reported that 20% of people with grade school education classed themselves as "liberal." Among high school graduates the figure was 26%, and among college graduates the figure was 39%.

the suburbs. And ghetto residents are, of course, vastly different in attitude from those who live elsewhere (Hennesey, 1965).

The region in which one lives can have a strong effect on attitudes. For a time it was believed that regional differences were disappearing, but a study based on nine Gallup polls and on one conducted by the National Opinion Research Council found that there were no data to support that belief (Glenn-Simmons, 1967).

Organization Membership

Belonging to an organization has a profound effect on individual attitudes. There is a strong tendency toward uniformity of opinion on subjects bearing upon the interests of the organization. This is why working through organizations is so important in public relations. People who belong to a gun club will have vastly different attitudes on gun legislation than people who belong to a golf club. PTA members are much more "activist" about schools than parents who are not members (Costello and Zalkind, 1963).

Occupation

What people do for a living also influences their attitudes. First, is the alliance with others in the same field — bankers group with bankers, doctors with doctors and so on. Second, is the grouping into occupational classes. Personal service occupations have little prestige in the United States. Surveys of occupational prestige show that waiters, bartenders, barbers, janitors, gas station attendants, and domestic servants rate near the bottom, while lawyers, doctors, corporation executives, teachers, and ministers rate far above them (Packard, 1959).

People will often work for less money in a white-collar job than in a blue-collar job, because the white-collar job has "prestige" while the blue-collar job is "labor." People in one occupational class tend to be "for" those in that class and "against" those in another class.

Political Affiliation

Politics creates strange and unreasonable attitudes. Party members will loyally support the party's position on issue after issue and cheerfully reverse their stand whenever the party leaders change their minds. A study of attitudes toward the Supreme Court showed that affiliation with a political party was the chief structuring agent (Dolbeare and Hammond, 1968). Individual attitudes on many points can be predicted by determining the official attitude of the party to which the individual belongs.

Union Membership

If a man belongs to a union, he is likely to follow the union line on economic issues. With more general problems there is more independence of thinking. In general terms, union members are antagonistic to the interests of management and ownership because their interests are diametrically opposed. There are exceptions, but usually membership in a union means that the individual is suspicious and distrustful of management. Union leaders hold their jobs by "fighting" management, and it is not easy to fight someone you like (Kornhauser et al., 1956).

Ethnic Affiliation

Race has always been a problem in human relations. In a time of racial conflict it may easily outweigh all other factors. An individual cannot ignore or forget his race. It is part of his identity and is therefore a primordial influence on his attitudes.

In a study of voting patterns in Newark, New Jersey, it was found that ethnic affiliation was more important than political party, candidate slates, or policies advocated by the candidates (Pomper, 1966).

Like race and creed, national origin is a characteristic that the government says should not be used as a basis for discrimination. But, discrimination or no, many people are acutely conscious of their national origin; they tend to like those of similar origin and be reserved about those of different origin.

Social Class

Ask any American what class he belongs to and he will probably say "the middle class." He will be essentially right because this is a country with few class distinctions. But there are divisions and they affect the attitudes of their members. One widely used classification divides the population into five classes: (1) "the 400," (2) upper-middle, (3) lower-middle, (4) upper-lower, and (5) lower-lower. These classes are not based entirely on money, but on history, occupation, place of residence, family, and so on. (The "400" are those who are in "society.")

A member of "the 400" may be flat broke and sponging off friends, but he looks down on the uncouth millionaire who is still in class 3. The truck driver in class 4 may make more money and live in a better house than the college instructor in class 2, but his attitudes are still class 4. The cleaning shop proprietor in class 3 considers himself very different from the banker in class 2 or the handyman in class 5. Social class is a matter of identity. There is some migration from class to class, but most people adhere firmly to the class mores and class standards of their own group.

Experience

The things that people do and the things that happen to them can have a profound effect on their attitudes. A Black who has been unjustly man-handled by a white policeman will therafter probably class all white policemen as brutal. A factory worker mistreated by a bad foreman will lump all supervisory personnel in the same unfavored category.

Conversely, the people who have pleasant experiences tend to like everything and everybody connected with that experience. The employee who is aided by his employer in time of need, the citizen rescued from a holdup by an efficient and courteous policeman, the beginner who is trained by an understanding and kindly foreman — all will have attitudes that reflect the treatment they received.

Age

The old people who think the younger generation will ruin the world and the young who are convinced that the oldsters have already ruined it have one thing in common: their thinking is warped by their age. Older people have judgment and experience, younger ones have enthusiasm and optimism. They cannot look at things in the same way, so their reactions to any situation will usually be different.

Summary

There are a great many factors that influence attitudes. The amount of influence depends on the individual. One man may be more religious than another. One woman may be more politically active than another, but all people are affected to some degree by most of these factors. The more that is known about people, the easier it is to determine what factors have influenced their attitudes.

PSYCHOLOGY OF PUBLIC OPINION

Dr. Earl Jandron, of the Department of Psychology at San Jose State University, has compiled a summary of social psychological findings which bear on public opinion. It is presented here with his permission.

The Persuader

1. There will be more opinion change in the desired direction if the communicator has high credibility than if he has low credibility. Credibility is:
   a. Expertise (ability to know correct stand on issue).
   b. Trustworthiness (motivation to communicate knowledge without bias).
2. The credibility of the persuader is less of a factor in opinion change later on than it is immediately after exposure.
3. A communicator's effectiveness is increased if he initially expresses some views that are also held by his audience.
4. What an audience thinks of a persuader may be directly influenced by what they think of his message.
5. The more extreme the opinion change that the communicator asks for, the more actual change he is likely to get.
   a. The greater the discrepancy (between communicator message and recipient's initial position), the greater the attitude change, up to extremely discrepant points.
   b. With extreme discrepancy, and with low-credibility sources, there is a falling off in attitude change.
6. Communicator characteristics irrelevant to the topic of his message can influence acceptance of its conclusion.

How to Present the Issues

1. Present one side of the argument when the audience is generally friendly, or when your position is the only one that will be presented, or when you want immediate, though temporary, opinion or attitude change.
2. Present both sides of the argument when the audience starts out disagreeing with you, or when it is probable that the audience will hear the other side from someone else.
3. When opposite views are presented one after another, the one presented *last* will probably be more effective. Primacy effect is more predominant when the second side immediately follows the first, while recency effect is more predominant when the opinion measure comes immediately after the second side.
4. There will probably be more opinion change in the direction you want if you explicitly state your conclusions than if you let the audience draw their own, except when they are rather intelligent; then implicit conclusion drawing is better.
5. Sometimes emotional appeals are more influential, sometimes factual ones. It all depends on the kind of audience.
6. Fear appeals. The findings generally show a positive relationship between intensity of fear arousal and amount of attitude change *if* recommendations for action are explicit and possible, but a *negative* reaction otherwise.
7. The fewer the extrinsic justifications provided in the communication for engaging in counternorm behavior, the greater the attitude change after actual compliance.

8. No final conclusion can be drawn about whether the opening or closing part of the communication should contain the more important material.
9. Cues which forewarn the audience of the manipulative intent of the communication increase resistance to it, while the presence of distraction simultaneously presented with the message decreases resistance.

The Audience as Individuals

1. The people you may want most in your audience are often least likely to be there. There is evidence for selective seeking and exposure to information consonant with one's position, but not for selective avoidance of information dissonant with one's position.
2. The level of intelligence of an audience determines the effectiveness of some kinds of appeals.
3. Successful persuasion takes into account the reasons underlying attitudes as well as the attitudes themselves. That is, the technique used must be tailored to the basis for developing the attitude.
4. The individual's personality traits affect his susceptibility to persuasion; he is more easily influenced when his self-esteem is low.
5. There are individuals who are highly persuasible and who will be easily changed by an influence attempt, but who are then equally influenced when faced with countercommunication.
6. Ego involvement with the content of the communication (its relation to ideological values of the audience) decreases the acceptance of its conclusion. Involvement with the consequences of one's response increases the probability of change and does so more often when source-audience discrepancy is greater.
7. Actively role-playing a previously unacceptable position increases its acceptability.

The Influence of Groups

1. A person's opinions and attitudes are strongly influenced by groups to which he belongs and wants to belong.
2. A person is rewarded for conforming to the standards of the group and punished for deviating from them.
3. People who are most attached to the group are probably least influenced by communications which conflict with group norms.
4. Opinions which people make known to others are harder to change than opinions which people hold privately.
5. Audience participation (group discussion and decision-making) helps to overcome resistance.
6. Resistance to a counternorm communication increases with salience of one's group identification.
7. The support of even one other person weakens the powerful effect of a majority opinion on an individual.
8. A minority of two people can influence the majority if they are consistent in their deviant responses.

The Persistence of Opinion Change

1. In time, the effects of a persuasive communication tend to wear off.
2. a. A communication from a positive source leads to more rapid decay of attitude change over time than one from a negative one.

b. A complex or subtle message produces slower decay of attitude change.

c. Attitude change is more persistent over time if the receiver actively participates in, rather than passively receives, the communication.

2. Repeating a communication tends to prolong its influence.

3. More of the desired opinion change may be found some time after exposure to the communication than right after exposure (sleeper effect).

Some Questions

1. How specific does the change need to be?
2. How long does the change have to last?
3. How many people have to change — one, some, many?
4. What is to be changed — how people think, how they talk, how they behave nonverbally? Should subjects be aware or unconscious of change?
5. Must a whole new set of attitudes be created?
6. Do you control some media?
7. Is it likely people will listen?
8. Are there others trying to produce change in opposition to you?
9. What are the time limits you have?
10. How much money, resources, help is available?
11. How will others perceive you?
12. What is the nature of your audience? How intelligent? How friendly or hostile? How informed about the issue?
13. Will you be required to have future interaction with the people you are trying to change?
14. What is your stake in the problem topic? Are you committed?
15. What are the consequences of being a successful manipulator?
16. Might you be changed yourself by applying your technique?
17. How will you react to failure?

SELF-INTEREST

These are the two most important words in public relations. If we appeal to the self-interest of those we are trying to influence, we are likely to succeed. If we fail to do this, or if we appeal to our own self-interest, we are likely to fail.

EXERCISES

1. Name a subject of broad interest on which public opinion has changed materially in recent months.
   (a) What groups, organizations, or individuals were responsible?
   (b) What message did they convey to the public?
   (c) How did they reach the public
   (d) Why did they succeed?

(e) Who opposed it?
(f) What message did they convey to the public?
(g) How did they reach the public?
(h) Why did they fail?

Case Problem

An electrical utility has had "brown-outs" every summer for three years. Solving the power shortage, caused largely by increased use of air conditioners, requires construction of a nuclear power plant. The most economical location is on the seashore in an area of much natural beauty.

How would you oppose this and how would you support it? For both sides of the question:
Who would you try to reach (individuals, organizations, and groups)?
How would you reach them (the tools to be used)?
What message would you convey to each group or organization?

Publics | 8

When someone says "the public," it is important to know just which "public" he means, because there can be an almost infinite number of publics. If fact, whenever two or more people become conscious of a common interest, they become a public. Two fishermen excluded from a favorite stream, two thousand teachers frustrated by rowdy students, or two hundred million Americans angered by the increased cost of living — all are publics, and most people belong to a considerable number of different publics. Our fishermen could easily be schoolteachers and angry Americans.

A Definition

The dictionaries give many definitions, but none of them quite fits the needs of public relations. Here is one that will serve our purpose.

The public is everyone interested in, or affected by, an organization, or whose opinions can affect the organization.

This applies to individuals, ideas, issues, products, or services as well as to organizations.

Note particularly the dual nature of the public. It can be affected and it can affect. For example, the employees of a company may negotiate for higher wages. They are definitely affected by the company's actions and their actions may affect the company. On the other hand, a group of outsiders who are totally unaffected by the negotiations may inject themselves into the situation and affect its results. In this illustration there are two publics involved: the employee public and the outside public.

Publics may be grouped into two classes: general and special. Most individuals and organizations will have publics in each class. And most individuals belong to several publics.

137

GENERAL PUBLICS

The general publics of commercial organizations are employees, owners, customers, the community, educators, government, suppliers, dealers, and competitors. With noncommercial organizations, the publics are essentially the same, but with one addition — the constituents.

Constituents

Anyone who expects a noncommercial organization to accomplish something on his behalf is a constituent. A volunteer worker for a charity is a constituent and so is the beneficiary of the charity. Voters are constituents of their national, state, and local governments. Members of an environmental protection group are constituents of the group. In fact, anyone who contributes to or receives from a nonprofit organization is a constituent.

Employees

Anyone who works and gets paid for it is an employee. The President of the United States is an employee of the U.S. Government. The president of a corporation and the newest and lowliest laborer on the payroll are both employees. The basic test is work for which a predetermined payment is made.

Owners

Owners are normally thought of as stockholders, partners, or individuals who employ workers. In nonprofit organizations, such as trade associations, the members are owners. In government the taxpayers are the owners. Essentially, ownership involves putting money or its equivalent into an activity or enterprise in order to gain some benefit from the investment.

Customers

The woman pushing a shopping cart to the checkout counter of a grocery store is obviously a customer. So, too, is the householder calling the police to search for a suspected burglar. The contractor buying a trainload of cement, the child purchasing an ice-cream cone, the student in a college — all are customers.

A member of an association becomes a customer whenever he gets information or help from that association (of which he is an owner by virtue of membership). The distinguishing characteristic of customers is that they receive or expect to receive something from the organization or individual with which they deal.

Community

The community includes all people and organizations affected by or who can affect the organization by virtue of location. The community may actually include employees, owners, customers, suppliers, dealers, and many others who have some direct relationship to the organization. It also normally includes a great many more people who have no direct involvement. The community of General Motors includes all the people in the plant cities plus, to a less intense degree, all the people of the United States. The corporation is so big and its products so numerous that its actions have an effect on people throughout the country.

The community of a state university includes the campus, city, and, less intensively, the entire state. The community of a small retail store may be a few square blocks. We normally think of a community as a city or neighborhood. Sometimes we think of it as a state or nation, but this should not be allowed to create misconceptions. In public relations, the community is not a geographic entity, it is an "effect" entity. It extends just as far as the organization can reach.

Educators

Anyone who teaches in or administers educational institutions is an educator. The person may be a college president with several advanced degrees, a part-time coach, an art instructor, or a teacher of a first-grade class.

Government

Customarily we think of government as national, state, or local, but this does not completely cover the field, because there are many quasi-governmental bodies that have some similarities to government. Entities such as irrigation districts, flood control districts, the Rural Electric Administration, the Tennessee Valley Authority, and numerous others have many governmental powers and privileges; they must be dealt with more as government agencies than as the corporations or associations that they legally are. Also, in thinking of government, we must think of both the legislative and the executive branches.

139

Fig. 8.1 One of the top public relations photographs in a contest conducted by the *Public Relations Journal*. Its purpose was to show audience reaction to a new high school TV program, "It's Academic." It was used in a booklet published by Cleveland Electric Illuminating Co. to persuade local educators to participate in the program. It succeeded. Peter Hastings of Hastings-Willinger was the photographer.

Suppliers

In general terms, a supplier provides things for resale or for manufacture. The farmer who sells peaches to a canner is a supplier, so is the printer who sells labels, and the manufacturers who sell cans, sugar, and machinery to the canner. The canner, who sells the canned peaches to a grocer, is a supplier. So are the manufacturers who sell soap and dog food and paper napkins to the grocers. The test of whether a person or organization is a supplier is this: if he sells the product, he is the supplier; he loses that identity as soon as the product is resold to someone else.

Dealers or Distributors

A dealer or distributor is a person or firm selling merchandise for one or a very few manufacturers. If a man sells General Electric household appliances exclusively, he is a dealer, but if he also sells Philco, Hotpoint, Whirlpool, Westinghouse, etc., he is not really a dealer. Dealerships are most typical in the automobile business and the service station business. A variation of dealership is the franchise operation, which is frequently found in the restaurant business. In any event, the distinguishing characteristic of dealerships is close and conspicuous identification of the enterprise with the brand name of the product sold.

Competitors

Competitors can be either direct or indirect. Two grocery stores can be direct competitors, but the restaurant across the street, the drive-in at the edge of town, the health food store, even the customer's backyard garden can be indirect competitors. In the broadest sense, any enterprise that reaches for the same buyer's dollar is a competitor; thus, a bar might get money that otherwise could be spent on theater tickets or clothing. For practical purposes, it is best to think of competitors as those engaged in the same kind of work and reaching the same potential customers. A Chrysler dealer in Des Moines is a competitor of all automobile dealers in Des Moines. He is also probably a competitor of all automobile dealers in adjoining communities, but he does not compete with dealers in Omaha or Davenport.

SPECIAL PUBLICS

Americans are joiners. We have a vast number of organizations of many purposes and sizes. It is very difficult to find an American who does not belong to at least one, and it is not at all unusual to find people who belong to a dozen or more. People belong to these organizations because of a common interest. Their membership in these groups makes them easy to reach and therefore important targets of public relations programs. These organizations fall into two classes: inward-oriented and outward-oriented.

Inward-Oriented Groups

These are organized mainly to promote the interests of members or to provide recreation, entertainment, or social interchange. They include such groups as labor unions, clubs, trade associations, Elks, Masons,

Knights of Columbus, the DAR, churches, medical societies, alumni associations, and on and on. There are thousands of such organizations, and their membership can run into the millions.

These inward-oriented groups can be subdivided into two categories: those who take positions on broad public issues and those who do not. In the first category, we find labor unions which not only protect their members but also involve themselves in such problems as product safety, costs of medical care, protection of the environment, pollution, consumerism, and even foreign policy.

Some trade associations will also be concerned with such problems. And, of course, there are a host of organizations representing minority groups and special causes, which concentrate their main efforts on the direct self-interest of their members but, in addition, will and do fight for causes they feel are parallel to their own or where they believe a great moral issue is involved. This leads to churches participating in labor controversies and to teachers' unions and associations taking strong stands on foreign policy.

Getting the support of these "activist" organizations requires a careful study of the organization and its past activities and a thorough analysis of the problem at hand. If the organization has already taken a position on a similar issue, there is a definite possibility of getting its support. If not, the organization will have to be convinced that its own self-interest will be served by its involvement.

The "nonactivist" inward-oriented groups are less helpful in public relations but they should not be disregarded. Typically, groups of this sort do not engage in crusades or drives. They may take positions on some non-controversial subjects but, outside of protection of their own membership or advancement of their own self-interest, they are not basically activists. Thus, the American Legion is vitally interested in veterans' affairs, national defense, and patriotic causes but probably has no other issues on which it would express a strong opinion. The American Medical Association is the watchdog of the medical profession. It takes a strong position on any issues affecting the practice of medicine but goes no farther. The local country club will be aroused over its taxation, over zoning affecting it, over laws that restrict its activities, but that is all.

These general-purpose groups are oriented inward. It is not likely that many of them can be induced to take official positions or to battle for a cause. But it is possible at times, and they always provide access to the individual members. Thus, while a club may not be willing to go on the warpath over some issue, it may be possible through a speech to arouse the members of the club to individual action; sometimes the whole group may be moved to action on a problem affecting the community.

Outward-Oriented Groups

These are groups organized to attain definite objectives. This category includes such special-purpose organizations as the American Red Cross, the Sierra Club, the Save the Redwoods League, The Anti-Defamation League, the American Civil Liberties Union, the Heart Fund, and the SPCA. Also in this category are general-purpose groups such as Chambers of Commerce, Rotary, Lions, Optimists, etc.

These are working groups. Their members may have little in common beyond the group purpose. They are organized to accomplish some purpose beyond personal benefit. Their sole satisfaction may be in this accomplishment. They are motivated by idealism and unselfishness. They will take controversial positions because they are oriented to action. Normally, they will take a position only on issues parallel to their own line of activity.

Special-interest groups can be organized whenever a strong cause exists and enough crusaders can be found. Every special-interest group that ever existed came into being because someone had a cause and persuaded others to join him.

Unorganized Publics

Many special publics exist without formal organization. To name a few, there are taxpayers, students, farmers, laborers, white-collar workers, environmentalists, contractors, and many minority groups.

Summary

Every person alive belongs to at least one public. Most belong to several. And it is not at all difficult to belong to many.

Suppose we use a hypothetical airplane pilot and find how many publics he could belong to. *Employee* — he flies a plane. *Owner* — he owns stock in the airline. *Customer* — he occasionally flies as a passenger. *Community* — he lives in an "on line" city. *Educator* — he occasionally lectures on aeronautics at the local junior college. *Government* — he is on the school board. *Supplier* — he owns a small winery that sells to the airline. *Competitor* — he owns a four-seater and occasionally flies friends to a vacation spot; he does not charge a fee but he is providing air transportation. *Dealer* — he owns part interest in a fried-chicken franchise.

Our hypothetical pilot also belongs to the Airline Pilots Association, the University of Illinois Alumni Association, the American Legion, the Elks, the Masons, the Congregational Church, and the Sierra Club. Without being too incredible, our man belongs to nine general publics, six inward-oriented groups, and one outward-oriented group.

The significance of membership in a public can vary considerably. Our hypothetical pilot is both an employee and an owner. But, since most of his income is earned as an employee and very little is earned as dividends on his stock, he is likely to think very much as an employee and very little as an owner. He might sacrifice stock dividends if he could get a substantial increase in pay.

Thus, while people belong to many publics, it is essential in public relations to determine which is most important to them and which is the most effective channel through which to reach them.

EXERCISES

1. List the publics of a college.
2. List the publics of a general hospital.

Case Problem

Your state senator has introduced a bill to permit use of gasoline tax funds for construction of urban rapid transit.

Which publics will be in favor of this?
Which publics will be opposed?
For each public, give the specific reason for its attitude.
What arguments can be used to support the position of each public?
What arguments can be used to counter these positions?
Which tools would you use to reach each of these publics? Why?
Prepare a brief plan for a campaign to get this law enacted.
Prepare a brief plan for a campaign to keep this law from being enacted.

The Constituent Public

Some people believe that public relations for business organizations is different from public relations for nonbusiness organizations. Some students, especially those who don't intend to work in business, have criticized textbooks for a supposed business orientation. And some authors, in an effort to counter this criticism, devote much attention to nonbusiness organizations.

That is not the case in this book because there is very little real difference. The basic principles and techniques of public relations apply to, and can be used by, any organization.

How else is it possible to explain the success of a woman who went from managing public relations for a large hotel to a major assignment in the Department of Health, Education and Welfare? How can we account for the man who moved from a key job in the Department of Commerce to an important position in the U.S. Chamber of Commerce? It is evident that their knowledge and skills were applicable in any public relations situation regardless of whether commercial or noncommercial.

The one major difference is in the publics of business and nonbusiness organizations. Most publics are common to both. The following ten chapters discuss publics. With the exception of the dealer public, all these publics exist to some degree for nonbusiness organizations. Every organization, whether profit or nonprofit, must think about employees, owners (or the equivalent), customers (or users of its services), the community, education, government, suppliers, and competitors.

The one public common to nonbusiness organizations and not a business public is one we will call the constituent public. It varies somewhat from one organization to another but, in general terms, it includes all the people who expect a noncommercial organization to accomplish something on their behalf.

In order to attain these objectives there must be a contribution of money or time or both. In some cases, the constituents contribute for their own benefit. In others, the beneficiaries may be quite different from the contributors. Generally, the contributions are voluntary. With tax-supported entities, the contribution is involuntary although the expectation of benefit is still there. To understand the constituent public in its varying forms, it is necessary to look at several different kinds of organizations having constituents. However, before we get specific, we should look at a problem common to all nonprofit groups.

THE COMMON PROBLEM WITH CONSTITUENTS

The biggest problem of any nonprofit organization is to maintain balance between input and output. It is easy to spend so much time and money in holding the organization together or in fund-raising that the actual function is neglected. Conversely, it is not at all difficult to concentrate attention on the program or the beneficiaries and forget about the supporters. Many an organization has failed for one of these reasons. With all such institutions, it is essential to remember that there is giving and receiving. Neither can be neglected. Maintaining the satisfaction of both kinds of constituents is a continuing public relations problem.

SOCIAL WELFARE

This category includes such groups as community chests, the Red Cross, the Salvation Army, the Boy Scouts, the Girl Scouts, the YMCA, the YWCA, the USO, the various organizations concerned with fighting specific diseases, religious bodies, and a host of other charitable entities. Their distinctive characteristic is that they exist and function because people contribute time and money for the benefit of others. Their constituents divide rather clearly into those who give and those who get.

The Givers

Most social welfare organizations need substantial and continuing contributions of money and manpower or womanpower. These contributions come largely from unpaid volunteers. These volunteer workers generally can be grouped into three categories — although there may be some overlapping of function and activity.

The fund-raisers who, usually in an annual drive, give and persuade others to give the money that enables the organization to carry on its program. Frequently the fund-raising is done as a combined activity through a community chest or crusade.

The time-givers who devote their own time to helping others. Usually there is an organized group whose members agree to spend a definite number of hours working in hospitals, day nurseries, children's homes, etc.

Those who raise money, in many different ways, for the benefit of one or several institutions *but who also give time to the same or to different institutions*.

While there are numerous independent givers in all three categories, most of the giving is done through organizations. Without organization, the giving would be only a tiny fraction of what it is. Getting these groups organized and functioning is a public relations problem of great importance. Motivation comes largely from ego- or self-fulfillment, but this must be focused on a specific objective and put to work by a well-planned program. In 1977 Americans gave $35.2 billion to charity.

The fund-raisers   There are a number of permanent organizations which, for a fee, will contract to raise money for a specific purpose. In New York City, the Manhattan classified telephone directory lists some thirty firms that appear to fit this description. The principal objection to these firms is their fee. In some cases, it is a rather large percentage of the total and this can lead to bitter recrimination when the figures are publicized. On the other hand, these people are experts who may be well worth their hire because the net proceeds may still be larger than could have been obtained otherwise. Fund-raising specialists are commonly used when large sums of money are needed.

The procedures in fund-raising are substantially the same whether used by a fund-raising specialist or by a voluntary group. The keys are: organization, objectives, communication, and follow-through. An annual community chest campaign illustrates the technique. The paid administrative staff organizes and serves as the communications center but most of the work is done by volunteers. The first step is the committee — a group of civic leaders who lend their names to the cause, who represent the principal groups that might contribute, and who, because of their involvement, can put pressure on their own and related organizations. A committee is likely to include leaders in banking, education, religion, labor, industry, agriculture, transportation, etc. The lineup varies depending on the situation. Thus, a Portland, Oregon, committee might well include a lumberman — because lumber is a major industry segment of that city. In Detroit there would probably be an automobile man.

The committee, either personally or through delegation, establishes contact with every organization in the community. The head of the organization is persuaded to become responsible for both unit and individual contributions from his organization. Frequently, at this level, the "headman" appoints some employee or member to work on soliciting individual gifts. The whole purpose of organization is to make sure that every possible source of money is tapped and that there is a mechanism for follow-through so that the objectives will be reached.

Objectives are imperative. There must be a specific dollar goal — for the community, for the various segments, for organizations, even for individual people.*

Often, partial objectives are decreed for various stages of the drive — for example, a certain sum by a certain date or a final goal to complete the campaign: "Only $3,500,000 more and we're over the top." Objectives give the workers a definite goal to work for and a definite measure of accomplishment. Without these targets, the results will be far less.

Communication is a vital component of any fund-raising effort. Potential givers must know that a campaign is going on, they must be urged to give, and they must be reminded until they give or decide not to. The leaders of the effort must know how the campaign is going, where help is needed, and how to reinforce weak spots.

The outbound communication is done through publicity (the news media are usually wholeheartedly behind these drives), through mailing pieces, posters, reminder cards, leaflets, and of course meetings, rallies, and speeches by the leaders. Inbound communication consists mainly of reports by the various workers on their progress. In a well-run campaign, the entire communication process is highly systematic and thoroughly planned.

Follow-through is the fourth element of a fund-raising effort. In spite of the frequent mention of volunteers, it must be stated that many of the volunteers are drafted and that the money does not gush forth without an effort. Someone has to recruit the workers, and the workers have to solicit contributions from everyone.

People often volunteer because they are asked to do so by someone they respect or admire. When the "boss" asks a subordinate to volunteer, it's

---

*Community chests often issue cards showing the percentage of income that individuals should give as their "fair share."

hard to decline; when the president of a large corporation asks his opposite number to head the drive in his firm, it's much easier to say yes than to say no. Many workers are obtained in this way, although, of course, many do really volunteer without any pressure. The follow-through on the campaign is often quite systematic. Through use of quotas, weekly reports, "pep" meetings of workers, graphic goals such as the ubiquitous "thermometer," it is possible to keep people informed and working until the effort is completed.

Follow-through can often be a matter of pressure from above. The effectiveness of this pressure is illustrated by the author's own experience. He was asked to "volunteer" to head the community-chest drive in an office with about 100 people. On checking the records of the previous year, a report of his predecessor to the head of the office contained this phrase: "After considerable arm-twisting, I managed to get 100% participation." Consultation with the new manager, who had just taken office, yielded a decision that there would be no "arm-twisting" but that a good effort should be made. Participation dropped to just over 60% and total gifts were down even more sharply!

The time-givers These are probably the most genuine volunteers in the field of social welfare. Many people, both men and women, who have time or will make time give millions of hours every year to helping others. Some of these people come to social welfare agencies looking for a chance to help. Others need only to be told they are needed and still others get into the act because friends urge them or because there is an organized group of workers such as the many hospital volunteers and auxiliaries. Scout leaders, Red Cross workers, and a wide assortment of other helpers belong to this classification although, in many cases, they also contribute money, either individually or through fund-raising activity.

It is probable that most of these time-givers are women. Getting the time contribution is a public relations problem of the organization to be benefited. The "walk-ins" must be received and put to work at some needed task which they can do. The others must be informed of the need for their services either through publicity or through the organized group that recruits the workers. Often a group must be formed — usually from a nucleus of people closely associated with the organization. For example, a new hospital might get some doctors' wives to organize the New Hospital Volunteers.

Maintaining membership in such groups is nearly always a problem. People die, move away, become disabled, or just lose interest. The solution is active solicitation of workers, meaningful work for them to do and expressed appreciation and recognition. Much of this is done through personal contact, but house organs, bulletin boards, and general publicity are also valuable tools for recruiting volunteers and for acknowledging their help. According to the Gallup poll, 27% of the American people participate in this work.

The money-makers These groups raise money by conducting profitable activities. Some sell candy, cookies, or cosmetics; others conduct rummage sales or auctions, still others hold dinners where the food and service are donated. It is doubtful if anyone can even guess the number of organizations involved or the amount of money raised. It is a favorite device of churches and schools, and above all, of the Girl Scouts.

With this kind of money-making activity, the beneficiary is almost invariably one organization and the workers are its members. If the First Methodist Church needs new choir robes, the Ladies Aid Society may hold a baked-goods sale. The ladies supply the ingredients and the work; they sell their products and put all the proceeds into buying the robes. When the Girl Scouts sell cookies, they buy them from a large bakery; the scouts themselves do the selling and they keep the profits.

With these groups, where the workers and the beneficiaries are often identical (and where personal contact is close and almost constant), the public relations work is largely directed toward the customers. A simple sale may be publicized by placards or by exposure in the local news media. On a large scale, the annual Girl Scout cookie sale has become such an institution and the Girl Scouts are so highly regarded that publicity is easily obtained. In general, this type of money-raising activity has a simple PR problem.

A quite different sort of situation is found with the numerous charitable groups that raise money for social welfare. Members are expected to do some socially beneficial work, and participation in group activities is made a privilege. The entire structure may have started with "society." It is possible that members of "the 400" decided that with all their wealth they should aid those less fortunate. At any rate, we now have a great many organizations — usually women's organizations — that raise large sums of money, require their members to do some sort of charitable work, and recruit and keep their members through admitting them to some level of society. They raise money with thrift shops, concerts, balls, luncheon-fashion shows, tours, lectures, and many other paid-admission affairs.

The society pages of newspapers report these activities in much detail. We read about the activities of the Junior League, Assistance League, Charity League, The _____ Volunteers, etc. In general, members come from the upper and upper-middle class. In some organizations they may be listed in the Social Register; in others, they may be far down the scale. But all stress the prestige of membership.

While this privilege of membership is a powerful means of getting members, it also creates the main public relations problem. All too often membership becomes not a commitment to work but a means of social climbing. When an organization becomes long on climbers and short on workers, it rapidly loses its effectiveness.

Another serious problem with these groups is the determination of the beneficiaries. If the group is affiliated with one organization — a hospital, for example — there is no problem but, in many cases, there is no affiliation. This leads to disagreements as to where the money and time are to go. It can lead to unhappiness among potential recipients. If the "Children's Hospital" wants therapy equipment while the "General Hospital" wants television sets, there can be difficulty in deciding which need is most worthy.

Most of these organizations have some member in charge of publicity and most of the publicity is directed toward the society editors of local papers. However, a substantial effort may also be made to get general publicity for an event that is open to the public on payment of an admission fee. If the "Major Hospital Auxiliary" is giving a formal ball, the publicity is aimed at the society pages and the members sell tickets to friends and acquaintances. If the "North End School" is conducting some sort of event, it tries to get publicity throughout the community and sells tickets at the gate to anyone who shows up.

The Organized Receivers

The organizations that benefit from fund-raising campaigns fall into two classes: those which are the only recipients and those which share with others in the proceeds of a combined campaign as in a community-chest drive.

If "St. Samantha's Hospital" carries out an annual drive to raise funds for maintaining an outpatient clinic, it is the only receiver and there is not much of a PR problem so far as givers are concerned. If, on the other hand, "St. Samantha's" depends on the community chest for funds to operate its outpatient clinic, there is a PR problem. It has to convince the community chest that its clinic should be supported — and it must justify the sum needed. The community chest has to convince other receivers, and givers too, of this community need.

In fact, one of the biggest PR problems of joint fund-raising is to determine which organizations are to be included and how much they are to receive. This also extends to the donors. Either individuals or organizations may object to giving money that benefits a group they oppose. In some communities this problem is solved by permitting donors to earmark their gifts for specific organizations.

Handling this very difficult problem is mainly a matter of policy. If the policy is equitable, the operation has a reasonable chance of success; if there are very many who feel that the balance is unjust, there will be a lack of support or even competing drives. From the standpoint of PR practice, the problem must be solved with continuous and effective two-way communication.

Organizations that utilize volunteer time may have such problems as too many or too few workers — or workers who want to do one thing but resist doing something else. Another problem is getting the help when it is needed and still another is the union restrictions on what unpaid helpers may be allowed to do. Person-to-person negotiation is the tool that has to be used in situations like these.

When a receiving organization deals with the society groups, it has to persuade the groups that it needs their help (either time or money), and occasionally it may have to compete with similar organizations. Here, too, personal contact by the organization's PR personnel with the leaders of the groups is invaluable.

The Ultimate Receivers

In the end, all social welfare organizations must deal with the individual people who benefit from the gifts of money and time. Many of these constituents are poor, friendless, and poorly educated. Physical or mental disability may be present. They must be treated as self-respecting individuals, not faceless numbers. In the case of tax-supported welfare the benefits may be looked on as a right. (This will be discussed later.)

With these gift-supported benefits, there is no legal right but there is a human right: the right to have the receiver's dignity preserved. The Lady Bountiful approach must not be used. These benefits are gifts, and they must be presented without "strings" and without anticipation of gratitude. If the presentation is done properly, there will usually be an expression of gratitude but it should never be required.

And, finally, remember that not all the receivers are poor and friend-less. The elderly lady in the hospital who is helped by a cheerful volunteer aide just might be a wealthy woman who could leave a substantial bequest to the hospital.

Suggested Readings

Six booklets available at nominal cost from the Public Relations Society of America (845 Third Ave., New York, N.Y. 10022) contain a wealth of information for those who must deal with constituents. The booklets are grouped under a general heading, *Managing Your Public Relations: Guidelines for Nonprofit Organizations.*

Specific titles are: *Using Standards to Strengthen Public Relations, Planning and Setting Objectives, Measuring Potential and Evaluating Results, Making the Most of Special Events, Using Publicity to Best Advantage, Working with Volunteers.*

FOUNDATIONS AND ENDOWMENTS

A foundation or endowment is an organization which has a sum of money that is treated as capital; its income is used for socially beneficial purposes. In some cases, however, capital as well as income may be expended. Some foundations have a very broad purpose, as in the case of the Ford Foundation which contributes to many different activities. In contrast, the Carnegie Foundation for the Advancement of Teaching has a very specific area of interest. Endowments are commonly devoted to a single educational institution and frequently turn some of their capital into buildings which, while not yielding income, may make a greater contribution to the school than the investment income.

The Givers

Foundations and some endowments often start with a large gift of money from some person or family. This may be the only contribution ever made. On the other hand, there may be other voluntary large gifts, plus occasional drives to add to the fund or to construct a specific building. Also, there are continuing programs to build up the endowment or foundation by regular gifts from alumni, etc. Large gifts are usually obtained through personal contacts with wealthy people. Sometimes these gifts have no strings attached. Sometimes they are for specific purposes — as for building a library at some university.

Obtaining these very large gifts is a highly personalized art which we will not attempt to cover in these pages. Smaller gifts are usually obtained through a campaign as described in the section on fund-raisers. Frequently, the two sources are tied together as when a wealthy person says, "I'll give a million dollars providing that others match it." This method is also used by foundations, which often make grants to educational institutions on the condition that the school raise an equal or greater sum of money from other sources. For example, the Ford Foundation gave Stanford University $25 million, but Stanford had to raise $75 million in order to get the Ford money.

The Receivers

Foundations generally dispense their money in lump-sum grants or in continuing support of some activity for varying periods of time. The total amounts requested can far exceed the amount available and individual requests can be for unjustifiable amounts. Furthermore, there are applications of doubtful merit. This creates a hydra-headed public relations problem. Disappointed seekers of grants may voice loud and bitter complaints. Even the winners may object to other winners on the grounds that their own funds might have been larger if money had not been "wasted" on some of the others. Winners, too, may complain about restrictions tied to the grants. If that were not enough, large foundations are frequently criticized by politicians for supporting specific institutions or activities.

Because some foundations have assets running into hundreds of millions of dollars and because a few have been used as tax loopholes, all are subject to intense government scrutiny — especially by the tax collectors. This has led to the proposals that all foundations have a termination date — a date when all funds must be distributed to specific beneficiaries. The problem, of course, is to convince all parties that the grants are fair, that the "strings" are necessary, that the purposes are socially desirable, and that the foundation itself is socially beneficial. To accomplish this, there must be a continuing program to inform all these constituents about how and why the grants are made, about the results obtained, and about the benefits that accrue to the public.

Suggested Readings

Russell, John M. *Give and Take.* New York: Teachers College Press, 1977.
Taft, J. R. *Understanding Foundations: Dimensions in Fund Raising.* New York: McGraw-Hill, 1967.

ASSOCIATIONS

There is an old gag that goes as follows: if two Americans were ship-wrecked on a desert island they would organize a chamber of commerce before their clothes dried out. The facts justify the gag. We organize associations for almost any purpose where joint action might be benefi-cial. In New York City, the Manhattan classified telephone directory uses more than four pages to list associations. Even as small a city as Reno has some 92 associations in its Yellow Pages. The *Encyclopedia of Associations* listed 12,644 associations in the United States in 1977.

Association activity is largely public relations activity. This generally requires the chief paid executive to devote most of his or her time to public relations. His work is frequently supplemented by a PR depart-ment or counselor, or both.

In nearly every association the givers are also the receivers although, in many situations, there may be beneficiaries who do not contribute. Some associations are organized primarily to protect the interests of an indus-try. Some are formed to advance a profession. Others are organized primarily to promote a product, a service, a community, or an area. Each of these has special problems, so we will discuss associations as though they were all either protective, professional, or promotional. However, we must recognize that the distinction is not always clear-cut, and that most promotional associations also have a protective function.

Under this admittedly arbitrary distinction, we would class the Ameri-can Medical Association as protective. It protects the interests of the medical profession but it does not try to get people to increase use of medical services. Even though it runs advertising urging people to take care of their health, the purpose of the advertising is to improve the public image of doctors — not to increase their income.

Another "protective" association is the Association of National Adver-tisers, whose main objectives are to give the business of advertising a unified voice and to help members improve the quality of their advertis-ing. Among professional associations, we would list the Public Relations Society of America, whose primary objective is the advancement of the public relations profession.

The Florida Citrus Commission is promotional. It does protect the interests of the citrus growers of Florida, but its main purpose, through promotional activities, is to get people to consume more Florida citrus products and thus increase the income of the growers.

On a much smaller scale is the Redwood Empire Association, which encourages tourism in and around the Redwood National Park and hopes to increase the income of its members.

Promotional Associations

Rather generally, these groups use advertising, publicity, and printed materials plus, in some cases, a staff of personal contact people to promote consumer demand for the product or service its members want to sell. Expenditures may range from a few thousand dollars a year to many millions. The burden on members may be almost nominal or it can be very taxing. One California "Advisory Board," organized to promote a food product, has levied assessments approximating 3% of the gross income of the farmers who support the program.

With all promotional associations, there are three major public relations problems: (1) obtaining and maintaining financial support, (2) deciding just how to spend the money, and (3) evaluating the program in order to determine whether it has accomplished enough to make continuation worthwhile, which feeds directly back to the first problem.

Obtaining and maintaining financial support

In many promotional associations membership is voluntary. The cost of membership can range from a nominal to a substantial figure. Frequently it is prorated according to the size of the potential member. Thus a 100-room motel might pay ten times as much as a 10-room motel. As long as a substantial majority of the potential membership (either in numbers or volume) participates, there can be a viable program; but if only a minority backs the effort it will not get very far. There is a limit to the amount of "free riding" a group will tolerate. Therefore, there must be a continuing effort to get and maintain membership. This is frequently done by the paid employees but the more enthusiastic members often participate actively through contacts with their associates and competitors.

People become members of promotional associations because they expect to benefit — either directly in terms of their own income or indirectly through general growth of the industry, the community, or the area. Persuading people to contribute to an effort of this sort requires a carefully balanced appeal to their self-interest and to their pride. The greatest danger is in overselling the benefits of membership. If the member does not get all that he expected, he will probably withdraw at the first opportunity. The appeal to pride is based on self-fulfillment, on group acceptance, and on self-respect.

When promotional programs become large, the cost to members may be quite high and universal participation becomes very desirable, if not imperative. This requires either a strong drive for membership, which is similar to a fund-raising campaign, or some form of compulsory contribution. The American Dairy Association, with a multimillion-dollar advertising campaign, gets its money as voluntary contributions, but it carries on continuing drives for participation.

The compulsory contribution is typified by the numerous "advisory boards" in California. A state law permits agricultural commodity groups to raise money for promotion by an assessment on *all* producers of the commodity. The assessment must be approved by a specified majority in both number and volume. The program is carefully regulated by the state and periodic referenda are conducted to be sure that the program is still wanted.

Getting and maintaining these "marketing orders" are major PR problems. The growers have to be convinced that the program will be worth the cost and, when the periodic referenda occur, the growers must be convinced that the program has attained its objectives. A continuing flow of information to the growers plus periodic meetings where questions can be answered and policy decided are the means by which these promotional programs are "sold" to the people who pay for them.

Deciding how to spend the money   Generally, the people who support promotional associations are not experts in promotion. Usually they employ experts to manage the program for them. In most cases, the members are represented by a committee which meets with the manager and is responsible to the other members for the success of the program.

Under ideal conditions, the members of the committee decide policy and the paid employees execute the program. But conditions are not always ideal. The committee members may want to make all the decisions and tell the manager not only what to do but how to do it; when this happens, the program is likely to suffer. At the other extreme, the manager may make decisions without consulting his constituents, and thus he may lose their support.

The best solution is for the manager to present recommendations with very complete explanation and justification. If this is done well, there is a good chance of acceptance; if it is not done well, the manager may find that the committee is dotting every "i" and crossing every "t" or losing interest entirely.

One of the most effective promotional associations operates this way: a manager of advertising and promotion reports to the advertising and sales promotion committee. He recommends a complete program to attain the objectives that are determined by the committee. In this case the objective is to create a climate that will help canners sell the product the grower members produce and sell to them. Recommendations include details on advertising, publicity, research, printed matter, promotional campaigns, merchandising, personnel, etc.

The committee may decide to change the emphasis; it may conclude that the field promotion staff should be reduced or increased, but it does not pick that staff. It may decide to put more money into television, but it does not pick the station. It may decide to cut the amount spent for point-of-sale advertising, but it does not decide which pieces to eliminate. It may approve a magazine advertising campaign, but it does not select the words to be used in every ad.

The reason this operation is successful is because the manager of advertising and promotion has worked *with* the committee and earned its confidence. He continually consults with the members of the committee in order to know what they are thinking and what the other constituents are thinking and saying. A large part of his time is devoted to this, but it keeps the program going.

Evaluating the program   The hoped-for proof of the success of a promotion program is increased sales. Unfortunately, this is seldom possible to measure. Many factors influence sales; advertising and promotion represent only a small part of the total influence. A commodity promotion effort such as the one just described can have an effect on consumers and on retailers, but it cannot control quality or packaging, price or sales pressure, or economic conditions or competition. Yet all of these can have a powerful effect on sales. When sales do go up, there is a strong temptation to take credit for success — but this requires taking the blame if sales go down or remain static.

The only sound thing to do is to make sure that the members thoroughly understand what the program can do and how *that* accomplishment is to be measured — inquiries can be counted, attitudes can be measured, awareness of advertising can be determined, displays can be seen and photographed, new users can be located and identified.

There must be a continuing flow of information to the members telling them what is being accomplished with their money. This sells them on the whole program as well as on the separate activities that contribute to its success. Letters, booklets, leaflets, bulletins, house organs, meetings, clippings, reports of broadcast publicity, pictures of activities, and personal contacts are all useful means of conveying this information. This feedback is the thing that builds and stabilizes support.

Protective Associations

These associations do not try to increase use of the products or services of the members. They often deal with governments and with such publics as employees. A good example is the Association of American Railroads. It lobbies with state and national government. It tries to protect the interests of the railroads. It gets involved with labor. But it does not try to get people to ship by rail instead of by truck. The American Trucking Association tries to protect the trucking industry from unwanted regulations. It tells how skillful truck drivers are, how careful, and how courteous. (See the advertisements in Chapter 28.)

The promotional associations usually have a protective function. For example, the association mentioned as one of the most effective promotional groups has also done lobbying for protection of the industry from foreign competition.

Industry protective associations have the same problems as the promotional associations. They must get and maintain membership, they must carry on programs that benefit its members, and they must evaluate these programs.

Getting member support Because the costs are relatively small and because there is so often a definite threat to the industry, it is usually possible to get a very high percentage of the industry to participate. In many such situations every member of any size is a potential voluntary participant. Getting and keeping members is done by informing them of the need for the program and by continually reporting the successful solution of problems.

Deciding on the program Government regulation and competition are the two most important problems. The question is usually not "what to do" but "how to do it." Since the action is defensive, it is normally easy to get a decision to act — the problem then becomes one of determining how best to attain the objective.

Programs generally involve two phases: short-term action to combat a threat and long-term activity to keep threats from developing and to establish understanding and build relationships that will be helpful in time of need. An example of the protective aspect of associations is found in the commodity promotion group previously mentioned. Faced with low-priced competition from Australia, which had government subsidies and preferential ocean-freight rates, this association worked with the federal government and persuaded it to tell Australia to stop the subsidy or face a similar U.S. subsidy. On the ocean-freight rates, the association has put much pressure on carriers to equalize rates. These are short-term actions against specific problems.

On a long-term basis, the Association maintains continuing relationships with key people in Washington so that it will have ready channels of communication for any problem that may develop. The association has also established communication with the Australian producers, and a much healthier relationship between the industries of the two countries has developed.

Evaluation of the program Results are the test of a protective program. If there is successful accomplishment, the members will be satisfied. If there is failure, there will be dissatisfaction unless there is a convincing reason for the failure. The National Rifle Association represents people who enjoy shooting. It has fought against state and federal antigun laws. It has lost a few of these battles, but membership has increased because the people who own guns are convinced that even more drastic legislation might be passed without massive organized opposition. The evaluation has been favorable because the NRA has carried out a continuing program of informing members and potential members about the problems and the action of the association.

Professional Associations

Large in number but usually small in budget, professional associations seldom have major public relations problems. Membership is frequently restricted to those especially qualified and is often almost a prerequisite for practice of the profession. As a consequence, recruiting here is not like recruiting for a promotional or protective association. Dues are generally the same for all members and are often considered license fees.

The programs of professional associations are largely educational. Through meetings, conventions, and seminars, through research and through publication of booklets, books, and professional journals, they improve the skills and competence of their members. Evaluating a professional association is quite simple. If membership is a prerequisite to practice, there is little that members can do. If there is a voluntary aspect, the member can readily decide whether his investment of time and money is worthwhile.

The PR problem then becomes, to a considerable degree, a matter of policy. What the association does in terms of service to its members is most important. If the meetings are worthwhile, if they are properly promoted so that attendance is adequate and if the publications are valuable, the members will be satisfied.

Suggested Reading

Bradley, J. F. *Role of Trade Associations and Professional Business Societies in America.* University Park, Pa.: Pennsylvania State University Press, 1965.

SCHOOLS

For generations, our elementary and secondary schools have functioned in a climate of general public approval and willing financial support. However, a recent Gallup poll showed that only 37% of the population now approves of the public schools. This creates some of the most difficult public relations problems ever faced by any institution. Because these problems are so controversial and involve so much emotion, there are no solutions that will be universally approved. In many cases, the best that can be hoped for is a grudging acceptance of decisions but with full knowledge that the lid may blow off at any time.

With many publics it is possible to establish guidelines for building good relations — guidelines based on proven success. There are no guidelines for schools because, with the constituents of schools, that which builds good relations with one group will probably build bad relations with its opponents. These are difficult times for school administrators, and if there ever was a time when a public relations program was necessary for schools, it is now.

The most conspicuous public relations problems of schools center in these areas: finances, curriculum, discipline, quality of teaching, and integration.

Finances

On most tax bills the biggest item is school taxes. They are paid by every property owner and, until just a few years ago, there was an almost universal willingness to support any expenditure for the "education of our children." Now we find organized groups fighting against higher school taxes and urging elimination of "frills." The steady increase in rejection of school bond issues is a sign that taxpayers are no longer willing to support every educational expenditure. The Supreme Court decisions of June 1971, which upheld state laws requiring that bond issues be approved by a 60% or 66-2/3% majority, have added to the difficulty. Based on these decisions, future opposition to bond issues will probably be better organized and intensified.

Faced with what could be described as a taxpayers' revolt, any school needing more money will have to do two things. First, it will have to justify the need very clearly and simply. Second, it will have to carry on an intensive effort to get taxpayers' approval. A continuing flow of information must be maintained and when a bond issue is on the ballot, its passage will undoubtedly require a real vote-getting campaign.

Related to this public-school problem is the financial problem of parochial schools. These schools are supported without tax money although, in some cases, tax money has been channeled to them indirectly. The burden on the parishes is substantial, and more and more parochial schools are closing and thereby placing additional demands on public schools. The ever-increasing demands of teachers for higher pay and smaller classes adds to the monetary problem. Negotiations can be helped through use of PR to tell the teachers the facts about the financial problem and to tell the taxpayers about the costs of the demands.

Curriculum

We send our children to school to become educated but we do not agree on what they are to learn or how. Parents have ideas, teachers have ideas, and they often disagree. Neither can we assume that parents agree with each other nor that teachers agree among themselves. The result is intense controversy. It starts in the first grade over how reading is to be taught; it progresses into battles over the textbooks to be used; and it reaches a climax over sex education and the drug problem. Mrs. Jones may want Johnny to learn the three R's and Mrs. Smith may want Mary to educate herself. Mr. White may be a fundamentalist and may violently oppose sex education, yet his own daughter may want to learn about the subject.

Obviously no school can please everyone and there is no certain solution to the curriculum problem. There is, however, one approach that offers the best probability of progress, and that is two-way communication. The school must provide avenues for communications. It must try to listen to all sides, to understand the reason for the varying attitudes, and to assess the intensity of those attitudes. It must explain its position and provide justification for what it does and how it does it. It cannot rely on a "teacher knows best" or "principal knows best" or even "school board knows best" answer — nor can it give in to a "father knows best" dictum, because "father" Johnson may disagree with "father" Jensen.

It is a tough problem. It probably cannot be solved to everyone's satisfaction but the effort to solve it should be based on building understanding through two-way communication.

Discipline

Control of students is a vastly different problem now from what it was in the days of "spare the rod and spoil the child." Corporal punishment is an extreme rarity. Children reared in permissive homes are not likely to accept rigid controls at school and standards of dress and deportment seem to be less and less enforceable.

In years past, the teacher exercised authoritative control over his or her students. Now that condition is the exception. Repeated news stories about physical assaults on teachers or students seem to suggest that there is no control.

In some schools there has been a successful solution based on parental support. In a San Francisco high school torn with physical assaults and sabotage, a meeting of parents, teachers, and administrators analyzed the problem, the causes, and possible solutions. The parents, recognizing the fact that the turmoil was blocking their children's education, endorsed and backed a plan that gave effective means of control to the school. The key to this solution was understanding through two-way communication.

In another high school, students have protested against the uncontrolled atmosphere that even tolerated crap games in classrooms. Student leaders asked for more discipline because the existing climate prevented any meaningful learning. Here, again, the solution was based on two-way communication — in this case, between the students and the faculty and administrators.

Quality of Teaching

Evaluation of our schools has until recently been a matter of cold statistics — so many students, so many hours of instruction, so many subjects, etc. This produced impressive figures that were used to justify costs. But the figures did not prove any accomplishment and the taxpayers, faced with ever-increasing school budgets, have begun to question whether the results are worth the cost.

There is considerable evidence that our schools are not really educating the students. Repeatedly we hear of declining scores in Student Aptitude Tests. CBS has reported that 13% of teenagers are functionally illiterate. Elementary and secondary education is very definitely in a situation where it must improve its performance and tell the taxpayers what it has done.

Integration

This is probably the most difficult problem our schools ever have faced or ever will face. It is an intensely emotional subject. Many parents hate the idea and will never do more than grudgingly accept it. Others think it will solve all educational problems and are bitterly disappointed when it does not work an overnight miracle.

The rationale for the Supreme Court decision of 1954 was that segregated education was inferior education. Yet, in many cases, the turmoil of the process of integration actually depressed the quality of education. Nevertheless, segregated schools are illegal and nearly every school system must try to solve the problem of peacefully integrating its schools. There has been much progress but there is still a long way to go.

Continuing progress will come only through acceptance by parents and, to some degree, by students (although the latter appear to be less resistant than their elders). Two facts need to be considered. First, opposition to racial integration is not a light and transient whim. It is deeply ingrained and therefore not easy to change. Second, not all people want integration. In San Francisco some hundreds of Chinese parents have violently objected to a plan for busing their children to integrated schools.

No general solution for this problem of integration is in sight. Every community and every school district is different. What works in one situation may fail in another. There have been successes and failures. The thing that seems to work best is patient persuasion based on getting all concerned to understand the problem. Meetings with parents and with students plus a steady flow of communications — inbound and outbound — are tools that appear best suited to the task.

Suggested Readings

Bortner, Doyle M. *Public Relations for Schools.* Cambridge, Mass.: Schenkman, 1972.
Kobre, Sidney. *Successful Public Relations for Colleges and Universities.* New York: Hastings, 1974.

COLLEGES AND UNIVERSITIES

The public relations problems of colleges and universities have sky-rocketed in recent years and awareness of the situation has led to a greatly-increased reliance on public relations practitioners and to a considerable enhancement of their status.

Higher educational institutions have many publics, and most of these constituents have strong attitudes affecting them. Every one of these publics is important, so any college public relations program should have a plan for two-way communication with alumni, students, faculty, staff, parents, financial supporters, and the community.

Among the problems affecting the college publics are income, student costs, instruction, admissions, control, academic freedom, tenure, and role.

Income

With state-supported colleges, the operating funds come mainly from the taxpayers by way of the state legislature. Getting the needed funds used to be comparatively easy. The legislators were willing to vote for almost any sum that seemed reasonable, and the taxpayer's attitude was one of willing acceptance of the cost. Now the taxpayers are revolting against the ever-increasing costs, which look doubly large when the economy is in a slump.

Doubts are being expressed as to whether so many students should go to college. In some cases, organizations have fought to cut down public support for colleges with an avowed goal of reducing enrollments. What is taught and how it is taught are subject to question. In fact, all the other problems are involved with this one. The taxpayers have to be convinced that their money is being well spent and that the sums requested are essential. This requires a comprehensive program of building public support. It requires continuous two-way communication with all the publics and about all the problems.

The financial problems of higher education were highlighted by the Morgan Guaranty Trust Company in one of its monthly publications. It pointed out that the insistence on subordinating costs to educational considerations had caused much resistance to the costs. It criticized the contention that small classes mean excellence and cited the fact that on many campuses a small teaching load was a status symbol. The bank said that the financial problem was magnified by the unusually large increase in faculty salaries during the 1960s plus the greatly enlarged enrollments.

These problems are compounded by resistance of the taxpayers and the supporters of the private institutions to the ever-increasing costs and to innovative teaching methods.

The plight of the private schools is illustrated by the situation of Stanford University. One of the wealthier private universities, it owns thousands of acres of valuable real estate on the San Francisco peninsula. By selling or leasing this land for industrial and residential use, it obtains substantial income, but the neighboring city of Palo Alto is fighting against further development because of the effect on the environment.

Student Costs

Students, or their parents, pay large sums of money for higher education. For many years, the University of California has not charged tuition. When costs grew greater than the legislative appropriations could cover, there was a proposal to charge tuition. This brought a storm of protest. But when the tuition was disguised as "student incidental fees" there was not so much objection. Yale University and others are experimenting with deferred tuition charges, but the fact remains that these costs create a great PR problem — a problem of explaining why they are needed, why the student or family should pay them, and selling the payers on the method of payment.

Instruction

As enrollments have grown and class size has increased, there has been much justified complaint about impersonal instruction. There is complaint about not having contact with the teacher, about the use of teaching assistants, about the "publish or perish" judgment of teachers, about the refusal of colleges to permit student evaluation of teachers, and about many other things that affect the quality of instruction. Some of these problems are matters of policy but much of the dissatisfaction could be alleviated with real two-way communication — and possibly then communication could result in policy changes. Oregon State University has established a system for student-faculty dialogues which is yielding some very valuable areas of understanding and is a material aid in determining major policies.

Admissions

Who gets in and who does not can create some explosive problems. The

Yale alumnus whose son cannot get into Yale will not be easily placated. The girl who lives in Santa Barbara but cannot get into the University of California at Santa Barbara because she was not in the top 12½% of her high-school class will not be very happy, nor will her parents who cannot afford to send her away to college. The student who cannot get into the nearby state college because there is not any room will not be very happy. Here again, the college or university must explain the reasons for its decision — not only to the students and the students' families, but also to the other publics, because all these publics are constituents of the institution.

Control

One college president in the midst of a massive disruption said that the reason for his inability to act was that a college has no real organization and no channels of command or control. Certainly there is evidence to support this impression.

Student government was once a useful tool, but when only 15% or 20% of the students vote in the elections (as is common), student government is not really representative. Faculties are conspicuously unwilling to accept much control from the administration or to institute controls on their members.

This uncontrolled climate becomes fertile ground for disruption — which, in turn, creates extremely unfavorable public opinion. When San Francisco State University was almost closed by disruptions, the press comment — and presumably public opinion — was distinctly unfavorable. When control was restored and policies established and publicized, the reaction was overwhelmingly favorable and, most important, the climate for financial support was greatly improved.

Academic Freedom

The right of a teacher to teach in his own way is very important, but the occasional abuse of this right has caused considerable public disenchantment. It has resulted in heavy pressure on legislators and administrators to curb some of this freedom. This creates a two-way problem. The college or university must convince all the constituents that academic freedom is vital and essential. At the same time, it must show the faculty what the public reaction is to the abuse of academic freedom and persuade it to exercise some discretion. As with almost every other problem in higher education, the solution is two-way communication with both parties — the faculty and the external publics.

Tenure

The tenured professor looks on tenure as assurance that he will not be fired except for some very drastic transgression, but a member of the general public may look on tenure as an unreasonable protection. When a national news weekly tells about tenured professors drawing salaries but not teaching because no students enroll in their classes, the reader may be quite willing to support abolition of the whole system.

There is no doubt that tenure is under attack. It is not likely to be abolished forthwith but public opinion will probably force some changes; the nature of the changes will depend on how well the public relations job is done. Faculties must recognize that the threat is serious. They cannot rely on the past, nor on mere claims that tenure is sacred. They must cure the ills, tell the public how they have improved the system and continuously sell the public on the necessity for tenure.

Role

The role of higher education is being questioned from all directions. Is the purpose to question or to teach? Is the purpose to prepare for life or to prepare for work? Is a college education desirable for everyone qualified or should it be restricted to a smaller number? Should college education be accomplished in four years immediately after high school or should there be a completely different system? Is higher education for the young or should there be an adjustment in the system to admit the more mature? Is residence necessary or can an education be obtained otherwise? How good is the education being provided now? How can we do better? All these questions and many more are being asked by students, parents, teachers, and by the people who pay the bills.

It is readily apparent that major changes will probably be made in higher education because there are many dissatisfactions with the present system. Already a considerable number of colleges and universities are experimenting with new approaches, and the news media have given very favorable treatment to these experiments.

A major segment of the role problem centers on political activism. Logic would indicate that if a university gets into politics, politics will get into the university. Most people believe that a university should not get into politics.

The whole question of role is a public relations problem. Through inbound communication, the institution must learn what is needed or wanted by its constituents. Through planning, it must arrive at policy recommendations and decisions. Through outbound communication, it must explain what is being done and why. Through evaluation, it must learn how well the publics understand and accept the policies.

GOVERNMENT AGENCIES

Government agencies come into being because legislative bodies become convinced that they are necessary. They continue to exist because the same legislative bodies appropriate money for their support. They increase in size and budget if the lawmakers believe the function should be expanded.

As a consequence, government agencies devote considerable attention to the legislative bodies that appropriate the money for their operations. They strive for appropriations and carry on public relations programs with the beneficiaries of the agencies and with the general public in order to mobilize public support for themselves.

There has been much criticism of both these activities. Many complain about the "use of the taxpayers' money to pry more money out of the taxpayers." And there have been directives to reduce both activities. Yet, they appear necessary and ethical. The legislators must obtain information from the agencies in order to make rational decisions and the taxpayers must know what is being done with their money.

Before looking at governmental public relations in action, one point should be made. With very rare exceptions, the people who run these agencies are sincere and dedicated public servants. They honestly believe that they are filling a need. Most of them believe that their activity should be enlarged — not for their aggrandizement but for the public good.

The chief of police asking for more patrolmen, the admiral fighting for a new aircraft carrier, the secretary of transportation trying to get money for urban rapid transit — all are doing this because they think it will benefit the people. And each looks on his projects as more necessary than the projects of others who are competing with him for the taxpayers' dollars.

The public relations activity of governmental agencies divides into two general areas: (1) relations with the direct beneficiaries and (2) relations with the taxpayers at large.

The Beneficiaries

In dealing with beneficiaries, the objectives are to keep them happy with the service of the agency so that they will not complain, will protest any reduction in services, and possibly demand more services. In some agencies all the taxpayers are beneficiaries — as with a fire or police department. In others, there may be a limited number of direct beneficiaries — as with a state department of employment.

There are agencies where the beneficiaries are the general public but where most activity is in a very limited area — as with the Interstate Commerce Commission. And there are agencies, such as the Social Security Administration, where nearly everyone must pay, where nearly everyone will ultimately receive benefits but where, at any given time, only a part of the people are beneficiaries. In one sense the beneficiaries are the customers of the agency. Much of what is said in Chapter 12, The Customer Public, is applicable to this relationship.

To keep the "customers" happy, an agency must go beyond good service. It must know what people think about their benefits and the service they are receiving. It must find the areas of dissatisfaction and provide cures. It must explain its policies and rules and the reasons for them. It must convince the beneficiaries that the agency is doing its job well and that it is concerned about its "customers."

When the benefit is direct, as with a Social Security check, the problem is much easier than with an indirect benefit, such as national defense. In the first case there is something tangible — money that can be spent by the beneficiary. In the second case the benefits are never apparent until the country is at war, except of course for local benefits from military expenditures. In between, we have the benefits of police or fire protection that are available to all but which are rarely used by most people most of the time.

In every case, however, there must be a program to provide two-way communication. Almost every tool of public relations may be used. Particularly important are the employees of the agency. Nearly everything said in Chapter 23 is applicable here.

The Taxpayers

Every government agency is a burden on the taxpayers. Nearly everyone is aware of the costs of the Department of Defense but practically no one knows the cost of the commission that maintains military cemeteries in foreign lands. Yet, all these and countless others survive because people convince the legislative bodies that they should appropriate money for them.

In many cases the pressures come from potential beneficiaries. Often the legislators vote to appropriate money because they believe it will help them get reelected. But in practically every case the agency uses public relations to build support for the appropriations enabling it to survive or to expand.

When Robert McNamara was Secretary of Defense, he instituted many studies designed to improve efficiency and reduce costs. One of these studies convinced McNamara that the U.S. Marine Corps should be abolished. The reasoning was that the Marines consisted of infantry, artillery, and armored units, which could be supplied by the Army, and attack air units, which could be supplied by the Air Force. The conclusion was logical, but McNamara failed because the Marine Corps had built such powerful public support that it could not be abolished. The reaction was so strong that Congress not only rejected the plan but also made the Commandant of the Marine Corps a member of the Joint Chiefs of Staff in order to emphasize its regard for the Marines.

In contrast to these successes, Amtrak, the corporation established to supply passenger train service, was a resounding failure in its first months of operation. There was great public interest in Amtrak. Thousands of people tried to buy tickets but were frustrated by employees who did not understand the schedules. The people who obtained tickets were disappointed by the equipment, the schedules, and the service.

Amtrak started operations without proper organization and planning — these were management failures. Amtrak did not inform, train, or inspire its personnel. Even worse, it made little effort to inform the public about its operations and its problems. These were public relations failures.

For many years, the Armed Forces operated in a climate of strong public support. Budgets were approved with a minimum of opposition. Service in the Armed Forces was considered an honorable duty. Morale of military personnel was high. The public relations problem was relatively simple. Then the situation changed. The frustration of the Vietnam war, the demand that funds be spent on domestic problems, and a trend toward isolationism created major problems with Congress.

As far as Congress and the taxpayers are concerned, the problem continues. It is certain that the Department of Defense will have much more difficulty in securing appropriations and that it will have an even tougher job telling its story because of opposition to its public relations activities.

Military public relations suffered a devastating blow in the CBS documentary "The Selling of the Pentagon," which reported on the public relations activities of the Department of Defense and which, by its frequent use of the word "propaganda," left a definitely unfavorable impression. This kind of criticism of government public relations is not new. It has been going on just about as long as the activity, and it is used whenever there is an opportunity to make political hay.

The Credibility Gap

This phrase, coined during the Johnson administration, still survives. It expresses public doubt that the federal government is telling the truth to the people of the country. Undoubtedly, this disbelief extends to many other areas of government. It makes the public relations program of any government agency more difficult because it tends to make people mistrust anything said by anyone in government. The solution is easy to describe but very difficult to achieve. The public must be convinced that it is being told the truth and nothing but the truth. The public must also be convinced that, in some cases, the government cannot disclose the whole truth because of its effect on foreign affairs and because people in government will hesitate to express opinions in private for fear that they will be made public.

Suggested Readings

Krock, A. *The Consent of the Governed*. Boston, Mass.: Little, Brown, 1971.
Ladd, B. *Crisis in Credibility*. New York: New American Library, 1968.

CAUSES

During recent years, many people have become deeply concerned about problems that have not been solved by government. This has led to sit-ins, demonstrations, and numerous other activities designed to get action. In some cases there have been successes. Often nothing is accomplished beyond a flurry of publicity which may or may not be helpful to the cause. Success or failure of any cause depends on how well the advocates mobilize public opinion behind it. This requires three things:

an understanding of the nature of the problem, an understanding of some general principles of persuasion, and utilization of public relations techniques.

Understanding the Problem

Many of today's critical problems are deeply rooted in history. Segregation was a way of life for centuries. Dumping sewage into a stream or garbage into the nearest out-of-sight place is a long-established habit. The right of a property owner to do anything he chooses with his property is based on the old common-law thesis that a man's home is his castle. America was built by ruthless exploitation of natural resources. Progress has been an excuse for almost anything.

Now when we see the catastrophe facing us, we must recognize that motivating people to action requires them to abandon long-established ways of thinking. Individual rights will have to be restricted for the common good and people will have to be sold on this idea. This is not an easy task. It takes time and work to change people's minds.

Another key factor is public disinterest. On almost any issue, a few people will strongly favor certain action, a few will strongly oppose that action, and most people will have no interest at all. Yet, without support of the majority, a cause cannot succeed.

Most important of all — the opponents of many causes have a deep financial interest in maintaining the status quo. Consequently, they are willing and able to spend substantial sums of money fighting for their own self-interest.

This principle is demonstrated in a campaign to keep a lumber company from logging an area that could provide recreation for a community. The company owns the land — and private property cannot be taken for public use without just compensation. The company has paid taxes for years; it employs many people. It has a legal right to cut the trees and a moral obligation to continue employing its people. With a great financial loss facing it if it cannot do the logging, it is quite evident that it will fight tenaciously to cut the trees. Its employees and the people who sell to them will undoubtedly support the company. The advocates of preservation are probably few in number and ill-financed, and most of the general public is unconcerned. The only way that the conservationists can succeed is by persuading the uncommitted public that it is in their self-interest to stop the logging. Complaining and objecting will not do the job. A well-planned and conducted public relations program is needed.

Some General Principles

Building opinion in support of a cause cannot be done by antagonizing the general public. Many activists do just that and thus fail to get public support. It may be necessary to revolutionize our way of thinking but to talk in terms of "revolution" is a sure way to build opposition. The activists who express their contempt for the existing society — and the "establishment" — in words, deeds, and dress are not winning support from the great uncommitted mass of people. If Ralph Nader looked, dressed, and acted like some of the more radical activists, he would not be nearly as effective. It is easy to brush off a "long-haired kook." It is not easy to disregard a man who looks and talks like a member of the "establishment."

Another great error is to combine many causes. Protection of the environment and prevention of pollution are logical partners, but to couple them with unrelated issues has a twofold effect: it dilutes the effort and increases the opposition. For example, it may be possible to get support for an environmental cause from a hardened segregationist, but if conservation and integration are linked together, the segregationist may refuse to help.

Combining causes can also create internal problems involving priorities. Conversely, merging organizations for a common cause is highly effective.

Getting public support for a cause requires a focus on self-interest — the self-interest of the general public and the self-interest of its opponents. The public must be convinced that the cause is in its interest, that it will benefit if it succeeds. The self-interest of the opposition is an obvious point of attack. Someone, a group, a corporation, or a government agency is benefiting at the expense of the public. The campaign to save San Francisco Bay succeeded because the attention of the public was focused on the small group that was going to make money by filling "our Bay." The lumber interests in Oregon who wanted to log the valley of French Pete Creek were blocked by similar strategy.

Demonstrations alone usually fail. When students at the University of Texas chained themselves to trees in order to keep them from being cut down to enlarge the football stadium, they failed to save the trees. When citizens of Corte Madera, California, tried to keep the Corps of Engineers from turning a picturesque creek into a concrete ditch by laying down in front of the bulldozer, they failed. The demonstration at the Democratic Convention of 1968 turned public opinion against the demonstrators. In spite of press and TV treatment largely favorable to the demonstrators and unfavorable to the Chicago police, public opinion remained unsympathetic. Surveys by *The New York Times* and an analysis of mail by CBS showed a very strong reaction in favor of the Chicago police and against the demonstrators (Robinson, 1970).

Public Relations Techniques

In general terms, every cause tries to persuade people to take action. It may try to pass a law or prevent its passage. This requires lobbying and pressure on legislators. It may try to get some organization to act or refrain from acting. This requires pressure on the organization from the public. In all such situations, the most effective lever is public demand for action.

Getting any kind of action from a legislative body — federal, state, or local — is a difficult task. The legislative system is cumbersome and even unopposed legislation takes a long time to move through the machinery. Even then it may fail through some procedural error or simply because there are too many bills to be acted upon. Where there is opposition, as generally happens when a cause is involved, the problem becomes even more difficult because the opponents will use every legal and parliamentary trick in the book. To get a bill passed or blocked is almost impossible without the help of skilled lobbyists who know all the procedures of legislation and all the tricks of the legislators.

Another essential is public pressure. Most politicians want to be reelected. Consequently, they are very vulnerable to pressure of two kinds: pressure from campaign contributors and pressure from the public at large. The campaign contributors are usually small in number but large in dollar power. Generally they have an economic stake in legislation so they will express themselves forcefully and continuously. A state legislator who has received strong financial support from cement manufacturers or highway builders is under considerable pressure to vote for more highways.

Because the contributors are few in number, their pressure can be overcome if enough public pressure is brought to bear. This requires an intensive campaign to make the wishes of the public known to the legislators. Meetings, rallies, demonstrations, and other events can get attention and publicity, but the most effective tool of all is letters — letters by the thousands and tens of thousands. When a congressman or assemblyman finds his office full of letters from his constituents, he will probably respond.

A letter-writing campaign must be an honest expression of opinion —

not a contrived action. Form letters should never be used. Each person should use his or her own words. The tone should be friendly but firm. Diatribe and violent expressions should be avoided.

A good example of fighting for a cause was the campaign to save San Francisco Bay. It was saved by a massive outpouring of public opinion. Many people were involved. In 1851, the California Legislature started selling beaches, tidelands, and marshes to cities, corporations, private individuals, and land speculators. By 1958, the Bay had been reduced from 680 square miles to 437 square miles, and it was predicted that continuation of the trend would reduce the Bay to 120 square miles by the year 2020.

A study commission was established in 1965. It recommended establishment of a temporary Bay Conservation and Development Commission to report to the 1969 legislature. The commission presented a report recommending permanent controls and a permanent Commission. The temporary commission and its authority were to expire 90 days after the 1969 legislature adjourned. The land speculators and developers fought to prevent establishment of a permanent BCDC while the people who wanted to save the Bay fought for its creation.

On one side were the Leslie Salt Company, the Santa Fe Railroad, Westbay Associates (a combine of several large banks and a cement company), plus numerous others who had millions of dollars at stake. On the other side were the Sierra Club, the Save San Francisco Bay Association, the Save Our Bay Action Committee, the San Francisco Planning and Conservation League, the Stanford Conservation Group, and many smaller groups plus thousands of concerned but unorganized citizens.

In the legislature every parliamentary trick was used to block the permanent BCDC. To fight the bill through the legislature, a team of lobbyists was set up in Sacramento. To impress the legislators, the supporters of the BCDC ran full-page ads in newspapers and they wrote and persuaded others to write letters. Petitions bearing nearly three hundred thousand signatures were delivered to Governor Reagan and to Senator Dolwig, who was a leader of the opposition. Dolwig's office was deluged with phone calls, telegrams, and letters. Caravans of buses carried thousands of people to the legislative hearings. And always there was publicity. A steady stream of press releases was sent to all media with the result that few people in the state were unaware of the battle to save the Bay. This undoubtedly stimulated more phone calls and letters.

The fight was won — and it was a real fight. It succeeded only because it was an organized effort led by people who worked for months to accomplish a very difficult task against powerful opposition.

Nonlegislative Action

When dealing with nonlegislative organizations, there is no law to pass or to oppose but there may be some action to demand. For example, if a factory pollutes the air, direct action against the polluter is indicated. The solution is to mobilize public opinion against him.

The tools and techniques are the same as in action for or against legislation. Publicity, letters, petitions, resolutions, and many other means may be used to let the culprit know of public disfavor. Another potentially effective tool is the economic boycott. If people refused to buy throwaway bottles and cans, there would soon be none on the market. If people refused to buy redwood lumber, there would be an end to the cutting of redwood trees. If people refused to buy any product, that product would die.

EXERCISES

1. Does your college have good relations with the students? Why?
2. Have you ever actively supported a cause?
   (a) What did you do?
   (b) What did you accomplish?

Case Problem

In your community find an example of environmental destruction or pollution being done by some organization.

Describe in detail just what you would do to stop it without recourse to any legislative action.

The Employee Public | **10**

The relationship between employer and employee involves many phases; it reaches all the way from recruiting to death benefits. It often touches on highly sensitive areas, and it is loaded with emotion. A man's employment represents his own survival. His relations with his employer are therefore among the most important in his life.

In most organizations, wages are the biggest expenditure. If the organization gets its money's worth here, it has a chance of success. If it does not, it is doomed to failure. The attitude and performance of employees is, therefore, the subject of much concern to management; management conducts employee relations programs in order to improve the attitudes and the performance of its employees, and to get their political support.

The broad field of relations between employer and employees is normally divided into three categories. The actual names used to describe these may vary, and there is often some overlapping or consolidation. For our purpose, the categories will be treated separately. They are: personnel relations, labor relations, and employee relations. The first two are management functions which are largely off-limits to the public relations people. The third is a communications function and is a responsibility of the public relations department.

Suggested Readings

Burack, Elmer, and Smith, Robert D. *Personnel Management.* St. Paul, Minn.: West, 1977.
Hammer, W. Clay, and Schmidt, Frank L. (Eds.). *Contemporary Problems in Personnel.* Chicago: St. Clair, 1977.
Hersey, Paul, and Blanchard, Ken. *Management of Organizational Behavior.* Englewood Cliffs, N.J.: Prentice-Hall, 1977.
Pigors, P., and Myers, C.A. *Personnel Administration.* New York: McGraw-Hill, 1977.

As mentioned earlier, the public relations function is a staff function and it must avoid intrusion into the operations of other departments. This is particularly true in the field of personnel and labor relations. The rule is: BE CAREFUL. To be sure that the restriction is understood, it may be helpful to give some details as to what these two areas do include.

PERSONNEL RELATIONS

This function is often handled by a specialized department. It deals with the employee as an individual. Its activities include recruiting, selecting, hiring (and discharging), placing, training, and paying.

Frequently, it determines rates of pay, especially in situations where no union is involved. The public relations department may work with the personnel department, but it does not run that department. For example, the PR people may prepare booklets that the personnel department issues to new employees, or it may release news to mass media about employment opportunities. Most important, the PR people may advise on policy — because employment practices and methods can have a great effect on the public relations of the employer.

LABOR RELATIONS

This function is normally handled by experts whose specialty is negotiations. It deals with employees as a group — typically, as union members. Its activities cover administration of wages, hours, work rules, and seniority. It handles union relations, contracts, strikes, walkouts, and grievances. This is the department that deals with regulatory bodies such as the National Labor Relations Board, the Equal Employment Opportunities Commission and the Fair Employment Practices Commissions. The labor relations department also deals with labor laws and regulations and unemployment benefits.

Sometimes this division is called industrial relations but, regardless of its name, it is the one which deals with Labor, with a capital L. It often involves conflict. It frequently also involves government and the public relations people are not the prime movers in this area. Nevertheless, they may give such specialized help as preparing statements of policy, writing press releases, or preparing ads stating the company's position in a pending or actual strike. And, as in personnel relations, there is a large area of policy where the advice and help of the PR people may be very important.

EMPLOYEE RELATIONS

Having excluded most of personnel and labor relations, what is left? The answer: everything else that involves communication between management and employee. By communication, we mean two-way communication. To achieve this, there must be machinery with which to communicate and a willingness to use it. Management must be willing to listen to employees and it must provide the means for employees to express themselves to management. Management must be willing to tell the facts and employees must be willing to tell management what they think. In summary, both must be willing to talk and to listen — but management must provide all the machinery needed. The machinery is the employee relations program.

Employee relations are getting more and more attention from top management. Public relations budgets are showing major increases for this function. In some organizations, there is an independent department working only on this problem.

The reason is simple. Management is realizing that employees are the most important public of any organization. The pay and benefits of employees are usually the biggest expenditure. The quantity and quality of work done by employees is usually the most important factor in production. The support of employees in political situations can help protect the organization from adverse laws and regulations or help obtain favorable laws and regulations. If any organization has the support of its employees, it has at least a start toward success. Without that support it is not likely to succeed.

PROBLEM AREAS

The first step in an employee relations program is to eliminate, or at least reduce, the things that cause friction or dissatisfaction. Doing this requires the cooperation of all managers, especially those in personnel relations and labor relations.

This is a difficult task. It requires the utmost tact and diplomacy because people are zealous in protecting their own prerogatives. Nevertheless, the public relations people should be involved for two reasons. First, employees are a public. Second, public relations people are best qualified to handle the job of two-way communication which is needed.

To eliminate or reduce the things that cause friction between the employees and the organization, it is necessary to know what they are. The following are some of the most important.

Noninvolvement

People group together on the basis of common interest. There is certainly no more common interest than that of employment in the same organization because employment consumes about half of one's waking hours and is the basis of economic survival. This common interest can be built into a strong feeling if an effort is made. Employees want to belong; they have an inherent desire to be a part of and proud of the organization, so they resent a situation wherein they cannot feel that they belong. Where a strong union is involved, this may become "the organization" so far as participation is concerned.

Inability to Advance

Many employees are satisfied with one job, but many others would like to advance to higher levels of responsibility. These people are willing to make an extra effort. They are usually the ablest employees, and if they cannot advance they will either be unhappy in their existing position or leave to find greater opportunities. Often there will be more qualified employees than there are promotions available but even a few promotions from within can be encouraging proof that advancement is possible.

Elimination of Individuality

Employees are individuals, yet in many organizations this fact is completely overlooked, creating great resentment. People do not want to be numbers or statistics; they want to be known and identified. This is a major source of trouble in employee relations, yet it is one of the easiest problems to solve. An honest attempt to treat employees as individuals can be carried out with relatively little effort and very large results.

According to the Opinion Research Council, most hourly and clerical employees don't believe their employers treat them with respect as individuals.

Compensation

There are very few, if any, people who are satisfied with their pay. Whether it be an individual increase or a general upgrading of pay scale, there is always a desire for more. No matter how much the individual gets, or how short a time has elapsed since an increase was granted, employees individually and collectively remain unsatisfied with their compensation. There is no real solution to this problem, but it must be remembered at all times. A research study reported in *The New York Times* found that people felt they were paid from $3,000 to $5,000 less than they were worth.

Fringe Benefits

This can mean anything from a desk near a window to retirement pay, from a reserved parking space to psychiatric treatment. The number of extras given to employees — requested by them or demanded by unions — grows longer every year. The cost to employers is a very substantial part of the cost of operation, and both benefits and costs are bound to increase. Some of the fringe items are very costly but many are inexpensive. A generous hand with these can help to ease the push for more costly benefits, which can easily amount to 25% or more of basic pay.

Physical Discomforts

The list of physical discomforts about which employees complain is long — and getting longer as people become accustomed to what were formerly luxuries. The truck driver who once thought an automatic transmission was luxurious now wants an air-conditioned cab, and so on. Heat, cold, drafts, lights, distance to and nature of rest rooms or drinking fountains, eating facilities, parking lots, access to mass-transportation facilities, chair or desk heights, machine positions, material and waste handling, the machines or tools used, and the materials used on them — all these and more are the source of employee complaints. The volume of complaints is a pretty good indication of the degree of discomfort and the importance of remedial action. And, while luxury may not be in order, it is true that a comfortable employee will do better work (Herzberg, 1959).

Safety

The federal Occupational Safety and Health Act (OSHA) is intended to protect workers from hazards of all sorts while on the job. It sets stringent standards designed to guard employees against accidents, noise, disease, and dangerous materials such as chemicals, asbestos, and dust. There have been many complaints about the nit-picking nature of some regulations but safety is important to employees and employers alike. It is estimated that industrial accidents cost $15 billion a year. No monetary figure can be applied to the pain and suffering which accompanies these accidents, but it should be evident that promotion of safety is a vital part of employee relations.

Equal Employment Opportunities

Under federal law, every individual is supposed to have an equal opportunity for employment and promotion. Employers must obey this law. Progressive employers not only obey the law but also actively implement it by hunting for minority employees and by setting up training programs which will facilitate advancement. The Bank of America has an extensive training program for minorities and women. It is only one of many organizations which offers such opportunities.

Layoffs

Sometimes it is necessary to lay off employees. When this occurred at a General Electric plant, each affected employee was given a letter from the manager explaining the reason. The employee was allowed to use remaining payroll time for job hunting, and was helped by General Electric. The employee was given a booklet explaining termination pay, pension rights, and continuing insurance coverage. The news media received releases about the availability of workers. Advertisements were placed in numerous publications. Telegrams and bulletins were sent to hundreds of personnel managers. A job fair provided a site where interested employers and employees could meet. Through this program, about 90% of the laid-off employees found new jobs.

Failure of Management to Tell Its Story

In spite of all that has been said about the importance of management communication to employees, there are many failures — and employees are conscious of this. The number of complaints is evidence that employees do want to hear what management has to say. Even when there is disagreement or antagonism, employees feel that management should present its side. Management silence can be interpreted as admission of fault.

According to Opinion Research Council, only 28% of hourly employees feel that their company does a good job of telling them what is going on; 70% say that their companies are not willing to listen to them.

INFORMING EMPLOYEES

Employees have a right to know about anything that affects their jobs. If the employer doesn't give this information, the employees may get erroneous information from uninformed or hostile sources.

Informing employees is not necessarily easy. They are interested, but they have outside interests also, and they get information from many sources as noted in Chapter 2. Messages to employees have to compete for attention. This requires that all information be clear, concise, pertinent, and, above all, understandable. The federal government recognizes this fact, as shown in the Employee Retirement Income Security Act (ERISA) which requires that information given to employees must be understandable to everyone.

There are two kinds of information which should be given to employees — first, the information which they ask for; second, the information which they should have but may not ask for.

What Employees Want to Know

Employee interest varies from time to time and from organization to organization. A large chemical company surveyed its employees and found that the most wanted information concerned wage and salary policies, promotion opportunities, job security, and benefits. Hewlett-Packard, in a similar survey, found greatest interest in wage and salary policies, performance of the company, management philosophy, economic outlook, and employee benefits.

Interest varies according to occupation. In the chemical company survey, the research and technical people were most interested in organization goals, problems, and financial results. Managers were most interested in public issues, and hourly employees in the importance of their own jobs.

All this shows that every organization should find out what its employees want to know. This calls for continuous informal and formal research.

What Employees Should Know

There are many subjects which employees don't ask about. There are others which interest a few. There is much information which will be beneficial to organizational performance and employee satisfaction and which should be distributed. Rather than try to classify subjects by degree of employee interest, it seems best to list a number of topics which are generally considered important in employee communications.

IMPORTANT SUBJE(

This list is not necessarily complete but it is a starting point for determining what to tell employees. Some of the subjects may not be relevant to every organization and some may suggest others which are not shown here.

Salary and Wage Policies

Employees want to know how pay rates are established, how the pay for similar jobs in different locations compares, and how pay in one firm varies from the pay in another. At one company where an overall pay increase had just been made, there was still great interest in learning about basic pay policies.

Benefits

Informing employees about their benefits is important. J. C. Penney has used posters, pay envelope inserts, calendars, and information kits for store managers. They tell how employees should handle claims and take advantage of their benefits.

General Business Conditions

In general people are very ignorant about economics; they pay little attention to business news and often overlook the significance of events that might have an effect on them. Yet, they do want to know what the general business outlook is. Short, clear, and simple highlights will be appreciated.

Organization Situations

Employees are, in general, vitally interested in the situation of their employer. Any news or information that affects the employees' future prospects will command rapt attention. If the organization is losing money or making money, if some imminent development will change the financial situation, if short-term or long-time prospects are good or bad — all these are important to employees because they can drastically affect their income and security.

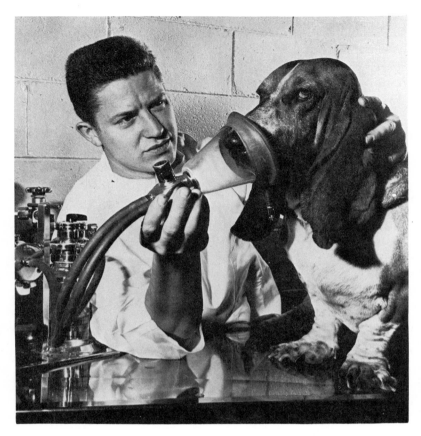

Fig. 10.1 One of the top five public relations photographs in a contest conducted by the *Public Relations Journal*. The purpose was to show veterinarians a new resuscitator—anesthetizer developed by National Cylinder Gas Engines, a division of Chemetron Corporation. The picture was used by hundreds of newspapers. Photographed for Carl Byoir & Associates, Inc. by George Kufrin.

Rules and Regulations

Every organization has rules and regulations. The list may be very short or quite extensive but, regardless of its length, employees want to be informed about all the requirements and privileges established by the organization. No one likes to be called to account for violation of a rule but the reaction is many times more violent when the rule was not known to exist. In informing employees about these points, it is important to explain why they are necessary. They will seem much less arbitrary and restrictive if the reason for their adoption is set forth in understandable language.

New Developments

Anything new is interesting, partly because it is different from the old and partly because "new" has become the watchword of a society and economy where change is the rule. To employees, any information about developments indicating a change in the organization is sure to be important. Employees want this information, and they will absorb it with great interest.

Sales Prospects

Projection of future sales (or equivalent accomplishments) are graphic forecasts of the prospects of the organization. Employees want to know about these prospects because, if the future looks bright or dark, they will be able to base personal plans on definite presumptions rather than blind chance. Regardless of what the prospects are, employees want to know about them.

Work Prospects

This indication is even more immediate than sales prospects. Employees want thorough and accurate information about anything that will affect the amount and kind of work they do and the amount of pay they get. Rumors on these subjects spread like wildfire, so it is essential that employees be given full, complete, and timely information about future work.

Products and Services

Information about the firm's products or services is always wanted. A simple description is helpful but a complete report covering everything from raw material through manufacture, delivery, and sale to ultimate use will be more relevant. New products and services are particularly interesting. The reason for their introduction, the research that led to their creation, the problems that had to be solved — all can command attentive interest.

Facts About the Organization

The background, history, and structure of the organization is of substantial interest to the employees. People like to know who they are working for; any information which gives them a little understanding of their employer will help create a better attitude toward him — assuming, of course, that the facts justify it. Most firms have much about them that is interesting and many have a history that is inspiring.

What is Expected of Employees

Despite supervisors who are supposed to inform employees about their duties and responsibilities, there is a lack of understanding by many employees of what management expects of them. Even though job requirements, rules, and guidelines are specified, they may be interpreted differently or enforced in nonuniform ways. Whenever this occurs, there are unhappy employees who say, "Why don't they tell us what they want us to do?"

Employee Accomplishments

Most employees want to know how they are doing. With some, their only motive is to avoid being fired. With others, there is a real pride in accomplishment and a desire for recognition. This recognition is a reward to those who did the outstanding work and a stimulus to others. The rule of employee recognition is: public praise and private censure. To publicize individual shortcomings or failures does incurable damage.

Importance of the Individual's Job

As business and industrial units grow larger and more automated, it becomes more difficult to see all the parts, and individual jobs seem less significant to the overall accomplishment. A cobbler making shoes knows how important each step is but the man in a modern shoe factory will have difficulty finding out the importance of his job unless someone tells him. And the invitation is there; employees do want to know where their job fits into the organization and how important it is. This wish is rooted in the desire for identity and accomplishment.

Chances for Advancement

Some people are satisfied with things as they are, but most people want to advance in income, status, title, or privileges — or all of these. For the ambitious, it is most important that their chances for advancement be clearly explained. When an employee knows what he or she must do to get a promotion, he or she can start doing it. Employees in every line of work and at every level of advancement want to know about their opportunities and the conditions for attaining them.

Income and Profits

Unions keep a close watch on the financial situation of the industries in which they work so that they will have useful information for wage negotiations. In nonunion situations, the information is still wanted by employees, partially, it is true, as a bargaining tool for higher wages, but also, to a considerable degree, as general information on the success of the organization.

Future Plans

Any story about the future is certain to attract great attention. If the story is about the employing organization, it will be doubly interesting. Employees' interest in future plans of their organization is intense and endless. Plans for new construction, transfers of activities or personnel, close-downs or startups are just a few of the possibilities. New product information is especially interesting, but marketing strategy often requires considerable secrecy about plans in this area. In general, any information that can be released about future plans will be most welcome.

OBJECTIVES IN EMPLOYEE RELATIONS

The fundamental objective of an employee relations program is to create and maintain in the minds of employees a favorable opinion about their employer. Within this general objective, there can be numerous special objectives. Some of these may be continuous and some may be short-lived. Some may be quite indirect and others may be conspicuously direct, but all should ultimately result in a contribution to favorable employee opinion. The following list covers the objectives most frequently sought.

To Avoid Misunderstandings

In every business there are repeated misunderstandings and comments about the necessity for better communications to avoid misunderstandings. Misunderstanding of management's rules can lead to violations and resentment when the violation is censured or punished.

Misunderstanding of policies and objectives can lead to wasteful perfor-mance. Misunderstanding of employee wants or desires can lead to er-roneous action by management and disappointment and rebellion by employees. If people understand, a great deal of friction can be avoided — and the function of public relations is to provide effective communica-tions and better understanding.

To Develop Pride in the Organization

An employee who is proud of the organization for which he works is a better employee. He is happier and more efficient. He tells his friends about the good organization and, either directly or indirectly, about its good products or services. Pride in the organization gives the individual a strong sense of identity. It also builds group loyalty and group coopera-tion. In almost any organization there are features of which employees can be proud. The task of public relations is to inform employees about these features in such a way that pride will be developed.

To Establish the Mutual Interest of Employer and Employee

Many employees look at the employer as an adversary or even an enemy. This is particularly true when unions are involved. Overcoming this attitude is not too difficult in a nonunion organization, but it can be extremely difficult, if not impossible, in a situation where a powerful union exists. Nevertheless, an effort must be made to accomplish this result. If mutual interest can be established, the employees will be less extreme in their demands. A conviction that success and profit for the organizations means success and profit for employees is a goal that an employee relations program should constantly try to achieve.

To Increase Understanding of Political-Economic Facts

Understanding the facts can result in more intelligent voting on economic issues and more reasonable negotiation on wage issues. Telling employees that a wage increase would bankrupt the employer may not be very credible, but a thorough explanation supported by provable figures has been effective on numerous occasions. A continuous effort to supply employees with well-documented information about the economics of the business and the implications of proposed legislation can be most useful in an employee relations program.

Clorox Company offers its employees a lunch-hour course in

economics. Meeting one day a week for ten weeks, the class is taught by a professor from a state university.

Motorola's economic-education program started with a letter from the president which was published in the company newspaper. This was followed by a series of 12 pamphlets covering supply and demand, marketing, where income goes, international companies, competition, productivity, financial statements, taxes, the risks of business, social responsibility, and the importance of individual jobs. Motorola also produced a motion picture about profits and a series of comic books on the same subject.

To Encourage Use of Employer's Products

An employee who uses the product he helps make is a valuable asset. First, as a customer, he uses his firm's product instead of a competing product. Second, he becomes a testimonial to the qualities of the product. Third, he may persuade others to use it. Employees are often given special price concessions. Employee relations programs usually include definite efforts to encourage this market.

To Get Cooperation for Improved Performance

Anyone who has ever dealt with a rude sales clerk or who has had a door handle drop off a new automobile will thoroughly appreciate how much depends on the performance of the individual employee. Individual performance is critical in many areas, and employees can be persuaded to make great improvements in their work by means of organized programs aimed at specific goals. Among the goals commonly used are higher product quality, fewer rejections, less waste, higher production volume, greater accuracy, more courtesy, improved safety, fewer customer complaints, greater promptness, better telephone manners, conservation of supplies, and a good many more.

The St. Regis Paper Co. improved the quality of its bags by putting the name of the bag machine operator on the bags which he made. The effort was so successful that six quality-control people were transferred to other jobs.

To Promote Safety

Preventing accidents saves time, money and suffering. It should have a high priority in employee relations. When the Santa Fe Railroad Co.

found that its safety record was poor, it surveyed its employees and found that they thought management didn't care. To disprove this, the president and vice-president held a series of meetings with supervisors and told each that he was an accident-prevention officer. The company magazine reported the meetings. A monthly update of safety performance was published. Outstanding individuals were recognized. All personal injuries were reported directly to the vice-president, who immediately called the supervisor of the injured worker. Accidents dropped to about one-fourth of the old level, and Santa Fe moved from nineteenth place to first place in safety among Class I (major) railroads.

When Weyerhaeuser instituted a plan to have employees inform their supervisors about dangerous conditions, the accident rate was cut to 2.2 per million man-hours in an industry where the average was 25.4 per million man-hours.

To Sell the Organization to Employees

Convincing employees that their organization is a good place to work has several benefits. It improves morale and thus improves performance. It stimulates employees to tell others about the merits of the organization and thus aids in recruiting. It also improves relations in the community because employees, by speaking favorably about their employer, help to create a favorable opinion in the community at large.

To Get Employees to Help in PR Activity

Employees have a dual role in public relations. First, they are the most important public of any organization. Second, they are the most effective communication channel. Some employees will voluntarily do things that promote favorable public opinion but most will need to be persuaded and aided. Getting employees to participate in selling the organization to the public is a goal that should be included in every employee relations program.

To Get Political Support

Laws and regulations often place burdensome restrictions on organizations. To counteract this problem, many firms are working to develop employee political action on issues affecting them. By thoroughly informing employees about the consequences of governmental action, it is possible to get employees to fight to protect their jobs by protecting the organization which provides the jobs. Employees can become lobbyists, letter writers, and voters who will express their concerns at election time.

At Standard Oil Company of California, employees voluntarily organized "Standard Oil Supporters" to fight the proposals to break up the big oil companies. Using demonstrations, letters, leaflets, and newspaper advertisements, they challenged the claims of the proponents and stated that breaking up the oil companies would create many additional layers of middlemen and drive up the prices of oil products.

BUILDING GOOD EMPLOYEE RELATIONS

The objectives mentioned heretofore are quite varied. Some are more easily attained than others but all *can* be attained if the program is sound and well-operated. The essentials for success are sincere interest in employees, written policy, action as well as words, fairness to individuals, fairness to groups, and two-way communication.

Attitude

This is the responsibility of top management. If it is not really and sincerely interested in the employees, no public relations people will be able to make the program work. Also, if management is not sincerely interested, it will not support the program long enough for it to be effective.

Policy

A written statement of policy is as necessary in an employee relations program as a written Constitution is to the United States. It serves the same purpose: to state clearly what the policy is and to make certain that it is adhered to. It says what management will do and what it will not do. It is more than a set of rules and might even be described as a statement expressing the employer's attitude toward the employees. Here is the policy of General Foods:

Concerning Employees
General Foods will employ on the basis of individual merit and will continue to take positive steps to seek out qualified and qualifiable applicants.

General Foods' compensation practices will be as good as or better than those prevailing for similar work under similar conditions in the communities where the company has operations. Employees will be compensated on the basis of performance and will be rewarded for results.

G.F. management is responsible for selecting, training and developing competent people in order to assure maximum opportunities for promotion from within. Promotion will be based on an individual's performance and management's judgment of his ability to carry greater responsibility.

G.F. will inform its employees as promptly as possible about company matters which concern them.

General Foods' employees are free, without restraint or discrimination, to deal with the management in any reasonable way they desire — through chosen representatives or otherwise.

G.F.'s key people in the communities where the company has operations are encouraged to participate in community and civic affairs, selecting those activities where assistance or involvement will help both the communities concerned and the corporation.

Action

No quantity of words will overcome a lack of action. Management must act to implement its policy. If management says it wants employees to improve their education, it must provide the means for improvement. If management wants employees to know that there are opportunities for promotion, it must provide the opportunities.

Fairness to individuals   Favoritism is a sure way to ruin an employee relations program. Every employee has a right to equitable treatment and every employee is conscious of that right. Because ability varies, some employees will make greater progress than others (assuming of course that no union restrictions prevent merit promotions). Some employees will need more help than others. And some, because of personal characteristics, will require different consideration. All these and many other differences in treatment will be tolerated if the basis is fair and the rules are known. The Opinion Research Council says only 17% of clerical employees feel that they are dealt with fairly.

Fairness to groups   Within any organization of moderate to large size there will be groups. They may be formal and definite or informal and vague. But they will be important to the members. Groupings may be by department, race, seniority, kind of work done, union membership, rank, or even by religion. All groups must be treated fairly — the instant one appears to be favored, all the others will rebel; if one feels that it is being penalized or deprived, it will react vehemently against the injustice, real or imagined.

Two-Way Communication

Employees must receive information that will help them understand the organization. They must be assured of action on their problems and management must provide the communication channels.

The best channel is face-to-face contact with supervisors at all levels. This must be encouraged constantly. Employees are often afraid to express themselves fully and frankly. They must be assured that it is safe to ask questions, to make suggestions, to point out problems.

Hewlett-Packard has an "Input-Output" system wherein employees can write questions and get answers on a confidential basis. Bank of America has had considerable success with open meetings in which employees can raise questions with their bosses and get definite answers and actions.

Pitney-Bowes has an outstanding program which includes an annual meeting of jobholders, an annual report to employees, an employee-management council of nine top executives and nine employees, a question-and-request program, a management newsletter, bulletin boards, and slide presentations.

EXERCISES

1. Give an example of a policy that builds good employee relations.
2. Give an example of a policy that builds bad employee relations.
3. Give an example of communications from employees to management (from your own experience if possible).

Case Problem

You are public relations counselor to a building contractor who does business with the federal government; 2% of his employees belong to racial minorities. He has been told that he must increase this to 10% or be barred from any future federal contracts. Increasing volume of business is unlikely. Employing more minority people will require employing fewer "majority" people.

Which organizations and groups would support this policy? Why?
How would you reach them?
What would you tell them?
Which organizations and groups would oppose this policy? Why?
How would you reach them?
What would you tell them?

The Owner Public

People invest their money in a business for one basic reason — to make more money. This monetary gain can take two forms, income or capital gains. Often both are obtained. If neither is gained, the investor is unhappy and expresses his unhappiness by selling his stock or fighting for a new management team.

Almost as important as owners are prospective owners — the people who do not own stock but who may be induced to buy it. The owners' list of any organization is constantly changing as some people sell their holdings and others acquire them. For this reason, an owner-relations program must be addressed to the entire community of people who may buy stocks or influence their purchase.

FINANCIAL PUBLIC RELATIONS

This area is so specialized that many counselors deal only with this one activity. Some large general counselors have separate divisions to handle financial relations. The Public Relations Society of America recognizes the uniqueness of financial relations with a special interpretation of its code. It is quoted here:

AN OFFICIAL
INTERPRETATION
OF THE PRSA CODE OF
PROFESSIONAL STANDARDS
AS IT APPLIES TO
FINANCIAL PUBLIC
RELATIONS

This interpretation of the Society Code as it applies to financial public relations was

originally adopted in 1963 and amended in 1972 and 1977 by action of the PRSA Board of Directors. "Financial public relations" is defined as "that area of public relations which relates to the dissemination of information that affects the understanding of stockholders and investors generally concerning the financial position and prospects of a company, and includes among its objectives the improvement of relations between corporations and their stockholders." The interpretation was prepared in 1963 by the Society's Financial Relations Committee working with the Securities and Exchange Commission and with the advice of the Society's Legal Counsel. It is rooted directly in the Code with the full force of the Code behind it and a violation of any of the following paragraphs is subject to the same procedures and penalties as violation of the Code.

1. It is the responsibility of PRSA members who practice financial public relations to be thoroughly familiar with and understand the rules and regulations of the SEC and the laws which it administers, as well as other laws, rules and regulations affecting financial public relations, and to act in accordance with their letter and spirit. In carrying out this responsibility, members shall also seek legal counsel, when appropriate, on matters concerning financial public relations.

2. Members shall adhere to the general policy of making full and timely disclosure of corporate information on behalf of clients or employers. The information disclosed shall be accurate, clear and understandable. The purpose of such disclosure is to provide the investing public with all material information affecting security values or influencing investment decisions. In complying with the duty of full and timely disclosure, members shall present all material facts, including those adverse to the company. They shall exercise care to ascertain the facts and to disseminate only information which they believe to be accurate. They shall not knowingly omit information, the omission of which might make a release false or misleading. Under no circumstances shall members participate in any activity designed to mislead, or manipulate the price of a company's securities.

3. Members shall publicly disclose or release information promptly so as to avoid the possibility of any use of the information by any insider or third party. To that end, members shall make every effort to comply with the spirit and intent of the timely disclosure policies of the stock exchanges, NASD, and the Securities and Exchange Commission. Material information shall be made available to all on an equal basis.

4. Members shall not disclose confidential information the disclosure of which might be adverse to a valid corporate purpose or interest and whose disclosure is not required by the timely disclosure provisions of the law. During any such period of non-disclosure members shall not directly or indirectly (a) communicate the confidential information to any other person or (b) buy or sell or in any other way deal in the company's securities where the confidential information may materially affect the market for the security when disclosed. Material information shall be disclosed publicly as soon as its confidential status has terminated or the requirement of timely disclosure takes effect.

5. During the registration period, members shall not engage in practices designed to precondition the market for such securities. During registration the issuance of forecasts, projections, predictions about sales and earnings, or opinions concerning security values or other aspects of the future performance of the company, shall be in accordance with current SEC regulations and statements of policy. In the case of companies whose securities are publicly held, the normal flow of factual information to shareholders and the investing public shall continue during the registration period.

6. Where members have any reason to doubt that projections have an adequate basis in fact, they shall satisfy themselves as to the adequacy of the projections prior to disseminating them.

7. Acting in concert with clients or em-

ployers, members shall act promptly to correct false or misleading information or rumors concerning clients' or employers' securities or business whenever they have reason to believe such information or rumors are materially affecting investor attitudes.

8. Members shall not issue descriptive materials designed or written in such a fashion as to appear to be, contrary to fact, an independent third party endorsement or recommendation of a company or a security. Whenever members issue material for clients or employers, either in their own names or in the name of someone other than clients or employers, they shall disclose in large type and in a prominent position on the face of the material the source of such material and the existence of the issuer's client or employer relationship.

9. Members shall not use inside information for personal gain. However, this is not intended to prohibit members from making bona fide investments in their company's or client's securities

insofar as they can make such investments without the benefit of material inside information.

10. Members shall not accept compensation which would place them in a position of conflict with their duty to a client, employer or the investing public. Members shall not accept stock options from clients or employers nor accept securities as compensation at a price below market price except as part of an overall plan for corporate employees.

11. Members shall act so as to maintain the integrity of channels of public communication. They shall not pay or permit to be paid to any publication or other communications medium any consideration in exchange for publicizing a company, except through clearly recognizable paid advertising.

12. Members shall in general be guided by the PRSA Declaration of Principles and the PRSA Code of Professional Standards for the Practice of Public Relations of which this Code is an official interpretation.

Because of the complexities of the subject, this chapter can only be an outline of the relations with owners. The whole area is constantly changing and here, perhaps more than in any other phase of public relations, it is imperative that the practitioner be aware of the current situation.

The Public Relations Journal publishes about a dozen articles a year on the subject. Usually there is an annual special issue which summarizes the situation. The Securities and Exchange Commission (SEC) issues new rules and interpretations frequently. Keeping up with these changes is a never-ending task. Practices that are satisfactory today may be unsatisfactory or illegal tomorrow.

OWNER CONCERNS

When people buy stocks or bonds, they do it with the objective of making money, but the objective is somewhat more complicated than this bald statement. A New York Stock Exchange study of shareowners found that 38.1% bought for family security; 35.1% invested for retirement; 30.6% invested for the education of children; 29.7% were looking for added income; 24.3% said they were trying to build an estate. Only 10.6% invested for short-term gains.

With goals of this nature, it should be apparent that the investors are deeply concerned about what happens to their money. In appraising the management of their funds, they raise questions about many subjects. Sometimes they write to the company, but more and more often the questions are asked at meetings of shareowners. Among the most frequently asked are questions on the following:

Low Earnings on Stock

There may be many reasons for low earnings. Some of these may be beyond the control of management and some may be the fault of management. With the first group, the task of management is to clearly explain the causes of the poor earnings and their probable duration. With the second group, management must tell the owners what it is doing to improve performance.

Low Price of Stock

Complaints about low stock prices are often expressed by selling, which further depresses the price. Stock prices are not nearly as controllable by management as are earnings. True, price does often reflect earnings, but a brief study of a representative list of stocks will show some remarkable examples of nonrelationship between prices and earnings. Prices are often a reflection of expectations; when buyers expect that a stock price will go up, their buying makes it go up. If and when the owner-relations program of a corporation convinces enough buyers that the future looks brighter than the present, it is quite likely that the price of the stock will advance. Propping up the price of the stock is not the primary purpose of an owner-relations program, but when the program creates enthusiasm about the firm and its future, that enthusiasm should have a positive effect on the price of the stock.

Low Dividends

Stockholders get their share of corporate earnings through dividends. If dividends are not up to investor desires or expectations, investors are obviously unhappy.

If low or passed dividends are a direct result of low earnings, the problem is really one of explaining the reason for the low earnings and assuring the owners that things will improve. In some cases, the earnings are good but management decides that the welfare of the company will best be served by retaining earnings for use in the business rather than paying them out to stockholders. When this happens, management must tell the owners why this is being done, how long it will go on, and what it will do to future earnings, dividends, and corporate assets.

Executive Perquisites

More and more stockholders are questioning such items as salaries, bonuses, stock options, club memberships, use of company cars, boats and planes, the existence and use of company-owned resorts. Even attending meetings at exotic locations is challenged. This indicates that corporate management is in a spotlight and that the audience is very critical.

Board Memberships

Some business leaders may be on the board of directors of several different companies. Now this is being challenged. Demands are made that boards include women, minorities, nonofficer employees, "public" members, and "social responsibility" members.

Fees to directors are being questioned. There are demands that company officers who serve on outside boards give their fees to the company. Board membership was once a privilege, but today it may be a burden. No board of directors can take its actions for granted. Shareowners may challenge almost any action.

Accounting Methods

Accounting procedures vary widely and financial reports are so variable that comparisons are difficult. The Financial Accounting Standards Board (FASB) is trying to bring uniformity to this area, but it is an enormous task. Meanwhile stockholders and the SEC continue to press for more complete and more comparable information.

Lack of Information

In spite of all that has been learned about informing stockholders, there are still complaints that they do not get adequate information. Some organizations do give their owners a thorough briefing, but there are still a good many that do not provide enough information. What stockholders (or members) need is information that will enable them to realistically appraise their investment and to judge the competence of management.

Social Responsibility

This is a very sensitive problem. While most stockholders still seem to be relatively unconcerned, there is a growing minority which loudly and persistently demands that the corporation take specific steps to prove itself socially responsible.

Most effective are the pressures through churches, colleges, and other groups which own substantial blocks of stock. It was pressure of this sort which caused General Motors to establish its Public Policy Committee. The Bank of America and many other large companies have also set up similar committees. (See Dialogue I.)

Almost any activity may be questioned. The areas of interest include the physical environment, nuclear development, civil rights, human rights, products, marketing and advertising tactics, corporate ethics, and even the personal conduct of officers and directors.

THE SECURITIES AND EXCHANGE COMMISSION

The SEC was established by the federal government to protect investors. To do this, it has set many rules designed to standardize the information given to investors. Two of the most important rules deal with reporting methods and "full and timely disclosure."

The latest summary of these rules would fill about nine pages of this book. They are not shown here because they are constantly changing. Anyone involved in financial public relations must act on the basis of the latest rules. However, these two rules are not likely to change in principle.

Reporting

Any information which affects the value of the security must be made known to the owners and to the SEC. One summary of the reporting requirements has 37 different topics. The list includes such details as changes in auditors, employee stock-purchase plans, the effect of the energy crisis, environmental situations, civil rights, and legal procedures. To repeat: the owners and the SEC must be told all the facts.

Full and Timely Disclosure

This is a broad requirement. It means that the corporation must immediately disclose to the public, and to the SEC, any changes which could affect the value of the securities it issues. The purpose is to keep insiders from buying or selling the securities on the basis of advance information.

The origin of this rule is the Texas Gulf Sulfur case. Officers of the company learned of the discovery of a valuable ore deposit on company property. They bought additional stock before the discovery was publicized. They made a lot of money — and precipitated an SEC investigation which led to this rule.

OBJECTIVES IN OWNER RELATIONS

The primary objective of an owner-relations program is to convince the owners or potential owners that the management is doing a good job and that investing in the company is a wise thing to do. Within this very broad area there are numerous minor objectives, each of which contributes toward the main goal. Any of these objectives may require a special campaign but often the objectives are pooled in one general program.

To Build Interest in the Company

People sometimes buy stock in a company without any real interest in it. When this situation exists, there is no understanding of, or sympathy for management's problems, and no commendation for its successes. By interesting stockholders in the company, it is possible to create a much more understanding ownership. Such an ownership will be more stable and not so easily influenced by the latest rumor or stock market quotation.

To Create Understanding

Every business has problems that may be thoroughly understood by management but complete enigmas to the stockholders. The president may know all the reasons why a plant must be closed or a building replaced, but the stockholders who pay the bills will not know unless management informs them. The effect of remote events may be obvious to management but not to stockholders. The failure of a supplier, the imposition of taxes, the changing of tariffs, the rulings of various governmental agencies — all can have important effects on the business. The stockholder must be informed if he is to understand the significance of these forces upon his company.

To Sell Company Products to Stockholders

The use of the company's products by its stockholders is desirable for several reasons. It familiarizes the stockholders with the product and, assuming that the quality is satisfactory, it makes the stockholder feel that his company is doing a good job. Being familiar with the products should lead to favorable comments about them, and this can create expanded sales and possibly an increased interest in the stock. Finally, the use of company products by stockholders can affect sales volume.

It would seem logical to expect stockholders to buy the products of the company in which they own stock; logical or not, this is not an automatic reaction to stock ownership. Granted, there might be a problem with a man owning stock in General Motors, Ford, and Chrysler, but even in the absence of conflicting interests, most stockholders have to be encouraged.

To Reduce Stock Turnover

Rapid turnover of stock means rapid turnover of ownership. This makes it extremely difficult for management to maintain contact with the people who own the business. Without this contact, management has no security and no chance to convince the owners that it is doing well or that it is working on the problems of the business.

If stock is turned over too rapidly, the financial community becomes aware of this instability and its attitude toward the organization becomes distrustful, which can lead to money problems. Also, this excessive turnover creates added work and increased costs in issuing stock certificates and keeping the stockholder list reasonably accurate.

To Stabilize the Price of the Stock

A company may, in some cases, buy or sell its own stock in order to stabilize the price. This can have an immediate effect but it is expensive and should be considered a purely managerial decision and not a normal activity of stockholder relations. Slower acting, and much less costly, is the effort to convince stockholders of the inherent stability of the company and to encourage them to pay less attention to day-to-day fluctuations in the price of the stock. By reducing the volatility of stockholder reaction, a company may induce less impulsive trading and more long-range investments.

To Win Approval of Management

In most corporations the management has very little personal contact with the owners; if it is a large corporation with thousands or hundreds of thousands of stockholders, there is no real contact. Yet, some communication is essential to the survival of management because management must not only operate the business but also convince the owners that it is doing a good job.

Management strives for that approval by telling the stockholders what it is doing and why. Naturally, management presents its story in the most favorable light possible. Occasionally, stockholders challenge the use of corporate funds for this purpose, but most owners recognize the necessity for this information. Management's optimistic outlook will survive only if it is supported by facts.

To Increase Prestige

Prestige is a nebulous thing. Some firms obtain it with relatively little effort and some fail even after the most desperate attempts. Prestige can be totally detached from other characteristics normally used in evaluating a company. A firm can have great prestige in spite of low earnings, passed dividends, and a declining price for its stock. The reverse can also exist. The value of prestige, aside from flattering the egos of management, is that it helps to stabilize the company. People will be more sympathetic, more willing to believe its side of any public controversy, and more likely to retain stock in spite of fluctuations in the stock market. Prestige also attracts new investors and assures favorable attention for the firm by the financial community.

To Get New Investors

Every company loses stockholders. Some sell out in order to invest their money elsewhere, others to cash in on profits, to stop losses, or to settle estates. The reason for selling is unimportant, the important thing is that they *can* sell because someone is willing to buy. Getting these new investors is a major project in any owner relations program. Nonowners must be made aware of the stock and the characteristics of the company behind it if they are to buy. Most potential investors want adequate information about possible investments before they commit themselves.

To Develop a Favorable Climate for New Capital

Periodically, business firms have to acquire additional capital. Sometimes this is obtained through selling bonds or debentures and sometimes through selling additional stock. In either case the problem is to create a situation that will enable the company to acquire this capital in the most efficient and economical manner. To accomplish this, the company must convince the financial community that the investment will be sound and that the bonds or stock can be sold to investors. In some cases capital is raised through bank loans. Here the principle is the same. Financial decision-makers must be convinced that the loan will be a good one.

To Create Favorable Attitudes in the Financial Community

The financial community includes stock exchange firms, investment counselors, financial writers, security analysts, brokers, dealers, mutual funds, investment bankers, commerical bankers, institutional buyers, and anyone else who may be advising on or making decisions about bonds, stocks, or loans.

Stock exchange firms, through their client representatives, advise their clients to buy, hold, or sell specific stocks.

Investment counselors study the entire economic situation of corporations and inform their clients as to the advisability of investment.

Financial writers in newspapers and magazines tell their readers what is going on with different business firms and report their successes and failures, their problems and prospects.

Security analysts are employed by many financial organizations to study securities and make recommendations about them.

Brokers act as buying and selling agents for their clients and also as advisors in connection with investments in bonds and stocks.

Dealers in securities buy and sell to all sorts of investors. They act as principals, not as agents.

Mutual funds buy and sell stocks and bonds for their investors. Usually a separate firm acts as the investment counselor for the fund. Commonly, the investment counselor serves only one fund or a group of closely related funds.

Investment banks buy and sell large blocks of securities. Often, several will combine to purchase an entire new issue and then resell in smaller blocks to other investors.

Commercial banks cannot own stocks. The only bonds they can invest in are those issued by governmental agencies. They can, however, make loans against securities to corporations and individuals.

Institutional buyers, such as pension funds, insurance companies, and foundations, may make large investments in securities.

All these different members of the financial community want and use detailed information about the various firms in whose stocks or bonds someone may wish to invest or to liquidate an investment. Any owner relations program of any size must include a definite plan to continually inform all the various members of the financial community who could influence the financial operation of the firms concerned. A small organization with a limited amount of stock and a highly localized operation will obviously have a much smaller group of people to inform than will U.S. Steel or General Motors. The key questions are: "Who would be interested?" "Who could make a decision or recommendation affecting the financial situation of the organization or its stocks or bonds?"

To Get Political Support

Many laws and proposed laws are encroaching on the operations of business firms and endangering the investments of the stockholders. Alerting stockholders to these dangers and asking them to protest to their congressmen or legislators should be a part of every owner-relations program.

Suggested Readings

Roalman, Arthur (Ed.). *Investor Relations Handbook*, New York: Amocom, 1974.
Wiesen, Jeremy L. *Regulating Transactions in Securities*. St. Paul, Minn.: West, 1975.

BUILDING GOOD OWNER RELATIONS

Relations with owners are much less complicated than with other publics. Their wants are simpler, their complaints are few, and the objectives of an owner relations program are relatively uncomplicated. Sincerity is, of course, a necessity; policy must be definite; there must be positive action and two-way communication.

Attitude

Management must really believe in giving the owners clear and adequate information. It must be convinced that the owners *are* the owners and that management works for *them*. When management really *wants* to build good relations with owners, the job is more than half done.

Policy

Policy in owner relations should be clearly written so that its meaning will be understood by all investors.

General Foods expresses its policy toward owners in a general statement on management. Pertinent paragraphs are:

> Corporate performance will be judged on long-term achievements as well as by short-term requirements. It will be measured by these criteria: Earnings per share; profit before taxes; return on stockholders' equity; net sales. Operating performance will be judged by these criteria: Profit before taxes; volume; strength of franchises; return on funds employed; net sales.
>
> The financial management of General Foods will be based on principles and practices which accurately reflect the nature of its operations, which on balance are consistent with the standards of the industries within which it competes, and which fairly and consistently present its performance and results.
>
> We will take reasonable risks to achieve desired growth and long-term appreciation in GF stockholders' equity. The long-term strength of GF's consumer franchises will not be subordinated to short-term profit needs.
>
> General Foods will keep the owners of the business and members of the financial community properly informed in a forthright and timely manner.

Action

Deeds must back up the words in the policy. Management must check the performance of those who deal with the owner public to be sure that they are following the rules. The range of activities available in owner relations is practically unlimited. The purposes, too, can cover a wide range. For example, Bank of the Commonwealth in Detroit activated a "Local Ownership Committee" to keep control of the bank within Michigan. It persuaded shareholders to accept the offer of a local group instead of an out-of-state group. Employees were kept fully informed and follow-up information was given to all stockholders.

Two-Way Communication

In every area of public relations, the volume of inbound communication is far less than the outbound one. This is probably most apparent in owner relations where, in many cases, little effort is made to learn who the stockholders are and what they are like.

Owners may be individuals, corporations, trust funds, mutual funds, or estates. The percentage owned by any of these may vary widely from one corporation to another and knowledge of the nature of these owners can materially aid in planning an owner relations program.

Early information about owner attitudes can provide guidance for the program of conveying information to them. Questions and complaints from owners must be answered accurately and promptly. On any point of doubt, the number of people who actually raise questions is only a small part of the number who have this doubt.

Many companies systematically survey their stockholders in order to learn what they want from their investment. The New York Stock Ex-

Southern Pacific
Quarterly Report

Three Months Ended March 31, 1976

Southern Pacific
Quarterly Report

Three Months Ended June 30, 1976

Southern Pacific Pipe Lines Terminal
Brisbane, Calif.

Fig. 11.1 Periodic reports to Southern Pacific stockholders keep them informed about current conditions.

change also periodically does general studies of shareowners in order to discover a collective profile. From the NYSE 1970 "census" of shareowners, we learn that 49.9% of shareowners are women and that 43.6% of shareowners never went to college. From this, it is possible to draw some conclusions regarding communications.

Half the stockholders are women — and many may not be familiar with the specialized language of business. Many stockholders never went to college — so their vocabularies are somewhat limited. Furthermore, even among well-educated businessmen, there is little knowledge of the specialized language of any business except their own. Obviously then, any communication to stockholders should not be in technical terms. Beyond avoidance of specialized language, there must be an effort to explain facts in the clearest, simplest way possible. Information of interest to owners comes from many corporate sources and in many forms. It must be translated into readable, understandable, everyday English, and presented in such a manner that it will not only convey information, but also affect owner opinion in the most favorable way.

There are two extremely difficult problems in communicating with owners. First, more than half of corporate securities are held by mutual funds, pension trusts, insurance portfolios, trust funds, endowments, and other agencies. These may represent thousands of owners with whom the corporation has no contact. In such cases, the owners, for all practical purposes, are highly sophisticated organizations with experts to appraise the investment; yet there are still many individual investors who must be informed in terms they can understand.

Second, distributing information through the news media is increasingly difficult because the media aren't able to publish all the news sent to them. This means that a news release alone can't do the job of "full and timely disclosure." Other channels such as quarterly reports, special reports, letters, brochures, and speeches must be used in order to reach all shareowners.

EXERCISES

1. Do you own any stocks?
   (a) Do you receive adequate information from the company?
   (b) Are you happy with your investment? Why?
   (c) Do you use the products of the company or companies in which you own stock? Why?
2. If you do not own stock, ask the above questions of someone who does.

Case Problem

You are public relations director of General Motors. The environmentalists are making a loud and concerted drive to force General Motors to abandon annual style changes and dividends, and to put all funds saved by these actions into development of a "nonpolluting" engine. They now have proxies for 11% of the stock and have one director (out of 23) on the board; they are urging boycotts on all GM cars.

How would you determine how serious this problem is? What research would you recommend? Which publics are concerned? What would you recommend to top management?

Where can you get help? How could you persuade the environmentalists to take a less drastic position?

What plan would you recommend to oppose the environmentalists? Whom would you try to reach? What would you say? How would you reach them?

The Customer
Public

12

In any business where products or services are sold, the customer is the key to success. Many years ago one of America's greatest merchants, Marshall Field, expressed the whole principle of customer relations in a few words: "The customer is always right."

Customers can make or break any commercial enterprise. If they are pleased with what they buy and happy about their treatment, they will continue to buy and tell their friends. If the product, service, or treatment is unsatisfactory, the customer will not only stop buying but also will tell friends and acquaintances about the unhappy experience.

Relations with customers are often as much a marketing problem as a public relations problem. Good salesmanship and good customer relations go hand in hand. It is difficult indeed to draw a line between them. Quality of merchandise or service and the prices charged are essentially marketing problems. The treatment of customers, the attitudes of sales personnel, and the policies of the firm toward customers are mainly customer relations problems.

There is much overlapping between these areas and fortunately, in most organizations, there is no attempt to draw a hard line between them. True, the public relations manager does not tell the sales people what to do but, in most cases, the sales manager is more than willing to receive suggestions — he knows that anything that improves customer relations will make his job easier.

The principles of good customer relations apply also to situations where no direct purchase is made. Members of an association are in one sense owners, but they are also customers for the services of the association. Taxpayers, too, are owners, but in most contacts with governmental agencies their role is much more that of the customer. A woman mailing a letter is a customer of the Post Office, a man called in to explain his income tax return, is a customer of the Internal Revenue Service. Many governmental contacts with individual citizens have a dictatorial tone. It would certainly be difficult to "sell" a traffic summons, or to "persuade" a man to pay more taxes without the power of penalizing him for nonpayment. Yet, whenever any government agency is dealing with a member of the public, there should be a maximum effort to treat the citizen like a customer.

THE CHANGING CUSTOMER

In recent years the customer has become more important than ever before. The reason for this influence is the shift from a production-oriented economy to a market-oriented one. Relatively speaking, it is easier to make things than to sell them. Fifty years ago there were scores of automobile manufacturers. Now there are only a few. Those who disappeared usually failed in marketing, not in production. The same thing has happened in many fields, and every such case reemphasizes the importance of the customer. Beyond this major shift in the economy, there are several other factors that make good customer relations a necessity.

Increased Disposable Income

As incomes have increased and the relative costs of food and shelter have declined, most families have acquired "discretionary buying power" — money that is not precommitted to fixed costs of living. They have reserve funds that give them independence of action and freedom of choice. Today, most families are able to buy goods and services that were far beyond the reach of their parents. Whether the purchase is a house, an automobile, or a package of facial tissues, the customer does not have to take the first thing he is offered, nor does he have to buy from a particular vendor. He can buy what he chooses where he chooses.

Increased Education

People are better educated now than they were 50 years ago. The college diploma today is about as common as the high-school diploma was at the time of World War I. This means that the buying public is much better informed than their parents and grandparents. It has a better basis from which to judge the merits of products or services. There was a time when the vendor could make statements that the customer could not challenge, but today's more educated buyer is a very different customer. People are harder to please and harder to fool than ever before.

Increased Mobility

With practically every family owning an automobile, the family can buy where it chooses. It is not limited to places within walking distance. It does not have to buy only at places convenient to public transportation. If a family does not like the business concerns near its home, it can drive to another more pleasing business firm. Even large firms gain from this mobility. A purchasing agent can fly across the country in hours to investigate a potential supplier.

Increased Variety of Goods and Services

Once the idea of renting a car was a novelty. Now many firms compete to offer the best car rental service. Once a grocery store carried a few hundred items. Now a typical supermarket offers nearly eight thousand items.* Grandma made a cake with flour, sugar, eggs, and butter. Grand-daughter has many kinds of cake mixes to choose from on the grocer's shelf. Grandpa had a suit for every day and a special one for Sunday. Grandson may own half a dozen suits plus sports clothing for several different activities. All these developments mean that more and more goods are competing for the customer's dollar. While he has more dollars to spend, there are more ways to spend them — which puts a bigger burden on the would-be vendor. Competition for the consumer's money is more intense and more skillful than ever before. Contributing to this is the great increase in new products. Several major manufacturers have pointed out that a large part of their current sales are accounted for by products which did not exist ten years ago.

Increased Skepticism

The attitudes of consumers toward the makers and sellers of goods and services have become clouded with doubt and suspicion. At one time people took things at face value, complaints were minor and private. Now there is widespread distrust. A poll by Lou Harris & Associates found that 78% of the respondents believed that products didn't last as long as they once did, while 64% said that it is harder to get things repaired. Half the

*Progressive Grocer.

sample felt that consumers were not getting as good a deal as they did ten years before. A third of the consumers were dissatisfied with the auto manufacturers, the mechanics, and the oil companies. A poor opinion of doctors and hospitals was held by 25%.

Increased Activism

Consumer groups are militantly active at both state and national levels. They press for consumer protection agencies and for specific laws covering such things as unit pricing, weights and measures, product freshness dating, electronic pricing of groceries, funeral costs, automobile repair estimates and costs, generic drug substitutes for brand names, special utility rates for the poor, elimination of fair trade laws, charges by telephone companies for directory service, property taxes, food prices, and many others.

Increased Litigation

The number of consumer lawsuits has increased dramatically. It is estimated that one million product liability lawsuits are filed every year. In one four-year period, the increase was 26% while the losses went up 279%. In Cook County, Illinois, the average judgment increased from $93,133 to $144,091 in five years.

This has brought staggering increases in the cost of liability insurance. One company paid $10,000 one year and $80,000 the next. A bottled gas company's rates went from $392 to $55,200 in two years while its coverage was reduced from $500,000 to $300,000.

The problem is so serious that many firms can't afford insurance and must risk bankruptcy to stay in business.

CUSTOMER PROBLEMS

Most customer problems originate in just a few categories, but these categories are very important to both buyer and seller. They are quality, price, service, billing, credit, warranties, and legal obligations.

Quality

Marshall Field once said, "The quality will be remembered long after the price is forgotten." The statement applies to both high- and low-price items. If the quality is high, people will remember their satisfaction. If the quality is low, people will remember their dissatisfaction.

Customers complain because the biggest strawberries are on top of the box, they object to meat packaged "best side up," and they lose their tempers over repairmen who do not get things fixed properly. They return clothing that comes unsewed. They complain because things shrink, fade, leak, or rattle. Whenever a customer feels that he is not getting what he paid for, he will protest.

Price

Pricing complaints are of two kinds: those arising from the belief that the purchase was not worth the price, and those arising from the knowledge that a competitor offers a better price.

In recent years, certain consumer groups have become quite vociferous on the subject of price and relative value. They have succeeded in establishing federal labeling requirements for foods, which will help purchasers to determine the price per ounce and thus assist in cost comparison between similar items. This, of course, does not settle the question of relative quality. Nevertheless, this and the other activities of "consumer" groups show that all consumers are vitally concerned about getting their money's worth.

Service

Complaints about service are increasing. Probably a large part of this is due to shortages of personnel and inadequate time for training. Buyers expect sales personnel to be available when needed. They expect them to know their merchandise. They want salespeople to be helpful but not pushy, friendly but not familiar, courteous but not fawning. They expect them to sell, not oversell, to give facts, not fiction. They want prompt attention, and they expect commitments to be kept.

Surveys repeatedly show that the chief reason people buy at certain retail stores is the nature of the sales personnel. Quality, price, and all other factors are secondary to the nature of salespeople in the store.

Billing

The extensive use of automated accounting, the increased use of charge accounts, the growth of checking accounts and credit cards — all combine to move more transactions away from cash and into a "pay-by-mail" situation. The complications of billing and of receiving checks and crediting them to the right account lead to frequent errors and inequities. Another source of trouble is the staggered billing date which does not coincide with the monthly or semimonthly paycheck.

Charge customers complain that their checks may be received and cashed but not credited to their account for several days. When such a customer receives a delinquency bill or is assessed a service charge for the delay, he or she quite rightly resents it.

Customers also complain about retailers who, in effect, "sell" their accounts to some other entity which then assumes responsibility for collection. Still another sore spot is the failure to credit an account for a payment even though the check has been cashed. And, finally, customers find much ground for unhappiness in the collection letters they may receive. The customer who has a ten- or twenty-year record of promptly paying bills will react rather violently to an impersonal dunning letter.

Montgomery Ward has led in fighting to eliminate laws requiring that debts owed on the first of the month must be treated as debts for the whole month even if the bill is paid on the second of the month.

Citibank sends cards to delinquent debtors offering a chance to avoid a suit for collection. The result has been a great reduction in lawsuits.

Credit

The use of credit has increased tremendously in recent years. Easy charge accounts, gasoline credit cards, bank credit cards, and numerous other aids to "buying now and paying later" have created a new problem in customer relations and have led to new kinds of complaints. Obviously, credit is granted in the expectation that the money will eventually be paid by the buyer. Fortunately, the majority of customers understand and tolerate the usual investigative procedures. Yet, many buyers resent the necessary credit investigation and object to the fact that local credit associations exchange information about the bill-paying habits of all users of credit.

Warranties

A Harris poll found that over half of the respondents couldn't understand their warranties. Nearly half said that the warranties were designed to protect the seller and 57% said the warranties weren't adequate. Customers want warranties that are understandable and protect the buyer.

Legal Obligations

Many dealings with customers must be in writing so there can be no misunderstanding about the obligations of both parties. Unfortunately, many of these documents aren't understandable to anyone but a lawyer. Insurance policies, loan applications, credit statements, real estate mortgages, time-payment contracts, construction or repair contracts, and warranties are some of the most conspicuous examples.

There has been some progress toward simplifying such documents. Citibank in New York and Wells Fargo Bank and the Bank of America in California have led in the simplification of such forms. By using conversational language in large type, they have greatly improved customer relations. One Wells Fargo form was cut from 91 words to 57 words.

Suggested Readings

Blum, Milton L. *Psychology and Consumer Affairs.* New York: Harper & Row, 1977.
De Lozier, Wayne. *Consumer Behavior Dynamics.* Columbus, Ohio: Merrill, 1977.
McGuire, E. Patrick. *The Consumer Affairs Department.* New York: Conference Board, 1973.
Reynolds, Fred D. and Wells, William D. *Consumer Behavior.* New York: McGraw-Hill, 1977.

OBJECTIVES IN CUSTOMER RELATIONS

The primary objective in a customer relations program is to help make sales. Note the word "help," because customer relations is secondary to the sales function. It is possible to make sales without a customer relations program, but it is not possible to have a customer relations program unless there are customers. There are a number of minor objectives within the general one just mentioned. Sometimes, several may be combined into one campaign but, in many cases, there will be separate drives toward separate goals. Some of the more common objectives are:

To Retain Old Customers

In any business most of the sales are made to established customers. These people have been satisfied and the problem is to keep them satisfied. The things that made them customers must be continued and the things that might weaken their enthusiasm must be avoided. To do this, it is necessary to know why they buy, what they like and dislike, what pleases and displeases them. It costs more money to get new customers than to keep old ones; if there is a big turnover in the customer list, the profits of the business will be reduced.

J.C. Penney Co. has an "in-house" consumer advocate who once worked for Consumers Union, an organization whose purpose is to help consumers get the best values for their money.

To Attract New Customers

Even the most satisfied customers change, move away, or pass away; if they are not replaced, the volume of sales will be reduced. Accordingly, every business firm must constantly get new customers. Part of this acquisition is a matter of sales management but a large part comes from the customer relations program. Old customers may influence their friends and acquaintances. First-time buyers may become repeat buyers because of the kind of treatment they get. Casual and random buyers may be induced to concentrate their purchases. In most businesses the prices of goods and services are about the same as the prices offered by the competition. The difference is the way in which customers and prospective customers are treated.

To Get a Bigger Share of the Buyer's Dollar

Few buyers concentrate their purchases at one location. The average woman usually has two or three grocery stores from which to choose. For clothing, she may have a dozen possible sources. Automobile owners may have credit cards with several oil companies. The relative share of the customer's dollar received by each of the vendors depends to a marked degree on the attitude of the buyer. If it is purely a matter of price, the seller offering the biggest value will get the biggest share. But values can be intangible and sellers who give those intangible pluses usually ring up some very tangible profits at the cash register.

To Expedite Handling of Complaints

Most large business firms have an established procedure for handling complaints. Many smaller firms have none, even though they should have. These used to be called complaint departments but more and more they are being called adjustment departments because "complaint" implies a listen-but-no-action attitude while "adjustment" implies satisfaction. Regardless of the term used, it is very important that the problem be handled as quickly as possible and that the customer be satisfied.

Most complaints have at least some justification. The fact that some buyers will take advantage of the seller and make unreasonable complaints should not affect the procedure. Every complaint should be handled as if it were valid; the attitude must be gracious rather than grudging. Unadjusted complaints grow in the eyes of the complainer — and in the mouth, too.

People are much more likely to tell their friends about mistreatment than about good treatment. In the handling of complaints, it is imperative that sales personnel be properly informed. Sometimes a salesperson will spot an obvious attempt to get an unjustified adjustment but this is not a cue for playing detective. The customer should not be grilled or cross-examined. The goodwill obtainable through a satisfactory adjustment far outweighs the cost of the merchandise involved.

To Reduce Complaints

Adjustment departments cost money; even if there is no department, someone must take time to handle complaints. Every minute spent in this way could be more profitably spent somewhere else. The fewer the complaints, the more efficient the operation. In addition, a reduction in complaints means a reduction in dissatisfied customers who may stop buying and induce their friends to do the same. Reducing complaints is accomplished by reducing the causes for complaint, not by choking off the flow. The stimulus to complain can be lessened by a program that informs customers about policies affecting them, and even more, by teaching sales personnel the fundamentals of good relations with customers.

Citibank invites customers to discuss their problems with officers of the bank. Montgomery Ward has established an arbitration panel to settle complaints, but store managers have done so well in settling complaints that the panel has yet to be used.

To Reduce Costs

Costs of delivery, of collecting bills, of returned goods, of service calls can all be reduced if customers know that these costs are ultimately reflected in the price they pay. Customer relations programs can induce shoppers to carry small packages; they can speed up collection of bills; they can educate shoppers to buy with deliberation and avoid bringing back items purchased in a burst of enthusiasm. They can induce the customer who wants a service call to be there when the serviceman arrives, thus preventing costly callbacks. Many other business expenses can be pared through a tactful effort to get customers' cooperation.

To Make Customers Like the Seller

This is a goal that is easy to state but hard to attain. If customers really do like the seller, they will be loyal and helpful, forgive errors, encourage their friends to buy, even offer suggestions to the vendor for improvement of goods or services, and often help the seller make additional sales. A customer of this sort is the most valuable customer of all, because he is a living testimonial — a walking advertisement for the seller's goods or services. To make customers really like the vendor should be a continuing objective in every customer relations program. There are many ways in which to accomplish this, but they all start with treating customers like friends. Organizations that genuinely like their customers always have customers who like the organization.

BUILDING GOOD CUSTOMER RELATIONS

Good relations with customers can be attained if management really wants them. Proper attention to a few fundamental principles will insure a successful program. The essentials are attitude, policy, action, and two-way communication.

Attitude

Management cannot make a program work unless it really means it to work. A cordial friendly policy is not worth a hoot unless it is based on an honest intention to carry it out. Customers must know that they can rely on a statement from the seller. Attempts to back down on commitments or to claim that the customer is misinterpreting the policy can result only in failure of the program.

Policy

A written policy guiding relations with customers is imperative. Without it, employees will have no consistent guidance and customers will be unable to find out what rights and privileges to expect. Customer policy can cover everything from service charges to alteration costs, from policy on returns to how sales people address customers. The policy does not always have to be voluminous. Macy's expresses its policy in five words: "The Customer must be satisfied." J.C. Penney Co. puts it this way:

THE PENNEY IDEA

1. To serve the public, as nearly as we can, to its complete satisfaction.
2. To expect for the service we render a fair remuneration and not all the profit the traffic will bear.
3. To do all in our power to pack the customer's dollar full of value, quality and satisfaction.
4. To continue to train ourselves and our associates so that the service we give will be more and more intelligently performed.
5. To improve constantly the human factor in our business.
6. To reward men and women in our organization through participation in what the business produces.
7. To test our every policy, method and act in this wise. "Does it square with what is right and just?"

Marshall Field & Co. has had for many years a policy of always accepting returned merchandise in good condition regardless of how long it had been out of the store. Once a woman customer returned a pair of new shoes that had been purchased some 30 years before. Marshall Field & Co. refunded the purchase price without question. The woman was not at all surprised because she trusted the store's policy. And Marshall Field & Co. got nationwide publicity — and undoubtedly many new customers — because of the story.

Action

Good intentions, fair policies, and sincerity are all desirable, but they will fail without tangible backing. Actions speak louder than words. In customer relations, nothing will be accomplished unless management implements its program with positive deeds. It must live up to all its claims and stand behind all its dealings. A guarantee of satisfaction must be carried through to the point of complete customer satisfaction. The dangers of favoritism are obvious. Every customer feels that he or she is equal to any other customer. If there is any evidence or even suspicion that someone else is getting a better deal, there will be a drastic reaction.

Favoritism is so repugnant to American thinking that we even have federal laws such as the Robinson-Patman Act to guarantee equal treatment to all buyers. Since almost everyone wants and expects equitable treatment, the solution is to enforce a policy of absolute equality and to make sure that the customers are aware of it.

In order to deal adequately with the problems of customers, many organizations have established consumer affairs departments. The list includes such diverse entities as the Ford Motor Company, Giant Food, American Petroleum Institute, Hershey Foods Company, American Airlines, Clorox, and Mattel. There is even a Society of Consumer Affairs Professionals. Some of its members are members of PRSA and some studiously avoid any connection with the words "public relations." This may be an effort to euphemize because customers are a public, and customer relations is a public relations function.

Two-Way Communication

Unless there is communication *from* customers, management will not know how it is doing and what the customers are thinking. To get this feedback, management must provide the means. It cannot rely on voluntary action of the customers. Even though many will express themselves without being asked, there are many more who will not take the time or make the effort. Management must inquire. It must make it easy for customers to register complaints and suggestions.

If management makes the tools of communications accessible to its customers and encourages their use, it will be well informed about customer attitudes and opinions and it will be able to improve its performance and its credibility. Many hotels and restaurants regularly supply every guest with a questionnaire designed to find out how well the customer was satisfied.

Communication *to* customers is also necessary. A definite plan for conveying information is essential. Haphazard and spasmodic efforts will not be effective. Someone must decide what to say to the customers, how to say it and how to get the message to them on a continuing basis. And then the plan must be put into effect.

The National Livestock and Meat Board has a program for educating consumers which is channeled through high school consumer education coordinators. Coordinators are given a color filmstrip with a 33 1/3 r.p.m. record. The strip explains the factors in meat prices. Leaflets and a student opinion survey are also supplied. Reports indicate that the program is well received, and that it is helping to educate consumers.

EXERCISES

1. Were you happy or unhappy with your treatment by the salesman or sales-

woman the last time you bought something? Why? Did the salesman or sales-woman know his or her job?

2. Which retail store do you prefer to shop in? Why?
3. Do you know the name of any salesperson in a store where you shop?
4. Were you pleased with your last contact with the service personnel of any organization (service station, public utility, bank, etc.)? Why?
5. Have you had an unhappy experience with billing from any concern where you charge merchandise or services? How would you improve this situation?

Case Problem

You are public relations director of a large retail grocery chain. There is loud and continuous public outcry about the "high price of food." Charges are made that you are making large profits at the expense of the public. Fact: for every $100 of merchandise sold, the store pays $83. It spends $16 for rent, heat, light, fixtures, labor, insurance, taxes, etc. It makes $1 profit. Additional facts: a large part of the items sold are nonfood items, and many food items are ready-to-eat "convenience foods."

How would you convince the customers that your profits are small and reasonable and that the prices are fair?

What groups, organizations, and individuals would you try to reach?

What message would you convey to them? What tools would you use?

The Community Public | 13

Good relations with the community in which it operates are vital to any organization. Whether it be a military post, a retail store, a manufacturer of shoes or any of a hundred possibilities, the friendly regard and good opinion of the community can materially aid in the successful running of the enterprise.

In thinking of a community, it is normal to visualize a town or a city, but in public relations terms this is not quite correct. For PR purposes, the community includes all people and organizations affected by, or who can affect, the organizations. Employees, customers, stockholders, suppliers, and many other key groups may be actually located in the same area but, for our purposes, we will describe the community as all those who do not have a direct financial interest, although there may be considerable secondary financial interest.

The community of General Motors is the entire United States and, to a lesser degree, parts of the rest of the world. The community of a Chevrolet assembly plant may be the city in which it is located plus several surrounding counties. The community of a Buick dealer may be half a city. The community of a shoe repair shop may be a city block. The community of the United States Army is the whole world. The community of Ft. Dix is in the New Jersey area — until some soldier on furlough has an automobile accident in Fargo, North Dakota, whereupon Fargo temporarily becomes part of Ft. Dix's community.

COMMUNITY COMPLAINTS

Complaints from the community seldom come directly to an organization. Instead they are voiced by individuals to other individuals within the community. Rather generally, these criticisms are expressed without any expectation that they will be acted upon or even heard by those who are responsible. People will tell their friends that they dislike or even detest an organization because it is indifferent, paternalistic, unfair, high-handed, or ignorant, but they seldom tell the organization. There can be many causes of community complaint, but these are the most common.

Indifference

Since most organizations have plenty of problems of their own, it is very easy to concentrate on them and to forget about the community. Also, it is possible to be actively indifferent — to refuse opportunities for community activity and even to order employees not to participate as individuals. Either of these negative policies will become known to the community and will create an image that is most unattractive. Any organization that becomes so identified will have few friends and many opponents, perhaps even active enemies. Today, organizations are expected to be concerned about community affairs, and those who do not live up to this expectation are rightfully subject to community criticism.

Paternalism

At the opposite pole is the organization that takes too much interest in its community. Whenever any organization seems to have a conspicuous hand in every activity, whenever it seems to be running everything in the community, there is an adverse reaction. The old "company-town" image is a bad image even when the organization's activities are highly beneficial and unselfish. To avoid paternalism, the organization must be ready and willing to help with both manpower and money, but it must strive for an image of helpfulness rather than dominance.

High-handedness

When an organization defies community opinion and does what it chooses without regard for the wishes of others, it can quickly develop a large group of active enemies. These people will go farther and do more than those who merely dislike the organization. Active enemies are not satisfied with talking to their friends. They talk to everyone; they make speeches; they get injuctions; they publicly demonstrate their opposition; and they create major problems for the organization that has aroused their wrath.

Ignorance

To be a help to the community, an organization must know the community — its needs, its problems, its people, its interests, and its attitudes. Many organizations do not know and do not try to learn these things or, knowing, ignore them. This results in actions or policies that may be well-intentioned but not necessary or desirable. It also results in missed opportunities for creating favorable community opinion. In any community there are needs — and priorities for those needs. The organization which, through ignorance, works on a low-priority problem at the expense of a more urgent one creates an image of ignorance or plain stupidity, which leads to bad community relations.

Unfairness

The American people have a deeply ingrained belief that everyone and every organization should be fair in dealing with others. Any organization that appears to be, or is, unfair to some individuals, groups, or organizations is on shaky ground in its community relations. The American resistance to monopolies, the dislike of bigness, are reflections of the basic belief that no one should have an undue advantage and that all should compete on reasonably equal terms. No organization can have good community relations unless the community believes that it operates fairly in all its dealings.

OBJECTIVES IN COMMUNITY RELATIONS

The overall objective of a community relations program is to promote favorable public opinion in the community where the organization operates. If an organization has good community relations, it is natural to assume that it has good public relations, but that assessment can be erroneous. It is possible to have good community relations and poor relations with stockholders or suppliers or the government; so it should be emphasized here that public relations includes every public while community relations includes only those close to the operation but not directly involved on a day-by-day basis.

Within the general objective of promoting favorable public opinion in the community there may be several more specific goals.

Without attempting to indicate relative importance, these goals typically include the following ideas that are to be "sold" to the community:

importance as an employer, taxpayer, and buyer; fairness to employees, to customers; regard for, responsiveness to, and dependence on the community.

Importance as an Employer

The amount of money paid to employees can be a significant factor in the economy of the community. The presence or absence of that payroll is a factor in the business health of the entire community. If an organization is growing and hiring more workers, that not only means more jobs but also more purchases from local sellers of everything from houses to groceries. Conversely, if an organization declines or fails, it will mean fewer jobs and fewer dollars being spent.

Importance as a Taxpayer

There are two reasons why this objective is vital One is that it shows how large a portion of the community's tax load is borne and, by implication, how much more others would have to pay without this help. The other reason is that by publicizing the tax burden, there will be less pressure to increase the taxes. Of equal significance to the effect of taxes in general are the effects of specific taxes. Inventory taxes force businesses to use out-of-state warehouses; local income taxes may force businesses to move away.

Importance as a Buyer

Whether the organization is an insurance office buying a new type-writer from a store next door or General Motors buying millions of items from thousands of suppliers, the purchase can have an effect on the community involved. Buying from suppliers in the community and letting that practice be known is a certain way to build goodwill in the community. Use of minority suppliers is increasingly important.

Fairness as an Employer

Two important things can be accomplished if this objective is attained. First, it will help in recruiting; second, it will build community support in case of controversy with employees. If the people of the community are convinced that "X" is a good employer, there will be more job applicants than if they have a negative opinion or no opinion at all. Job applicants often ask questions about prospective employers and then apply at the place that sounds best to them.

Controversy between employer and employee may occur for many reasons. When it does happen, the community is usually aware of it; if the employer has established its fairness in the minds of the community, it will have more public opinion on its side than if it has a reputation for hard dealing. Public opinion in such a case may not control the outcome, but it can affect it.

Fairness to Customers

By establishing a reputation for fair treatment of customers, a business will, of course, gain new customers. It will also gain goodwill from people who cannot really become customers. Any kind of enterprise may need public support at some time. If its community knows that the organization treats its customers fairly, there will be much more opinion on its side. Often the establishment of a good reputation in the community leads to an extension of the community. People will go far out of their way to patronize a business that really values its customers.

Regard for the Community

There are many ways in which an organization can prove regard for the community. It can be proved by participation in community activities and by contribution of time and money to local causes. Doing things for the community of its own volition is certain to develop a profoundly favorable reaction. The tone must be one expressing sincere interest in community welfare and an enlightened attitude toward the organization's responsibilities. Mere "do-goodism" just will not suffice and an obvious expectation of some sort of reward for good deeds is sure to create ill will.

Responsiveness to the Community

A cold impersonal organization that will not listen to community ideas or that insists on proceeding without local counsel is certain to create adverse public opinion. Whenever an organization has one or more projects designed to benefit the community, there must be a thorough study of possible results and consultation with people who can give impartial advice.

In addition to the things that the organization thinks of doing for the community, there are always numerous suggestions and requests that come from the community. All of these cost money. If all such requests were filled, the financial burden would be impossible to tolerate. Community requests generally fall into two categories: contribution of money or manpower that may be made by numerous organizations, and specific action or inaction asked of one organization alone.

The first group is typified by numerous charitable drives, which are aimed at everyone who might be able to contribute. The second group includes such things as suggestions for changes in things done by the organization. These can range from air pollution to location of parking lots or to work hours which may affect local traffic.

Whatever the nature of the request, those who make the proposal must be given a hearing and an explanation of the reasons for the decision. Even if the decision is to say "no," it can be palatable if the proponents are convinced that they have had fair treatment.

Needs from the Community

Membership in a community entails getting as well as giving. A community gains certain things from the enterprises in its locality but it must provide services to the enterprise. Schools, police, and fire protection, streets, sewers, and water are among the first that come to mind. These are rather universal and generally accepted by any community.

Beyond these general needs there may be special ones. A manufacturer may require additional employees and a business office may need office help with special training which can be provided by local schools. A retail store may need special consideration in zoning. A relocation or expansion of an enterprise may necessitate added hospital facilities or enlarged schools or new utilities, all of which place additional costs on the community.

To get these things requires public approval and public money, which can only be gained if the public knows why they are needed and how it will benefit. Communities do not spend money without some hope of return. But they will do it if the facts are there — and if they are properly presented.

BUILDING GOOD COMMUNITY RELATIONS

Implementing an effective program of community relations requires enlightened attitude, a definite policy, thorough knowledge of the community, positive action, and effective two-way communication.

Attitude

No community relations program can exist unless management is convinced that it is desirable and necessary. Some organizations will carry on a much more comprehensive program than others because they believe in it. The degree of activity depends on the attitude of management. This attitude is, of course, affected by the nature of the organization, the amount of money available and the problems it has or can have.

Policy

Once management has decided to implement a community relations program, it must establish a definite policy stating what it will and will not do. While policy must be stable and consistent, it must also be up-to-date and adaptable to new tasks, personnel, and situations.

Following is the Policy of Sears Roebuck and Co.:

> All Company public relations policies have one aim — to create and maintain a favorable climate of public opinion about Sears in order that the Company may prosper and grow.
>
> In formulating those policies over the years, we have used as our credo General Wood's statement, "Business must account for its stewardship not only on the balance sheet, but also in matters of social responsibility."
>
> Sears is among the nation's largest corporations. It will have an increasingly important impact on the American economy. Because it is a leader, Sears cannot afford to take a narrow view of its role in society without risking unfavorable public opinion and possible disfavor in the eyes of its customers.
>
> The Company is judged by its conduct in every community in which we do business and the sum total of this conduct is what results in our image nationally.
>
> > William F. McCurdy
> > *Vice President*
> > *Public Relations*

Knowledge of the Community

The community may be one city or many cities; it may be a nation or a neighborhood. Regardless of its size or nature, a community relations program must be appropriate to the community. This requires a thorough knowledge of the community or communities involved.

To know a community is to answer questions like these:

What are the problems of the community?

What are the interests of the community?

What is the economic situation?

Who has economic power?

What is the political situation?

Who has political power?

Who are the opinion leaders?

Are there special emotional attitudes?

Community problems Community problems may include such things as taxes, land use, schools, traffic, police protection, urban renewal, flood control, urban sprawl, corruption, fire protection, rapid transit, water supply, preservation of historic sites, garbage disposal, zoning, moving of middle-class families to suburbs, air pollution, and many others. All or some of these may be present, but usually some are more pressing than others. If an organization knows which problems are important, it will be able to plan its community relations program intelligently and help to solve those problems.

Community interests Community interests are as different as the communities themselves. One will be much concerned about juvenile delinquency, another will be enthralled by art. One will be for progress at any price, while an adjacent community will have an opposite viewpoint. Los Angeles builds freeways everywhere regardless of what they do to the environment. San Francisco fights them and even talks about tearing them down because of encroachments on parks and views.

Community A will go all out to attract new businesses to its area. Community B will take the opposite course because it does not want additional crowding. One community will be sports mad but the next one may be working day and night on urban renewal. And interests change with time. Projects are completed, blocked, or die because the instigators lose their energy. Any effort to aid a community must be based on knowing what the community wants. Giving a million dollars for something no one appreciates will not build as much goodwill as a contribution to a cause dear to the heart of the community.

Economic situation A growing community has a drastically different attitude from one that is static. A mining town is not an agricultural town. A distribution center has little in common with an educational center. California and Florida both have an important tourist trade, both have a warm winter climate, both produce oranges — yet the differences in these states are much greater than the similarities. Their economic bases are very dissimilar and this creates completely different problems in community relations.

The aircraft industry is vital in Seattle and totally inconsequential in Portland. Flint lives on automobiles, Topeka on wheat. In Bakersfield, cotton is important. In Bisbee, copper keeps the wheels turning. Appalachia is depressed but a hundred miles away, Megalopolis is booming.

The economic situation of any community must be known if there is to be any meaningful relationship with the people who live and work within the area.

Economic power The economic power in any community is normally concentrated in a few hands. Usually, a very small number of organizations can insure the success or failure of a community enterprise by their support or opposition. The automobile business dominates Detroit business. Two milling companies in Minneapolis outweigh almost everything else.

In the larger cities there may be a considerable number of manufacturing, retailing, and financial institutions which together are the backbone of the economy. In some small cities one firm alone may be the foundation of business. In every community, however, economic power is concentrated. Knowing who controls the power is essential to success in community relations. If this "establishment" can be induced to a favorable attitude most of the community will follow. If the "establishment" turns thumbs down, it is unlikely that there will be much success. The key to this situation, therefore, is to learn who runs things and to win their favorable opinion.

Political situation No community operates without politics and politicians. In some cases there may be so-called nonpartisan elections, but even if the major parties are excluded, there is still partisanship and political activity. Parties vary from community to community. A Mississippi democrat may have nothing in common with a Massachusetts democrat except for the name.

Factions vary from time to time. The "ins" may resist "reform" until they are "outs," whereupon they may be very much in favor. Political power in any community is sought and fought for. It is as important as economic power — and often the two become heavily intermingled. In community relations it is essential to know the local political situation. Government can be neutral but it can also be a powerful friend or an equally powerful enemy.

Political leaders Whether political parties are involved, as in national or state government, or whether the parties are "officially" absent, as in many cities, there are always political leaders. The "ins" have the power and the "outs" hope to get it. All play the game of politics. Politicians come and go, but there is always a struggle for the power that comes with public office. Knowing the political leaders and what they stand for can materially aid a community relations program. Getting support from, or giving support to, the people who run politics may be very important to an organization. And, to look at the other side of the coin, knowing who not to support and whose help to avoid may be equally important. In summary, it pays to know the politicians.

Opinion leaders   Besides the members of the economic and political establishments, it is not unusual to find others who exert a strong influence on public opinion. These individuals may be ministers, educators, elder statesmen, journalists, newspaper columnists, or merely people with strong opinions and a willingness to voice them. In any community, there may be one or several of these independent opinion leaders. They can be loyal friends or bitter enemies; because of their relative detachment from the economic and political center of power, they are usually stronger in their convictions and louder in their expression of opinion. Every community relations program must recognize the existence of these people and strive for their support.

Special emotional attitudes   In many communities, there are special emotional attitudes that must be considered in attempting to build favorable public opinion. These attitudes may be the result of long-established beliefs or the aftermath of a violent incident or controversy; they may be rooted in economics, race, religion, or any of a dozen other influences.

Public opinion about racial integration will be quite different in Alabama and Alaska. Centralia, Washington, and Centralia, Illinois, are about the same size — 10-12,000 people. But there the resemblance stops. Centralia, Illinois, is a strong union town. Centralia, Washington, is cold to unions because of an incident that happened many years ago when members of the IWW (a very radical labor union) fired into a veteran's parade and killed several men. Catholic communities want government aid for parochial schools. Protestant communities are opposed. Japanese cameras are unpopular in Rochester, New York, because that city is the home of Eastman Kodak.

Many communities are free from strong emotional situations, but some do have them and woe betide the unwary public relations man who blunders into one of these situations.

Action

Knowing the community permits action that will demonstrate good citizenship and good neighborliness.

Good citizenship   In an individual, good citizenship is demonstrated by obedience to laws, avoidance of injury to the interests of others, payment of just bills, and a general practice of the Golden Rule. The same deeds characterize good citizenship in an organization. It must conform to the laws and not rely on legal trickery to evade them. It must be financially responsible. It must not impose on others. Most of these actions could be described as the avoidance of things that can make others unhappy.

Under the ecological concept of public relations, this is adapting the organization to its environment.

Good neighborliness   It is possible to live next door to a good citizen and never know his name. Good neighbors are different. They are known and liked. To attain this status requires a positive effort. It is in this area that some of the most important things are accomplished in community relations. Basic to all these activities is an inner conviction that the organization has an obligation to its neighbors — both individually and collectively. This helps adapt the environment to the organization. Good neighborliness includes two general groupings of activities: self-improvement and community action.

Self-improvement   Self-improvement may include constructive actions such as designing buildings to be beautiful as well as functional; concealing unsightly equipment; avoiding pollution of air and water; preserving natural beauty; protection of open space; utilization of land so as not to infringe upon the desirable features of some neighbor's land; use of art, decoration, and landscaping to make installations more appealing to the eye; suppression of odors, noise, or dust; concealment of unsightly rubbish, refuse, garbage, and junk; minimizing the inconvenience and obstruction caused by construction; preservation of the view from nearby property; and many more.

All of these actions are becoming more important every day as we become more conscious of our environment. A century ago a factory chimney belching smoke was a symbol of business activity. Today it is air pollution. Once, a man could do anything he wanted with his property as long as he did not violate any laws. Now he must consider public opinion. People are becoming more aware of the environment every day; any organization that disregards this public awareness is building poor public relations.

Fig. 13.1 One of the top five public relations photographs in a contest conducted by the *Public Relations Journal.* The purpose was to get contributions to the "March of Dimes." Distributed by the wire services, it was widely used. In addition it was used in the publication of the National Foundation March of Dimes. John W. Blecha was the photographer.

Community action Community action can involve many different services. Here are some examples: a meat packer makes its facilities available to the state government for testing and experimentation; a food company gives secretarial training to poor girls and helps them find jobs.

The same food manufacturer brings professors from Black colleges to observe company operations.

A food manufacturer matches donations from $10 to $1,000 by its employees to any U.S. college or university. Summer jobs for youth, college scholarships, tuition assistance to employees, sponsorship of 4-H projects, support of church choirs, and building playgrounds are done by many organizations. Several food manufacturers contribute food to disaster areas whenever needed. A soup company joins with other firms to rehabilitate substandard houses and sells them to the poor with long-term, low-interest loans. Small firms give awards to high-school students, sponsor Little League baseball, lend equipment to schools, and so on.

A large retail chain builds roads, gardens, playgrounds, community centers, hospitals, churches, and fire departments. It provides college scholarships, aids Boy Scouts, Future Farmers, YMCA, and YWCAs. It grants funds to colleges and to youngsters in poverty areas. It aids city planning, health centers, and educational television. Similar activities are carried on by hundreds of other organizations. Many of these actions could, of course, be classed as enlightened self-interest, but they really go far beyond this. In one sense, they are an expression of gratitude to the community — a tangible "thank you" for favors received. The one common denominator in all these contributions is that they indicate an awareness of social responsibility.

Two-Way Communication

Communication to the community is easier than communication from the community. There is usually very little voluntary inbound communication. People do not often tell an organization what they think of it or what they think it should do. Nevertheless, they do have opinions which can be discovered.

Much can be learned by listening and by questioning in an informal manner; much more can be learned by organized research; still more can be learned through active involvement in the community.* No community relations program can succeed without a constant flow of facts and ideas from the community, and the responsibility for this inflow belongs to the organization — not to the community.

Outbound communication to the community is equally important. Good deeds will be known to those directly benefited by them but many

---

*Many corporations have named members of their boards of directors as a "public policy committee" to advise the board on public issues.

others may remain uninformed. All people in the community should know about those good deeds if the whole community is to have a good opinion of the organization. A continuing program to inform the community about the performance of the organization is, therefore, indispensable.

EXERCISES

1. Name an organization that has good relations with its community. Why are they good?
2. Name an organization that has bad relations with its community. Why are they bad?
3. How would you improve public opinion about the organization listed under Exercise 2?

Case Problem

The telephone company serving your state claims that earnings are inadequate to provide the equipment and service needed. It wants to increase its charges and has filed a rate application with the public utilities commission.

As public relations director, how would you support this? As leader of the opposition how would you oppose it?

Prepare a brief plan to attain your objective. Specify research to be done, publics to be reached, messages to each public, tools to be used, and methods of measuring accomplishment with each public.

The Educator
Public

14

Educators are especially important in public relations. First, they mold the minds of the younger generation. Second, they strongly influence government today. Third, many educators are also authors. As teachers, there is a tremendous capability for influencing the thinking of the upcoming generation. In government, educators are found in key positions everywhere. They advise mayors, governors, and even the President of the United States. They head major activities and, even when not officially in government, their opinions and comments from the sidelines often carry tremendous prestige. As authors, educators spread their ideas and influence far beyond their own classrooms.

In thinking of educators we must consider grammar school, high school, and college teachers. All of them have attitudes and opinions. Many teachers, especially in grammar schools and high schools, have had little opportunity to learn about the business world. Among college-level teachers, the background information may be very broad in some cases and very limited in others. Yet, every teacher may be asked questions by his students on almost any subject, and every teacher has numerous occasions to express his opinion.

It should be readily apparent that any public relations program should include a definite plan to communicate with educators and, through them, with their students. Considerable emphasis is added to this conclusion by the fact that business people and educators often have quite different viewpoints on many subjects.

Most public relations activity involving educators is conducted by business organizations. There are, however, some nonbusiness organizations which have problems with educators. The difficulties of the Department of Health, Education, and Welfare are largely centered on its regulations affecting the operations of schools and colleges. The De-

241

partment of Defense has problems which arise mainly from educator attitudes toward the armed forces. Other governmental agencies also have relations with the educator public, but their total involvement is much smaller than that of business organizations.

PROBLEM AREAS

Relations with the educator public are strongly influenced by educator attitudes and by the wide variation in educators' knowledge about economics and about the motivations of noneducational institutions.

Educator Attitudes

Educator attitudes, like those of other people, are derived from their own experience, education, and interests. When the Carnegie Commission on Higher Education surveyed 60,000 college faculty members, it found that teachers of engineering, business, agriculture, and physical education tended to class themselves as conservative. Teachers of sociology, anthropology, and philosophy generally identified themselves as liberal.

Most teachers place a very high value on academic freedom. They don't want anyone to tell them what to teach or how to teach. They will accept some forms of help but resist any taint of commercialism.

For example, teachers generally refuse to use materials which are strongly identified with brand names. Educators are critical of the nature of the materials supplied by business firms. A survey of teachers in Washington, California, and New York found that 47% felt that industry materials were not balanced and objective. Nearly three-fourths (73%) said that the materials presented the viewpoint of the industry. Almost all (98%) said the materials were antienvironmental. (See Public Relations Journal, June 1977.)

Educators resist outside dictation. At Brigham Young University, the Department of Health, Education and Welfare ruled that the student dress code was unfair. The faculty and administration vigorously challenged HEW.

A substantial number of teachers are opposed to any connection between education and the military. Recruiters for the armed forces have been hampered or blocked at some high schools and colleges while other recruiters have been welcomed. The R.O.T.C. has been opposed at many colleges and universities.

Economic Knowledge

Except for college instructors in economics, there are many teachers who don't have training or background which enable them to discuss economic problems. Yet, many of them express opinions or answer questions on the subject. Students who get their economic ideas from this source or from parents who are equally uninformed may have very unsound opinions on which to base economic decisions.

The problem is so acute that many organizations are making major efforts to inform both teachers and their students. Among them are the U.S. Chamber of Commerce, the National Association of Manufacturers, the National Federation of Independent Business, the Joint Council on Economic Education, and many corporations.

Motives of Business

The motivation of business organizations has been largely centered on profits. Teachers, like many others, are often badly informed about the size of profits that are made or the losses that can occur. Also, they are unaware of the function of profits — as a tax source, as a prerequisite for capital formation, as a certain means of determining whether a product or service is necessary and worth what it costs.

Many teachers feel that business is not socially responsible, that it does not pay adequate attention to the public interest, that it is cold, selfish and inhuman, that it cares little about the physical environment. Here, too, business organizations have a problem and an opportunity. Many companies and associations are meeting this challenge with intensive programs directed towards educators.

OBJECTIVES IN EDUCATOR RELATIONS

The objectives in this area can be stated briefly: to inform teachers; to help teachers; to inform their students and students' parents.

Informing Teachers

This is the first step in any program of educator relations. Continental Can Company provided a sixteen-week seminar for high school teachers in plant cities. The seminar was aided by Allied Chemical Co. Seminars covered details of business operations, relationships with the community, and social responsibility. Teachers were enthusiastic about the seminars, and many favorable comments were made about the absence of prop-aganda.

Helping Teachers

Pacific Lighting Corporation and its subsidiary, Southern California Gas Co., have an outstanding program. Selected executives spend a week on a college campus living with students, delivering lectures, attending classes, meeting with students and teachers. At the secondary level, a Youth Motivation Task Force of 200 company employees (mostly from minorities) go to ninth-grade classrooms in poor areas. These volunteers stress the value of education and the importance of finishing school.

Materials for classroom use are supplied by scores of business firms, including such giants as General Foods, General Mills, Pillsbury, Pet, Carnation, Ford, Chrysler, and General Motors. These materials include films, booklets, charts, models, and many other teaching aids.

General Electric had a problem in recruiting factory workers. There were many job openings but a shortage of qualified applicants. In one plant, it hired 4,100 people but could retain only 1,200. General Electric found that many starters couldn't add and subtract; others couldn't write legibly. To remedy this, General Electric provided courses for teachers and guidance counselors on what factory work is like. This aroused interest in factory jobs and motivated students to acquire the skills needed to get and hold a job.

Reaching Students

Programs for students are increasingly important. Many firms grant college scholarships. Pacific Lighting Corporation grants 54 four-year college scholarships to students classed as poor or minority. Special attention is given to those whose grades have suffered because of the need to work to support themselves or their families. Another PLC innovation is the Intercollegiate Advisory Council. Six students from different colleges are employed for eight weeks to observe the operations of the company and report their findings and opinions, which are published without censorship.

THE EDUCATOR RELATIONS PROGRAM

Improving relations with educators requires the same essentials as with every other public, but with some differences. A great emotional and intellectual gap does exist between educators and non-educators.

Attitude

If any organization is to have good relations with educators, it must be willing to try to improve the opinions of educators. It must recognize the importance of teachers and be determined to make a real effort. There must be an acceptance of educators as intelligent human beings who can and will understand an honest and factual message. Educators have a favorite word to denote intelligent conversation. That word is "dialogue." It implies equality of both parties, which is exactly what the attitude should be.

Policy

Once it is decided that there will be a program of relations with educators, it becomes necessary to determine the specifics and to put them in writing. The possibilities are multitudinous and can involve far-reaching commitments and large appropriations, but these activities can be most helpful in bridging the gap between the business world and the academic world.

A very good example of a policy dealing with the educational world is that of Standard Oil Company of California:

> Standard Oil Company of California and the Chevron companies have a long-standing and very complete Aid to Education program that extends from elementary schools through the graduate level of our universities. We consider the support of these educational institutions to be extremely important as it contributes to the growth and progress of our communities and to the freedom and security of our country. We have recognized this need for many years and have willingly assumed a part in providing for it.

> We consider the well-being of our educational system of particular significance today as it strives to enlarge and expand facilities and courses of study. These enlargements and expansions will give our youth access to better training and information and help them be better prepared to meet their responsibilities as tomorrow's leaders.

> In this way we believe corporate financial aid to education can be a very significant investment in our country's future. In line with this assistance, we offer a broad program of scholarships, fellowships, grants, services, and materials. These are offered through programs that are reviewed each year and updated to meet the changing conditions in our educational system.

> J.R. GREY, President
> Standard Oil Company of California

245

Action

The most effective means of affecting educators' opinions are those that render active assistance to the educational process. Helping the teacher to teach not only educates the teacher, it also educates the students. The list of possibilities is almost unlimited. Here are some of the more common: providing trained personnel for forums, career counseling, special exhibits, business-education days, school visitations, open houses, plant tours, use of research facilities, hiring teachers for special projects, fellowships, scholarships, grants-in-aid, lending or giving equipment, awards, study projects, cars for driver education, meaningful part-time work for students (especially summer jobs), and work-study programs.

Plymouth stimulated interest in vocational education with automobile "trouble-shooting" contests for high-school boys. Johnson and Johnson taught first aid to sixth-grade students. It developed a program manual accompanied by a complete teachers' guide, a set of progress tests, and a color filmstrip.*

Two-Way Communication

Communicating with educators is both easier and harder than communication with other publics. Easier, because teachers are usually communicators; they read, write, talk, and listen more than nonteachers. Harder, because teachers are often suspicious of the motives of business. A teacher who considers himself an impartial public servant has little in common with the businessman who is trying to make money by dealing with the public. With such a large gap between the two groups, a major effort is needed, and the organization must make it. It must seek out questions and problems. It must assume responsibility for both inbound and outbound communication.

EXERCISES

Many college instructors use guest lecturers from business organizations.

1. Have you ever heard such a speaker?

*For those who wish to design materials for use in classrooms, it is suggested that a careful study be made of a booklet entitled: *Choosing Free Materials* published by The American Association of School Administrators, 1201 Sixteenth St. N.W., Washington, D.C.

Fig. 14.1   Educator "helps" supplied by Standard Oil Company of California

2. Was the speaker and organization utilizing good public relations?
3. Contact a nearby business firm and find out if they have speakers available for your college. Also find out who is available, what subjects can be covered, how the speakers' bureau (if any) is organized.

Case Problem

You are public relations counselor to the State Chamber of Commerce. The board of directors has decided to conduct a program designed to improve relations between the business community and the State University — including both faculty and students. They have asked you to prepare a plan.

What research would you recommend in order to define the problem, its nature, its extent, and its location?

What messages would you convey to students and to faculty? Would you treat all students and all faculty in the same way, or would you break them up into specialized groups?

What communication channels would you use?

The Government Public

Government at all levels is increasing in size and cost. It is also increasing in power and in its day-to-day participation in, or interference with, the lives and activities of the entire population. For all practical purposes, government controls or limits almost everything we do. As a consequence, no public relations program is complete unless it includes provisions for dealing with government. Government, as far as public relations is concerned, includes both the legislative and executive branches. The judicial branch is, presumably, a neutral and fair arbiter between the public and the other two branches of government.

A few years ago most problems in this area were largely confined to nongovernmental organizations but the enormous expansion of government at all levels has created a situation wherein government agencies must view other agencies as publics affecting their operations. State laws conflict with federal laws. States and cities send lobbyists to Washington. In the arid western states, federal and state laws on irrigation differ and create conflicts.

In order to limit the length of this chapter, most of what is said will concern the problems of nongovernmental agencies. The principles can be applied by governmental agencies dealing with other governmental agencies as well.

THE BURDEN OF GOVERNMENT

Government has become so burdensome and so costly that people in all parts of society are demanding a halt to the ever-increasing interference of government with their lives.

Controls

Individual citizens have rebelled against the Food and Drug Administration's restrictions on Saccharin and Laetrile, against air bags in cars, against laws requiring motorcyclists to wear helmets, against mass innoculation against diseases. They have successfully blocked the federally required interlock between seat belts and automobile ignition systems.

Business leaders have not been silent. Reginald H. Jones, Chairman of General Electric, said that the power of decision making is moving from the boardroom to federal agencies. Professor Irving Kristol of New York University says that the regulatory agencies are unfriendly to business and that they want to substitute their decisions for those of the marketplace. Cornell C. Maier, President and chief executive officer of Kaiser Aluminum & Chemical Co., says that the regulatory agencies have become a fourth branch of government.

The situation is not confined to the United States. The Conference Board (a research organization) surveyed business leaders in 33 countries and found a consensus that government controls were stifling investments, creating chaotic business conditions, adding to inflation, and injuring the individuals they were trying to help.

Costs

The federal budget in 1933 was $3.3 billion. Now it is about $500 billion. In fewer than 50 years, the cost of government has multiplied about 16 times at the federal level alone. New York and California have budgets in the $15 billion range and many states are in the billion-dollar class. The figures are so large that they are hard to grasp, but taken in smaller pieces, they are more comprehensible.

The *Wall Street Journal* reported that a statistician employed by Chevron U.S.A. has calculated that the $10.6 billion first year budget of the new federal Department of Energy was equal to $3 a barrel on all U.S. crude oil production and twice the cost of all our oil imports from Saudi Arabia, our largest foreign supplier. The budget exceeded the annual capital and exploration costs of the entire petroleum industry. It was $800 million more than the entire 1974 profits of the seven largest oil companies — in the year when critics described the profits as "obscene."

Paperwork

The regulations of the Occupational Safety and Health Administration

fill a bookshelf 17 feet long. The Federal Paperwork Commission estimates that the cost of filling out government required reports is $32
billion a year. The 10,000 largest companies average $1 million spent on
reports per year. The five million small businesses average a cost of
$4,000 per year, and each of the proprietors has to spend a day and a half
a week on government paperwork.

Thirteen thousand small firms have abandoned their pension plans
covering 400,000 workers because of additional costs and paperwork
required by the Employees Retirement Income Security Act.

Compliance

It has become nearly impossible to comply with all of the laws and
regulations. There are so many that it is very difficult to know of their
existence. In 1970, the Federal Register (in which all new laws, rules, and
regulations must be published) contained 20,000 pages. In 1977, there
were more than 70,000 pages. One 100-word section of the Internal
Revenue Code includes 16 cross references to other sections of the code,
and these also have cross-references.

Since these laws and regulations are usually drafted by lawyers, they
are generally clear only to lawyers. They are frequently in direct conflict
with one another. Federal laws require employers to report certain information about their employees, but in some cases, state laws forbid
employers to get this information. Sometimes the regulations are simply
ridiculous. A real estate broker was fined by OSHA because he did not
have a separate toilet for his female employee — his wife.

Dealing with Government

Every organization must be prepared for governmental action which
may affect its operations.

General Foods says this about governmental relations:

General Foods will exercise its citizenship responsibilities with government at all levels: By
encouraging active, knowledgeable participation by individual employees and the corporation; by helping government officials to draft sound legislation and regulations designed
to serve the public interest and improve the business climate; and by supporting policies
which encourage sound economic growth.

General Foods will operate within the spirit as well as the letter of the law.

We will vigorously protect the company's good name and take positive steps to defend
and strengthen it through sound programs of public information.

251

OBJECTIVES IN GOVERNMENT RELATIONS

The objectives in government relations are to secure favorable laws, regulations, and interpretations thereof and, conversely, to prevent unfavorable laws, regulations, and interpretations.

Laws are the province of legislative bodies although they may be proposed by the executive arm of government. Regulations and interpretations are generally controlled by the executive departments. It will be seen therefore that an organization must deal with both branches of government if its interests are to be protected.

Securing favorable actions and preventing unfavorable actions are accomplished in the same way — by focusing all efforts on a specific goal: "To persuade Congress to pass HR-1897." "To persuade the Colorado Legislature not to pass S-186." "To convince the Food & Drug Administration that Product X-37 is safe for human consumption." "To convince the City Council that Main Street should be repaired." In nearly every case, the problem is to convince members of legislative or executive bodies that some specific action should or should not be taken.

Attaining these objectives may require any, or all, of the following activities: Lobbying, nonlobbying communications, public support, political action, and ballot initiatives. (See "Public Policy Communication," *Public Relations Journal*, July 1977.)

Legal Restrictions

The first amendment of the Constitution says that Congress shall pass no law abridging the right of the people to petition for a redress of grievances. This would seem to sanction activity designed to influence the decisions of Congress — and the decisions of agencies created by Congress. But Congress has passed a law requiring that all lobbyists register with the Department of Justice.

Additional laws which would seriously restrict lobbying may be passed. The definition of lobbying may be expanded to cover almost any activity which may tend to influence government. There are proposals which would require rigid accounting for even the smallest expenditure. Some proposals would require most public relations practitioners to register as lobbyists. Even a press release might be classed as lobbying.

Public utility commissions have ruled that public relations activity is not a legitimate cost of doing business. Advertising designed to promote sales has generally been considered a business expense, but public relations advertising has been restricted.

Many states have laws restricting lobbying. As one example — Salt Lake City papers reported that IBM had hundreds of lobbyists in Utah. The facts were that, under provisions of a new state law, every IBM salesman had to register as a lobbyist because he might at some time talk about, or try to sell, office equipment or computer services to some state agency.

LOBBYING

Lobbying is normally defined as attempting to influence legislation but, for all practical purposes, it also includes attempting to influence the interpretation and administration of laws and regulations. Therefore we shall treat it as aimed at both legislators and executors (or administrators).

The Ethics of Lobbying

To many people, any effort to influence legislation or administration of laws is evil. In their eyes, "lobbying" is a nefarious practice. Yet, there really is nothing wrong in trying to secure favorable laws and regulations or to prevent unfavorable ones.

Any other conclusion would require that all legislators and executive department employees be absolutely fair and completely informed about all subjects on which they pass judgment. With all the actual and potential laws we have, it should be obvious that many of these lawmakers and law enforcers must get help from people who are familiar with the subjects on which action is to be taken.

A congressman from Kansas cannot be expected to know much about the lumber industry. An assemblyman from Manhattan may be completely ignorant about the dairy industry. A councilman whose experience has been in law may not understand the automobile business. Yet, each of these people may be voting on laws or ordinances that affect those businesses. The same situation exists in the executive departments — people make decisions without enough information.

The Nature of Lobbying

Lobbying has two functions — informing and persuading. It is the persuasion that arouses most opposition; yet, it is difficult indeed to tell

253

where informing stops and persuasion begins. Cold facts can be highly persuasive. They can be even more effective when presented in a dramatic manner, even though not a word of persuasion is used.

Lobbying is done by individuals, business firms, labor unions, government agencies, and associations. There is lobbying for railroads, motor trucking, airlines, insurance, orange growers, brewers, automobile workers, schoolteachers, liquor dealers, undertakers, and so on ad infinitum.

Lobbying can be continuous or spasmodic. If there is a onetime, short-term goal, the effort can be brief and the work stopped when the project succeeds or fails. Thus, people lobbying for a law on drunken driving stop all their activity when the law is passed, but transportation associations maintain a continuing program because their task is never done.

Lobbying can be at work on both sides of an issue at the same time. The railroads may be opposed by the motor carriers, the meat packers by the cattlemen, the East Siders by the West Siders, the apartment builders by the owners of single-family homes. In fact, opposition is much more common than one-sided action.

What Lobbyists Do

Lobbyists are often visualized as furtive individuals using all kinds of pressure to reach their goals. In the great majority of cases, the lobbyist is an honest and sincere person whose main work is communication. He gives information to governmental agencies and to his principals. A typical lobbyist may do any or all of the following:

1. Inform his sponsor or principal about major developments in legislative and executive departments, such as a new committee chairman or a new interpretation of regulations.
2. Report the introduction and progress of bills that might affect the sponsor.
3. Arrange for the appearance of witnesses at legislative or executive hearings and investigations.
4. File statements with committees or departments.
5. Communicate with legislators or executive personnel either in person or by phone.
6. Analyze proposed laws or regulations.
7. Inform the legislators and the public about possible effects of laws or regulations.

8. Provide facts about his sponsor's (firm or association) business.
9. Assist in formulating his sponsor's policy regarding legislation or regulation.
10. Educate legislators and executive department personnel about the economics of the business or industry he represents.
11. Inform legislators and executive department people about the way in which his business or industry operates.
12. Help legislators draft laws.
13. Help executive department officials draft regulations.
14. Publicize testimony given at hearings on proposed laws and regulations.
15. Actively support or oppose laws by enlisting the help of the lawmakers and by planning with them the legislative strategy needed.
16. Mobilize opposition to harmful laws or regulations.
17. Persuade legislators to introduce and support laws helpful to his sponsor.
18. Persuade legislators to oppose laws harmful to his sponsor.
19. Persuade executive department personnel to prepare favorable regulations or to revise unfavorable regulations.

NON-LOBBYING COMMUNICATIONS

Governmental agencies, both legislative and executive, can be influenced by means other than lobbying. Information can be given to elected or appointed officials with the objective of improving their knowledge. With many organizations, there may be no governmental problems for long periods, yet there is always the possibility that a problem may arise. When this occurs, it will be much simpler if the legislative or executive personnel involved have solid information available. Accordingly, it is good insurance to maintain a flow of information to those most likely to be influential. Members of committees likely to handle legislation involving the organization and appointed officials charged with administering laws affecting the organization are obvious targets for such information.

Even this type of communication has come under fire. In fact, until there is a crystallization of laws and regulations, any activity which might conceivably influence voters, lawmakers, or administrators should be carefully checked against existing laws and regulations. What is legal today may be illegal tomorrow.

PUBLIC SUPPORT

Lobbying must be backed by voter support. While lobbying makes the personal contacts and nonlobbying communications deliver information, these are only the points of the arrows. Opinions and facts presented by interested parties will be effective only if the government agencies know that many voters support the cause represented. This requires that voters express their opinions — by mail, by telephone, by telegram, by personal contact.

Newspaper ads are often used to express opinions on some issue and urge the readers to write to their representatives. There are also frequent letters sent to individuals calling for similar action. If the letter to the representative is temperate and personal, it can be very effective, but if the voter merely signs a preprinted coupon or card it will be a wasted effort. Every politician knows the difference between a contrived message and a personal expression of opinion.

To get persuasive public support requires education of the voters on the issue involved. This necessitates research on the policy in question and distribution of the facts to the voters. People will respond if they know how a law or regulation will affect them. They seldom respond to abstract ideas.

The federal Common Situs picketing bill provided that if workers for one contractor went on strike at a construction project, they could picket all other contractors at the site and thus stop all work. Organized labor backed the bill with all its power. The bill was opposed by many organizations. Their lobbyists were supported by hundreds of thousands of letters sent to members of Congress. The letters came from voters throughout the country who were convinced that the bill was harmful to their interests and to the country. The bill was defeated.

POLITICAL ACTION

Political action committees are standard features in labor unions. They are still rarities in other organizations. Contributions by individuals to candidates and work by individuals for candidates are the functions of such committees. To make a PAC work, the sponsoring organization must take a firm position and make its position known. The reason for the position must be explained in terms of the self-interest of the voters whose support is sought.

INITIATIVES

In many states, it is possible to bypass or overrule the legislature through the initiative process. Using this process effectively is very difficult without retention of a political specialist. The specialist is, or should be, completely familiar with all the machinery of such operations. The specialist defines the problem, determines strategy and tactics, selects the key workers such as fundraisers, speakers bureau heads, and media directors. He or she directs the day-to-day activities of all campaign workers.

One essential item often overlooked in such campaigns is intelligence — the gathering and distribution of information to be used by the workers. This includes careful attention to what the opposition is saying and the refutation of inaccuracies.

In a heated California initiative campaign, one side made repeated false statements about the source of money being spent by the other side. The facts were not received until the Friday before election day. They completely disproved the opposition statements, but they were almost too late to be used — over the weekend, all media were operating with skeleton staffs and regular programming was already filled.

THE ROLE OF THE PR PRACTITIONER

Many public relations practitioners operate entirely in the field of politics and a number of counseling firms have special divisions to handle political problems. This phase is highly specialized, and the Public Relations Society of America has established as a guide the following interpretation of its Code of Professional Standards:

AN OFFICIAL INTERPRETATION OF THE PRSA CODE OF PROFESSIONAL STANDARDS AS IT APPLIES TO POLITICAL PUBLIC RELATIONS

PREAMBLE

In the practice of political public relations, a PRSA member must have professional capabilities to offer an employer or client quite apart from any political relationships of value, and members may serve their employer or client without necessarily having attributed to them the character, reputation or beliefs of those they serve. It is understood that members may choose to serve only those interests with whose political philosophy they are personally comfortable.

DEFINITION

"Political Public Relations" is defined as those areas of public relations which relate to:

257

a. the counseling of political organizations, committees, candidates or potential candidates for public office; and groups constituted for the purpose of influencing the vote on any ballot issue;

b. the counseling of holders of public office;

c. the management, or direction, of a political campaign for or against a candidate for political office; or for or against a ballot issue to be determined by voter approval or rejection;

d. the practice of public relations on behalf of a client or an employer in connection with that client's or employer's relationships with any candidates or holders of public office with the purpose of influencing legislation or government regulation or treatment of a client or employer, regardless of whether the PRSA member is a recognized lobbyist;

e. the counseling of government bodies, or segments thereof, either domestic or foreign.

PRECEPTS

1. It is the responsibility of PRSA members practicing political public relations, as defined above, to be conversant with the various statutes, local, state, and federal, governing such activities and to adhere to them strictly. This includes, but is not limited to, the various local, state and federal laws, court decisions and official interpretations governing lobbying, political contributions, disclosure, elections, libel, slander and the like. In carrying out this responsibility, members shall seek appropriate counseling whenever necessary.

2. It is also the responsibility of members to abide by PRSA's Code of Professional Standards.

3. Members shall represent clients or employers in good faith, and while partisan advocacy on behalf of a candidate or public issue may be expected, members shall act in accord with the public interest and adhere to truth and accuracy and to generally accepted standards of good taste.

4. Members shall not issue descriptive material or any advertising or publicity information or participate in the preparation or use thereof which is not signed by responsible persons or is false, misleading or unlabeled as to its source, and are obligated to use care to avoid dissemination of any such material.

5. Members have an obligation to clients to disclose what remuneration beyond their fees they expect to receive as a result of their relationship, such as commissions for media advertising, printing and the like, and should not accept such extra payment without their clients' consent.

6. Members shall not improperly use their positions to encourage additional future employment or compensation. It is understood that successful campaign directors or managers, because of the performance of their duties and the working relationship that develops, may well continue to assist and counsel, for pay, the successful candidate.

7. Members shall voluntarily disclose to employers or clients the identity of other employers or clients with whom they are currently associated and whose interests might be affected favorably or unfavorably by their political representation.

8. Members shall respect the confidentiality of information pertaining to employers or clients even after the relationships cease, avoiding future associations wherein insider information is sought that would give a desired

advantage over a member's previous clients.

9. In avoiding practices which might tend to corrupt the processes of government, members shall not make undisclosed gifts of cash or other valuable considerations which are designed to influence specific decisions of voters, legislators or public officials on public matters. A business lunch or dinner, or other comparable expenditure made in the course of communicating a point of view or public position, would not constitute such a violation. Nor, for example, would a plant visit designed and financed to provide useful background information to an interested legislator or candidate.

10. Nothing herein should be construed as prohibiting members from making legal, properly disclosed contributions to the candidates, party or referenda issues of their choice.

11. Members shall not, through the use of information known to be false or misleading, conveyed directly or through a third party, intentionally injure the public reputation of an opposing interest.

EXERCISES

1. Draft a letter to your congressman asking for a "yes" vote on some bill now before Congress.
2. Draft a letter to your state senator asking for a "no" vote on a bill before the legislature.

Case Problem

You are public relations director of an association of western farmers. In your state all crops require irrigation (there is no summer rain). There is a federal law that prevents farms exceeding 160 acres from getting water from federal irrigation projects — but 160 acres is too small for efficient operation. How would you get this law repealed?

Who could help you?

Who would be opposed?

Where would you get facts needed to prove your case?

What message would you convey?

Who would you try to reach?

How would you reach them?

The Supplier Public

It would be difficult to find an organization that does not have suppliers. Even the smallest office or plant buys supplies produced by someone else. Whether the buyer is a one-man office, a local school board, or a nation-wide manufacturer, the supplier is important to the buyer and good relations with suppliers can contribute to the success of the buyer.

The buyer wants quality at a fair price. He wants certain and timely delivery of his purchases. He also wants to receive exactly what he ordered, and often he wants something which requires an extra effort on the part of the supplier. Getting all these things will be much easier if the buyer has a definite program for cultivating good relations with suppliers.

Small organizations may have only a few suppliers but, as their size increases, so does the supplier list. General Motors, U.S. Steel, General Foods, and other large firms may number their suppliers in the thousands.

Regardless of the number of suppliers involved, it is good business to maintain good relations with all of them. Before attempting to state the essentials of good supplier relations, it might be in order to discuss some of the things that make for bad supplier relations.

BUYER PRACTICES

Suppliers find numerous buyer practices to be unfair, unreasonable, inequitable, or just plain dishonest. Among the most common are buyer attitudes, shakedowns, freeloading, lying about competitive prices, attempts to beat down prices, demands for special deals, making unreasonable claims, boycotting, and blacklisting.

Buyer Attitudes

Some buyers treat salesmen in a manner that would earn them a punch in the nose from anyone else. Rude and inconsiderate treatment, broken appointments, endless waiting, failure to provide even the most rudimentary facilities for those who are waiting, and an attitude of contempt and enmity are all too common. When a supplier gets this kind of treatment, he may suppress his rage, but he will not be able to suppress his poor opinion of the buyer and the organization.

Shakedowns

"Under the counter" is a phrase too well known to be ignored. There are, indeed, a number of buyers who make a very substantial concealed income by demanding — and getting — bribes from suppliers. Suppliers hate shakedowns, but unfortunately some of them will pay the price in order to get the business. No reputable organization will participate in a shakedown or tolerate such an action by an employee.

Freeloading

Slightly less vicious than the shakedown buyer is the freeloader, who is always asking for personal favors, substantial gifts, and lavish entertainment. These buyers do not ask for money; they ask for complimentary tickets to major athletic and theatrical events; they hint at invitations to expensive restaurants; they suggest lavish Christmas gifts or fantasize about an expensive item so that the seller will provide it.

Lying about Competitive Prices

In an effort to get a reduced price quotation, some buyers will deliberately lie about a supposed lower price quotation from a competitor. Whether or not the seller believes the lie, he will definitely resent this attempt to deceive him.

Attempts to Beat Down Prices

Some buyers assume that their sole function is to beat down the prices quoted by sellers. Quality, service, delivery, terms, published price lists, and all other considerations are ignored while the buyer applies every pressure possible to get a lower price. Sellers expect to be competitive and they expect buyers to seek the lowest reasonable price, but they do not like cut-throat buying practices.

Demands for Special Deals

The special deal can cover such things as delayed billing, bonus merchandise, billing for one quality but delivery of a higher quality, LCL delivery at carload prices, and a host of other extras that give the recipient more than he pays for. All these expenses come out of the seller's pocket and thus reduce the profitability of his business. Unprofitable accounts are of no value to the seller, and the buyer who bargains for too much is taking the first step toward losing his supplier.

Making Unreasonable Claims

One of the more obnoxious forms of chiseling is the unreasonable or falsified claim. These can include claims that delivery was not on time, that the quantity was not complete, that the quality was not as specified, that the items received were not as ordered, etc. All of these things can happen inadvertently and, if they do, the supplier expects to make compensation. But sometimes the claims are false; it can mean the end of the relationship between the chiseler and his victim.

Boycotting and Blacklisting

Occasionally a buyer or several buyers may boycott a supplier or place his name on a blacklist and collectively refuse to buy from him. This is a rather rare practice but it does happen. The supplier who gets this treatment can easily go bankrupt. Entirely apart from any question of legality, practices of this sort usually result in an explosion of unfavorable publicity. It should never be forgotten that there are laws forbidding them.

SUPPLIER PRACTICES

Buyers too, can find things they dislike about the practices of their adversaries. To them, some of these actions seem just as unreasonable, unfair, inequitable, or dishonest as the buyer practices that suppliers deplore. These include such things as misrepresentation, full-line forcing, arbitrary terms, delivery problems, discriminatory pricing, and exclusive dealing.

Misrepresentation

Deceptive selling can cover numerous items. Particularly irritating are misrepresentations of quality or quantity. A seller will offer nylon but deliver orlon; another will fail to tell the buyer that the reason his product is cheaper is because it is packed 18 to the case instead of the competitor's 24. Both are guilty of deceit that can have only one result — eventual loss of an account. Other misrepresentations that annoy or infuriate buyers are those dealing with origin of the merchandise and identity of the vendor. The buyer expects to be told the truth, and he will not tolerate deception very long.

Full-Line Forcing

The buyer who wants one item does not like to be forced to buy others he does not want or need, yet some suppliers sell their products on an "all-or-nothing" basis. The practice appears in many different kinds of business. It may have advantages for the seller, but many buyers are solidly opposed to it and will, whenever possible, do their buying elsewhere.

Arbitrary Terms

The use of unusual and arbitrary terms, discounts that vary from the normal customs of the industry, delivery practices that inconvenience the buyer, and credit operations that ignore his needs are all sources of dissatisfaction and complaint. The unhappiness usually occurs when the seller deviates materially from the manner of doing business common to the industry.

Delivery Problems

One of the greatest sources of friction between buyer and seller is the problem of delivery. The buyer wants his order delivered at the promised time, at the right place, and in the form and manner that was ordered. If the seller defaults on any of these terms, the buyer will be justifiably furious.

Discriminatory Pricing

In spite of numerous laws, such as the Robinson-Patman Act forbidding unfair pricing, there are recurring complaints in all lines of business that certain suppliers give better prices to some customers than to others. Legally, about the only justifiable reason for varying prices on the same merchandise is that it costs less to sell and deliver large orders than smaller ones. But many buyers challenge prices based on volume — if they are in the smaller-volume, higher-unit price category.

Exclusive Dealing

This is a typical problem in retailing. The buyer who has a good line wants to be the sole source in his area. His competitor, who sees the profitability of the line, quite naturally wants to be able to sell it as well. The outsider complains if he can not get in — and the insider complains if he loses his exclusivity. There is no universally acceptable solution, and so it is a continuing source of difficulty.

OBJECTIVES IN SUPPLIER RELATIONS

The purpose of a supplier relations program is primarily to assure the purchaser of completely dependable sources of supply at reasonable cost. Beyond this minimum requirement, there are other things which can benefit the buyer who has established good relations with suppliers.

The preferred customer usually gets first chance at new or improved items. He gets the first deliveries if there is a shortage. He gets extra consideration if he has trouble. All of these and many other pluses accrue to the buyer who is important to the supplier and who, by his treatment of the supplier, merits special consideration.

In view of the preceding observations, it can be said that a supplier relations program should convince suppliers that the buyer treats them equitably, that he is fair, reasonable, honest, that the relationship is stable, and that there is a mutual interest between buyer and seller.

Equitable Treatment

Essentially, this means that all suppliers are treated alike, that they compete in an orderly manner under rules that are known to all and fair to all. This is not to say that every possible supplier must be considered. (For example, there are seven pages of printers listed in the Yellow Pages of the San Francisco telephone book.) Nor is it to say that limiting purchases to a few or even to one supplier, in spite of the fact that others could fill the bill, is wrong. Both these problems are matters of policy; but, regardless of the nature of the policy, it should be clear and known to suppliers and would-be suppliers.

Fairness

Fair treatment of suppliers can easily be defined in terms of the Golden Rule. It requires courtesy and consideration in dealing with them. It eliminates shakedowns and free-loading. It necessitates recognition of the supplier as a legitimate business enterprise entitled to a reasonable profit. Respect for the suppliers' rules and procedures is also essential. Perhaps most important of all, the supplier is entitled to treatment as a truthful and ethical organization.

Reasonableness

Any buyer may have special needs or unique specifications peculiar to his own situation. It is reasonable to ask a supplier to fill these unusual needs, but it is not reasonable to demand special treatment which the supplier can not provide to other customers in the same situation. Nor is it reasonable to manufacture excuses for delayed payment or nonpayment or to make false claims of shortage or deficient quality. Suppliers do sometimes make errors and they do occasionally fail to deliver the order that was specified, but the buyer's reaction should be based on the assumption that the error was accidental and not deliberate.

Honesty

This goes a step beyond merely answering questions truthfully. It includes telling the loser why he did not get the order, as well as telling the winner why he did. It implies a willingness to tell a seller what the problem is rather than merely telling him what is wanted; there are many times when a buyer specifies a certain item not knowing that there is a better one available.

Stability

A continuing relationship between buyer and seller brings great benefits to both. If a seller has hopes of making another sale, he will be much more attentive to the order in hand. He will make a much greater effort to assure satisfaction, and he will keep on doing his best to please a regular customer. On the other hand, if there is no likelihood of developing a permanent relationship, the seller will have much less reason for the extra effort. Assuring suppliers that there is stability in the situation is a sure way to build good relations with them.

Mutual Interest

In many buyer-seller situations, there is, unfortunately, an attitude of antagonism. The two parties think of themselves as adversaries with each trying to gain the greatest advantage from the conflict. Each party should recognize its dependence on the other and, while protecting its own interests, make a definite effort to give the other party a profitable deal.

BUILDING GOOD SUPPLIER RELATIONS

A supplier relations program needs the four essentials found in every public relations program: attitude, policy, action, and two-way communications.

Attitude

Management must be convinced that it pays to have good relations with suppliers. It must know what has to be done to develop and maintain good relations and it must be sold on the advantages to be gained. Also, management must be willing to stick to its guns because building good relations with suppliers takes time and its benefits are not immediately apparent.

Policy

There should be a definite written policy in order to prevent misunderstandings. It may be brief and general or long and detailed. Some even go so far as to forbid buyers to accept a cigarette from a salesman. General Foods expresses its policy in this way:

> General Foods will deal firmly with suppliers of goods and services, but not seek unfair advantage. The company will remain open-minded to new sources of supply and alert to new ideas.

Action

The buyer organization must, by its actions, prove its appreciation of good supplier relations. It must practice what it preaches. Suppliers must be treated with courtesy and consideration. They should be given all reasonable aid, whether it be a place for salesmen to hang their coats or a complete explanation of why a certain requirement is specified.

Two-Way Communication

A very large part of the communication between buyer and seller is at the personal level. In larger organizations, the point of contact is usually

Salesmen are an integral part of the California Canners and Growers Purchasing organization. We welcome creative and profit-producing presentations. It is our desire to work with and select suppliers who will help us to continue to grow and prosper.

PURCHASING OBJECTIVE

The objective of the Purchasing Department of California Canners and Growers is to select suppliers who will furnish materials, supplies, services, equipment and facilities which will increase our efficiency and help us to insure maximum long-range profits.

SALESMEN INTERVIEWING SCHEDULE

To conserve your time and the time of the Purchasing personnel we encourage appointments. All possible efforts will be made to interview salesmen promptly and courteously. Understandably, salesmen who have made appointments will receive priority.

Fig. 16.1 Cover and an inside page of a leaflet handed to supplier salesmen who call on California Canners & Growers — a large cooperative cannery.

between the purchasing agent and the salesman. But, even in the smallest unit, someone has to do the buying and thus becomes responsible for the communication function. Essentially, the problem is to stimulate an interchange of thought in order to learn the problems of the suppliers and inform them of the buyer's needs and policy.

EXERCISES

1. Have you ever tried to sell anything to a purchasing agent? Were you treated courteously and fairly?
2. Draft a brief policy (50-100 words) to be followed by the purchasing agent of a manufacturer who buys from suppliers in several different fields.
3. What kinds of raw materials, equipment, and supplies would a canner of fruits and vegetables buy? Why are good supplier relations important in that business?

Case Problem

You are public relations director of a large, full-line canner. Your company has been losing money on canned fruits for several years. Your costs are increasing but you have been unable to increase your selling prices because of oversupply in the market. Management has decided that it must reduce production to a level that can be sold profitably. This will mean buying fewer fruits and vegetables from the growers. The growers have been selling at the same price for several years. Their costs have increased.

How would you solve this problem?
What publics would be involved?
What message would you convey to each?

17
The Dealer Public

In the broadest sense, a dealer is anyone who sells things but, in this chapter, we will use the word to describe a seller who handles the products of one manufacturer or principal only. Thus, Macy's would not be considered a dealer, but a Dodge automobile agency or a Gulf service station would. To take the category a step further, we will include under this heading distributors (as of appliances), selling agents, and franchise retailers such as Kentucky Fried Chicken.

Thus, in the eyes of the public, a dealer is not Joe Smith but Dodge, not Henry Brown but Kentucky Fried Chicken. The dealer is, therefore, especially important to the principal whom he represents. First, because he is the custodian of the company's name and reputation, and second, because he is the key to sales success in his territory.

Much of this chapter also applies to brokers. Brokers generally represent only one principal in any general product group so they too have an "exclusive" relationship with the firms they represent.

The best product will fail if it is not supported by a strong and enthusiastic dealer organization. Every dealer is important and good relations with dealers are developed and maintained only if there is a solid dealer relations program. Planning for good dealer relations should start with a look at things that cause bad dealer relations.

DEALER PROBLEMS

There is often friction between suppliers and dealers. The following list covers some of the most common problems: nature of dealer or franchise agreement, pricing policies, inadequate help from principal, direct sales, over-loading, short-ordering, unrealistic quotas, too many dealers, arbitrary termination of contracts, forced payment on guarantees, forced advertising payments, and forced purchase of supplies.

INDEX

	Paragraph
ACCESSORIES	
Price Reductions, Factory Installed	7(a) (d)
Lower Price on Model Change, Factory Installed	7(b) (d)
Dealer's Stocks	2(h)
Reacquisition by Company, upon Termination	21(a) (b)
ACCOUNTING AND RECORDS, DEALER	
Manual of Accounting Procedure	2(f) (g)
Inspections by Company Representatives	2(n)
ACKNOWLEDGMENTS	25
ADVERTISING AND SALES PROMOTION	
Trade Practices and Advertising	2(m)
Genuine Parts	2(h), 15
Advertising and Promotion Funds	16
Advertising Discontinued upon Termination	19(b)
AGENTS OF COMPANY	
Authorized Agents	D, E
Dealer Not Agent	13
APPLICATIONS AND CLAIMS, DEALER	
Loss or Damage during Shipment	6(c)
Price Reductions, Refunds and Credits	7(c)
Dealer's Premises upon Termination	22(c)
Maintenance of Records on	2(n)
AMENDMENTS	
Authorized Officers	E
Power to Make	33
APPOINTMENTS	
Of Dealer	A
Of Additional Dealers	3
Company May Refuse	18
ASSIGNMENT	27
AUTHORIZED MERCURY DEALER	
Authorization of Dealer	A
Dealer Not Agent of Company	13
Ceases upon Termination	19
Effects of Termination on Actions, Use of Trade-Marks, Forms, etc.	19(b)
Appointing Additional Dealers	3
Company may Refuse to Appoint Purchaser as	18
COLLECTION CHARGES	6(a)
COMPANY PRODUCTS	
Definition of	1(a)
Changes in	9
Warranty by Company	10(a)
Warranty by Dealer	10(b)
Pre-delivery Inspection	12
Sales and Service Responsibility of Dealer	2(a)
Dealer's Orders	2(i)
Genuine Parts	2(h), 15
Limitation of Company's Liability	30
Reports Concerning	2(g)
Assignment of Retail Orders	19(c)
CUSTOMER RELATIONS	
Service Policy	11
Pre-delivery Inspection	12
Dealer's Sales and Service Responsibility to Customers	2(a)
Customer Deposits	2(l), 19(c)
Customer Handling, Complaints, etc.	2(k)
Trade Practices and Advertising	2(m)

Fig. 17.1 Part of the index to the "Mercury" dealer sales agreement. It shows the detail involved in relationships with dealers.

Nature of Agreement

Both dealers and franchise operators register many complaints about the agreements or contracts governing their relationships with principals. Generally, the complaints are that there is little flexibility and a great many specific requirements and limitations. Agreements that specify the exact location of the dealership, that restrict moving or selling the dealership, and that require approval of the participants in the dealership can cause friction. Most complaints in this area arise from a lack of understanding of the reason behind these requirements.

Pricing Policies

Every salesman would like to have a free hand in pricing what he sells. Many of them would soon learn that price alone is not a long-term solution to all sales problems; whether prices are set, suggested, or influenced by the principal, it is easy for the dealer to object to the policy that sets them.

Inadequate Help from Principal

Sometimes it seems that dealers want the principal to do all the work and still pay them full compensation. Actually, however, dealers do not expect this. But they do frequently have justifiable complaints about inadequate information, instruction, and cooperation.

Direct Sales

The dealer who works hard and long to build a sales territory rightfully feels that he is entitled to a profit on all sales made in his territory. Consequently, whenever the principal makes a direct sale and deprives the dealer of his profit on that sale, the dealer is likely to be angry. No dealer organization will last if there is very much shortcutting.

Overloading and Short Ordering

Dealers complain when the factory ships more than they want and they complain if it ships less than they want. Overloading is usually the responsibility of the sales department which may be trying to force dealers to work harder; short orders are commonly a result of production problems. But both make dealers unhappy and result in protests, controversy, and even a rupture in the relationship.

Unrealistic Quotas

The manufacturer who gives his dealers sales quotas that are unreasonably large may hope for superhuman efforts, but he is much more likely to get superhuman squawks. Unthinking and arbitrary determination of sales quotas is one of the greatest sources of dealer complaint. Most dealers want to make sales and they are usually willing to work hard because larger sales mean more income. The complaints occur when the principal demands more than can possibly be delivered.

Too Many Dealers

Every dealer wants to earn a larger income. Therefore, he naturally wants to tap the largest possible territory. When the principal opens new dealerships and reduces the territory of existing dealers, this can mean a financial loss for the older dealers — and that leads to objections. The question of too many dealers can be raised even when none are being added; whenever a dealer loses sales to another, he is convinced that there are too many dealers.

Arbitrary Contract Termination

Dealership contracts or franchise agreements are usually set up with the idea of permanence but sometimes they must be canceled. When the principal ends the relationship, it is usually for a good reason; but occasionally the action may be, or may appear to be, arbitrary. Since loss of a dealership represents a substantial financial loss, the slightest hint of arbitrary action is sure to bring violent protests and possibly lawsuits.

Forced Payment on Guarantees

Some manufacturers force their dealers to pay part of the cost of guarantees. A typical example is that of the manufacturer who supplies replacement parts but expects the dealer to provide the labor necessary for installing the parts. The dealer reaction is that the entire fault is attributable to the manufacturer and that he should carry all costs of honoring the guarantee.

Forced Advertising

When the manufacturer of an advertised product requires his dealers to spend some of their own money to advertise that product, there can easily be strong objections. Many dealers do spend the money, but some of them protest vigorously at having to do something which they believe to be the sole responsibility of the manufacturer.

Forced Purchases of Supplies

Occasionally this means purchase of spare parts; more commonly, it shows up in the franchised food business where franchise holders are required to buy supplies from the principal. Numerous lawsuits, injunctions, and complaints to the Federal Trade Commission have resulted from this situation.

PROBLEMS WITH DEALERS

While dealers have quite a few complaints about their principals, there are relatively few about dealers, but these few are rather substantial. Principals complain that their dealers do not sell enough, that they do not follow instructions, and that they want too much help.

Inadequate Sales

This is the perennial and universal complaint about dealers. In spite of the fact that dealer compensation is usually a matter of straight commission and therefore a powerful incentive to work hard for increased sales, there is still a belief in the minds of many sales managers that their dealers are not working as hard as they should.

Failure to Follow Instructions

Most manufacturers provide dealers with complete and comprehensive instructions covering every detail of operation from accounting to restroom sanitation. Dealers, being independent, frequently apply their own interpretation or even completely disregard the rules and regulations. This results in profound dissatisfaction because the principal has carefully planned his instructions to urge the kind of performance that will be uniformly successful in every dealership.

Unreasonable Requests for Help

If some dealers had their way, the principal would do all their work for them. Dealers do need help and they can get it, but in many cases the demands become unreasonable. When the principal is asked to do most of the dealer's work, he feels that the dealer is not earning his commissions. When this condition exists, there is bound to be an unsatisfactory relationship.

OBJECTIVES IN DEALER RELATIONS

The main purpose in a dealer relations program is to build and maintain a dealer organization that will enable the principal to conduct a profitable business. The objectives of such a program are to retain good dealers, to acquire new dealers, and to improve the performance of both.

Retaining Good Dealers

A good dealer is important to any selling organization. Such a dealer assures that a definite and profitable sales volume can be attained. Good dealers need to be retained, not only because they are profitable, but also because it costs a great deal less to keep a dealer than to acquire a new one. A good dealer relations program can forge a strong two-way loyalty that binds dealers firmly to the supplier's organization.

Acquiring New Dealers

Inevitably, some dealers will be lost through business failure, through conflicts within the dealership, through death or retirement, and through failures in dealer relations. These must be replaced. Also, a growing organization needs new dealers to cover additional territory or to provide sales or service beyond the capacity of existing dealers. As volume grows, it may be necessary to divide territories and install new dealers. Getting new dealers will be much easier if there is a dealer relations program.

Improving Dealer Performance

While this is essentially a matter of sales management, dealer morale can be helped through a program designed to develop enthusiasm and a sense of real participation in the overall progress of the product sold. Sales meetings, of course, are always planned to build enthusiasm, but, to maintain a high level of performance, it is essential that every possible means be used to make the dealer feel that he is important and appreciated. This is where a dealer relations program fits in — as the "extra."

BUILDING GOOD DEALER RELATIONS

Most dealer relations are handled by the sales department. Public relations people participate as consultants, as assistants, and as creators of the various materials used in communicating with the dealers.

Attitude

The attitude of the principal toward dealers must be based on recognition of the importance of the dealers and a real wish to work with them for the common good. The principal must want and be willing to pay for good dealer relations. A principal may have hundreds or thousands of dealers, yet each must be recognized as an individual and the relationship should reflect a feeling of partnership in a joint effort.

Policy

Because there are so many problems in conducting a business through dealers and because there are so many opportunities for misunderstanding or disagreement, it is imperative that policies be clearly defined in writing. Dealer relations policies may require considerable detail and may become quite voluminous in order that all points be covered. General Motors spells out its dealer relations policy in a 33-page booklet. It explains in great detail the exact nature of its franchise agreement. It tells dealers what they can and cannot do and what they must do to retain the franchise. Topics covered in the booklet include such items as:

Terms and Tenure — normally five years, renewable.

Agreements as Personal Service Contracts — the dealership is considered on an individual basis.

Requirements for Dealership Operations — the dealer must establish a sales and service outlet and operate it in accordance with certain minimum standards.

Survivors and Nominees — the dealer can nominate a prospective heir or relative for participation in the dealership.

Action

Attitude and policy may be perfect but, if they are not carried out, there will be no accomplishment. Because selling is so competitive, it is easy to concentrate on volume and forget about dealer attitudes. This is inexcusable. Sales people have a dual responsibility and should be aware of it at all times.

277

Two-way Communication

Communication from principal to dealer is relatively easy. Ample facilities and personnel are usually available. Dealers, on the other hand, may have no time or ability to communicate their thinking to the principal. This means that the principal must, in effect, "pump" ideas from dealers. A dealer may be confused or unhappy but unable to express his feelings. He may have a good idea but no means of getting it implemented. Accordingly, a dealer relations program must include an aggressive effort to seek out the thoughts of the dealers, aid in their expression, and have them considered by the principal.

EXERCISES

1. Have you had contacts with a dealer (automobile, appliance, etc.)? Was the dealer really interested in you?
2. Have you needed service from a dealer?
   (a) Were you pleased with the service? Why?
   (b) How would you improve this situation?

Case Problem

You are public relations director of a major manufacturer of "white goods" (stoves, refrigerators, washers, and dryers). You have heard and read numerous reports of dissatisfaction with dealer service.

How would you find out how serious the problem is with your products and your dealers?

Describe in detail the research you would do in order to determine
(a) the extent of dissatisfaction,
(b) the reasons for dissatisfaction, and
(c) the remedy for dissatisfaction.

Plan a program to solve this problem. Include
(a) what you would do to improve service by the dealers,
(b) how you would sell dealers on the need for better service, and
(c) how you would inform the public.

18

The Competitor Public

Both philosophers and governments have much to say about the virtues of competition. Certainly it is necessary, desirable, and inevitable, but it can also be so intense as to become harmful. When competition is fair, the public benefits; when it becomes vicious, it may destroy the participants and deprive the public of needed goods or services. It is against the law for competitors to set up agreements that prevent competition, but it is legal, ethical, and proper for competitors to treat each other fairly and decently, to communicate with each other, and to participate in solving common problems.

To determine the content of a competitor relations program, there should be some consideration of the things that make for bad relations between competitors.

COMPETITOR PROBLEMS

There are only a handful of points about which competitors complain, but they make up in size and intensity for their small number. They are price-cutting, quality misrepresentation, abnormal terms, theft of secrets, and theft of employees.

Price-Cutting

The frequency with which stories of price-fixing appear is an indication of the common desire to eliminate price competition. Almost everyone feels that a lower price is a sure way to increase sales; when competitors are struggling against each other, a price cut can be a powerful weapon — until it is matched. Real or imagined or falsely reported, price-cutting is the action most likely to precipitate retaliation and create an atmosphere of violent antagonism. Everyone expects price competition but not competition that upsets existing differentials.

Quality Misrepresentation

The competitor who sells inferior merchandise under a quality identification is another source of bad relations. Not all buyers want the same quality and most sellers recognize that their merchandise will not fill all needs. But, when a sale is lost to a competitor who delivers a lower quality than that on which the price competition was based, it creates a situation ripe for competition that can lead to drastic losses for all the people involved in that particular line of business. Whether it be ten-ton trucks or toothbrushes, competitors hate to lose business because of misrepresentation of quality.

Abnormal Terms

Practically every kind of business has its own special terms for credit, delivery, payment, discounts, etc. Usually these are the result of many years of experience and mutual satisfaction of both buyers and sellers. The introduction of new and more generous terms that reduce profits or increase costs has some of the effect of price-cutting and produces the same kind of reaction. Meeting these terms may, in addition to reducing profits, require changes in office procedures and necessitate new financial arrangements.

Stealing Secrets

A formula or process in any manufacturing business may be of considerable value. In certain conditions such things may be the principal assets of the firm. As competition becomes more intense, there is a temptation to equalize the game by duplicating the product of the "other" firm. There have been a number of instances in which an organized plot to steal such secrets has succeeded. Stealing secrets is not limited to formulas and processes. It also includes marketing strategy and plans, financial reports, and many other kinds of information. Stealing secrets is not only bad competitor relations, it is also a crime.

Stealing Employees

Whenever a firm hires an employee away from a competitor, it may be called "stealing." Some organizations refuse to take the initiative in such matters, but others — either directly or through "head hunters" (executive recruiters) — carry on an active campaign to recruit employees from other companies in the same field. The company that loses personnel in this manner feels that it has been robbed and complaints are loud and prolonged. Employee recruiting may be necessary, but it can lead to very poor relations with competitors.

OBJECTIVES IN COMPETITOR RELATIONS

The key to a successful program of competitor relations is to avoid cut-throat competition and develop a feeling of mutual respect and confidence. The objectives in competitor relations are to convince competitors that the organization is honest, that it competes fairly, and that it will cooperate with others.

Honesty

It is useless to give speeches, write letters, and make statements if honesty is not practiced. If the firm is honest, this attitude will permeate all its dealings with its competitors. It will build a good reputation for the firm and render it trustworthy.

Fair Competition

It has been said that civilization is a condition under which people compete in accordance with accepted rules. When the rules are accepted, competition can be civilized — or fair. If any organization acknowledges the rules and conforms to them, it will be a fair competitor. But beyond this, the competitors must be shown that the organization has willingly adopted this code of ethics.

Cooperation

There are organizations that are honest and that compete fairly yet refuse to cooperate with their competitors in any way or for any purpose. This policy leaves the noncooperating company in a limbo, with no friends and hardly even an acquaintance in their industry. Much more common and advantageous to all is a willingness to cooperate with competitors for the benefit of the entire trade or industry. Cooperation is a continuing activity and must be more than just a statement of agreeability. It requires time, money, and manpower but it makes friends.

BUILDING GOOD COMPETITOR RELATIONS

Attitude, policy, action, and two-way communications form the cornerstone of good relations with competitors. If these are adequate, the program should be successful.

Attitude

In a competitive situation it is very easy to develop deep antagonism towards other organizations. The normal "Beat Harvard" or "Beat Yale" spirit can help in building morale but, if carried too far, it can lead to a kind of competition that is very unsound. The solution is to inject into the competition a determination to compete fairly, honestly, and vigorously, but to avoid actions that precipitate retaliation.

Policy

Competitive policy need not be long or highly detailed, but it should be definite, it should be written, and it should be adhered to by everyone whose actions could affect the situation. Policy needs to be policed at all levels. No salesman or supervisor or sales manager should be allowed to violate policy once it has been established. Policy should be made known to competitors and, when changes are necessary, they should be promptly notified. C. W. Cook, former Chairman of General Foods, had this to say about competitive policy in a talk to a management meeting:

> We are determined to be successful, yes; but not at the expense of honest principles. Competitively aggressive, yes; but not stooping to rough or shady tactics. Tough, yes; but considerate of the rights of all with whom we do business.

Action

Positive personal contacts, exchange of nonconfidential information, and membership in associations are all desirable activities. Opposite numbers should know each other well enough to permit complete frankness. Presidents should know competing presidents, sales managers should know competing sales managers, salesmen should know competing salesmen. Contacts may be face to face, over the telephone, or by mail. The goal is acquaintance but not necessarily comradeship.

Almost every trade, line of business, or occupation has an association. While membership is usually voluntary, most associations represent an overwhelming majority of the potential members. Association membership is expensive but usually well worth it. Membership brings much information and many specific aids. It also greatly improves competitor relationships.

Two-way Communication

Communication between competitors is often informal and unscheduled but this only adds to its importance. Building and maintaining good relations with competitors requires a continuous interchange of ideas and information. Many a battle between competitors has been prevented by a telephone call, a direct question, and an honest answer. Communication is probably the most important element in competitor relations. It should be encouraged.

Price lists, annual reports, house organs, bulletins, and syndicated letters are tools primarily planned for other purposes, yet they can perform a valuable function in communication with competitors. In most cases they contain no information that could be competitively disadvantageous, so their release can do no harm. The printed materials cited above are not the only means of exchanging information. Letters, telephone calls, or face-to-face conversation should also be used.

EXERCISES

1. Have you ever worked in a job where you had contacts with competition (e.g., an *outside* salesman)?
    (a) Was the competition fair?
    (b) Were your contacts with competition pleasant or unpleasant?
    (c) Why?

Case Problem

You are public relations counselor to a large retail automobile dealer. He informs you that competition has become "murderous," that lies, misrepresentation, and price-cutting are ruining his business and that of all other dealers as well. There is no dealer association.

What would you advise?

What publics are involved?

What is their interest in this situation?

Who would you try to reach?

What message would you convey?

Dialogue III

Dialogue with Mr. John F. Henning, Executive Secretary-Treasurer, California Labor Federation, AFL-CIO. Former Under Secretary of Labor under Presidents Kennedy and Johnson.

> This dialogue deals with a public which is not covered in the preceding chapters. Public relations practitioners do not ordinarily deal with labor unions — that is the bailiwick of the labor relations people. Yet, organized labor is a big factor in employee relations and must be considered. Read between the lines of this dialogue. It will be most enlightening.

Q. Do you think that your ideas are typical of the ideas of the leaders in labor?

A. Yes, there may be some exceptions, but in general what I say is representative of the overwhelming body of thought in U.S. labor.

Q. Labor's opposition to the proposed expansion of Redwood National Park has led some people to believe that labor is opposed to protecting the environment.

A. That idea is not correct. We do believe in protecting the environment. We want to save those tallest trees, but we're not satisfied with the arguments presented in support of the proposed expansion. For example, we don't think that the effect of logging outside the park has been clearly determined, yet that has been a major argument in this case.

Q. Do you have a general position on problems involving the environment?

A. Yes, we think that every Environmental Impact Report should include a report on the social and economic impact of the proposal.

Q. How do the environmentalists react to this?

A. They have responded very favorably. In fact, the Sierra Club has set up liaison with us on problems of this nature.

Q. Is any group opposed to this solution?

A. Some developers are very much opposed. They don't want to admit that their developments may require roads, water lines, sewers, utilities, schools, fire and police protection, and other costly services.

Q. Let's go back to the park expansion and its possible effect on jobs. I know that the lumberman's job is very important to him, but can't he be retrained for other work?

A. It's a nice theory, but there is no industrial diversity in the Humboldt County area. It is a one-product economy. Essentially, there are no other jobs to be trained for and no other industries to use the skills which might be taught.

Q. What about jobs in tourism?

A. That is a minor possibility, and there is little potential for expansion. Oh, sure, some of the loggers might become bartenders or motel operators, but we're talking about sufficient jobs. If those lumbermen can't work at their trade, they can't work at all. That's why they are so militant.

Q. Do you have any comments on governmental handling of environmental problems?

A. Indeed I do. The Dow Chemical case comes to mind. Red tape, bureaucratic bungling, and long delays in decision-making forced Dow to give up its plans for a large plant. This cost many jobs. Regardless of the merits of the plant or its possible effect on the environment, the real problem was governmental failure to make decisions. We must have a way to get answers promptly.

Q. Some people accuse labor of putting jobs above every other consideration.

A. I wouldn't say "above." Of course, we put jobs first in our thinking, but we do consider other things. Take freeways, for example. Some critics think we're interested only in the jobs derived from their construction, but that isn't the whole case. Our society and economy depend on the automobile. Without freeways, our urban centers would choke to death. The working population in cities like Los Angeles would suffer terribly without the access freeways provide.

Q. What about rapid transit?

A. Labor has never opposed the idea and again not merely because of the construction jobs. We feel that mass transit is a necessity in metropolitan areas. We need both freeways and rail and bus systems.

Q. There are many complaints about overregulation by government, about multiplicity of laws and petty rules which handicap business.

A. This is a very complex society. We must have competition, but we can't let private forces devastate the economic and social order. We must have controls. It's obviously hard to draw the line between public and private responsibility. Many things should be handled by private action, but many aren't so handled. Take the case of asbestos application. It appears that asbestos fibers may cause cancer. We believe that asbestos processing must be done in ways that protect the health of the workers. That calls for government regulation.

Q. How does labor feel about the energy situation?

A. We agree that there is a crisis and that we must act. Here in California, we are supporting a terminal which would handle liquefied natural gas from Alaska — and remarkably, many environmentalists who first opposed the idea are now changing their positions. We opposed a ban on nuclear development. We are strongly supporting development of solar energy.

Q. How do you feel about taxing big cars out of existence?

A. Some people need big cars. You can't pack a large family into a compact. Many people need big station wagons to double as a family car and a work car.

Q. There is much talk in Washington about coal as a solution to the energy shortage, yet there is fear that this means massive pollution and damage to the land. What do you think?

A. We believe that we can have both coal and environmental protection. We are against destructive strip-mining. Nor do we want the whole of America to look like Pittsburgh did before it cleaned its air. But if it comes down to survival, we'll have coal.

Q. If the country relies more heavily on coal, aren't we in danger of coal strikes which could paralyze the entire economy?

A. I don't see an easy solution here. We have had militant unions for many years. We have had strikes but the economy continues to grow. We can't give up what we regard as an essential right.

Q. As a citizen who has been inconvenienced and irritated by strikes, I resent them. I suspect there are many others who feel as I do.

A. No strike is ever popular. We don't completely disregard public opinion, but no one can operate solely on the basis of public opinion polls — not industry, not labor.

Q. How do you feel about health care?

A. Labor believes it must be greatly and broadly improved. For example, many union-negotiated health and welfare plans apply only to those

287

who are at work. If a worker is unemployed there may be no insurance to cover the bills — and we now have several million people out of work in the country.

Q. Do you support a specific plan?

A. Without singling out any one of the several ideas now being discussed, we feel that it should be a blend of public and private protection.

Q. That sounds as though you don't believe that government can solve all problems.

A. You're right. We have a case in California which proves it. We're supporting a bill which would permit private insurance companies to write workmen's compensation insurance for local government entities. Today the State Compensation Insurance Fund has a monopoly on such bodies, but we think private companies could do a better job.

Q. Recently one of the regents of the University of California has sharply criticized University research which led to development of an electronic tomato harvester which would require fewer laborers in agriculture. As a newly appointed regent, how do you feel about this?

A. I'm not like the nineteenth-century Luddites who destroyed labor-saving machinery. We must have new technology, but we must consider its economic and social impact. We have a near perfect example on the waterfront. Containerization has revolutionized shipping. Many workers could have lost their jobs, but they didn't because labor and management negotiated a civilized transition between the old way and the new. By eliminating new hirings, by early retirements, and by protecting those who had jobs, the work force was gradually reduced to an efficient size and no one was hurt.

Q. If you were advising a public relations practitioner about American labor, what would you say?

A. I'd say that the Industrial Revolution made unions inevitable. They are here to stay. Unions are a social, political, and economic reality. They are part of the system in which our institutions must operate. Everyone must recognize this — and everyone should be glad that American labor is markedly different from labor in the other free countries. Virtually all of them believe in government operation and ownership of industry. We don't trust government that much nor have that good an opinion of its efficiency. We'd rather deal with private business. We believe in private enterprise but insist that it must serve the broad public good.

IV

The Public Relations Program

Implementing a public relations program includes gathering and interpreting information (inbound communication), defining the problem and determining how to solve it (planning), carrying messages to the public involved (outbound communication), and examining what is being accomplished (evaluation).

If a public relations program is being started, the activity will be in the sequence given above. But, once a program is underway, it becomes a continuous process with no beginning or end except for individual activities within the general structure. All of the different phases should be going on at the same time. Inbound communication, planning, outbound communication, evaluation — all are constant activities. This viewpoint is essential in considering public relations as a self-adjusting system.

Inbound communication includes every activity that can provide information pertinent to the organization's relations with the public.

Planning includes deciding what should be done, just how it should be done, where and when and why it should be done. Planning involves determining the objectives to be attained. It also includes condensing all this into a recommendation and then selling management on the recommendation. The recommendation may involve policy, action and program.

Outbound communication means selection and proper use of the communication channels; it means deciding what to say, how to say it, when and where to say it, to whom it should be said — and, finally, making the statement.

Evaluation is the process of checking the PR program and all its parts to learn whether it is worth what it costs, which things are effective and which are not, who is persuaded and who is not.

Each of these major divisions of public relations activity is vitally important.

Part IV

If all are done well, the program will be good. If any are skipped or done poorly, the program will suffer. They will be treated separately in the next four chapters. Again it must be remembered that once a PR program is established, there is no one, two, three, four sequence. All of these activities are carried on simultaneously. They are all responsibilities of the public relations practitioner.

Another responsibility of the public relations practitioner is to advise management on policy. This will be an increasingly important area in the future. For the public relations practitioner to do this job properly, he or she must be more than a communicator; to some degree at least, he must be a social scientist.

LEGAL ASPECTS

In all phases of the practice of public relations, there must be consideration of what is legal and what is not legal. Laws and court decisions are changing. Restrictions on what can be said or done are increasing. Along with these changes has come a major alteration in public attitudes. There is a widespread willingness to criticize, to doubt, to accuse, and to sue.

A chapter, or at least several pages, could be devoted to this subject *if* conditions were stable. Unfortunately the situation is changing so rapidly that anything printed in a book may be obsolete by the time it is read.

A basic reference is: Simon, M. J. *Public Relations Law*. New York: Appleton-Century-Crofts, 1969.

Since this book was published, there have been many new laws and court decisions. These are generally reported in the *Public Relations Journal*. Each year, the January issue of the *Journal* contains an index which will enable the practitioner to find pertinent articles if he or she has not previously noted them. It is also advisable to keep informed about lawsuits and court decisions reported in the general news media,

Obviously this situation suggests close cooperation with the legal department or counsel of the organization. The practitioner should know what can or cannot be said, but should not let lawyers take over control of the public relations activity. Many lawyers would elect to say nothing at a time of crisis and wait for a court to decide the issue while the organization is being tried and convicted in the court of public opinion. When a charge is made against an organization, a lawyer might suggest a "no comment" answer, but to many people "no comment" is an admission of guilt.

19

Inbound Communication

If any organization is to succeed in adapting to its social, political, and economic environment — and in adapting that environment to the organization, it must know the nature of that environment.

This knowledge is acquired through inbound communication. The process starts with the public relations practitioner. He or she must be highly sensitive to and aware of public attitudes and opinions.

Much of this awareness comes from constant attention to the news and consideration of how the reported trends, surveys, and actions might affect the organization. But just watching the news doesn't do the whole job. There must be a continuing effort to find out every fact which can affect the relations of the organization with any of its publics. These facts are gathered through informal research, through voluntary inbound communication, and through formal research.

Every one of these activities is essential. In fact, Dr. Otto Lerbinger of Boston University says that if public relations practitioners ignore research, they will be ignored by management.

INFORMAL RESEARCH

Much useful information can be obtained by collecting all pertinent data, statements, comments, and published materials available. Among the sources to comb are:

Organization Records

Annual reports, house organs, proceedings of meetings, press clippings, copies of speeches, histories, copies of important letters, records of important actions — all these and many others are a primary source of information in any PR situation. Whenever possible, this information should be in a well-indexed file where it can be found when needed.

Photographs

Any photographs showing organization activities or ceremonies plus pictures of personnel, buildings, interiors, products, etc. should be properly identified and the location of the negatives noted so that additional prints may be obtained. Pictures disappear like snow in May so the picture file must be well-secured in order to prevent losing the last copy of an important photograph.

Reference Books

In almost any situation there are books that give comprehensive information about the particular line of activity in which the organization operates. A history of sugar tariffs may be of no interest to a retail store, but it can be very helpful to the public relations activity of a sugar refinery.

Public Records

Many government agencies maintain voluminous records which are available for public use. They include such things as hearings of legislative and executive bodies, statistics on many different subjects and publications on a very wide variety of topics. Both the federal and state governments are able and willing to supply such information. Usually the easiest way to find needed information is to write to the executive branch most likely to be concerned. For example, the Department of Agriculture (U.S. or state) would be the logical place to find information about the cotton crop, the Department of Labor would be the place to get information on industrial accidents, and so on.

Trade Journals

There are approximately 3,500 trade journals in the United States. They cover 159 different fields — from advertising to woodworking. These are invaluable sources of information. They should be read thoroughly and continuously. Pertinent items should be saved and filed (unless the whole publication is kept). Trade journals can answer many questions and should be considered as primary sources of information about their own industries. Many have research departments, many have done elaborate studies of their industries, and many maintain large reference libraries. Often they have a complete index of items they have published. The *Business Periodical Index*, available in most large libraries, provides an index by subject and by author of many articles published in the larger trade journals.

Newspapers

Reading the newspapers is a must for any public relations practitioner because it provides news of current happenings, news about or affecting the organization, and because it sharpens awareness of public interest. Newspapers also provide considerable information on specific topics and their back files are nearly always available for public use.

Public Opinion Polls and Voting Records

A continuing study of public opinion polls and voting records can often provide broad guidelines that will help in formulating plans. If the polls show strong sentiment in favor of a particular policy, this is a warning to avoid action that is inconsistent with that policy. If voters turn down candidates or propositions, then public relations plans that parallel the thinking of the defeated candidates or propositions may also be rejected.

General Magazines

Many of these magazines have large libraries and complete files of back issues. Their location may not be convenient for most usage, but when it is believed that a specific magazine has published something on a given subject, it may be possible to locate the article and obtain a copy or extract. The *Reader's Guide to Periodical Literature* is an index by subject and author of many articles that have been published in major magazines. It is available in most large libraries.

Libraries

There are many libraries that may be helpful. The local public library is an obvious place to start, but there are many others. Public libraries may have special technical branches, and there are specialized libraries covering numerous different fields. Many trade associations maintain libraries. School and college libraries may also be available as sources of reference material. Do not overlook the indexes of magazine articles on *Technology and Science, Education,* etc.

Colleges and Universities

Many institutions of higher learning publish numerous research reports, technical bulletins, and other materials that may be useful references in public relations. Also, it should be remembered that faculty members themselves may be a fruitful source of information.

Associations

There is an association for almost every line of work and for practically every special interest. They are prime sources for information about their particular domain. Most associations are more than willing to provide any information they have and many will make quite an effort to assist in any situation if they can. For lists of associations, see *National Trade and Professional Associations of the United States*, available in most libraries, or classified telephone directories. The Public Relations Society of America and the specific trade association of the industry or field in which the organization operates are, of course, the first sources to consider.

Television

Television news is usually only headline news but watching it will indicate the topics which are getting public attention and presumably affecting or reflecting public opinion.

VOLUNTARY INBOUND COMMUNICATION

This heading includes all truly voluntary communications such as letters and complaints, plus some that are aided by the organization such as items received through a suggestion system. Most of this activity is very informal. The information obtained may not be representative and it may lack objectivity. Nevertheless, it is a valuable aid. Its inflow should be encouraged and the information should be seriously considered.

Personal Contacts

Any employee may have personal contacts with members of the public and in the course of these contacts acquire information of significance in public relations. Service personnel and sales people, adjusters and delivery men, teachers and janitors, telephone operators and truck drivers — any one of these may hear something important. This information must be recognized and channeled to the PR department. Employees should be taught to recognize such information and their supervisors helped in forwarding it to the PR department.

Public relations personnel must make a special continuing effort to contact members of the public. They must get out of their offices, ask questions, listen, stimulate discussion, and always try to find out what the public thinks and says.

Mail

Most organizations receive a lot of mail. Systematic analysis of incoming mail to determine the number and nature of complaints and, conversely, the number and nature of letters indicating satisfaction or praise can often shed light on situations that might not otherwise be known. Such analyses may be continuous or periodic. They may cover all mail or a fixed percentage only.

Reports

The periodic reports of personnel often contain information that is significant to the PR department. These reports may come from sales people, from supervisors, from managers, or even from the top executives. Regardless of the source, if there is anything bearing on public opinion, it should be routed to the PR department promptly. Cooperation of the managers at all levels is the key to this problem. Obtaining that cooperation is a continuing responsibility of the PR people.

Advisory Committees or Panels

Special groups are often set up to be consultants on public relations. Detached from the organization, they hopefully represent the public viewpoint. The topics on which such groups are asked to comment may include such diverse subjects as employment policies, pricing structure, the merits of a recipe, or the virtues and faults of prepackaged produce. Panels or committees can provide quick answers but they can also become "conditioned" through repeated use and thus lose their independent viewpoint.

Performance Records

Any football coach who loses ten games in a row knows that his public relations are in bad shape. Similarly, an organization that loses sales or employees or any other measurable asset may be suffering because of a decline in public approval. Lawsuits and government investigations are also indicators of unsatisfactory performance.

Suggestion Systems

Many suggestion systems are organized to encourage employees to recommend money-saving improvements in the operation. This is a very restricted use of a valuable tool. Suggestion systems should be open to others besides employees and should embrace the entire range of company activities, not just cost reduction. People should be encouraged to advocate improvements and helped to get their ideas into the proper channels for consideration.

Study of Opinion Leaders

Opinion leaders may speak or write to very large audiences. Their statements are often extremely influential, and for this reason, the things they oppose or support should be carefully noted in order to take advantage of the favorable or to counteract the unfavorable.

FORMAL RESEARCH

Research costs money, and it takes time, but it can provide comprehensive answers and it is dependable. Through use of scientifically based research, it is possible to determine how people feel. Information obtained in this way is objective and truly representative of public opinion.

In public relations, research has two functions: (1) to determine what public opinion is, and (2) to determine how the PR program has affected public opinion. Knowledge of research procedures is indispensable to the practitioner.

Suggested Readings

Anderson and Anderson (Eds.). *An Introduction to Projection Techniques.* Englewood Cliffs, N.J.: Prentice-Hall, 1951.
Cantrill, Hadley. *Gauging Public Opinion.* Princeton, N.J.: Princeton University Press, 1972.

Dichter, Ernest. *Handbook of Consumer Motivation*. New York: McGraw-Hill, 1964.

Heise, David R. (Ed.). *Sociological Methodology*. San Francisco: Jossey-Bass, 1977.

Meyer, Philip. *Precision Journalism*. Bloomington, In.: Indiana University Press, 1975.

Robinson, E. J. *Public Relations and Survey Research*. New York: Appleton-Century-Crofts, 1969.

Selltiz, Claire; Wrightsman, L. S.; and Cook, S. *Research Methods in Social Relations*. New York: Holt, Rinehart & Winston, 1976.

Sonquist, John A., and Dunkelberg, William C. *Survey and Opinion Research*. Englewood Cliffs, N.J.: Prentice-Hall, 1977.

Stephan, Frederick F., and McCarthy, Philip J. *Sampling Opinion*, Westport, Conn.: Greenwood, 1974.

Principles of Research

Every research project is different but, in spite of the difference, there are certain general rules that apply in any situation. These rules should be followed in setting up and conducting any study of public opinion.

1. *Do not guess*. Be sure of the facts. If in doubt, keep on digging until you *know*.
2. *Do not try to sell*. The purpose of research is to find out what people think — not to change their opinions.
3. *Do not lead*. Lawyers are not allowed to lead witnesses and researchers should not for the same reason — the answers will not be accurate.
4. *Make questions simple*. They must be easy to answer and impossible to misunderstand.
5. *Use understandable language*. The questions must be asked in the words commonly used by the people being questioned.
6. *Conceal the objective*. People try to give the answers they think will be most pleasing and this may not be what they really think.
7. *Talk to representative people*. People most interested in giving opinions may not represent anyone but themselves. People picked by some sound statistical method are more likely to be representative.
8. *Preserve anonymity*. Answers will be more honest if the respondent is sure his opinion cannot be traced back to him.
9. *Pretest*. Always try out the questionnaire before launching the full project. In nearly every case some revision will be needed.
10. *Anticipate answers*. Research must yield a base for action. It is important to think about just what *will* be done if answers give a definite indication that something *should* be done.

Organization for Research

Research may be done by a number of agencies. It can be handled by the public relations department or by a public relations counselor. Sometimes it is conducted by trade associations, advertising agencies, or even by publications. If the research project is very simple and very limited, it may be possible to do the work without use of a specialized research organization. However, when the problem is large and funds permit, specialists should be used. There are many opinion research firms and nearly all can be relied upon to do a competent professional job. Also, some large organizations have full-fledged research departments that are staffed by experts and thus able to handle the entire task.

Utilization of Research

Research may be used by any organization and any public or problem may be involved. For example, telephone companies regularly survey customer opinion about their services. Among the items covered are: experience making local and long-distance calls, experience with directory assistance service, transmission on local and long-distance calls, results of reports on trouble, installation service, contacts with business office, experience with coin-box phones, satisfaction with the telephone book, and billing service.

Pacific Telephone Company asks this question about transmission:

> During the past month or so on your local calls did you have any trouble hearing or being heard — because of —
> faint voices on the line?
> noises on the line?
> fading in and out?
> low volume?

(Similar questions are asked on other points.)

Research Procedure

To be effective, research must be very carefully planned and executed. The sequence is:

Defining the problem   The first step is to determine what is to be studied. The subject may be very broad such as community attitudes about the organization or it may be very narrow such as color preferences in paper towels; either way, it must be clearly defined and understood.

Investigating the problem   All available information should be studied to find out what is known about the subject and what may have been done in identical or similar situations. Past experience often provides many answers and may help to greatly simplify the project or even make it unnecessary.

Examining organization policy   The policies of the organization may strongly affect the whole approach to research. Since research is done for the purpose of guiding action, there is no point in researching a problem on which no action can or will be taken.

Informing management   Since top management will have to pay for the research and implement recommendations coming from research, it is imperative that the subject be thoroughly understood by the heads of the organization.

Planning Research

When a research project has been approved, a number of decisions must be weighed:

1. What is the objective?
2. Who will conduct the research?
3. How much will it cost?
4. How long will it take?
5. Who will be surveyed?
6. What kind of questions will be asked?
7. How will questions be asked?

Deciding on the objective   The most important element in any research is the objective. Unless there is a clear and definite objective, the entire survey may be wasted. Essentially the purpose is to find out what people think or feel about something, but this must be made quite specific. For example:

What do our customers think about our new billing procedure?

Will the employees in plant No. 9 object to the proposed changes in rules?

Is there any improvement we should make in our community relations program?

Who will conduct the survey?   This should be decided early because the people who do the work ought to participate in all the planning. Simple surveys may be handled by the PR department or counselor but, whenever a major study is indicated, the safest course is to work with a professional opinion research firm, unless there is a complete and competent research department within the organization.

299

Selecting a research organization is very important. Usually several firms are available. Consultation with a firm's former clients plus examination of questionnaires used and reports prepared will normally provide a good basis for determining competence. One very important point to determine is whether the work was finished on time. Occasionally a firm will be technically adequate but notoriously slow in delivering reports.

How much will it cost?   Research can be very costly. There must be an early consideration of the kind of expenditure needed, so that over-ambitious plans can be trimmed to a realistic level. Preliminary estimates should be made as soon as planning starts and definite bids should be obtained and approved before field work is started. Actual costs can vary considerably in the examples that follow but these will be useful in the early stages. Telephone surveys cost around $10 to $15 per respondent. Personal interviews can cost $25 to $30. If the people to be surveyed are specified by occupation, the cost may be much higher. (It costs up to $100 to conduct an interview with a businessman.) These are overall costs. Thus, a telephone survey reaching 2,000 housewives throughout the country would cost about $20,000 to $30,000; an interview survey of 100 businessmen in Philadelphia would cost nearly $10,000. These cost figures, of course, include charges for preparing questionnaires, paying interviewers, tabulating data, and preparing the report.

How long will it take?   There must be a definite timetable for every survey. This should show when the field work starts, when it ends, how long tabulations and analyses take and when the report will be delivered. Timeliness is important in research as in many other things; long delays not only frustrate and annoy the clients, they may also cause a complete loss of interest in the project. Also, long delays may invalidate the findings. What was true in April may be untrue in November. Most surveys can be done in six to eight weeks. A typical time schedule for a telephone survey might be as follows:

Preparation and pretesting of questionnaire — two weeks.
Field work (interviewing) — two weeks.
Coding and tabulating — two weeks.
Analysis and reporting — two weeks.

For a mail survey, add one week; for a personal interview survey, add two weeks. (Large surveys need not take much more time than short ones; the research firms merely use more interviewers so that a survey of 500 and one of 5,000 may take about the same time.)

Who will be surveyed? By questioning a part of the public, it is possible to determine what all of the public thinks. By questioning a few thousand people, the public opinion polls of Gallup, Harris, etc. can predict with reasonable accuracy how the entire national electorate will vote.

In all such surveys, the key is selection of the respondents. If the sample is large enough and if it is truly representative, it can give a fairly accurate indication of how the entire public feels. The public to be studied may be the total population, it may be former customers, it may be apartment-dwellers in Des Moines, or lumbermen in Oregon. In every case, its opinions can be measured by questioning a limited number of people who are a good cross-section of the group to which they belong. The problem is to select a representative sample large enough to be statistically sound.

(a) *Nature of the sample*. A representative sample can be either a quota sample or a random sample. There are many possible variations, modifications, and combinations but, in general, all samples fit into one of these two types.

In a quota sample the characteristics of the public to be studied are determined and then a small number of people conforming to the same statistics is selected for questioning. Thus, if half the public is male and half female, the sample should be half male and half female. If 20% of the public went to college, then 20% of the sample should consist of people who went to college. In surveying customers, if 40% of them are cash customers, then 40% of the sample should be people who do not use charge accounts. There are many different breakdowns possible, and whenever one of these could influence the answer, it should be considered in setting up the sample. Thus, age might be important in a survey about schools. People in their thirties are much more likely to be concerned about schools than people in their sixties.

In a random sample, the selection is by pure chance, with every member of the public having an equal chance of being included. For example, if every fiftieth name in the telephone directory were selected, the result would be a random sample of telephone users. If every tenth person coming off airplanes were selected, that would yield a random sample of airplane passengers. One danger in taking a random sample is that it may not be truly random. Stopping and questioning every twentieth person walking down Main Street in Jonestown may appear to be a good way to find out what the people of Jonestown think, but the sample is not representative of Jonestown. It represents only the people walking down Main Street. Nevertheless, with proper care, a random sample can be a sound sample.

(b) *Size of the sample.* The size of the sample must be large enough to represent accurately the particular public involved for the type of questions asked. Some questions require only a small sample while others may need many more people to be statistically safe. Through use of statistical tables based on the laws of probability, it is possible to determine in advance how many people must be questioned to get an answer within desired "error limits." Other things being equal, the larger the sample the smaller will be the error due to interviewing part of the public rather than all of it.

The degree of accuracy needed determines the size of the sample. For public relations purposes, we don't need extreme accuracy. If a survey shows that 75% of the respondents have a certain opinion, it tells us that most of the public has that opinion. We don't worry over the possibility that it is only 70%. All we need is enough accuracy to permit making an informed decision.

With a random sample of 250 respondents, it is possible to get a statistically sound measurement. This of course presumes that the sample is representative of the particular public. Thus a survey of 250 employees in one plant would be valid for that plant, but might not be valid for employees in another plant. A survey in Missouri might be accurate in that state, but not projectible to any other state.

What kind of questions will be asked?   Except in the most informal situations, research requires a questionnaire. It may be short or long but, if the answers are to be worthwhile, every person questioned must be asked the same questions in the same way. Usually, a number of questions will be needed in order to prevent oversimplification and to elicit the reasons for the attitudes and opinions expressed. Some of the most common forms of questions are: true-false, multiple-choice, ranking, essay, and rating.

(a) *The true-false* question may also be used as a yes-no question. Here are two examples: The respondent (the person being questioned) is instructed to check one square.

"The Jones Company treats its
employees fairly."   TRUE ☐   FALSE ☐

or

"Do you think the Jones Company
treats its employees fairly?"   YES ☐   NO ☐

(b) With *multiple-choice* questions, the respondent is asked questions like:

"Which of these stores has the friendliest sales people?"

> Ashley's_____
> Baker's_____
> Chandler's_____
> Davis's_____

(c) *Ranking* questions require thoughtful consideration. This is one example:

"Rank the four following items as 1, 2, 3, and 4 in order of their importance to you."

> job security_____
> opportunity for promotion_____
> retirement benefits_____
> current rate of pay_____

(d) *Essay* type questions require both thought and some ability of expression. Such a question might be:

"How do you feel when a friend asks what company you work for?"

When this type of question is asked, it is essential to use an interviewer trained to probe for clear meaningful answers. Most people do not know when they have answered a question like this.

(e) *Rating* questions take several forms. One way is to ask a question like this:

"Here are the names of three organizations; what is your opinion of each:"

very favorable_____favorable_____neutral_____
unfavorable_____very unfavorable_____

Another way is to ask a question like this:

"Please indicate how much you agree or disagree with the following statement . . .

> The Jones Company is a good company to work for.
> agree very strongly_____
> agree strongly_____
> agree somewhat_____
> undecided_____
> disagree somewhat_____
> disagree strongly_____
> disagree very strongly_____

Still another way to ask rating questions is by using what is called a semantic differential. It uses several bipolar scales, each containing two opposing adjectives separated by boxes, like this:

growing   □ □ □ □ □ □   static
thoughtful   □ □ □ □ □ □   inconsiderate
dependable □ □ □ □ □ □ □   undependable

Respondents are asked to check the box coinciding with their rating of the organization.

All questions in the same series should be asked in the same way. Shifting from one type of question to another confuses the respondent and multiplies the chances of erroneous answers.

The order in which questions are asked is very important. Great care must be taken in order to keep one question from affecting the answer to another. It is also advisable to consider such things as:

Is the question really necessary or just interesting?*
Should any questions be broken into several questions so that more accurate answers can be obtained?

Does the respondent have enough knowledge of the subject to answer intelligently?
Can the question be answered without a lot of work?
Will the question seem unreasonable?
Does the question suggest to the respondent that a specific answer is expected? Are the words simple?
Is the question valid in the sense that it measures what it is supposed to?

Demographic data, which means things like age, sex, occupation, income bracket, place of residence, etc., are always important. By tabulating the answers in accordance with such data, it becomes possible to find out what different kinds of people think and to draw such conclusions as, "Employees under 30 consider current rate of pay most important. Employees over 50 say that retirement benefits are most important."

When it is decided what questions to ask and what demographic data

---

*Do not overload the questionnaire. There is often a tendency to keep on adding questions because "it would be nice to know," but this makes the respondent resist because of length and confusion.

will be required, a preliminary questionnaire is prepared; then the problem is to determine the method of questioning. Sometimes this is decided first.

How will the questions be asked? There are several ways in which to conduct a survey. It can be done by mail, by personal interview, by telephone, in a group interview, or by combining two or more of these methods. Each procedure has advantages and disadvantages. None is

BANK OF AMERICA

A. W. CLAUSEN
President

Dear Customer:

We need your help.

We at Bank of America are anxious to maintain the highest level of service in each of our branches. To do this we must, of course, be aware of the areas that need improvement. We will greatly appreciate your taking a moment to complete the enclosed questionnaire.

Please be frank. There is no need to sign the questionnaire. If you do sign, your reply will be treated as confidential upon your request. If you have a particular problem that you wish conveyed on to your branch, we will do so. A postage paid envelope is enclosed for your convenience.

An evaluation and summary of the questionnaires will be prepared by our Marketing Department for my personal review. I will then forward the results of the study to your branch to assist the staff there in providing you with the best banking service possible.

Sincerely,

A. W. Clausen
President

BANK OF AMERICA NATIONAL TRUST AND SAVINGS ASSOCIATION · BANK OF AMERICA CENTER · SAN FRANCISCO, CALIFORNIA 94120

Fig. 19.1 Letter to customers asking for help in a survey of customer opinion.

best or worst. The choice of method has to consider the nature of the respondents, the type of questions to be asked, the length of the questionnaire, the time available, and the cost. Here are some of the things to remember about each procedure:

(a) *Mail.* Mail surveys are relatively economical. They can guarantee complete anonymity to the respondent and there is no chance for an interviewer to inject personal bias or to lead the respondents.

On the negative side, the number of returns may be low (many people just will not fill out and mail a questionnaire),* the answers may not be representative of the public being surveyed, and mail surveys take a long time. Also, there is no real assurance that the person chosen to answer the questionnaire actually does so. If the questions are not easy to understand and answer, the results will be biased by the intelligence — or lack of intelligence — of the respondents.

(b) *Personal interview.* With personal interviews, more information can be obtained. Longer questionnaires can be used and questions can be explained if the respondent does not understand. By controlling who is interviewed, it is possible to make the sample truly representative. And the response is high (few people will refuse to answer an interviewer's questions).

Personal interviewing is expensive. (It can easily cost several dollars per interview.) Interviewers can bias the answers or lead the respondents. They may select the wrong respondent and they may do the job superficially or even completely falsify questionnaires. Personal interviewing takes a lot of time. Interviewers require special selection, training, and supervision. Their work must be checked to find out if they are really making the calls they report.

(c) *Telephone surveys.* Making a survey by telephone is relatively inexpensive and fast. By use of a reverse telephone book which lists numbers by address rather than alphabetically, it is possible to concentrate calls in specific areas (such as the area within walking distance of a store).

Unlisted telephones create a problem. In New York City, 30% of the phones are unlisted. In Chicago, 33%, and in Los Angeles, 38% of the

*Unless the survey gets a 75% to 80% response, it is likely to be unrepresentative. This, then, necessitates a check of nonrespondents. Because of these faults, mail surveys are being used less and less frequently.

telephone numbers are not in the book. There is no trustworthy information as to who these people are or why they choose to be unlisted. Some research firms have developed ways to get around this by dialing random numbers in given exchanges without knowing who they talk to, but with some idea as to the area in which these people are located.

Generally, telephone surveys cannot use long or complicated questionnaires. Their use in rural areas is not very satisfactory because of costs, poor transmission, the party line that cannot be tied up for lengthy conversation, and the fact that telephone installations are not as universal as in cities.

Getting calls through is always a problem regardless of whether they are to rural or urban numbers. Many people are not at home when called and this necessitates callbacks or substitutions. If lower-income people are important to the study, the telephone should not be used. Many of these people do not have telephones and therefore have no chance to be included in the sample. The biggest disadvantage is the limitations of the questioning technique. Scaling questions such as bipolar are difficult to use and ranking of more than three or four factors is impossible.

(d) *Group surveys*. A group survey can be done quickly and inexpensively. By assembling the respondents, explaining the questionnaire, and asking for "on-the-spot" completion, the whole task can be done in a hurry.

A serious disadvantage of this system is that in such a situation there is a tendency to give inaccurate answers. In spite of assurances of anonymity, there is a subconscious feeling that individual answers will be identifiable. Also, these studies are expensive because the respondents usually are paid to come in to a central location. The sample, too, may be biased. Some potential respondents are too timid to come to a business office, but may be willing to meet at another location such as a church or other public place.

Doing the Research

Having decided whom to survey, what will be asked and how the survey will be conducted, the next thing is to do the job. This involves several steps. A questionnaire must be prepared in final form and pretested to eliminate anything that confuses the respondents. When the questionnaire is acceptable, the entire sample is questioned and the questionnaires are collected, edited, and tabulated. The findings are analyzed and conclusions are drawn and ultimately incorporated into recommendations.

Preparing the questionnaire and pretesting During preliminary stages, the questionnaire may go through several revisions. When it is believed to be adequate, a few copies are mimeographed or duplicated in some convenient manner and a limited number of respondents are interviewed. Twenty to fifty is normally adequate. This first batch of questionnaires is carefully checked to see what kind of answers are being given

BANK OF AMERICA

CUSTOMER RELATIONS SURVEY

1. HOW DO YOU RATE THE **TELLERS** ON: (Please check one in each category)

	Excellent	Good	Fair	Poor
Courtesy	☐	☐	☐	☐
Knowing their job	☐	☐	☐	☐
Personal Appearance	☐	☐	☐	☐

2. WHEN YOU VISIT YOUR BRANCH, ARE YOU **USUALLY** WAITED ON:

Without Waiting ☐   Short Wait ☐   Long Wait ☐   Very Long Wait ☐

3. DO THE TELLERS **CALL YOU BY NAME?**

Always ☐   Usually ☐   Sometimes ☐   Almost Never ☐ (or Never)   Don't Remember ☐

4. DO THE TELLERS **THANK YOU?**

Always ☐   Usually ☐   Sometimes ☐   Almost Never ☐ (or Never)   Don't Remember ☐

5. FROM YOUR PERSONAL EXPERIENCE WITH THE **OFFICERS**, HOW DO YOU RATE THEM ON:

	Excellent	Good	Fair	Poor	Unable to Rate (No Experience)
Courtesy	☐	☐	☐	☐	☐
Knowledge of your type of transaction	☐	☐	☐	☐	☐
Personal Appearance	☐	☐	☐	☐	☐

6. HOW DO YOU RATE YOUR BRANCH COMPARED TO **OTHER BANKS:**

Better than most	About the same	Not as good	Worse	No previous Experience
☐	☐	☐	☐	☐

7. TO FURTHER ASSIST US IN THIS SURVEY PLEASE CHECK

Your sex: Your approximate age:

MALE ☐   FEMALE ☐   Under 30 ☐   30-45 ☐   46-65 ☐   Over 65 ☐

WE WOULD BE GRATEFUL FOR YOUR COMMENTS AND SUGGESTIONS_____

_____

_____

_____

Fig. 19.2 Questionnaire used to determine customer opinion.

and which questions, if any, seem to be confusing. Corrections are made and another small number of respondents is interviewed. If the problems are solved, the questionnaire is then duplicated in sufficient quantity to supply all respondents who are to be questioned. Usually the question-naire is printed and each question is always numbered so that answers can be tabulated.

Interviewing   Regardless of the manner of questioning, the survey should be done as rapidly as possible to avoid changes in opinion or attitude that can occur with the passage of time. Whenever possible, there should be no identification of the principal for whom the research is being conducted although, of course, in some cases it will be obvious.

Interviewers must be instructed to *read* the questions exactly as worded. A very slight change of wording can sometimes seriously bias the results. Most people do not object to being interviewed (very few feel that their privacy is being invaded) although they will occasionally decline to an-swer some question (Hartman, Isaacson, Lawrence, and Jurgell, 1968).

Editing and tabulating   In any survey there will be incomplete ques-tionnaires, errors, and unresponsive answers. On some, the defects will be slight or amendable but, if the questionnaire is not usable, it should be discarded. All satisfactory questionnaires are then tabulated, in order to determine the numbers of answers of each kind to each question; for example, 814 said "yes," and 139 said "no" to Question No 6. In large surveys the data is placed on punch cards and put through tabulating machines. With small surveys, the data can be recorded by hand.

Analysis and Conclusion

With all data tabulated, the figures are analyzed to see what the weight of opinion is on each question. From this comes the drawing of conclu-sions as to its significance and possible action that may be indicated. The analysis and conclusions should not be entrusted completely to an outside organization because, at this point, familiarity with the organization sponsoring the survey should be a major factor in determining what the figures mean and what should be done.

Here judgment is crucial. It must be made by people who know the organization, who know the public surveyed and who know why the questions were asked. Everyone involved in the evaluation must ask: "Is this true?" "Do we believe this?" "Can we rely on these facts?" On four different occasions, the author has refused to believe the findings of nationally known and impeccably honest and accurate research organizations—because he *knew* they were wrong. In every case there was an ultimate discovery of the cause of the error.

One final comment on research. Research can define a problem. It cannot solve a problem. It can tell you what is right or wrong. It cannot tell you what to do.

Reporting and Recommendations

The finding of the research should be reported to management, and, if action is indicated, it should be recommended as promptly as possible. The recommendation may involve policy, action or program — or all three.

SPECIAL TYPES OF RESEARCH

In addition to the normal survey, there are other means of sampling opinion that should be noted.

Focus Group Interviews

This is a fast and economical way to get information. It is often used to discover whether a sizable survey should be made. Participants, usually about 8 to 10, are selected to be representative of the public involved (e.g., housewives under 35, or employees with over 10 years service, etc.). The respondents are seated around a table and their comments are recorded. The discussion is led by the person conducting the interview whose purpose is to get participants to talk freely about the topic.

A group interview of this sort gives respondents ample time to think, it allows free-wheeling discussion, and the participants stimulate each other to voice more ideas. It is more valuable as a means of getting possible public viewpoints than for measuring opinion.

A disadvantage is that one person may monopolize the conversation or influence the answers of others. Also, the discussion can easily stray far from the subject. And the microphone may not register all that is said or do it so poorly (because of several people talking at once) that it cannot be transcribed. Also, obviously, the results cannot be projected to any public — the number of participants is too small for a reliable representation and, as mentioned before, the opinions obtained may be group opinion rather than individual opinions.

Motivation Research

People often conceal their true thoughts, even in an anonymous survey, so motivation research is used to dig into the subconscious and find out what people *really* think. It is done by means of what is called a "depth interview" — prolonged questioning without a questionnaire. Often the interview is recorded. The work can be done only by an expert. It requires knowledge of psychology, anthropology, and sociology. Obviously it is costly and time-consuming.

The basis of motivation research is that most attitudes are emotional rather than rational; in order to understand attitudes, it is necessary to uncover the subconscious psychological influences that cause them. The analysis is an interpretation of the results in light of our knowledge in the social sciences rather than a strict analysis of results.

There has been considerable controversy over the use of motivation research, but it can be a valuable tool when used properly.

Projection Techniques

This process, like the "depth interview," is an effort to probe into the subconscious. Typical methods are to ask the respondent to complete a sentence or write his caption for a picture or fill the balloons in a cartoon with the words he thinks are appropriate. Thus, a cartoon of a supervisor talking to an employee might yield words indicating that the supervisor is incompetent or overbearing or that he really helps those who work under him. Conducting and evaluating this kind of research is a task for experts only (Anderson and Anderson, 1951).

"Delphi"

This is a method developed by a Rand research group for use in forecasting public opinion trends. It asks each respondent to name one problem that he or she considers important. When all ideas are received, each is listed on a questionnaire. This is submitted to all respondents, who are asked to rate the importance of each suggestion on a rating scale. The scale usually ranges from a high of five (very important) to a low of one (not very important).

By grouping all suggestions into categories (e.g., fringe benefits) and asking the respondents to rate the categories and the specific ideas in each category, it is possible to get a very clear indication of the relative importance of each suggestion. (See "Delphi: Polling for Concensus," *Public Relations Journal*, February 1978.)

311

"Quester"

This is a copyrighted technique for determining attitudes by a computerized analysis of words used in answering questions. It is an effort to economically get the kind of information received through depth interviews. Tested over a period of several years, this innovation has yielded very encouraging results (PR Reporter, November 28, 1977).

NEW USES OF RESEARCH

A study of public opinion research for the Foundation for Public Relations Research and Education has indentified three new uses for research:

1. *Environmental Monitoring* — the study of trends, events and actions which may affect the social, political, and economic environment of the organization.
2. *Public Relations Audits* — the identification of the publics involved with specific issues and the assessment of their political power.
3. *Social Audits* — the assessment of the social responsibility and performance of the organization.

REDUCING THE COST OF RESEARCH

Research can cost a great amount of money. Often a special survey is the only way to get the needed information, but before any survey is launched, there should be thorough investigation of all existing data. This analysis can frequently produce answers which may negate the need for a special survey. At the least, this review may help shape the new survey or reduce the number of questions which need to be asked.

Another way to hold down research costs is to split the cost with some other organization. These arrangements can be made through the firm which conducts the research.

EXERCISES

1. Visit your college library and look at the *Business Periodical Index*.
   (a) How many articles on water pollution were listed in the latest issue?
   (b) How many articles on energy conservation were listed?

2. Telephone some trade association listed in the local telephone book.
   (a) Ask if they can give you statistics about some specific phase of their business.
   (b) Ask if they keep a library of information about their industry.

Case Problem

You are public relations director of a large bank. You believe that the bank has a reputation for stodginess. Draft a questionnaire that will find whether this is true or not.

Who would you survey?

What kind of sample would you use?

How many people would you survey? Why?

What demographic breakdowns would you make? Why are these important?

Planning 20

Planning is indispensable in a public relations program. In fact, planning is what makes a program. Without planning, there can be only disorganized activity. With planning, there can be definite objectives, specific accomplishments, and measurable results.

Planning permits public relations activity to be positive rather than defensive. It eliminates the grab-bag approach and it insures that the right action will be taken at the right time. Planning, by setting goals, enables management to evaluate its programs. And, finally, planning insures management support because when top management has approved a definite program, it then becomes a party to the activity; it shares responsibility and therefore has a vested interest in its success.

THE IMPORTANCE OF OBJECTIVES

Management by objectives (MBO) is an old and proven idea that is attracting new attention in business and in nonbusiness organizations. Essentially, management by objectives means that the organization determines exactly what it intends to accomplish and allocates to every department or division what it must contribute so that its objectives may be met. By this system, every manager knows what the objective is for the organization and what his own department must accomplish.

Without management by objectives, a corporation could have a very strong desire to grow, but the approach might be haphazard. With MBO, the corporation might establish a goal of increasing sales by 50% and profits by 75% in five years. This would then require specific objectives for the various departments. Each would have certain things to do in

315

order for the corporation to attain that increase, and each would have very specific numerical goals that could be easily measured (Humble, 1970).

It is easy to visualize how MBO can work in a manufacturing concern. It is easy to visualize a sales manager planning and building an organization that would be selling 50% more goods in five years — but what about public relations? Can its contributions to overall objectives be measured? Yes! Can its accomplishments be expressed in figures? Yes! And as MBO becomes the rule rather than the exception, PR practitioners will be forced to set specific objectives and to show exactly how their activities contribute to attainment of the overall objective of the organization.

It has been indicated that there are eight general areas of objectives that must be set for a business organization; the list can be modified for other types of organizations (Drucker, 1954):

market standing
innovation
productivity
physical and financial resources
profitability
manager performance and development
worker performance and attitude
public responsibility.

Public relations might be a factor in almost any of these objectives. Through product publicity it could improve market standing. Through awareness of public needs and interests it might find opportunities for innovation. Through employee relations it might help increase productivity. A financial relations program might help develop financial resources. As an internal communications tool, it might help motivate everyone toward the objective of increasing profitability. Management performance and development could be aided by publicizing progress. Worker performance and attitude could be improved through an employee relations program. Public responsibility is a particularly responsive area. Through public relations the organization can learn public attitudes, determine policy responsive to those attitudes, and then convince the public that their interests are being well served.

In establishing objectives it should be possible to set a numerical base point from which progress can be measured. For example, a survey might establish the fact that only 15% of stockowners at large know what Company A makes or does. The objective might be to raise that figure to 45% in one year. Or a survey might show that in the community of Company B,

80% of the people think that it is a major source of air pollution. The objective might be, after eliminating the pollution, to reduce that figure to 0%.

This will probably yield some side benefits. When MBO was applied to a large industrial relations department, the quality of work improved, payroll was reduced, some long-standing programs were found to be ineffective or unnecessary and were eliminated, there was a heightened sense of purpose in the department, and its acceptance by the rest of the organization was improved (McConkey, 1967). Similar results would seem likely to occur in public relations.

MBO concentrates the organization's efforts on opportunities rather than problems, and this can be of great help to a public relations program. Drucker says that the biggest successes come to the innovators and that forcing oneself to respect the apparent irrationality of others may be the best way to see the organization from their viewpoint (Drucker, 1964). Innovation in public relations might well be extremely effective. Great benefits might feed back to those who look for opportunity to serve the public interest and who do not restrict their efforts to solving current problems.

Looking into the future and planning ten or fifteen years ahead could be the best way to do this. Most businesses have been growth-oriented for many years but recent developments have shown that this may be changing. Public utilities that once tried to sell ever-increasing quantities of power are now urging people to use less. The governor of Oregon has publicly stated that he is opposed to efforts urging industries to move into his state. These are just two straws in the wind but they may be very significant. Perhaps growth will no longer be the prime objective. In any case, MBO will probably play an important role. The PR practitioner should plan his work by objectives even if it is not the rule in his organization. He should do it for one simple reason — he will get better results.

Suggested Readings

Anscher, Melvin (Ed.). *Managing the Socially Responsible Corporation*. New York: Macmillan, 1974.
Benje, Eugene J. *Elements of Modern Management*. New York: American Management Association, 1976.
Feinberg, Samuel. *Management's Challenge—The People Problem*. New York: Fairchild, 1976.
Mati, Paul. *How to Manage by Objectives*. New York: Wiley, 1975.

FUNDAMENTALS OF PLANNING

There are many kinds of planning in public relations. There are long-range plans which may be semi-permanent in nature and, conversely, there are short-range plans geared to a specific objective within a short period of time; in addition, long- and short-range plans may work together toward the same goal. Planning is constant in public relations and any plan may need frequent reappraisal to insure that the right actions are being taken at the right time. All plans are subject to revision as goals are attained or as problems change.

In making plans, several principles must be followed. The plan must recognize that every organization is different and that no two situations are alike. The plan must fit the situation both internally and externally. It must be both practical and palatable and, finally, it must be appropriate.

The Difference in Organizations

It is obvious, of course, that a big firm is different from a small one and that a college is quite unlike a machinery manufacturer. But these are not the most important differences, because big firms are not necessarily alike and machinery manufacturers often have little in common aside from the kind of products they make. Management and the past history of the organization are the factors that make them different. Any plan must be based on a thorough knowledge of the organization and its differences from others.

The Difference in Situations

Every situation is unique. Organizations seldom face identical problems. Even if they were quite similar in every other way, it would not be possible to use the same public relations plan. It is conceivable that two breweries could exchange successful advertising campaigns without any effect on sales because, essentially, they are selling similar or practically identical products to the same customers. But the organizations themselves, their publics, and their problems are not identical; consequently, their public relations plans must be quite different.

Recognition of the Situation

A public relations plan must be fitted to the situation both internally and externally. It must be based on complete knowledge of the facts and of the people involved. It must recognize the personalities of those in management and it must be suited to the public it aims to influence. If the plan is right for the situation, it can succeed. If it does not conform to these requirements, it will fail.

Practicality

A plan must be feasible. Its execution must be within the power of the organization and it must be financially possible. It is not at all difficult to think up many desirable alternatives. The problem is to concentrate attention on those that can be done and afforded, and then to decide which ones have priority.

Palatability

It is possible to put together a plan that has many virtues, including practicality, which may not be palatable to top management. Personal tastes or idiosyncrasies may prevent its acceptance. By knowing the people involved and by consulting with them during the planning stage, resistance to the plan can be eliminated.

Future Trends

A plan should always consider the changing environment. It should be based on awareness of cultural, social, technological, economic, and political factors which will assume importance in the future.

Appropriateness

A plan must be appropriate to the organization. People have a great capacity for spotting insincerity and artificiality. An organization cannot get away with a program which the public recognizes as out of step with the nature of the sponsor. The plan must be fitted to the existing public image.

FORMULATING A PLAN

Planning starts with facts and ends with a recommended program. The steps include gathering of information, analysis of the problem, determination of causes, study of similar situations, development of possible plans, selection of the best plan, and recommendation of that plan to management. This takes time and it is, therefore, imperative that enough time be allowed for deliberate, orderly planning.

Gathering Information

Every piece of information bearing on the subject must be considered.

The various channels of inbound communication are all involved in this process. Clippings, reference works, research reports, personal experience, and past activities should be funneled into a central assemblage and condensed into a summary that could be described as "everything we know about the situation."

Analysis

When all the information is assembled, the next step is to analyze it and determine its significance. This process includes evaluation of the information. It asks questions such as "How much can we rely on this statement?" "How accurate is that report?" "Does Joe Blank know or is he guessing?" "How valid is that research report?" "Which of these conflicting pieces of information do we believe?" When this process is complete, it is possible to accurately define the problem or problems or even to decide that there is none.

Determination of Causes

Often it is possible to find out just why a problem exists. Thus, a store might be losing charge customers because of a billing procedure or a factory might be having trouble recruiting employees because of a misunderstanding about working conditions.

Study of Similar Situations

Experience is widely praised as a teacher and, if someone else has faced a similar situation, information about his success or failure may be very useful. Consultation with others or study of their reports can often save time, money, and scars.

Possible Plans

There is usually more than one way to accomplish something. The first solution proposed may or may not be the best, so all possible plans should be considered along with their advantages and disadvantages. Then the various possibilities should be examined in detail and discussed with those who can contribute to the process of selecting the best one.

Strategy and Tactics

Strategy means what to do. Tactics means how to do it. Choosing the correct strategy is essential. For example, take the problem of preventing construction of a nuclear power plant in an area which has great recreational value.

Nuclear power is highly controversial. Opinions on both sides are intense. Preserving recreational areas is not nearly so controversial. Most people are for the concept — at least in the abstract.

In this case, the mose effective strategy will be to oppose construction of the plant *at that particular location*. This avoids the nuclear power controversy and concentrates the whole struggle on preservation of a recreational area.

Recommended Plan

When the best possible plan has been decided upon it must be presented to management for approval. Often the plan includes recommendations on policy, and this requires that management not only approve a public relations plan but also establish a policy as a foundation for the plan. Regardless of the nature or content of the plan, and regardless of whether a policy decision is involved, the recommendations should be presented as a complete plan that can be put into effect upon approval. It should be definite and precise and the reasons for the recommendations should be clearly documented.

CONTENT OF A PLAN

A plan consists of four parts:

1. the reason,
2. the objective(s),
3. the means,
4. the costs.

The plan may have one objective or several. It may be aimed at one public or at all publics. It may be a plan for hours or for years. It may be simple or complex. It may be unified or it may have numerous phases. But regardless of its nature, a plan should always tell the reason, the objective(s), the means for attaining the objective(s), and the cost. (The objective(s) must, of course, include the "expected result(s).") There will often be a separate plan for each public.

The Reason

Management is not likely to approve a public relations plan until it is convinced that the activity is necessary. Also it can better judge the merits of the program if it understands the situation that leads to a recommendation for action. In some cases, there will be specific problems which must be solved and, if management recognizes the problems, it will probably be willing to implement a solution. Even if there are no problems that handicap the organization, there will be situations or attitudes that can be improved.

In this part of the plan, it is advisable to include the summary of what is known, the analysis of the situation, and the determination of causes together with a convincing statement as to the necessity for action. For example, a "reason" might include a report on a customer survey showing great dissatisfaction with billing procedures, an analysis of billing procedures indicating that this dissatisfaction is justified but that a customer-pleasing modification can be made without excessive cost, and a persuasive statement that the change should be made and that customers should be told.

This is, of course, a very simplified illustration. Situations may be much more complex; there may be numerous problems all of which affect the whole. Even the most complicated circumstances should be clarified and boiled down to an understandable statement of the facts and their causes.

The Objective(s)

This is the most important part of the plan. It is the statement of specific goals. Often it is slighted or forgotten, yet no public relations activity can really succeed without a clearly defined objective. The ablest public relations practitioner supported by a gigantic budget will fail unless he or she knows exactly what is to be accomplished. The rankest beginner can make progress if goals are specified.

Objectives may be as simple as "to double the percentage of employees who are using the company stock purchase plan" or "to go a year without a lost-time accident." Objectives may be as complicated as "to persuade a two-thirds majority of the voters to support a bond issue for airport improvement" or "to reduce the number of people who think Corporation X has little regard for the public, from the current 15% to 10% in one year."

Frequently a plan contains several objectives which may be related or unrelated. There may be different objectives with different publics and multiple objectives with any public. Thus, there can be a broad objective of improving employee relations by attaining a number of specific goals with that one public. And sometimes the same effort can attain objectives with more than one public. For example, a plant tour might cover half a dozen publics and attain slightly different objectives with each. The important thing is to be sure that there is a definite purpose and that all involved know exactly what it is.

Sometimes it is difficult to state the objectives; that is precisely the time to take heed. If the objective cannot be stated clearly, there may be no need for action. Working without an objective is like riding aimlessly in a car. Considerable time and money can be used up but the driver may finish the trip exactly where he started.

The Means

This part of the plan deals with the method by which the objectives are to be attained. It is the "how" of the plan. Essentially it consists of four interrelated sections: (1) who to reach, (2) how to reach them, (3) what to say to them, (4) when to say it.

Who to reach   In its simplest form, this means the publics who will be affected by the plan. Usually, however, it is not quite that simple because no public is uniform and homogeneous. Some individuals and groups are more influential or vociferous than others. There are forces which can help and others which can hinder. There are people or groups of unusual prestige or ability whose support or opposition can sway others just because they are recognized as important. These should be identified and given special consideration. On many issues there will be a few people with strong opinions on each side and many people with no solid opinions. These facts must be recognized. Special efforts must be made to gain the support and help of the "friends" and to counteract the opposition either by converting them or by neutralizing their actions.

Thus, on a "conservation" issue there will be individuals and groups who feel strongly and will work diligently to advance the proposed conservation effort. Opposed will be the individuals and organizations who will gain financially if the conservation effort is blocked.

A typical illustration may be found in the long struggle for a Redwood National Park. The "pros" were spearheaded by the Sierra Club while the "cons" were headed by the lumbering interests. Also prominent in this issue were the governor of California, the Secretary of the Interior, the California Redwood Association (lumbering), the Save the Redwoods League (conservation), the Redwood Empire Association (travel), the California State Parks Commission, the U.S. Forest Service, the congressman for the district where the redwoods grow, several other congressmen, the Chambers of Commerce of numerous cities in the redwood country, and a great many other individuals, organizations, and groups.

Whenever a public relations plan is created, the "who to reach" question must be expanded to "who can and will help and how do we get their help?" "Who can and will hinder and how do we convince them or counteract their opposition?"

How to reach them Selecting the right channels is a vital decision in any public relations plan. Making this decision requires a thorough understanding of the characteristics of the channels. It also requires consideration of the people who are to be reached and the message that is to be conveyed to them. Some channels are more efficient than others in reaching specific audiences and in carrying specific messages. Often there are alternatives of equal efficiency and frequently a number of channels may be used at the same time and for the same purpose.

The problem is to choose those which will accomplish the task most effectively. Cost must be a factor but it should not be the controlling factor. A letter may be cheaper than a personal contact but there are times when one personal contact will accomplish more than a thousand letters, even though the contact may cost more than the thousand letters.

Choosing the right channels necessitates reflection. It involves asking such questions as: "Can this be explained verbally or should it be written down?" "Should we produce one 32-page booklet or four 8-page booklets?" "Should we have one general meeting or a series of departmental meetings?" "Shall we try to explain it all at once or shall we do it a step at a time and give people time to digest the ideas?" "Do we need a motion picture or can we do it with slides?" "Who will be the best person to present the idea?" "Shall we rely on publicity or do we need to run some advertising?" "Which channels will get the most attention from the audience?"

The public relations practitioner must look at his channels much as a carpenter looks at his tool chest. All tools have a purpose. Many of them are interchangeable to some degree, each is better for some uses than any other tool, and frequently it is necessary to use several tools to accomplish the task. Knowing what has to be accomplished and what each tool can do will enable either the PR man or the carpenter to pick those best suited for the particular job at hand.

What to say The purpose of any public relations plan is to affect public opinion. Public opinion is affected by giving people ideas. This requires deciding which ideas are to be communicated to the public or publics involved and how they are to be presented. Making this decision requires that two questions be asked: "Which ideas do we want to communicate?" and "Which is the mose effective way to have them accepted?"

Answering these questions requires first, a study of the objectives and second, a study of human nature and the art of communication.

A good illustration of the process can be made from a prior example:

Objective — To persuade a two-thirds majority of the voters to support a bond issue for airport improvement.

Which ideas do we want to communicate?

A. That the bond issue is absolutely essential.
B. That the bonds will be paid off by airline fees.

Which is the most effective way to have them accepted?

A. Do we point out the advantages of passage or the disadvantages of failure?
B. Do we tell the voters that the airlines will pay off the bonds, or do we tell them that the bond issue will not raise taxes?

In every PR situation a similar process is involved. The "what to say" section does not deal with the actual words. It concentrates on the basic ideas to be conveyed.

When to say it   Timing is seldom given enough consideration in public relations plans. Yet, it can make the difference between success and failure. There are two phases of timing to be concerned about. One is involved with the "timeliness" of the program, the other with the sequence of its parts.

Timeliness should always be considered. This means that PR activities should be scheduled to coincide with public interest because ideas will be better received by the public when their interest has been intensified by other factors. Thus, winter is the time to talk about cold prevention, tire chains, antifreeze, and insulation. A disastrous fire opens public minds to thinking about fire insurance and fire-fighting equipment.

The sequence of any public relations plan should be thought out very carefully. Essentially, the problem is to put first things first and to make sure that each step leads clearly and logically to the next. Thus, if understanding idea A is necessary to the understanding of idea B, it becomes imperative to explain idea A before idea B is exposed to the public. A sequence that is often used is (1) state the problem (2) state possible solutions (3) evaluate possible solutions (4) recommend the preferred solution and explain why it is best.

The Costs

No organization is likely to approve a public relations activity until the cost is known. Accordingly, every PR plan must include a budget. If the plan is large and complex, the budget may contain a great many items. Conversely, the plan may cover one activity and require only a small onetime appropriation. The guideline is to include in the plan a cost figure for every separate item proposed. If the plan involves twenty different activities, a cost figure for each activity must be shown.

Management does not like blanket appropriations or blank checks. It is entitled to know where the money is going and usually it demands a detailed accounting. Some managers treat budgets rigidly while others allow a little flexibility. The financial practices and policies of the organization must be known and adhered to in preparing and managing the public relations budget. In its simplest form, the PR budget says "Here is what we propose to do. This is what it will cost."

An excellent example of a public relations plan is that of the Chemical Industries Council of the Midwest prepared by Daniel J. Edelman, Inc.

Why Necessary: The chemical industry has a continuing need for new talent.

Reason: Many young people are unaware of the opportunities in the chemical industry.

Objective: To interest high-school students in chemical industry careers.

Means:
Who to reach: High-school students and their teachers.
How to reach them:
(a) *Conference and luncheon for high-school guidance counselors and chemistry teachers.*
The purpose is to provide these teachers with up-to-date information on careers in chemistry.
(b) *Chemistry career seminar.* This annual event brings students and industry personnel into direct contact through personal interviews.
(c) *CIC speakers panel.* The panel members appear regularly in high schools throughout the Chicago area.
(d) *CIC inner-city careers team.* This team goes to inner-city schools in order to inform students who have had no contact with the chemical industry.
(e) *The Davidson Award.* This award is presented annually to the outstanding high-school chemistry teacher.
(f) *CIC scholarships and fellowships.* The council annually presents scholarships and fellowships to outstanding students.

(g) *Spring Scholarship Luncheon.* At this annual luncheon attended by over 600 industry representatives and guests, the scholarships and fellowships are presented.

(h) *Environmental Health.* A CIC committee has been formed to find ways in which the industry can aid in this area.

What to say: In general terms the message is that the chemical industry is interesting and challenging and that there are many opportunities for jobs in that industry.

When to say it: All year and every year.

Costs: Not available.

Participation in Planning

Creating a public relations plan is the responsibility of the public relations department or counsel. These people do all the work, but they do not operate in a vacuum. Consultation with those who can affect the plan or who will be affected by it is essential. By giving these people a chance to express their ideas, two important things are accomplished. First, the consultation prevents errors and gains expert help in devising the most effective program. Second, consultation gets people involved. It gives them a vested interest in the success of the plan and assures their cooperation and assistance in its execution.

PERT

This is an acronym for Program Evaluation and Review Techniques. What it really means is planning activities so that they will be done on time.

PERT requires a determination of what is needed, when it will be needed, and how long it will take to do it. When this is determined, it becomes possible to set specific dates for every step in the activity and thus guarantee completion on time.

Here is a simple example of how it works. It is necessary to produce a brochure which must be in the mail on July 1. It is calculated that these amounts of time will be needed: Outline and layout, one week; copy writing, one week; copy and layout approval, one week; photography and charts, two weeks; typesetting and engraving, one week; approval and corrections, one week; printing and binding, two weeks; safety allowance, two weeks. Total time required, 11 weeks.

Counting 11 weeks back from July 1 gives a starting date of April 15 and the following check dates:

start outline and layout — April 15,
complete outline and layout — April 22,
complete copy — April 29,
copy and layout approved — May 6,
complete photography and charts — May 20,
complete typesetting and engravings — May 27,
correction and approval of proofs — June 3,
printing and binding complete — June 17,
delivery (even with delays) — July 1,

Whenever a program consists of many different parts or steps, or when it involves many people (an annual report for example), it is imperative to follow this procedure. It is best implemented with a large chart in calendar form which shows which items are due on given dates.

EMERGENCY PLANS

Any organization big enough to be well-known to the general public or having any potentially hazardous activities should have an emergency public relations plan. A fire in a five-employee store may not be of much general interest but if a fire occurs in a major department store, the interest will be great enough to necessitate a plan.

Most typically in need of emergency plans are transportation companies, public utilities, and manufacturers where large or dangerous products are handled or where large machines are used. Accidents can happen, and if they involve people or property to a substantial degree there will be great public interest. No one knows when an accident will occur, and when it does, there is no time for planning; accordingly, emergency plans must be prepared in advance and they must be known to all who might be involved.

Emergency plans need to include these points: (1) who in the organization is to be notified; (2) who is to be the spokesman, (3) how the news media are to be handled; (4) notification of families.

Notification

The general rule is that all concerned, management plus the PR department, should be notified. Thus, an accident in Department No. 9 should be reported to the superintendent of the department, to his bosses all the way up the corporate ladder, and to the public relations department. There would be no point in notifying other department superintendents unless they are affected.

Spokesman

It is advisable to have all inquiries and especially all reporters directed to one person who can speak for the organization. In most cases the director of public relations will be designated for this assignment, although, if a very large organization is involved and the accident is a real catastrophe, there will be demands for a statement by the chief executive officer.

Dealing With News Media

The rule for reporters is very simple — "help them get the truth." Anything that will facilitate their efforts to get all the facts should be done. The first step is to notify all interested media. In some cases they will be aware of the situation but this should not be assumed. They should be told.

The second step is to facilitate their coverage of the story. Desk space, typewriters, and telephones should be made available if possible. The spokesman for the organization must be accessible and stay accessible. A press conference should be held if there are any developments justifying the joint attention of all reporters.

Reporters want the news as fast as it becomes available. They want to know what happened, who was involved and how, when, where, and why it happened.

Reporters want human interest. They want to know about the people involved: their number, their names, addresses, jobs, extent of injuries, the hospitals where the injured have been taken, the notification of families.

Reporters also want to know what caused the accident, the effect it will have on the business, corrective measures that will be taken, the history of the facilities involved, and who was at fault. All these can be answered except the last. Because damage suits may be involved, it is extremely important that no one admit fault. Thus the reporters' request for information should be answered with what, who, how, where, and when, but not with "why."

Notification of Families

This is a particularly important part of any emergency plan. Some spokesman for the organization should personally notify the wives or other "next of kin" of any people who have been killed or injured. Often it is desirable to have the spokesman accompanied by a minister, priest, or rabbi or by a very close friend of the family. All of this, of course, requires either very complete personnel records or some very fast work to locate the people whose presence will ease the shock of the news. Families should be notified before names are released to the news media.

THE PROOF OF THE PUDDING

The value of an emergency plan was demonstrated when two tankers owned by Standard Oil Company of California collided in the Golden Gate. No one was hurt, but thousands of gallons of oil were spilled into San Francisco Bay. Within hours, Standard Oil was engaged in a massive "clean-up." Hundreds of employees aided by several thousand volunteer workers swarmed onto the beaches and succeeded in eliminating most of the pollution in a few days.

Comments of the news media were highly favorable and a survey showed a generally favorable opinion of SOC. Only a very few "die-hard" activists were critical.

The reason for the success was the emergency plan. It included what SOC would do (clean up the mess immediately) and what it would say. It worked very well. In fact, the most difficult problem Standard Oil's Public Relations Department had was handling the great number of phone calls from the news media and from would-be helpers.

IT CAN HAPPEN HERE

In planning for emergencies, thinking should not be limited to accidents. Among other things which can create a public relations emergency are defective products or services, verbal or physical assaults by militants, suits for damages, attempts to break up meetings, irrational demands, seizure of property, efforts to stop activities, unfounded charges against the organization, bomb threats or actual bombings, demonstrations, boycotts, picketing, and numerous other activities. Any of these unpleasant things can happen to any organization. No one can be sure of immunity. The only safe procedure is to keep abreast of the news. Whenever any organization gets into trouble, ask the question, "What will we do and say if it happens to us?" Then have a plan for action in case it does happen.

EXERCISES

1. Can you find an example of a planned public relations effort? (Hint: look for a series of events or news items dealing with the same subject and progressing toward an objective.)

Case Problem

You are public relations director of a major railroad which wants to discontinue service on several money-losing branch lines. The Interstate Commerce Commission will rule on this, but the communities now being served will oppose the move.

Prepare a brief plan to counteract the opposition and generate public support for the discontinuance of service.

21 Outbound Communication

Outbound communication is the most conspicuous element of public relations. A good many people do not realize that there is anything else involved. Inbound communication, planning, and evaluation are not visible activities. But outbound communication is designed to attract attention and, as a consequence, it is seen and heard in varying degrees by everyone. In addition, much more time and money are spent on outbound communication than on all other public relations activities, so it naturally becomes the center of attention.

Dictionary definitions are adequate for most purposes, but in public relations it is necessary to go a step further than "informing," or "making known," or "transmitting information." It must be done in such a way that it will cause a favorable reaction on the part of the recipient of the message.

In its simplest form, communication exists when one person conveys an idea to another. Thus, a smile, a scowl, or a beckoning finger can communicate. But when the idea becomes more complex, the communication must be in words, either spoken or written. And, as the audience to be reached becomes larger and more distant, the problem of communication grows.

The purpose of outbound communication is to improve public opinion. This requires that ideas be conveyed to the public that will affect the opinions of its members.

ELEMENTS OF COMMUNICATION

Successful communication requires three main elements: a sender, a message, and a receiver. All must function effectively if the idea is to get through and create favorable opinion. To define the problem, it will be helpful to examine just what is involved in the process of communication — the conversion of an idea into a responsive action.

The Sender

There must be a physical means of transmitting the idea. It may be done by sound or sight or by both. Regardless of which is used, the following principles apply. The sender must reach the right public. It must have enough power to be heard or seen by a substantial percentage of those to whom it is aimed, and it must be used frequently enough to make a solid impression that will be retained and that can result in a change of opinion.

The Message

The message must convey the idea. This requires that the idea itself be clearly defined in terms of the desired public opinion. In other words, formulation of the message starts with the idea to be created in the minds of the public and works backward to determine what is necessary to create that idea. If the message is to be successful, it must be understandable. This means that it must be stated in the daily language of the persons to whom it is addressed. Examples and illustration (both visual and figurative) must be familiar.

The Receiver

Obviously there is no communication until the message is received and responded to. The receiver must be the right person — this requires that the message be carefully aimed to hit the correct audience. The receiver must actually get the message. (An unopened letter has not communicated.) The receiver must also absorb and think about the message and must, at the very least, be willing to believe it. The more interested the receiver is, the more likely he is to get the message. If he is vitally interested, he will make special efforts to find out about the subject.

Sending and Receiving a Message

To illustrate the communicative process, let us trace the elements necessary to successful transmission of an idea by radio.

There must be an announcer. There must be transmitting equipment. There must be power to operate the transmitter, and the power must be

Fig. 21.1   One of the top five public relations photographs in a contest conducted by the *Public Relations Journal*. Its purpose was to show that the Independent Federal Savings & Loan Association of Washington, DC is integrated. Its success was outstanding. The photograph was taken for Jeanne Viner Associates by Paul Schmick of the *Washington Evening Star*.

turned on while the announcer is speaking. If the announcer is very good, he will do better than one who has a poor voice and weak personality. If the transmitting equipment is good, the message will be clearer than if the equipment is antiquated. If the transmitter is very powerful, it will reach farther and be heard by more people than if it is weak. Assuming a good announcer, good equipment, and ample power the message should get through — and the more frequently it does (within reason), the more effective the communication will be.

The message must be in understandable language — language that is used regularly by the people to whom the message is aired. The message must reach its destination. If there is interference from static or from another station, it will not be heard clearly. It must be delivered at a time when it can be heard by the desired audience. A message to factory workers at 10:00 a.m. will not reach many of them. But 10:00 a.m. might be a very good time to reach housewives.

To receive a radio message requires a receiving set. If the receiver is a weak one, it will pick up only the closest and loudest signals. If it is powerful, it will be able to receive the weakest and most distant ones. The receiver must be hooked up to a source of electricity. It must be turned on and tuned in. The volume must be correct, and a listener must be present. He or she must be paying attention and be open to conviction, because often people listen carefully — in complete disbelief. There is no effective communication until the message is believed.

These principles apply to any means used for communication. The task is to get the right message to the right audience through the right channels.

THEORIES OF COMMUNICATION

There have been many attempts to determine how ideas get to people and affect their attitudes and opinions. Both empirical experience and research have proved that the media don't do the job alone. The media can distribute information, but this is only part of the task. The information must be received, understood, and accepted. Ideas must be absorbed and considered. Attitudes and opinions must be formed or changed. Somewhere between the media and the attitudes of the individual there is a factor which translates the information into opinion and action. That factor is the opinion leader — someone who affects the opinions of others.

Efforts to describe this process have led to numerous theories. Among the most significant theories are: the great idea theory, the two-step flow theory, the multistep flow theory, the communicator theory, and the diffusion theory.

The Great Idea Theory

While not directly applicable in day-to-day public relations activity, this theory is worthy of note as a general concept of the communication process. This theory, developed by Elmo Roper, is that "great ideas" originate with "great thinkers," such as Adam Smith, Plato, Jefferson, and Einstein. The ideas are spread by "great disciples," such as St. Paul, Huxley, Spinoza, and Lincoln. The ideas are further distributed by the "great disseminators," such as Churchill, Lippman, Hearst, and Cronkite. The ideas are extended by "lesser disseminators," such as politicians, writers, organization leaders, and so on. The ideas are received and perceived by "participating citizens," and through them, reach the "politically inert" (Katz & Lazarsfeld, 1964).

The Two-Step Flow Theory

This theory is that there is a definite, limited, and readily identifiable group of opinion leaders who get information from the media, evaluate and interpret these ideas, and communicate with other people to affect their attitudes and opinions. The two steps in the theory are from media to opinion leaders and from opinion leaders to the public. At first, this seemed like a neat solution — reach the opinion leaders, and they will reach the public. But experience proves that things aren't quite that simple because there is no permanent, definite group of opinion leaders who are influential on all subjects. This knowledge led to a modification of the two-step flow theory. . . .

The Multistep Flow Theory

This theory is based on the role of the small group in forming public opinion. It recognizes the fact that there are opinion leaders on many different subjects. John Doe may be an opinion leader on labor, Jane Doe may be an opinion leader on education, and Mary Doe may be an opinion leader on women's rights.

Also, it has been learned that there may be levels of opinion leadership on any given subject. John Doe may be influenced by John Smith. Mary Doe may be influenced by Mary Smith.

An idea on education goes through the media to the people who are opinion leaders on education and from them to the individuals who are interested in education. Thus the Jane Doe mentioned above may read a magazine article about schools and talk about it with her friends, thereby influencing their opinions.

Applying the great idea theory to this example, we might classify John Doe as a "participating citizen." The John Smith who influences John Doe on labor matters might be a "lesser disseminator," and George Meany of the AFL-CIO could be a "great disseminator."

Recognizing the importance of the small group in forming opinion, it would seem necessary to devote considerable effort to reaching the group opinion leaders. At first glance, this would seem very difficult. How could one reach opinion leaders on education in Iowa?

It might be possible to get a list of PTA presidents, but in any PTA there may be several opinion leaders who are not on any relevant list. However, this problem really solves itself. Opinion leaders are more exposed to media, they are more interested; they actively seek information. For public relations purposes, the group opinion leaders don't have to be identified. They find in the media the items that concern them. Under the "communicator" theory which is described next, the group opinion leader is an amateur communicator.

The Communicator Theory

This theory has been described in several different ways, and it has a number of names. It can be expressed as: "Convince the communicators and they will convince others." It is widely used in public relations, and it seems to work. There are two kinds of communicators — professional and amateur.

The professionals are people who earn their living in the field of mass communications — editors, reporters, commentators, writers, speakers, teachers, columnists, authors, and many others.

The amateurs do not earn their living by communicating, but they are by their nature better communicators than the mass of the population. They may be found at any level and in any location. They may be barbers or bankers, housewives or home economists, sailers or surgeons. These are the people who tell their friends and acquaintances what they heard or read and what they think about it. No one can guess how many communicators there are in any public, but their existence is obvious whenever there is a gathering of people. Some people talk and others listen. Usually the communicators do most of the talking because they have something to say.

In applying the communicator theory to public relations, it is not very practical to try to reach the amateurs. Fortunately, however, it is not necessary to go hunting for them. They reach out for information. They are the curious, the readers, the inquirers. They go to meetings, they serve on committees. They influence others not by force of position or money, but by force of their communicative talents. They are seldom experts in communication, but they do communicate.

These amateur communicators must never be forgotten. They are the people who pick up pertinent facts or memorable phrases and pass them on to their associates. By including memorable phrases and facts in public relations messages, it is possible to gain much help from these amateurs.

As for the professionals, the solution is clear. They are primary avenues of communication to the public. Every public relations program places great reliance on reaching these communicators with messages they can pass on to their readers or listeners.

The Diffusion Theory

This theory deals with the process by which ideas are adopted by individuals. It has five steps: awareness, interest, trial, evaluation, and adoption.

1. *Awareness* — the individual learns of the existence of an idea.
2. *Interest* – the individual seeks more information.
3. *Trial* — the individual tests the idea on others.
4. *Evaluation* — the individual determines whether the idea is compatible with his or her own self-interest.
5. *Adoption* — the individual incorporates the idea into his or her thinking.

BARRIERS TO COMMUNICATION

Several factors can inhibit communication. Any single one of these factors may prevent adoption of the idea and at any time several, or even all, of these may be present.

Exposure

There is no guarantee that any message will reach its target. It may not be possible to reach the desired audience because of technical difficulties such as limitations of media. There may be no media which can reach the target audience. Political restrictions or censorship may block communication. Mobil Oil Company was unable to use television to tell its side of a controversy because the networks refused to sell advertising time for the purpose even when Mobil offered to buy equal time for the other side. Economics may be a barrier. Either limited funds for the sender, high cost of media, or lack of receiver funds to buy papers and magazines may hamper delivery of the message.

Volition is another potential barrier. Some people don't, or won't, listen to some messages. The most important target groups may be the least attentive. Uneducated people don't look at educational television programs. Prejudiced people frequently refuse to listen to the other side of the argument.

Nature of Media

To reach any audience, it is essential to use media which will get to that audience with the greatest impact. This requires thorough knowledge of the characteristics of the media, the characteristics of the audience, and the media habits of the audience. An advertisement in *Time* will reach upper-income business people but not high-school dropouts. An automotive trade magazine may be ideal for reaching mechanics, but a total failure in reaching carowners.

Part V of this book is called "Channels of Communication." This is just another way of describing media.

Nature of Message

Receiving and accepting the message may be hindered by several things. The idea may be too complex for easy understanding. It may be hard to prove or demonstrate; it may be too condensed and thus omit important elements. There may not be enough repetition to drive the point across. It may be too long for the time available. For example, television has usually failed in presenting complex issues because it can't provide adequate time.

Nature of Audience

The intelligence, interest, education, and vocabulary of the audience may limit reception of the message. The adult functional competency study, conducted by the University of Texas in 1976, found that 21.7% of the adult population of the United States are functionally incompetent in reading, 32.9% are functionally incompetent in computation (practical arithmetic); 32.2% just "get by" in reading, and 26.3% just "get by" in computation. Overall competence varies by age, sex, race, and region. These variations may all be due to education or lack of education, but they do exist and must be considered.

Audience Attitudes

Individual attitudes have much to do with the receipt, understanding, and acceptance of a message. Inattention, indifference, stubbornness, antipathy, fear of new ideas, and even superstition may close minds. Some people don't want to be confused with facts because their minds are already made up.

Opposition

Even if all the foregoing barriers are surmounted, there may still be a communication failure because of opposing communication. There are two sides to every question, and if the other side does a better job, its ideas are likely to prevail. The opposition may also rely on tricks of propaganda as described in Chapter 1. Keeping track of opposition statements is essential in any controversy.

PERSUASION

Getting people to adopt ideas requires more than a bare presentation of facts. It requires interpretation of the facts in terms of the self-interest of the receivers. Successful persuasion depends on several ingredients.

The Source

Credibility of the source is a necessity. To attain credibility, there must be complete and absolute honesty. Recipients of a message are likely to assume that the source of the message is biased in its own interest. A message about the energy shortage from an independent authority will probably be more credible than a message from a producer of energy.

The Idea

The idea must be related to the hopes, fears, problems, values, and attitudes of the receivers. In simplest terms, it must appeal to their self-interest. A sheep grower is not likely to favor protecting coyotes because he believes that coyotes kill his lambs. He might favor protecting coyotes if he were convinced that coyotes get nearly all their food from the rabbits and ground squirrels which eat up the grass needed by his sheep.

The Meaning

The meaning of the message must be clear. There must be no possibility of misunderstanding. This requires careful checking of every phrase to be sure that it will be understood by the receiver. This necessitates a thorough understanding of the language used by the receivers.

Penetration

The message must get through. It must be repeated often enough to guarantee a solid impression. The more pervasive the idea, the better chance it has of reception. The person who receives the same basic message time after time — possibly in slightly different terms but always bearing the same idea — is more likely to get the idea than if he hears the message only once.

Proposed Action

There must be a recommendation for action, and the action must be possible. Generalities won't work. "Conserving energy" may evoke lip service, but not much more. "Turning down the thermostat to 68°" is something specific that can be done.

PRETESTING COMMUNICATION

It is always advisable to make sure that the message does what it is supposed to do, and to do this before it is released to the public. In the most elementary form, this test can be a mere rereading of the message to be sure it says what is intended. On a larger scale, there are several tests grouped under the general heading of "readability" (Flesch, 1946). Among the points to be checked are:

Short Sentences

Brief, clear sentences are far better than long rambling ones. Fifteen to seventeen words should be the maximum.

Good Paragraphing

Each paragraph should be a unit and cover one item only. Seven to ten lines are a good average.

Simple Words

The fewer multisyllable words the better. Short, basic words are more understandable. Three-fourths of the message words should be of one syllable.

Familiar Words

The language of the message must be the language of the receiver. Obviously, this necessitates knowing who the receivers are.

Human Interest

The more personal the message, the more it talks about people, the more effective it will be. Abstract words should be avoided.

THE IMPORTANCE OF WORDS

Words are the means by which ideas become messages and messages become attitudes. The English language has one of the largest vocabularies. With this language, it is possible to convey ideas with great precision. We can say exactly what we mean and, if we get careless, we can say something that we did not really mean. Another thing to consider is the phraseology — the way in which the words are put together.

If the ideas are properly expressed, they can be memorable — as in these example from historic events:

"Remember the Alamo" is much stronger than "Don't forget the Alamo."

"Retreat, hell! We just got here" is better than "We're not going to retreat."

"Of the people, by the people, for the people" is far more memorable than "of, by, and for the people."

The ideas are exactly the same, but the phraseology makes the difference in the effectiveness of the messages.

To choose the right words and phrases, it is necessary to recognize three points:

1. The words and phrases must mean the same thing to the receiver as they do to the sender.
2. They must be based on common experience.
3. Different audiences may need different words.

Same Meaning

Words must mean the same thing to the receiver as they do to the

343

sender. For any given word, there may be several or many different meanings. For any given meaning, there may be several different words. Take the word "strike," for example. To a baseball player, it means a pitched ball which crosses home plate at the correct height. To a union member, it means a work stoppage. But a "strike" in baseball can also be "right in the groove" or "cutting the corner of the plate." In labor, a "strike" may also be a "walkout" or "sick-out."

It is essential to think of semantics — the way in which people react to words. A good example is the word "agribusiness." It was coined to describe all the various business ramifications of agriculture. A tractor salesman is in agribusiness. So is a fertilizer manufacturer, a distributor of pesticides, a bank which loans money to farmers, a buyer of fruits and vegetables, and a truck driver who hauls farm products.

The word "agribusiness," which started out as a "good" word, has been changed into a "bad" word. Today, to most people who are not actually in or close to agriculture, the word means "big corporate farms." And big corporate farms are considered by many to be undesirable.

Common Experience

In order for a public relations message to be effective, the receiver must be able to relate the idea to himself. This requires that the idea be based on common experience. To a logger, the cry "Timber!" means "Look out, a tree is falling!" To a city dweller, the cry may mean nothing.

The reason for the difference in reactions is that the logger uses the word regularly while the urbanite has no reason to ever use it. There are words which are meaningful in the ghetto and gibberish to suburbanites. There are words which are familiar to bankers and foreign to their depositors or borrowers. There are simple words like "home," "mother," and "paycheck" which are more communicative than "residence," "maternal parent," and "compensation." It is always advisable to use words which fit into the experience of the receivers. This does not mean to use slang or jargon. Above all, keep the language simple. The following memorandum was circulated throughout IBM:

TO ALL IBM MANAGERS

A foreign language has been creeping into many of the presentations I hear and the memos I read. It adds nothing to a message but noise, and I want your help in stamping it out. It's called gobbledygook.

There's no shortage of examples. Nothing seems to get finished anymore — it gets "finalized." Things don't happen at the same time but "coincident with this action."

Believe it or not, people will talk about taking a "commitment position" and then because of the "volatility of schedule changes" they will "decommit" so that our "posture vis-a-vis some data base that needs a sizing will be able to enhance competitive positions."

That's gobbledygook.

It may be acceptable among bureaucrats but not in this company. IBM wasn't built with fuzzy ideas and pretentious language. IBM was built with clear thinking and plain talk. Let's keep it that way.

Tom Watson Jr.

Difference in Audiences

Intelligence, education, and experience all exert a profound influence on the ability of an audience to understand a message. A group of college professors might have great intelligence, a vast array of advanced degrees, and very little experience. To persuade them to accept a certain idea would require a very different message from the kind that would be used to convince a group of people who had a great deal of experience, high-school education, and average intelligence. A still different sort of message would be needed if the audience had very little education, sub-average intelligence, and not very much experience.

The point here is to know the audience — its intelligence, its education, its experience — and to know it well enough to be able to communicate ideas by use of the right words. Of course, no audience is uniform in these three characteristics, but it is possible to find the median and aim there. There will always be a few who will think the message is too complicated and a few who will think it is too simple. If it is aimed at the middle of the group, most members will receive it.

KEYS TO SUCCESSFUL COMMUNICATION

Because communications is so vast a field, it is only possible here to point out a few guideposts. Knowing them will not necessarily make the user an expert, but using them will give a much better chance for success. The keys are: right people, right channels, right time, right message, and right words.

Right People

It is imperative that the message reach the right people — those who are to be influenced. If the message does not reach enough of them, it will be ineffective. If it reaches many others than the target group, it can have "waste circulation" and be more costly than necessary. The right people may vary from time to time, from situation to situation, and from organization to organization. At one time, a handful of people may be all that need to be reached. At another time, the "right" people may be "all employees" or "the community."

In one situation, the "right" people may be one influential communicator — e.g., a columnist who has incorrect information. In the next situation, the "right" people may number in the thousands.

In Organization A, the "right" people might all be at one location. In Organization B, they might be scattered all over the country.

The "right people" are found by answering this question: "Who must we reach in order to attain our objective?" This, of course, requires that the objective be clearly defined.

"Right" people also applies to the organization. By selecting as spokesmen or "voices" the most effective people available, there is assurance of better delivery of the message and better acceptance of it. It may be the president who signs the "letter to stockholders" but some other person who makes the speeches at the stockholders' meeting. The decision should be based on a determination of who can do the most effective job. In a study of the acceptability of message sources it was found that the most important characteristics were safety, qualification, and dynamism.

Safety is described as safe, just, kind, friendly, and honest.

Qualification is expressed as trained, experienced, skilled, qualified, and informed.

Dynamism is interpreted as aggressive, emphatic, bold, active, and energetic.

The characteristic of dynamism may be more of an intensifier than a basic qualification (Berlo, Lemert, and Mertz, 1969-70).

Right Channels

There are many channels of communication which may be used. Each has its virtues and faults. Often, it may be necessary to use several in order to be sure that the message gets to the right people with sufficient impact and repetition. The message must not only get *to* the right people, it must be absorbed *by* them. Choosing the right channels must be based on knowledge of the people who are to be reached, the message to be communicated, and the characteristics of the tools. A study of sources from which farmers received information about farming practices showed the following ranking: company field men — 31%, neighbors —

25%, merchants and mill operators — 17%, extension workers — 13%, government publications — 11%, radio —1%, farm magazines — 1%, weekly newspapers — 1%, television — 0%, and daily newspapers — 0% (White, 1969-70).

Right Time

To communicate effectively, the message must arrive at the right time. If it arrives too early, the "receiver" will not be ready and willing to think about the subject. If it arrives too late, it will reach minds that have lost interest or have been closed to persuasion by the delay. Finding the right time is a matter of being in tune with the situation — knowing what the "right" people are thinking about or will respond to.

Right Message

The message must be believable, it must be realistic, it must be significant and it must be aimed at the objective. If it does not convince the "receivers," it is not the right message. Getting the message "right" requires an understanding of the attitudes of the "receivers" and the factors that have created those attitudes. It also requires an understanding of how they think and how they will react to ideas.

Right Words

The importance of using the right words can hardly be overemphasized. Ideas can be expressed in many ways and each variation may create a different reaction in a given audience. Conversely, by using different words, the same reaction can be developed in different audiences. The only guide to determination of the "right" words is knowledge of the audience and its language. When these are known and the objective clearly defined, the "right" words become obvious.

Suggested Readings

Allen, Ronald B., and McKerrow, Ray. *The Pragmatics of Public Communication*. Columbus, Ohio: Merrill, 1977.

Asante, Malefi K., and Frye, Jerry K. *Contemporary Public Communication*. New York: Harper & Row, 1977.

De Lozier, M. Wayne. *The Marketing Communication Process*. New York: McGraw-Hill, 1976.

Hiebert, Ray Eldon; Ungarait, Donald; and Bohn, Thomas. *Mass Media – An Introduction to Modern Communication*. New York: McKay, 1974.

Katz, Elihu, and Lazarsfeld, Paul F. *Personal Influence*. New York: Free Press, 1964.

Lerbinger, Otto. *Designs for Persuasive Communication*. Englewood Cliffs, N.J.: Prentice-Hall, 1972.

347

Mambert, W. A. *Elements of Effective Communication*. Washington, D.C.: Acropolis, 1971.
Robinson, E. J. *Communication and Public Relations*. Englewood Cliffs, N.J.: Prentice-Hall, 1968.
Rogers, Everett M., and Rekha, Agarwala. *Communications in Organizations*. New York: Free Press, 1976.
Simons, Herbert W. *Persuasion, Understanding, Practice and Analysis*. Reading, Mass.: Addison-Wesley, 1976.
Steinberg, Charles S. *The Creation of Consent*. New York: Hastings House, 1975.

EXERCISES

1. Find an example of a failure in communication by a political figure.
2. Find an example of successful communication by a political figure.
3. Find an example of a failure in communication by a nongovernment organization.
4. Find an example of successful communication by a nongovernment organization.

Note: Be objective and eliminate your own attitudes from this analysis. Why did each succeed or fail?

Case Problem

You are public relations aide to the President of the United States. The energy crisis has become critical. The President has sent a bill to Congress which would:

1. halt all use of air conditioning.
2. ration heating oil and gas to 75% of normal use.
3. ration gasoline at a level which would prevent pleasure driving.
4. prohibit use of gasoline in any recreational vehicles such as boats, campers, dune buggies, and snowmobiles.

The bill is stalled in Congress, but the fuel shortage is becoming worse every day. The President wants to get the voters to pressure Congress to pass the law.

Outline a one-hour television address for the President. This should include an introductory statement, the reasons why the law is necessary, the visual exhibits to be used, the reasons for the specific proposals, and a conclusion which will inspire the people to write their congressmen and senators.

Evaluation | **22**

Evaluating public relations activities is a necessity for two reasons: first, to determine whether the activities are achieving their purpose, and second, to justify the time and money invested in these activities.

Any public relations activity, regardless of whether it is a large program extended over a considerable length of time or a small one-time event, must have an objective. There must be an anticipated result, and there must be a determination as to whether the activity produced the hoped-for and planned-for result. If the result is attained, it can be assumed that the activity was successful. If not, it must be concluded that the activity was wasted. Usually the answers are not quite as simple as complete success or complete failure. Most of the time it is a matter of degree, but always there must be a measurement of accomplishment in order to decide what to do or not to do in the future.

Public relations activities cost money and time; management will provide the money and the time only if there is a justification for these expenditures. The only way to prove their value is by showing specific results. Management also wants to know how much each activity contributes to the objectives of the organization and why it is needed. If all these questions are answered satisfactorily, management will support the activities and possibly extend them. If not, it will withdraw its support, reduce or eliminate activities, or possibly kill the whole program. In attempting to answer management's questions, it is very easy to err in either measurement or reasoning.

ERRORS IN MEASUREMENT

Because public relations deals with intangibles, it is not easy to measure its accomplishments. A production manager can count the number of items he produces. A sales manager can record sales in precise figures. The public relations director or counselor does not have this advantage. Nevertheless, he must come up with specific statements regarding results and this can lead to error.

Volume Does Not Mean Results

One great mistake is to assume that volume means success. A great stack of press clippings is often used as proof of accomplishment. Much more important is the content of the clippings and the publications in which they appeared. Still more important is the number of people who read them and the nature of the readers. Most important of all is the effect upon the readers.

Numbers Are Not Accomplishment

Another example is the common practice of only counting noses. This leads to reports that "so many hundred people heard a certain speech" or "X thousands of people received a certain letter" or "X thousands of people attended the meeting." Numbers are important but only as a starting point toward the more vital question: "What was accomplished?"

Production Is Not Performance

Still another example of the "volumetric error" is the fallacy of equating output with results — the assumption that "if one press release is good, two are twice as good," "if one booklet is valuable, five are five times as valuable," and so on. Figure is piled on figure, but this gives no specific answers as to results.

Guesses Are Not Facts

The nebulous nature of public reaction and the very normal enthusiasm of the public relations practitioners can lead to an overly optimistic appraisal of results. When a person is enthusiastic about what he is doing, it is very easy to assume that what he is doing is succeeding. Unfortunately, the enthusiasm may all be in the mind of the doer and the people to whom the activity is directed may remain very unenthusiastic.

One Swallow Does Not Make A Summer

Many a public relations activity is counted as a success because it has engendered a few favorable comments. Conversely, a great number of worthwhile activities have been considered failures because of even fewer unfavorable remarks.

The error is obvious. Random statements are not necessarily representative of the attitude of the public. The only way to be sure of public attitude is to get enough answers that are representative.

There Are Two Sides to Every Question

It is a common human failing to believe only that which confirms our own convictions. In public relations this leads to the very dangerous practice of maximizing favorable evidence and minimizing the unfavorable. Counting the "yes" votes and throwing out the "no" votes may yield some impressive — and misleading — figures.

ERRORS IN REASONING

Closely related to errors in measurement are the errors in reasoning which can occur. The two most common are: (1) that knowledge is proportional to effort and (2) that attitude is proportional to knowledge. Both of these are possible but not inevitable, so no one in public relations should assume their universal application.

The Relationship of Effort to Knowledge

Public relations activities can and do contribute to public knowledge. It would seem, then, that if any public gains in knowledge from a certain amount of informative activity, an increase in that activity should result in more knowledge. Thus, there is a strong temptation to reason that public knowledge is directly proportional to the effort made to impart that knowledge. Unfortunately, this is not always true. Sometimes an increased effort will produce increased results — but often the stubborn public simply refuses to learn any more about the subject. People who at one stage eagerly absorb every bit of information on a given topic may consciously or subconsciously decide that they know enough. Thereafter, the information falls on deaf ears.

Also, it should be remembered that when public media are involved, there is an absolute limit to the amount of time or space they will devote to any subject. When that limit is reached, there is not a chance of getting any more publicity. Those limits may be purely arbitrary but when an editor decides he has given enough space to Topic A, he simply quits publishing items about it.

The Relationship of Knowledge to Attitude

Knowledge about a subject does not necessarily result in improved attitudes. In fact, it can lead to worse attitudes. For example, if a policy is basically bad, no increase in the amount of public knowledge about it can lead to its acceptance. It is far more likely to increase opposition to the policy. If a person is disliked, the more people know about him, the more he will be disliked.

There must be an objective appraisal of the merits in any given situation, and a realization that no amount of knowledge will substitute for the lack of merit. This problem is illustrated by the story of the PR man who was asked to improve the public image of the president of a company. His instructions were: "Humanize the SOB" — an obviously impossible task, which was promptly declined.

The whole issue of knowledge and attitude boils down to the fundamentals of public relations. The practice must be based on sound policy. If there is light, lifting the bushel will expose it; if there is no light, the more the bushel is lifted the more obvious the darkness becomes.

WHAT TO MEASURE

There are a number of measurements which can lead to a meaningful evaluation of public relations activities. Properly done and properly appraised they can produce facts and figures which will satisfy management that its public relations budget is a worthwhile investment.

The principal things which can be measured are production, distribution, interest, reach, understanding, and opinion. Of these, only the last is a real measurement of accomplishment. The other five are merely steps leading toward the ultimate appraisal. Public relations activities are carried on for one reason only, to affect public opinion.

When a public is favorably affected in a measureable way there is definite evidence of success. The other items cannot prove success but they can aid in determining how much effort was made, how much it cost, where the time was spent, and, sometimes, why things happened. They can also aid in appraising the effectiveness of the various segments of the program. And, last but not least, they can reassure management that the public relations activities are organized and planned.

Production

Every tool of public relations used can be reported in some numerical fashion. Production statistics can show how many publicity items were written, booklets printed, films produced, letters mailed, speeches made, and so on. These numbers can indicate how much work was done and its total cost. They can also reveal the amount of time and money devoted to various segments of the program. They can aid in budget control and in time utilization. They can show the PR director that he is spending too much time attending meetings. They can show management that the house organ costs too much per copy, and so on. But these figures are only the first step in evaluation. More important by far is what is done with this production.

Distribution

This measurement shows what happened to the production. It tells how many copies of the publicity items were sent out and to whom; what became of the booklets after they were printed; who attended the meeting; how many people saw the films, received the letters, or heard the speeches. This is a more informative measurement than production because it indicates how much of the production got into use and had a chance for effective performance.

It is, to some degree, a measurement of the efficiency (but not the effectiveness) of the public relations people. At the least, it provides assurance that publicity items do get printed, that booklets do get sent out, that people do attend meetings, look at films, or receive letters. It can indicate that the time and money is not completely wasted, but it is only one more step forward in evaluation. It does not reveal anything about the quality of the work. That characteristic is reflected by the interest which is or is not shown.

Interest

With most public relations activities it is possible to apply some sort of measurement that will indicate how interesting the activity is to the audience toward which it is aimed. Press clippings not only show that publicity items were printed, but by whom. They can reveal the amount of editing done to the publicity items and indicate whether they were well-written or too lengthy. Similar measurements of interest can be made on radio and television releases.

Clippings are evidence but not conclusive evidence. Clipping bureaus

353

often find less than half of the items printed. In one test conducted by the author's organization, two clipping bureaus were engaged to clip the same item. 80% of the clippings of Bureau A were not found by Bureau B and 80% of the clippings of Bureau B were not found by Bureau A.

An analysis of which media used the material and the circulation or audience covered can be additionally helpful. An item in a major newspaper is likely to be more valuable than the same item in a minor paper; a television network coverage of some event is considerably more important than a single-station coverage of the same event.

In product publicity it is a common practice to calculate the value of the space or time received for the items released. Thus an item that got 580 lines of space in a newspaper with a $1 line rate for advertising is valued at $580. One of the most outstanding cases in this area is a full-color, full-page publicity feature for a food product. It was used in 168 newspapers. The advertising value of the space was over $500,000. The actual cost was a bit more than $10,000. This is an unusual case, but it is not at all uncommon for product publicity campaigns to get space or time that would cost, at advertising rates, ten times as much as the cost of the publicity.

Requests for booklets are an indication of interest, so too is the "pick-up" from display racks. Conversely, a lot of booklets in rubbish cans or gutters is proof that the people who took them were not interested. If 80% of the people invited to a meeting actually came, it is evident that there was interest; if only 20% attended, it is quite clear that not many were interested.

The number and kind of questions asked give an indication of interest. The attention paid to a speaker is another clue.

A somewhat more sophisticated way to measure interest is through "reader-interest" studies. These studies will tell how many people read all or most of a given item. This information is compiled continuously for many publications and provides a general indication of relative interest in the various topics covered in an issue of the publication. Similar studies can be made on any printed material.

Reach

Who the information reaches is a measurement of considerable importance. Normally, public relations materials are planned for and aimed at specific audiences. If they reach the right audience, they will be much more effective than if they reach other people. A publicity item written for farmers will not do much good in a city paper. A radio or television message of primary male interest will be largely ineffective at 2:00 p.m. on a weekday because men are not watching television or listening to radio at that hour. Yet, 2:00 p.m. is a particularly good time for reaching women who are at home.

A newspaper article about a public utility's plan for beautifying its substations can be very valuable in its own territory but not very beneficial in a paper published on the other side of the country. An item about a new food product can be far more valuable on the food page of a newspaper than in any other location — the women who read that page are doing so because they are interested in food.

For the same reason, news about a new subdivision or a new type of house being offered for sale will not do much good unless it reaches the people who might be interested in buying lots or houses. A meeting attended by the right people, however few they might be, can do more good than a meeting attended by ten times as many wrong people.

This, of course, does not mean that numbers are to be disregarded. Reaching a hundred of the right people is ten times as good as reaching only ten of them.

Reader-interest studies not only tell how well a given item compares with others in the same medium, but also gives a general indication as to the number of people who actually read the item. A message addressed to employees is not fully effective unless it reaches all employees. A news story in a major news program on television or radio will reach more people than if it is broadcast at 2:00 a.m. But again, numbers are not the whole answer. It is possible that a 2:00 a.m. audience might consist of people difficult to reach at any other time, and these people might be the public that must be reached.

The question that must always be asked is: "Did the message reach the right people? "

Understanding

Any public relaions message must be understood if it is to have any effect. The point is well-illustrated by the story of the two men who had just listened to a speech by a spellbinding politician. The first man said, "Boy! Old Tom sure made a great speech, didn't he?" To which the second man replied "He sure did! Say, what was he talking about anyway?"

If the public does not get the idea, the communication has failed in spite of all the production, distribution, interest, and reach that would seem to indicate success.

In some cases, it is fairly easy to learn the degree of understanding attained. If an announcement of a new policy is followed by questions about the policy, it is obvious that the announcement was not understood. If employees ask questions about a statement in the employee booklet about retirement, it is evident that there is a lack of understanding. If attendants at a meeting ask questions about something that has just been explained, it is apparent that the explanation was not intelligible.

A more sophisticated way to measure understanding is through use of recall and comprehension tests. Recall is determined by finding out what people remember about a subject that has been presented to them. Questions like these are asked: "Why is this a good policy?" or "What were the main points in Mr. Jones' speech?" or "What did the letter say?" These test remembrance and indicate whether people do get the message. They can provide evidence that the message is well-organized and clearly and memorably expressed. However, even though people remember things, they still may not understand them.

To prove understanding, an additional tool is used — comprehension tests. These require the recipient of the message to explain what it means and to do so in his own words. Thus, an employee may be able to recall that his pension rights are "fully vested" after 20 years' employment. If in a comprehension test he states that his "pension rights cannot be taken away after 20 years with the company," there is an indication of understanding. But if he cannot explain "fully vested," he really does not understand the statement. Comprehension tests may cover one or more points. For best results, they should be kept simple and reasonably brief because most people who are unskilled in writing will have trouble explaining complex subjects.

Opinion

The one true measurement of the effectiveness of public relations activity is its effect on the opinion of a specific public. In doing this it is imperative to know the degree of exposure to the activity. If people don't see or hear the message they can't be influenced. Measuring change in opinion is best done through use of the research procedures described in Chapter 19. Basically, a public is surveyed to determine its opinion. Then the same public is surveyed again to determine whether there has been a change in its opinion.

Often the same questionnaire is used "before" and "after." For continuing evaluation, the same questions may be asked year after year.

Two cautions are necessary in this sort of procedure. First, it is essential that the "climate" in which the questions are asked is the same each time. For example, an employee survey done when a strike is imminent, will be materially affected by that situation and will not be comparable to a survey done under less emotional conditions. Second, the "before" study may focus attention on certain topics and warp the response in the "after" study. This can be counteracted by making sure that different people are questioned "before" and "after." As long as each group is a representative sample of the public involved, the results will be comparable. If the public is so small that the entire group must be questioned "before" and "after," this necessitates great attention to the questionnaire in order to avoid the dangers of a warped response.

AIDS TO EVALUATION

There are a number of special studies which can help in evaluating a public relations program. These include pretesting, impact analysis, process of influence, use of experimental campaigns, and seeking the expert opinion of other PR practitioners.

Pretesting

Every public relations message should be carefully checked before it is released. This is usually done by the PR counselor or someone within the PR department. In addition, it should be tested on someone who is not directly involved in order to find out if it is understandable. A response analysis will give much more information as to possible results. By selecting a small cross-section audience from the public involved and by carefully checking the effect of the campaign on their opinions, it is possible to learn on a small scale how the campaign can be expected to perform.

Of course, this has many limitations. It is not possible to run newspaper stories for just a few individuals and it is not economical to print booklets for a handful of people. But it is possible to expose ideas and concepts and methods of expression to a limited audience and find out how they react. Whenever the public is large enough and time permits, it is well worthwhile to pretest.

Inpact Analysis

Evaluation can be helped by analyzing the effect of public relations activities on various groups. Through this sort of analysis, it is possible to find that certain ideas are accepted by some and rejected by others or that one public understands and another public does not. Impact analysis may reveal that Group A is interested in a topic, while Group B ignores it completely, or that Group C has changed its opinion but Group D is still of the same opinion.

Process of Influence

There are many channels of communication through which messages can reach the public. Each has advantages and disadvantages and each may be more effective for certain types of messages or for certain audiences. Some of the differences are so obvious that they do not need testing or evaluation.

For example, an orientation of employees explaining rules, responsibilities, and rights should be in a booklet or a series of booklets, not in a stack of mimeographed sheets on a bulletin board. Conversely, a campaign to influence employees might have several possible routes to choose from. The problem could be to decide whether posters, letters, pamphlets, meetings, or a combination of all of them would give the best results.

In a study of factors influencing attendance at the convention of a professional association, it was found that a comprehensive brochure provided the information necessary to consider attendance but that personal contact with others was a major influence on the decision to go (Booth, 1969-70).

A further consideration could be the relative effect of certain people in the process of influence. Thus, one man might be a very good speaker, but not as effective as another whose earnestness and sincerity overcome his moderate speaking talent. A careful study of the process and the tools by which people's opinions are influenced can be a great aid in evaluating public relations programs.

Use of Experimental Campaigns

There is usually more than one way to solve a public relations problem. Sometimes the best method is not at all obvious. When this situation exists, it may be advisable to try out two completely different procedures in order to find out which is most effective. This is done with "matched samples," two audiences that are as nearly identical as possible. The audience is studied "before" and "after." If one campaign performs appreciably better than the other, the answer is quite evident. If both perform equally well, the choice then becomes one of personal preference or economy; if both give unpleasing results, the solution is to try a new campaign.

Another way to test campaigns is on a territorial basis. In this method the survey covers both the area where the campaign runs and areas where it does not run. In one statewide survey on public opinion regarding atomic power, it was found that in one county there was a much more favorable reaction than in the other geographic components or in the statewide average. This was the one county where an intensive public relations campaign had been conducted.

Expert Opinions

Doctors frequently call in other doctors for consultation and public relations people should have no hesitation about seeking the opinions of others in their own field. No one knows all the answers but, collectively, the professionals have a vast body of knowledge. In many cases it is possible to get an objective appraisal from an expert, which may result in considerable economies of both time and money.

Suggested Reading

The Winter 1977 issue of *Public Relations Review* is devoted entirely to the subject of measuring the effectiveness of public relations. It should be read and studied by any practitioner who wants to do a genuinely effective job of evaluating a public relations program.

EXERCISES

1. For one week read every issue of a daily newspaper and clip every article dealing with a subject of broad public interest. How many did you find?
2. For one week check all media to which you are exposed but this time look only for items dealing with a subject of particular interest to you (e.g., a hobby, a business with which you are familiar, a group to which you belong). How many items did you find?

Case Problem

You are public relations director of a large lumber company. You have been running advertising in national magazines telling how, by reforestation, you replace the trees you cut. Draft a questionnaire to determine

(a) whether the advertising is seen and read,
(b) whether it is believed, and
(c) whether the readers identify your company as the one responsible.

Who would you question?
How would you question them?

Dialogue IV

Dialogue with Mr. Michael McCloskey, Executive Director, the Sierra Club.

> This dialogue discusses the physical environment in which we live and work. Protecting that environment is an important task for all institutions; striking a balance between our needs, our desires, and the limitations of the planet creates a problem which bears upon many public relations programs.

Q. What changes have occurred in the Sierra Club in recent years?

A. We have grown. There are now about 175,000 members. We have 50 chapters, 260 local groups and 13 branch offices. Our membership is increasing at a rate of about 10% a year.

Q. Have your objectives changed?

A. Our general objectives are still the same: To maintain a heathful environment for all species of life, both flora and fauna, and in the process to preserve the richness and diversity of life. To maximize evolutionary possibilities and to stabilize ecosystems.

Q. Can you simplify that?

A. Yes, we try to protect the habitat for all living things, including man.

Q. Apparently you have made much progress toward that goal.

A. We have. Many of the worst manifestations of problems have been solved. A few years ago we were struggling to make people aware of what man was doing to the environment. Now there is great awareness of and support for our cause. The Environmental Protection Agency and the Carter administration have created a new climate for our work.

Q. Then your job must be easier?

A. To some degree, but our success in eliminating conspicuous pollution and destruction has created new problems. Now we are involved with things that are harder to see and to understand. It's easy to talk about clouds of black smoke. It isn't easy to get people alarmed about invisible pollutants that are expressed in parts per million. We used to work on the worst cases, the conspicuous ones. Now we're involved with the hard residue of problems which are very technical. We're talking about secondary standards and stack gas scrubbers. Many outrageous abuses have been eliminated but we are now getting into questions involving the rate of clean-up, and who should bear the costs and the burden of proof. These questions are hard to dramatize.

Q. What has the energy crisis done to your program?

A. It has created a huge new problem. There is some disposition to stampede into energy development without consideration of the environmental effects. Certainly the country must have energy, but we think that it can be obtained without such destructive measures as some people propose. Our efforts are focused on getting a rational blend of conservation and supply sources which are sustainable and which minimize environmental impacts. The problem is a continuing one. The Kaiparowits project near the corners of Utah, Colorado, New Mexico, and Arizona was stopped, but now there is a new project in the same general area. We call it "Son of Kaiparowits."

Q. What is your biggest problem today?

A. I think it is the belief of some people that environmental protection is unfairly penalizing some sectors of our society. I don't believe that this is happening, but some people are expressing concern.

Q. Can you give me some examples?

A. Yes. The proposed expansion of Redwood National Park was violently opposed by people in the vicinity of the park because it was seen as a blow to local employment in the lumber industry. Proposed restrictions on use of recreational off-the-road vehicles are objected to by the makers and by the users. Taxes on "gas-guzzling" cars are opposed by the manufacturers and their employees.

Q. It all comes back to the self-interest of the people involved, doesn't it?

A. Yes indeed. But a new ingredient has been injected into the problem. When a lumber company or an automotive manufacturer opposes environmental protection, we are facing an impersonal opponent. When the loggers or the factory workers militantly resist because of fear that protecting the environment is going to destroy their jobs it is a very different situation.

Q. How do you answer them?

A. Many labor leaders are overreacting. Environmental programs have created more jobs (over one million) than they have destroyed. Labor leaders need to take a hard look at the real sources of job losses:

depletion of the resource base; automation; mismanagement by conglomerates; monopolistic practices which drive local industries out of business. Too many labor leaders have stopped thinking for themselves. Their view of their fate is based on what management tells them.

Q. You have mentioned lumbering and automotive manufacturing as problem areas. Shouldn't the construction industry be included?

A. It should, and here we have a unique problem — the chronic insecurity of construction labor. These people go from project to project. When one job is finished, they may be out of work again, and there may be a long period of looking for another job.

Q. What do you tell these people?

A. There is really no way the construction industry can go on forever in this country building as if we were a frontier area. Eventually we will be built up and have a stable population. Then we will mainly need workers in building maintenance, not construction. However, during a transitional period ahead, there will be many new jobs in building sewage treatment plants, mass-transit systems, renovating older housing, rehabilitating eroded and strip-mined areas and in installing pollution control equipment.

Q. Is concern for the environment a largely urban affair? I have the impression that many people in rural areas just don't care. For example, the Kaiparowits project was strongly supported in Utah because many people there were more concerned about potential jobs than air pollution.

A. In most states there is real concern for the environment in rural areas as well as in urban areas. The ranchers of Montana and Wyoming are not rushing to get rich on coal. They are trying to protect their grazing lands and their water supplies. Utah may be an exception to this, but Utah may be changing, too.

Q. With the substantial success you have achieved, have you made changes in your methods of operation?

A. Not in general. We still lobby at federal, state, and local levels. We still rely on publicity. We generally get good treatment from the news media, except in some local areas such as parts of the lumbering country. We still alert our members to problems and encourage letter writing and other actions to inform government agencies of our position.

Q. How do you handle lobbying?

A. We have six people in Washington, D.C., plus several others who work at state capitals. Of course, we have to obey the federal and state laws on lobbying. The Sierra Club is a tax-exempt, nonprofit organization, but because we are a lobby, the membership dues are not tax deductible.

Q. Do you have any comments on the several bills in Congress which would place severe restrictions on lobbying?

A. We are opposed to most of the proposals. Common Cause is pushing a bill designed to discourage lobbying, and it would particularly penalize nonprofit groups. We agree with the American Civil Liberties Union that this would infringe on rights granted by the First Amendment of the Constitution.

Q. What do you see ahead for the cause of environmental protection?

A. I see progress. I also see that we will have to continue the fight. We have won some important battles but the war goes on. Nevertheless, we are gaining. We used to rely largely on action at the national level; now we are getting support at the state level. Some states are setting standards that are higher than the federal standards, and this is most encouraging. We will always have problems. Every year there are bills to support or to oppose, but with a sound policy and an effective communications program we expect to continue toward our goal.

V
The Channels of Communication

In Chapter 21, considerable attention was given to the basic theories and principles of communication. Now we come to the "nuts and bolts" of outbound communication. How *do* we transmit our ideas to the public?

(a) get a story into a newspaper or magazine?
(b) obtain television coverage of some incident?
(c) inform the public of our wonderful new factory or store?
(d) make a slide presentation or motion picture?
(e) plan and conduct a meeting, convention, or parade?
(f) use our own employees to build good public relations?
(g) communicate with our owners?

All of these questions and many more are answered in the following chapters. This part of the book is called "The Channels of Communication," but it might well be called "How To Do It."

Employees | **23**

Employees are the most important channel of communication. Properly motivated and properly utilized, they can accomplish more than all the others combined. On the other hand, if they are not motivated or used in the right way, they can undo all the other constructive elements in the program.

The outsider's opinion of the organization will be based almost entirely on the employee he knows or encounters. If he likes and admires the employee, he will probably like and admire the employer; if the employee is inefficient or surly, that will be his image of the organization.

Employees have repeated contacts with the public. These contacts provide the best means for two-way communication. They permit an exchange of questions and answers, thus providing an opportunity to explain and to persuade. They also make it possible to offend or to err. That is why it is essential for an organization to have a well-organized plan for utilizing employees in the public relations program.

Employees can fit into a public relations program in two ways: first, by their contact with individuals in the course of their normal work and second, by using them as communicators. In both situations the employees must be motivated, they must be provided with help, and they must be supervised. They must know the policies of the organization and its objectives.

EMPLOYEES AND THE PUBLIC

All employees have some contact with the public. Therefore, while there may be some temptation to forget production-line people or those who do routine jobs, it would be a mistake to leave them out completely. All employees can and should be involved in the PR program, particularly in community relations, because all of them are part of the community. However, some have greater opportunities for public contact and these should get special attention. This category includes salespeople, service people, purchasing agents, receptionists and guards, telephone operators, correspondents, supervisors and foremen, managers and executives.

Salespeople

Salespeople work almost entirely with the customer public and, since their work involves the customers' money, the relationship is most sensitive. Quite generally, sales personnel are given considerable instruction and guidance on sales methods. Unfortunately, not all of them receive comparable instructions and guidance in customer relations. Customers will forgive poor salesmanship, they will put up with lack of knowledge of what is to be sold, but they will not stand for rude treatment or being ignored.

Service Personnel

Service is a very sore point with most people. Complaints about discourtesy, disinterest, quality of work, costs, inability to get work done, failure to keep appointments, difficulty in obtaining repair service, and many, many others are a common topic at almost any gathering. As production becomes more mechanized and increasingly automated, an ever-increasing number of people are found in service of one sort or another, and the opportunities for offending people increase accordingly. The need for involving service personnel in public relations becomes more important every day. When they understand how important a part they play in public relations and when they are properly used, they can greatly improve public opinion of their employer.

Purchasing Agents

With the power of the purse behind them, purchasing agents or buyers are in a position to be quite dictatorial to salesmen. At worst, a buyer can create a very bad public image for his employer. At best, a purchasing agent can win many friends for his organization by his manner of treating the salesmen who call. The number of buyers relative to other employees may be quite small and buyers are commonly classed as executives, yet they must be thoroughly indoctrinated and as completely sold on the public relations program as anyone in the organization.

Receptionists and Guards

The person at the gate or reception desk is often the first contact with the organization. And the first impression, in spite of all the admonitions to the contrary, frequently establishes the image of the organization in a lasting way. A good receptionist can do much to give the first-time caller a favorable opinion and to maintain the good opinion of repeat callers. Every receptionist or guard should be well-informed about his or her importance in public relations and should be adequately trained and repeatedly checked to make sure of continued cordial and efficient handling of callers.

Telephone Operators

Good telephone manners are so important that many telephone companies will, without cost, train switchboard operators to handle phone communications rapidly, accurately and courteously. Telephone service is usually so good that every user expects immediate communication with the party called and blames the operator if he does not succeed. The telephone is, in many cases, the principal communication link between an organization and its public. As such, it can be a major influence on public opinion. Therefore, the manner in which telephone calls are handled must be carefully integrated into the public relations program.

Correspondents

Every organization receives and sends out letters. A letter is always a definite, and frequently a permanent, record of what was said. The manner in which statements are made can make friends or enemies out of the recipients and, once the message is received, there is little chance to alter the impression it creates. Those who write letters for the organization should be well aware of how their letters affect public opinion. Training, supervision, and checking are constant requirements if the organization's letters are to create favorable attitudes.

Supervisors and Foremen

Within the organization, these people have an important role in dealing with employees under their charge. Outside the organization, these same people, because of their status, have a definite role in dealing with the public at large and the community public in particular. In both cases they represent management, and, while normally not involved in major policy decisions, they should thoroughly understand those decisions and be able to explain and support them. This requires a special effort to involve supervisors and foremen in the public relations program, to motivate them, to train them, and to provide them with the information and tools necessary to secure their cooperation.

Managers and Executives

This group often participates in establishing public relations policies. Their support is, as previously mentioned, essential to the success of a program, but they can also be a major tool in executing the program. Most of these people are good communicators. They are expected to be the voice of the organization, and they should be used in the public relations program whenever possible. Motivation is necessary, of course, but it should not be difficult. With this group the major task of the PR personnel is to find opportunities for their use and to provide them with the tools needed to help them communicate with the public.

PUBLIC RELATIONS ON THE JOB

Only a small percentage of employees are able and willing to take on extracurricular assignments as active communicators, but all employees can participate in and aid the PR program in the ordinary course of their work or even in casual and informal contacts outside. To gain this cooperation, there must be an organized plan to motivate, to inform and to supervise.

Motivation

If the employee relations program is sound, there should not be much difficulty in persuading employees to do their part. If they are convinced that their organization is good, and that it treats them well, they will easily progress from awareness to activity. The problem is to show the employee how his job performance affects the public relations of his organization, to convince him that good public relations are important, and to persuade him to do all he can to build favorable public opinion by his work manners and by his informal contacts outside.

This requires a continuing effort. Employees come and go; even those who stay need to be reminded. All need to be resold. However, in this process of selling and reselling, it is imperative not to overdo it. Conveying a message to employees through every available medium may be effective once, but a continuous barrage of messages on some specific topic will soon backfire.

There is no "best" method for motivating employees, and there is no preferred tool. Articles in the house organ, meetings, skits, instructions by superiors, memorandums, bulletins, posters, letters, PA announcements, "communicators," and numerous other measures may be used.

Information

To be effective channels of communication, employees must be well-informed. They must know the policy of the organization, they must know the objectives of the PR program, and they must have facts. As stated before, the policy must be written and it should be made available to all employees so they will be aware of it. It is often desirable to further explain exactly what the policy means and why it was established. Objectives must be defined in terms specific enough to enable employees to act upon them. Thus, it is much better to state as an objective "to reduce complaints by 50%" than merely as "reduce complaints."

Facts provided to employees should be applicable to their own situation and in terms which are easy to understand. A grocery store employee can use a figure such as "We make only $1 profit on $100 of sales," but he cannot get much use out of the "fact" that "before-tax profits last year were 20% below the industry average." A telephone operator can be impressed with the fact that "The telephone operator is our primary contact with the public," but she will be more impressed with the statement "75% of our orders come in by telephone." The goal is to provide to employees those facts which can induce a better performance and can be used in their contacts with the public.

Not to be overlooked in the process of informing employees is the use of brief and well-organized statements which they can use in communicating with the public. Typically, these will be in the form of bulletins or leaflets that can either be retained or handed directly to interested members of the public. As with motivation, information must be supplied and resupplied. There must be enough but there should not be an overwhelming mass at any one time.

Supervision

This is primarily the responsibility of the line supervisors, the foremen, etc. Supervising retail sales or service people may be relatively simple. It is not at all difficult for the supervisors to see and hear what is being done. Supervising telephone operators is more difficult, especially when "monitoring" of calls is considered, but this is not an impassable barrier if the reason is carefully explained and monitors are properly trained. Guards and receptionists can be checked out fairly easily. In fact, most employees of relatively low rank can be observed and counseled without too much difficulty.

Since, in most cases, these checks are done by their immediate "line" superiors, these must be supervised as well. This job is the responsibility of their superiors, not of the PR people, although the latter may observe and report their observations to those same superiors. With managers and executives, the problem becomes sensitive and must be handled with great diplomacy.

Essentially, supervision of employees in their public relations role requires complete understanding of the policy, the objectives, and the facts, an enthusiastic conviction that the program is right, plus an ample supply of tact and supervisory skill that will obtain the loyal and enthusiastic participation of the employees.

PUBLIC RELATIONS OFF THE JOB

In addition to aiding the public relations program in the course of their daily work or informal individual contacts with members of the public, employees can provide much help on a more formal basis. This involves finding people who can and will take on special tasks. When these people are located, they must be motivated and informed. In addition, they must be provided special help. Their work must be planned and speakers should be well trained.

The most common utilization of these employees is in verbal communication to special audiences, or, to put it simply, talking to groups of people.

Finding the Communicators

In an earlier chapter, it was stated that communicators may be found at every level and in every occupation. They do not wear badges identifying themselves as such but they can be found if an effort is made. An alert public relations practitioner will, in the course of contacts within the organization, find certain employees who are able and willing to lend a hand or voice to the effort. Also, it is frequently possible to locate talent by asking for volunteers or by asking employees to submit names of people who might be induced to volunteer or even drafted. A Toastmasters Club either within the organization or to which employees belong can be a goldmine of talent.

Obviously, of course, if an employee belongs to an outside organization, he is a likely prospect for communication to that organization. The communicators are not only readers and listeners and talkers, they are also joiners. Every organization has communicators, and one of the important jobs of the public relations department or counselor is to find these people and use them.

Motivation

One of the best ways to flatter a person is to ask for his help. And flattery is one of the most effective motivations known. People who can speak before a public usually like to do so and generally welcome the opportunity. When such a person is located, he or she can often be motivated by simply being told why help is needed and convinced that he or she should make this contribution to the welfare of the organization.

Information

As members of the employee group, those who are to be used as speakers will, of course, receive all the information generally directed to employees. Because they are communicators, they will retain and understand more than the rank and file. This, however, is not enough. If an employee is going to make a speech, he will need more material than he can glean from mass employee communications. And this material will have to be especially suitable for his audience. The public relations department or counselor has the responsibility of providing the ammunition necessary for an effective speech. This may require considerable work, but it is a responsibility that cannot be shirked.

Special Help

Speakers frequently need more help than the mere supplying of information. Here the public relations department or counselor must fill whatever needs may exist. If the speaker needs charts, pictures, slides, films, or properties of any sort, the PR people should provide them. Often a speaker will need help in writing and rehearsing his speech. Sometimes the entire writing job falls to the PR department — and this is more the rule than the exception when the speaker is in the upper strata of the organization. These situations should be considered opportunities rather than burdens.

Planning

Use of employees in the public relations program must be planned. The program has objectives and any employee efforts that do not contribute to the attainment of those objectives are wasted. It is therefore imperative that each public appearance have a specific purpose — the communication of a definite message to a definite group. Simply making speeches is not necessarily advantageous, but persuading or convincing or informing certain representatives of the public can be most advantageous.

For these reasons, it is necessary to direct speakers so that they will carry the right message to the right audience. It is also necessary to plan schedules so as to avoid neglecting some and overloading others. There are no set rules for planning use of employees, but a careful study of who needs to be reached and who can best reach them will be the best guide.

Training

In Chapter 6, public speaking ability was listed as a requirement for success as a practitioner. To this should be added the ability to teach others how to speak because this is becoming an increasingly important responsibility of public relations practitioners.

The "trainee" might be a company president being taught how to handle harassment by activists or to deal with agressive reporters. (See Dialogue II.) At the other end of the scale, the "trainee" might be a blue-collar worker who wants to make a simple talk to a group of associates.

In between, there may be many others of varying status and ability. All may profit by help, and even the ablest may need polishing or refreshing. If any employee makes a speech, it reflects in some way on the organization — the better the speech, the more likely it is to prove beneficial.

THE SPEAKERS BUREAU

One of the most efficient ways to utilize employees in public relations and to provide information, special help, planning, and checking is through a speakers bureau. This is not as complicated as it sounds. In a very large organization, there can be a sizable activity under this name but the function need not be time-consuming. The essential thing is to set up the bureau and keep it operating. A speakers bureau consists of four things: a speakers file, a procedure for scheduling, booking sheets, and publicity.

The Speakers File

This is often a card index but it can be a book. It lists each speaker separately and contains the following information for each: name, biographical data, subject or subjects the speaker can discuss, record of speeches made, and response to his speeches. This file is used in selecting speakers for specific audiences and in maintaining a running record of their accomplishments.

Scheduling Speakers

Most organizations that accept outside speakers have a program chairman. His job is to recruit speakers who will provide his organization with interesting and stimulating talks. Business clubs, chambers of commerce, fraternal organizations, and many others are always in need of good programs, and their program chairmen are constantly looking for suitable speakers. Program chairmen can be approached either by mail or personal contact but the latter method is better.

The Booking Sheet

This is a simple form that lists the following: name of speaker, title of speaker, date of speech, time of meeting, name of organization, nature of organization (if it is not obvious from the name), name of program chairman or other contact in the organization, location of meeting (including room name or number), size of audience expected, and properties needed. A copy of this sheet should be given to the speaker as soon as an appointment is confirmed, so that he will be prepared. There must also be a followup to be sure he keeps the date. People do forget appointments and, of course, the public relations director must make sure that needed properties are at the right place at the right time.

Publicity

A press release either before or after a speech, and sometimes before and after, is very much in order. A release before a speech may help to draw a larger audience and a release after the speech may contain part or all of what was said and thus gain additional exposure for the message. For important speeches, the press should be invited to attend.

VOLUNTEERS

Speakers don't have to be scheduled through a speakers bureau. The VOICE of Standard Oil Company of Indiana (Volunteer Oil Industry Communication Effort) is an example. These "employee ambassadors" are not controlled by SOI. The volunteers are informed about company and industry views but they can say what they choose and select their own audiences.

Coaching and materials are offered and the volunteers report their speeches to the coordinator of the program. Through this system, hundreds of speeches have been made and thousands of letters have been written to politicians and others.

The work is recognized by membership cards, awards, mention in company publications, and personal thanks from supervisors.

MISCELLANEOUS PUBLIC APPEARANCES

In addition to speeches there are a number of other ways in which employees can reach audiences. Opportunities of this sort should never be passed up. Among the public appearances that can be made are round-table discussions, panels, conferences, question-and-answer sessions, and dramatizations.

Round-Table Discussions

Round-table discussions consist basically of groups of people discussing a specific subject. Usually there is a discussion leader, and frequently people move from table to table at a specified time. Such discussions are often held in connection with a convention or a large meeting where individual participation is desired.

Panels

The typical panel uses from four to ten people who sit at an elevated table facing the audience. Each panel member speaks for a few minutes on one aspect of the general subject and then all answer questions from the audience.

Conferences

A conference can be very formal or quite loosely organized. It may have speakers on certain topics within the general subject of the conference or it may have only a chairman with an agenda. Regardless of the nature of the conference, it is an opportunity to convey information and ideas to those present.

Question-and-Answer Sessions

A frequently used device, the question-and-answer session can be quite similar to a panel except that it omits the speeches. It is rather generally necessary in these sessions to have questions prepared beforehand and "planted" with audience members. Often a long list of questions is compiled and distributed to all members of the audience. The "answerers" are prepared to answer any of the questions. Audience members can merely call for "Question No. 9."

Dramatizations

The "skit" is used in psychiatry, in sales training, and in many other fields. It can also be used in public relations. A very brief dramatization of a situation can often do as much good as a longer speech. The decision to use a dramatization must be based on a careful study of the audience, the message to be conveyed, and the ability of the participants.

EXERCISES

1. Is there any organization with which you are familiar whose employees are enthusiastic about it?
   (a) Do they have any specific information about their organization (facts, figures, etc.)?
   (b) Do they try to sell you on the organization (or its products or services)?

Case Problem

You are public relations director of a large oil company that has been forced to ration fuel oil to all customers, both industrial and residential. You want to use employees to explain to your customers why this is necessary.

Which employees would you get to help on this problem (job categories)?

How would you get employees for a speakers bureau?

Prepare an outline for a leaflet explaining the necessity for rationing and suggesting ways to economize on fuel oil.

Write a title for the leaflet and the opening paragraph.

House Organs

A house organ is a periodical publication issued by an organization for people interested in that organization. Usually house organs carry no advertising and are distributed without cost to the recipient.

There are several names which may be used to describe these publications. Among the more common are: house magazines, employee publications, internal publications, newsletters, employee papers and company magazines or newspapers.

The house organ is one of the most common tools of public relations. If an organization has any semblance of a public relations program, it will probably have a house organ. Many a full-scale PR program has started with that alone. Editing and publishing house organs is one of the prime tasks of public relations people.

TYPES OF HOUSE ORGANS

There are many types of house organs. They may vary from simple mimeographed sheets to large and colorful magazines. Their circulation can range from hundreds to hundreds of thousands. They also can differ greatly in content, purpose, and audience. Most house organs are published primarily for employees but distribution frequently extends to stockholders, customers, and other interested groups and individuals.

Some organizations publish special house organs for these groups and very large firms frequently have a number of house organs, which may include national, regional, local, and special audience publications directed to specialists within the organization such as engineers, accoun-

Fig. 24.1 Some of the house organs of Standard Oil Company of California. Included are general, divisional, and special-purpose publications.

tants, salesmen, etc. Also, some firms publish external house organs directed to members of the general public.

The total number of house organs probably exceeds ten thousand. Of these, about four hundred have circulations of more than fifty thousand.*

*Gebbie House Magazine Directory.

Most house organs are internal publications and do not involve the general public. Occasionally, however, as these publications grow, they seemingly lose their "internal" character. Consider these two different examples. The *Journal of the American Medical Association* carries advertising but still retains its well-accepted status as a house organ. *The National Geographic Magazine* on the other hand, while officially the house organ of the National Geographic Society, is actually a general magazine with about 8 million subscribers.

FORMAT AND FREQUENCY

The format and frequency of publication of a house organ depend on the needs. Every organization must decide for itself what kind of house organ is necessary and how often it should be published.

Format

A house organ usually assumes one of three main forms. It may be a newsletter, a newspaper, or a news magazine. The first is often used in smaller organizations. The newspaper format is frequently used in larger firms where it may be a local supplement to a companywide magazine. The magazine is the most common form of house organ. Size of a house organ can range from a one-page mimeographed sheet to a regular magazine with full color illustrations. Because of costs, the tabloid newspaper format is growing in popularity.

Frequency

Most house organs are monthlies but some are issued only bimonthly or quarterly, and some are published weekly or "whenever there is enough news to put one out." In some cases, there may be a general monthly and supplementary house organs of variable frequency to care for regional, local, or special purposes.

GETTING A HOUSE ORGAN READ

A house organ must be read if it is to accomplish its objectives. This requires that the editor constantly strive to make it worth reading. It must be clear so that readers will understand it. It must be concise so that they do not have to study it. And it must be interesting so they will feel rewarded for the time spent in reading — and thus be willing to read the next issue.

A house organ should be of good quality. This means tight writing, eyecatching illustrations, and efficient production. A well-written understandable item will be more effective than six fuzzily-written confusing articles. One clear picture that tells a story will do more good than a dozen that merely fill up space. A good mimeographed newsletter is better than a sloppy magazine.

It must always be remembered that, while management pays for the house organ, it is not its exclusive property. It will be much more effective if the readers feel it is *theirs*. It should be *about* the organization, not *from* the organization. Messages from management should be identified as such. Editorializing should be confined to an editorial column or page.

A house organ is a channel of communication *to* employees and *from* employees. It must be credible. It must be frank. It must contain bad news as well as good news. It must help employees understand the organization. It must assure employees that the organization understands their problems and is trying to solve them. It must encourage response from employees. If it does these things, it will be read.

Readership Tests

Simple readership studies will reveal which items are interesting and which are not. A technique developed many years ago by George Gallup may be used. This involves going through the publication, page by page, with someone who claims to have read it.

For every item the question is asked, "How much of this did you read?" The portion read is marked with a soft pencil by a vertical line starting at the caption and going as far down the column or page as the reader indicates. Some items may be read completely, some may be read partly, and some may be ignored. This test is a quick and economical way to ascertain reader interest. Interviews should be continued until a trend is evident. Often it takes only a few dozen interviews to learn what is read and what isn't.

EDITING THE HOUSE ORGAN

Editing the house organ is a responsible job. Frequently the house organ is the only regular channel of communication with employees.

Always it is a major channel. Every house organ is a distinct and different publication, and every editor must make the publication fit the needs of the organization and the readers. House organ editing is almost a profession in itself. In fact, there is an organization called the International Association of Business Communicators (IABC), which started as a group of house-organ editors. It has now grown into an organization which involves the entire process of communicating with employees. Its publication, IABC News, contains much that will help the house-organ editor. There are also many books on the subject.

Suggested Readings

Darrow, Ralph C. *House Journal Editing.* Danville, Ill: Interstate, 1974.
Mann, Charles. *Editing for Industry.* New York: International Publishing Service, 1975.
Wales, La Rae H. *A Practical Guide to Newsletter Editing and Design.* Ames, Iowa: Iowa State University Press, 1976.
White, Jan. *Editing by Design.* Ann Arbor, Mich.: Bowker, 1974.

Content

A study by IABC shows that house organs are using more news about the organization, its outlook, its policies, and employee benefits. Employee chit-chat, which was once a major feature, is being greatly reduced. In Chapter 10 under the heading "Informing Employees" many topics suitable for use in a house organ are listed. Most of the material in an internal publication can be grouped into three categories: employee questions, employee news, and organization news. Occasionally, general news may be included if it is pertinent. A new law affecting an industry might well be discussed in a house organ in that industry. Del Monte, with many employees in rural areas, used its house organ to tell how the "one-man, one-vote" decision of the Supreme Court would change the state legislatures and swing power to the cities.

A study on house organ content was conducted for the International Association of Business Communicators by the S.I. Newhouse School of Public Communication of Syracuse University. It was found that the top ten subjects in current usage were: employee recognition, employee activities, expansion or new facilities, company policy changes, job related information, organization outlook, personnel changes, employee benefits, messages from management, and economics and productivity.

Graphics

Good illustrations and attractive design will add much to the interest of a house organ. In selecting pictures, it is important to use those which show action. A head-and-shoulders portrait of someone is dull. A picture of that same person doing something is much more interesting. In some cases, the editor must double as photographer and in other cases, it is possible to use a professional photographer. In either case, the picture must be interesting. The prize-winning photographs scattered through this book, while planned for general publicity, are the kind that attract attention.

EMPLOYEE QUESTIONS

This feature is what makes a house organ a channel for inbound communication from employees. The format and title may vary. It may be called "Hot Line," or "Action Line," or "Letters to the Editor," or anything else that seems appropriate. Whenever an employee asks a question which is likely to be of general interest it should be answered. Anonymity should be assured when requested. Employees need encouragement to use this channel. The key to success is assurance that the questions will be taken seriously and acted upon by management.

EMPLOYEE NEWS

Chit-chat may be unsuitable, but pertinent news about employees, especially in relation to their work, is most suitable for use. General Electric has had great success in improving relations with employees by telling how they contribute to the success of the company. Among the items used have been stories about orders won or lost, dramatic stories about individuals working to meet an important deadline, and the experiences of employees using benefit plans.

In reporting news about employees, it is imperative to be absolutely sure that there is no invasion of privacy or defamation of character. There should always be a release signed by the employee. The release should cover both pictures and names. Many organizations ask all employees to sign a blanket release authorizing use of their pictures and news about them in organization publications.

There is always news among employees. Here are some subjects to be considered.

Anniversaries

These are intensely personal dates. They mean much to the individual. They are an important part of his or her identity and the more years measured, the more important is the anniversary. A three-page story in one house organ listed 138 employees who had served for more than 20 years and used pictures of those who had passed the 40-year mark.

Sports—Individual or Team

The company team or department team is very important to its members. Any accomplishment means a great deal to the individual and publicity about such achievements is a much-appreciated reward. It also encourages added participation. Individual activities also merit publicity whether it is a big fish, a high bowling score, or breaking 100 at golf. Items of this sort are news. The daughter of a company employee who broke a world record in swimming was featured in a two-page story in the house organ of her father's company.

Promotions and Transfers

Whenever anyone is promoted or transferred, that fact should be made known. It is often evidence that the organization rewards outstanding service. Even if there is no promotion involved in a transfer, it is still news about the individual. Also, this information expedites communication by letting everyone know where the person is now located. Under a general heading of "New Appointments," one large corporation's house organ carried such items as: "_____ named Northwest Division IR Manager," "San Francisco appointment for _____," "Realignment Announced for Administrative Services Managers," "Two New Appointments made at Irapuato, Mexico."

Awards and Honors

Without reference to whether it is internal or external, any award to, or honor for, a member of the organization should be reported. It may be as simple as election to a minor office in some outside organization. It may be as important as a large suggestion system award or some conspicuous public recognition, but whenever an individual does something outstanding his associates should be told.

Human Interest

Feature stories about individuals are sure attention-getters. They are interesting to all and especially gratifying to the person featured. Essentially, these stories are short, semibiographical items. They succeed best when they deal with people who have done or are doing something out of the ordinary.

Work Features

Items about specific jobs not only please those mentioned but also encourage better performance. By showing the importance of an individual or group or department, the people mentioned are stimulated to do better work. Recognition of their importance helps them and makes others appreciate them too.

Employee Organization News

In any employee group, there may be a number of special organizations such as clubs, classes, teams, etc. What they do is very important to them and to the employer because, generally, these group activities help build a sense of belonging, not only to the special organization but also to the organization as a whole.

Letters to the Editor

Communication from employees to the employer should be aided and encouraged in every way possible. Letters to the editor can be a most effective way to do this. It may not be possible to publish all such letters but they must be answered authoritatively. The letters published must be representative. Brickbats as well as bouquets should be included.

Humor

Humor should be used with great discretion. Many house organs carry a column of jokes; all too often they are so old that they tend to downgrade the entire publication. If something funny actually happens, it could be very interesting if it is truly humorous. Bright sayings or wisecracks usually are not funny when they appear in cold print.

ORGANIZATION NEWS

News about the organization must be news, not opinion. In getting this news, the reporter should strive for objectivity. He or she should ask pointed questions. As far as possible, the news should be reported in terms of what it means to employees — their job security, their pay, their benefits, their opportunities, their rights, their responsibilities, their self-interest.

New or Remodeled Facilities

A new building, a new plant, a remodeled office, a new piece of machinery, or even a new letterhead is news. Employees like to know what is going on or what is going to happen, so they should be the first to know if at all possible. News of this sort is often good news, and knowing good news is a great builder of morale.

New or Improved Products

Whether it be an annual model change, a completely new product, a new flavor, a redesigned package, a new insurance policy or anything else, if the organization has something different for sale, the employees should know about it. Often there is an opportunity to tell how it was developed and who worked on it. Items of this sort are *news*. House organ stories such as: "Award winning new product — MEET 'PERKY' MEAT TURNOVERS," or "We're putting pudding in a cup (and fruit too) for a new product — 'FRUIT AND PUDDING CUP,' " get high readership — and sell the new products to employees.

Organizational Changes

Reorganizations or reassignments can affect many people. They want to know how these changes will affect them. Also, this information will help the changes become effective quickly. By informing everyone, there will be little excuse for confusion or for failure to follow new procedures.

Sales Reports

Most commercial firms have something to sell and even noncommercial organizations have an equivalent measure of accomplishment such as

387

enrollment or membership. These are an indication of the health or progress of the organization. They have a major effect on employees because their jobs depend on things like this. A healthy sales report is a good morale booster; even an unhealthy report is information that can give employees a realistic understanding of conditions. Sales information, of course, should be limited to figures that could be released to the general public.

Advertising

What is being done to advertise products or services is always interesting to employees. Advertising is a fascinating subject, and when it deals with company products, it is doubly so. Whenever there is anything new about advertising, it should be published in the house organ. Information should be as complete as the competitive situation will allow.

Policies and Rules

Employees should know about the policies of their employer and the rules they must follow. Changes should be widely publicized and even old policies or rules should be reiterated from time to time. Explanations of the reasons behind policies or rules can be of considerable value in fostering willing acceptance, and a house organ is an excellent means for doing this.

Bad News

Any organization may have to reduce activity or shut down facilities or take some action having an adverse effect on employment. Distasteful as this may be, it is better to tell the whole truth in the house organ than to let the bad news travel by grapevine where it will be garbled and exaggerated.

Training Opportunities

Upgrading one's job is important to many people. Telling them how this can be done through participation in special programs or classes is a valuable use of the house organ. There are times when people who should seize this opportunity are hesitant to do so, but stories about the gains made by others can encourage the doubtful and move them to action.

Benefits

People are normally quite aware of their paychecks but other benefits are often given little attention. These "fringe" items may be quite costly; employees should be informed about them so that the advantages of employment become known as something more than cold figures on a paycheck. In addition to insurance, sick pay, vacation, and retirement, these benefits can include subsidized meals, discount purchases, and numerous other things that mean considerable savings.

Information about Executives

The boss becomes more human when those under him know how he reached his present position and what kind of person he is. This, of course, assumes that he really earned his status. If he got the job solely because his father owned the company, it is rather difficult to be complimentary. But, assuming that he did deserve the job, his accomplishment can be a stimulus to others.

According to Opinion Research Council, 75% of managers rate top management favorably, but only half the clerical and a third of the hourly workers agree.

Organization History

Many organizations have colorful histories. Knowing how "XYZ" grew from an idea to an important factor in its field can be an inspiration to those who read about it. There are many ways to write about this. Among the possibilities are complete histories (either in one issue or in installments), highlights such as "How _____ was started or introduced," and the "10 years ago" or "50 years ago" technique.

Awards and Honors

Recognition by others should always be widely publicized. It is an indication that some people outside the organization think that it has done something outstanding and praiseworthy. This helps create confidence in management, increases loyalty, and builds pride in the organization. A good example of this is a house organ story entitled: "Equal Opportunity in Employment — NAACP Award to Granny Goose." The story told that the Oakland, California, Branch of the National Association for the Advancement of Colored People had officially designated

Granny Goose Foods as "Employer of the Year" in recognition of that company's consistent dedication to equal employment practices.

General News Affecting the Organization

When something happens outside the organization that can or will affect it, the occurrence should be reported. Such subjects as taxes, tariffs, costs of raw materials, freight and utility rates, competitive activity, and general economic conditions can all have a material effect on the well-being of the organization. Such facts should be made known.

Sources of Materials

Information about the sources of raw materials or component parts can be of high interest. Much of this will be self-evident but there should be no hesitation about going further afield. For example, a firm weaving woolens or making wool clothes might use a story on sheep-raising. An insurance company might use an article about the production of the paper used in its policies. And in the realm of the obvious, a large canner ran a four-page story with nine pictures to tell how tomatoes are grown, harvested, and processed.

Utilization of Product

Regardless of what is produced, the use of the product can make interesting reading. An oil company might tell how a special lubricant aided arctic exploration. A lumber manufacturer might show how its materials solved a technical problem in some unusual situation.

Importance of the Organization

Its significance to the community or to its own field of activity should be known to the employees. Many firms are the backbone of their communities or the "bellwethers" of their industries. Perhaps they are not the biggest, but they still "try harder." When employees know the importance of their employer, they should be much more cooperative and loyal.

Editorials, Pleas, and Admonitions

Great discretion should be the rule in this area. There is always a temptation to use the house organ as a channel wherein management tells employees what to do. There is a legitimate place for editorials or for messages "from the president." A good example is the message from the president of a large corporation headed: "Have Inside Information? Take Care How You Use It." The article detailed the dangers of using inside information in purchasing or selling stock of the corporation and warned of the corporate and individual liabilities involved. House organs can be used to urge employees to "give to the community chest" or "join the credit union," and employees can be admonished to work for "no defects" or "stop horseplay on the assembly line," but this should not be overdone.

MULTIPLE HOUSE ORGANS

In large organizations with several house organs, there are some special problems. Standard Oil Company of Indiana and Hewlett-Packard solve this problem with centralized guidance but decentralized control.

Standard Oil of Indiana has three house organs at its Chicago headquarters and 45 other publications at individual refineries, plants, and offices. The content is varied to fit the needs of the readers. Some are Ph.D.'s, some are marketing people, some are computer programmers, some are blue collar workers, and some are clerical workers.

The editors of these publications report to local managers and many of these editors are not professionally trained. The headquarters staff guides the editors with a monthly newsletter which serves as a clearinghouse of information and a continuing report of what the editors are doing. It shows and tells the editors "how to do it" and "how not to do it." It also provides material for local use which includes features, fillers, editorials, cartoons, and photographs. A regular feature is praise for good work and tactful criticism of errors.

Hewlett-Packard equips the division managers with guidelines for employee publications. Among the points covered are: objectives, responsibility, recognition of staff, format, and cost. The responsibility section states that the general manager of the division is responsible for attaining the objectives, staffing the publication, and monitoring the publication with special attention to the content. Points to be monitored are:

1. Confidentiality — sensitive information must be excluded. This covers financial data, marketing strategy, products under development, legal matters, and future organization changes.

2. Editorial taste — nothing questionable, offensive, or demeaning can be used.

3. Chit-chat — should be used only with restraint.

4. Staffing — should be done with care. A journalistic background is helpful but not essential. The key requirement is a strong desire to get information, to present it accurately and interestingly, and to meet deadlines. The editor needs support and encouragement. He or she must be given access to news sources and to the managers who review and approve. The editing is not an after-hours activity.

Hewlett-Packard summarizes its guidelines by stating that the successful house organ depends on: firm backing by management, adequate budget, attractive, consistent format, regularity of publication, and fitting the needs of the organization.

DISTRIBUTION

House organs are usually published for employees although, as mentioned before, some are published for other publics. Much can be gained by distributing to others. Among the categories to be considered are stockholders, customers, prospects, suppliers, dealers, distributors, related firms, associations, financial institutions and editors of trade and general magazines. Mailing to the employees' homes is a good idea because it serves to involve the families.

EXERCISES

1. Get a copy of the house organ of some firm.
   (a) Identify every item as to the purpose (check against the listing in the text).
   (b) Are there any items which do not conform to any category in the text?
   (c) How would you improve it?

Case Problem

You are editor of the house organ of the Gimmick Manufacturing Corporation. Employee efficiency has dropped drastically and, unless quality and quantity of production is increased markedly, the company will go broke.

Write a 200-word "Letter from the President" to appear on the inside front cover of the house organ. The letter must state the problem and persuade the employees to improve their performance.

Annual
Reports

Annual reports can take several forms. First, and most common, is the report to shareholders of a corporation. Another form is the corporate social responsibility report which may be sent to people who are not stockholders. A third variation is the annual report to employees which usually contains much information from the stockholders' report but interprets the material in terms of the employees' self-interest.

In addition to corporate reports there are the reports of associations, unions, government agencies, and special-interest groups, any of which may periodically issue reports to their constituents.

Most of this chapter deals with stockholder reports, but with the exception of the discussion about the Securities and Exchange Commission (SEC) and the Financial Accounting Standards Board (FASB), nearly everything else applies to any annual report.

PURPOSE

All annual reports have a common purpose — to enable the readers to appraise the competence of management and to determine whether their interests are being adequately served.

Typically, an annual report is a history of the past year, but a good annual report should go further. It should look forward to the next year or even several years. The past may be interesting, but the future is more important.

People invest their money or time in an organization in the expectation of satisfaction. They retain or increase their investment only if they anticipate continued satisfaction. Predictions and forecasts are dangerous, but it is possible to report on developments and trends which may affect the organization in the future. Every annual report should include this kind of information.

CRITICISMS

Annual reports are vital communication channels. They reach a very important public, but many of them fail to communicate. The reasons for this failure are easily correctible if there is a will to do so. Criticisms come from all segments of the owner public. Some of the most common are the following:

Unreadability

Many a report winds up in the wastebasket because the average reader can't understand the financial jargon and complicated statements which should make things clear.

Dullness

Many annual reports are dull and uninteresting. They don't get and hold attention. They kill the reader's interest and give an unfavorable impression of the management.

Flashiness

The constant striving for more striking and impressive reports has led too many people to concentrate on form and neglect the content. The result is a report which is beautiful but ineffective.

Overoptimism

One critic has said that it is almost impossible, by reading the typical letter to shareholders in an annual report, to tell whether the organization is succeeding or failing. All the reports tell the good news, but too many gloss over equally important bad news or drop it into the financial notes.

Unresponsiveness

Owner questions and complaints are often ignored in annual reports. This inbound communication is very important and should be answered. For every one owner who raises a question, there may be many who don't take the trouble.

TRENDS

In response to criticisms such as the foregoing, in compliance with requirements of the SEC and FASB, and in light of the owner concerns expressed in Chapter 11, annual reports are changing and improving.

General Changes

Reports are becoming longer and more costly. They are giving more information. They are becoming more readable and more interesting. They are becoming more frank. More and more companies are incorporating the 10-K report (a complete and detailed financial report) into the annual report. Some are even using it as a substitute for an annual report. The 10-K report *must* be filed with the SEC. It is loaded with figures, but it isn't very helpful to the small stockholder. It doesn't contain the background material and interpretation which enable the reader to understand the company. Even the SEC dislikes this trend, and some of its top officials have urged corporations not to abandon the more traditional annual report.

Some Examples

Many companies report on stockholder questions raised at the annual meeting. This is often issued as a special report on the meeting.

In one annual report, Ford Motor Company said that "not everything went right," detailing recalls, strikes, and customer-service complaints.

Amsul said in an annual report: "This was the worst year in Amsul's history."

Arco in a social responsibility report included a point-by-point critique of its program — a critique by an outsider who praised some things and harshly criticized others.

CONTENT

Some things *must* go into an annual report, other things *should* go into

395

the report, and there are many other items which *may* be included. When considering optional items, management often tries to put into the report only what it wants to include but omits information which the owners should receive. This is a bad policy because owner interests should be paramount.

SEC Requirements

The Securities and Exchange Commission requires that annual reports contain certain information. Because these requirements are constantly changing, it is impossible to list them here. To ascertain what is needed at any given time, it will be necessary to get the *latest* regulations of the SEC. These can be obtained from many certified public accountants and from local SEC offices.

FASB Requirements

The Financial Accounting Standards Board has stated that a financial report should be comprehensible to an investor with a reasonable understanding of business and economics who is willing to study the report; that the investor should be able to assess the possibility of receiving cash for dividends or interest, and that he or she should be able to evaluate the performance of management.

The standards for accounting are changing. While compliance with them is the responsibility of the accounting people in the organization, the public relations people must be sure that the report is understandable.

Reader Requirements

Annual reports are read by two radically different kinds of people: the individual owner who is generally quite unsophisticated, and the sophisticated financial analyst who is familiar with all the technical language. Each needs a different kind of information.

A recent survey found that the individual is primarily interested in quality of management, general business conditions, earnings, dividends, and the outlook for the industry. Technical factors such as volume of trading, etc., were not important. On the other hand, the financial experts who counsel individual investors or manage mutual funds, endowment portfolios, pension trusts, and similar large holdings want, and can use, a large amount of highly detailed information.

This creates a problem for the people who prepare the annual report. There may be a few hundred people who want a great quantity of detailed information and thousands who don't want it.

One proposed solution is to prepare two different reports, one for each audience. Another, similar proposal is to prepare a voluminous supplement to the basic report and give it to those who want the additional data. This supplement is usually called a "fact book."

Every annual report should serve the interests of the particular people who will read it. To determine these interests it is necessary to seriously study the questions raised by the owners. Surveys of stockholders are invaluable in learning what the owners think about the company and what else they would like to know.

Key Information

In addition to the information mandated by the SEC, an annual report should contain information which will aid in appraisal of the organization. Reports often contain a president's letter and an operating review, but these are not required.

There is considerable leeway in choosing what to include. Items which may deserve discussion are: long-range plans and objectives, problems and opportunities, corporate strategy, dividend policy, stock-market performance, long-range investment potential, and short-term prospects for earnings and dividends. Any of these should be explained in specifics, not generalities.

Forecasts should be handled with great care, but the report should point out the factors and trends which may influence results in the months or years ahead. For example, the Brooks-Scanlon Lumber Company gave its owners and employees a comprehensive report on how a proposed U.S. Forest Service timber-selling policy might affect the operations of Brooks-Scanlon.

General Information

Every company has situations of importance to the owners. Among the subjects which might be included in an annual report are: plant or building construction, raw material or component supplies, manufacturing, marketing, personnel, legal problems, transportation problems, energy supplies, taxes and tariffs, and public relations. (Reports on public relations involve any, or all, of the publics of the organization. The most likely are government, customers, and the community.)

Social Responsibility

Many corporations include a special section on social responsibility, while others issue a separate report on this subject. While some authorities feel that such material should not be in the annual report, others disagree strongly.

PREPARATION

Preparing an annual report is one of the most expensive, prestigious, time-consuming, nitpicking, and important responsibilities of the public relations practitioner.

Because the report covers the entire organization, it involves practically every department or division head. Each of these heads has definite ideas of what to include and what to say about it. This creates a problem for the person who must put the report together.

The public relations practitioner has the task of getting the cooperation of all these people, of coordinating and controlling the operation, of planning, designing, writing, producing and delivering the report. This demands the utmost in skill, tact, and perseverance.

Above all, it is imperative to retain control. Control can be retained only if the practitioner stays on top of the job and a good, long jump ahead of everyone else. To do this the practitioner must precondition the management, use the basic principles of PR program management, and start far enough in advance.

Preconditioning Management

Management must be aware of the climate in which the report will be received and the climate which is likely to exist in the following months. Work on the annual report may start from four to six months before it is issued, so this requires an estimate of what conditions are likely to prevail six months and a year in the future.

Assessing these conditions demands a continuing program of briefing management on public and owner attitudes. This briefing can be done through periodic meetings or through bulletins and memorandums. If management is kept aware of the changing social, political, and economic environment, it will be more willing to issue a report which will be meaningful.

Evaluating the Last Report

In Part IV, it was stated that the public program starts with inbound communication and continues through planning, outbound communication, and evaluation. With annual reports it is a good idea to start with evaluation of the last report. Certainly it should be changed and improved. The old report should be compared with those of other companies. It should be criticized. Every item should be analyzed for its importance, its clarity and usefulness to the reader. Always the question should be asked "How can we improve?" This critique can lead to new ideas and to a better report.

Inbound Communication

Chapter 19 covers this subject in general, but for the annual report there are some special things to consider. Questions asked by stockholders should be considered. The questions asked and the reports and comments made by security analysts are highly significant. Security analysts reports on the company, S.&P. reports, Value Line and other investor research services should be studied. If possible, analysts who follow the corporation should be interviewed.

Internal management reports should be read. Planning documents, capital budgets and market research reports may be significant. The 10-K report (annual) and 10-Q reports (quarterly) filed with the SEC should be reviewed. Prospectuses should also be analyzed — along with press clippings about the company and the industry.

When all of this background material has been digested, it is time to interview the top executives and get their input for the report. Here it is wise to have a list of precise questions derived from the foregoing review. At this point, it is no sin to confess ignorance. The important thing is understanding.

With these questions completed there should be enough information to start planning the report, although it is likely that on some points there will be a need for followup. Some information will not be immediately available, and of course the basic financial report will not be complete until the close of the fiscal year.

Planning the Report

The first step in planning is to determine the objective. In general, the objective must be to provide the reader with information which will

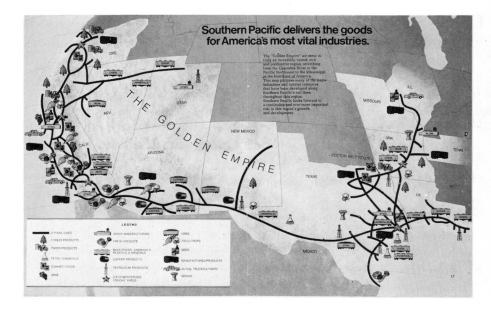

Fig. 25.1 Center spread of a Southern Pacific Co. annual report.

permit a solid appraisal of the performance and prospects of the company. This leads to the questions: "How much information and what kind of information?" And this leads to still another question: "What makes this company a good investment?"

The report should give the reader a true picture of the organization. This will include its virtues and faults, its successes and failures, its objectives and problems, its past accomplishments and future prospects. If all this is done well, the report will attain its objective.

Format and Design

Early in the planning stage, there must be a decision as to the physical form of the report and the typography and illustrations. The report must be printed but the actual design is optional. Usually the report is a booklet, but there are occasional variations.

No owner has to read an annual report, but if the report isn't read it is a waste of money. To get readership, the report must get attention and then hold it with material which is interesting. The report should include what is important and exclude trivia. A report which is attractive and informative, even entertaining, will be read. This requires an eyecatching layout, good illustrations, and a vigorous, plainspoken, no-nonsense writing style.

Many good ideas can be obtained by studying the prize-winning reports which are cited annually by the Financial Analysts Federation (219 E. 42nd Street, New York, N.Y. 10017). Another source of ideas is the *Public Relations Journal*, which usually features annual reports in its September issue.

The Production Schedule

In setting up a schedule, it is important to think of every element which will be included in the final report. Pictures, artwork, copy, layout, printing, delivery, envelopes, and mailing must all be considered.

Because all of these pieces must be fitted against a deadline, it is necessary to use the PERT system described in Chapter 20. In setting up the timetable, there must be realistic consideration of how long it will take to do things. Annual reports commonly take from four to six months in preparation. There must be a time allowance for delays. People will fail to deliver on time, people will be away from their offices, people will change their minds, printers will have problems, everyone else will have problems. But if the schedule is realistic and the person in charge of the report stays in control, it will be delivered on time.

DISTRIBUTION

Annual reports can serve several purposes. If they are to accomplish those purposes, they must reach the people who are to be affected. The principal publics to which annual reports are sent include not only those directly concerned but also numerous others not so closely involved but who still can affect or be affected by the organization. Aside from the SEC and the stockholders, who are *musts*, some of the more logical recipients are:

Employees

Annual reports are often sent to all employees. Occasionally some portions are omitted but more frequently the report is complete. The purpose is to give employees a better understanding of their organization, its problems, and its accomplishments.

Associated Groups

Sending the annual report to competitors, suppliers, dealers, and trade associations is a general practice. Usually this results in an exchange of reports which not only provides information but also gives the creator of the report new ideas.

Educators

Both libraries and interested faculty members are logical recipients of annual reports. A national organization may try to reach all educational institutions while a local or regional operation may limit distribution accordingly. The nature of the organization is also a factor. The key to this decision is: "Who would be interested?" The annual report of an electrical manufacturer may be invaluable to a teacher of electrical engineering or economics and totally wasted on a linguist or historian.

News Media

Newspapers, magazines, trade journals, news services, and broadcasters are generally included in the distribution of these reports. Selectivity is the rule here. There is nothing to be gained by sending an annual report to someone who is not interested — and much to be accomplished by putting it into the right hands.

Financial Interests

Brokerage houses, security dealers, security analysts, mutual funds, investment bankers, commercial bankers, and financial writers are always primary targets for the annual report of any firms whose stock can be bought or sold by the general public. As always, the guide is: "Who would be interested?"

EXERCISES

Get a copy of the annual report of a corporation.
   (a) Is the report easy to understand?
   (b) If you were a stockholder, would you conclude from the report that the management was doing a good job? Why or why not?

Case Problem

You are public relations counselor to a small corporation. Sales have been good but because of continually increasing labor costs profits are unsatisfactory. New automatic machinery can solve the problem. To pay for it will require so much money that there can be no dividends for two years. After that, it is expected that it will be possible to renew and increase dividends. This action has been approved by the directors.

Write the president's letter for the annual report.

Visual Aids $\quad$ 26

The term "visual aids" has come to mean things projected onto a screen — either still or moving pictures. Charts, diagrams, blackboards, and un-projected pictures are visual too, but in most cases when people speak of visual aids they mean motion pictures, slides or filmstrips (sometimes called strip films or slide films). That is the subject of this chapter.

During World War II, visual aids were widely used in U.S. military training. They proved so effective that their use in civilian circles since that time has increased phenomenally. Business and industrial firms now produce more than 9,000 motion pictures a year, of which roughly 40% are made for employees. Today, visual aids are used for almost every communication purpose and by almost every organization that wants to convey information or ideas to the public.

The reason for their effectiveness is that the eye absorbs more than the ear. A widely quoted phrase is: "People remember 10% of what they hear and 50% of what they see." Whether the figures are accurate is not important; the facts are that showing is better than telling. In most cases, the use of visual aids includes both showing and telling, which is better yet. Since practically all motion pictures have a sound track and many filmstrips have an accompanying record, they are frequently called "audio-visual" aids.

When visual aids are properly planned, produced, and utilized, they can be very effective tools of public relations.

CHARACTERISTICS OF VISUAL AIDS

Deciding what kind of visual aid to use requires some knowledge of the nature of each as well as the objective to be attained.

Slides

The greatest advantage of slides is flexibility. They can be arranged and rearranged in any way that seems desirable. It is possible to use as few or as many as are needed. They can be held on screen for any length of time. It is possible to back up and show a slide or a series of slides for a second time. It is possible to omit one or several from any given showing. It is also easy to add slides where and when they are needed. Slides can be used to show pictures, diagrams, charts, words, or any combination thereof. Color is always preferable to black and white, and light letters on a dark background are easier to read than black letters on white.

No slide sequence should be shown without explanation — either by voice, by words on the slides, or by title slides. If slides are to be used repeatedly, they should be mounted in metal frames to prevent damage. Slides can be lost, damaged, or disarranged. They normally are projected and explained only by someone who has selected and arranged them. Sending a set of slides to a stranger can be hazardous because there is no assurance that he will show and explain them properly.

Slides are very economical, and they can be used to show almost anything that does not require motion to tell the story or to sustain interest. Most slides are 35mm in size but some are produced as 2″ x 2″.

Filmstrips

A filmstrip is a length of 35mm film containing a series of individual still pictures. Also called strip films or slide films, filmstrips have, aside from nonadaptability to "on-the-spot editing," many of the advantages of slides. Filmstrips are often produced in large quantities for distribution to and showing by people who may be remote from the producing organization. The individual frames of a filmstrip cannot be disarranged. Usually there are explanatory words on the frames or title frames preceding untitled frames.

Often there is a script with commentary suggested for each frame, and sometimes a record is produced that can be played as the strip is shown. With a written script, the frames and corresponding commentary are numbered. When a record is used, it is common practice to have a chime at the end of each paragraph of commentary to signal that the next frame should be shown.

Filmstrips are used in the same way and for the same purpose as slides and the same rules apply as regards color and explanation. More costly than slides, filmstrips are still fairly inexpensive to produce and to distribute.

Motion Pictures

Motion pictures are the most interesting and exciting of visual aids. They are also the most costly and, for this reason, should be approached with considerable caution. It is not at all difficult to spend a quarter of a million dollars on a movie; even the simplest and briefest can cost several thousand. There are several forms in which a movie can be produced. Today, most motion pictures have soundtracks and most projectors have sound equipment, so the silent film is rather rare. Sound can be either "live" (the actors do the talking) or "off-screen narration" (an invisible commentator describes the action). The latter is much less costly.

Most films produced in recent years have been in color. The cost difference is not great and the superiority over black and white is overwhelming. Animation is an attractive and interesting device but, since it costs about $100 for a second of running time, it should be considered only when the need is great and the budget is large.

The great majority of public relations films being produced at this time are in color, with off-screen narration and no animation. Most of them are 16mm, although some very large organizations do produce 35mm versions.

Motion pictures have a usable life of several years. Many organizations schedule their films for five years or more of use before replacement.

Because a sound motion picture requires no commentary at projection time, it can be sent anywhere and used by anyone able to thread the film into a projector and focus the image onto a screen. Combining visual and aural communication and with the attention-compelling features of action and color, a motion picture is one of the most effective channels of communication. It can tell a story interestingly and persuasively — with no danger of omitting important words or adding comments that will create the wrong reaction. It can tell the same story to numerous audiences and it can tell it properly, regardless of time or location.

USE OF VISUAL AIDS

Visual aids can perform many different communication functions.

However, each of the three major categories is particularly adapted to certain types of use.

Slides

Slides are most frequently used as aids in reporting or explaining something to a meeting which has been called for a specific purpose. An advertising man might use slides to show a new advertising campaign to the board of directors. A city manager might use slides to show the council what a proposed new mall might do to the city. A teacher might use them to show a social studies class what Quebec is like. A college president might use them to present a building program to his trustees. Slide presentations can, of course, be repeated first in one situation and then in another. Slides, however, are generally considered aids to a specific speaker for use before a predetermined audience.

Filmstrips

Generally filmstrips are produced in quantities for use in conveying the same message to different, and frequently scattered, audiences. The strips are prepared so that a person unfamiliar with the material will still be able to present it in a satisfactory manner. Typically, filmstrips are "how to do it" aids. They can show how to bake biscuits or disassemble an automobile transmission or sell appliances. Because a print of a filmstrip is very inexpensive, it is possible with a small budget to produce and distribute scores or hundreds of copies for use whenever there is interest in the subject covered by the filmstrip. Their best use is in the areas of teaching, training, and informing.

Motion Pictures

Motion pictures are most effective when movement is necessary to tell the story or to maintain interest in the subject matter. Movies can have high emotional impact and thus can be extremely persuasive. It is much easier to assemble an audience for a motion picture than for a filmstrip; when the audience to be reached has complete freedom of choice as to attendance, it is generally necessary to use a motion picture. If people are vitally interested in a subject, they will take any opportunity to hear about it; they will look at slides or filmstrips. But if they are not really and deeply concerned, the attraction must be stronger. Controlled audiences such as students or employees will accept slides or filmstrips but will appreciate motion pictures more.

Motion pictures are used for such purposes as orienting employees, telling the history of the organization, job training, general education, product or service promotion, indirect public relations (e.g., a film showing how a public utility builds powerhouses and transmission lines with minimum damage to the landscape).

A particularly effective use for films is in developing support for or against something. Thus, a motion picture scene showing sewage flowing into a river is much more powerful than any still picture. A movie sequence showing a redwood tree toppling to the ground will arouse emotion much more successfully than a static scene showing the tree on the ground.

CERTIFICATIONS OF SHOWING

MODERN talking picture service, inc.

1212 Avenue of the Americas, New York, N.Y. 10036   PAGE   1

SHOW NO.	TOWN	ORGANIZATION	PLAY DATE MO. DAY	TIMES SHOWN	MEN	WOMEN	BOYS	GIRLS	TOTAL

CERTIFICATION OF SHOWINGS * 24
AUG 31 1970   JW

03292 PEACHY TRICKS

C01361 CLING PEACH ADVISORY BOARD

CIRCULATION REPORTED THIS MONTH

        BOOKINGS   350
        SHOWINGS   403

        ATTENDANCE REPORTED
        MEN   3,568
        WOMEN   4,007
        BOYS   3,552
        GIRLS   4,216
        IN TOTAL ONLY 1,998
        TOTAL   17,341

CIRCULATION REPORTED THIS YEAR TO DATE

        BOOKINGS   2,739
        SHOWINGS   5,796

        ATTENDANCE REPORTED
        MEN   9,809
        WOMEN   14,447
        BOYS   30,217
        GIRLS   114,531
        IN TOTAL ONLY 11,839
        TOTAL   180,843

CIRCULATION REPORTED SINCE START OF PROGRAM

        BOOKINGS   7,878
        SHOWINGS   16,646

        ATTENDANCE REPORTED
        MEN   26,732
        WOMEN   38,035
        BOYS   74,271
        GIRLS   333,658
        IN TOTAL ONLY 32,551
        TOTAL   505,247

THIS FILM HAS BEEN LISTED IN   60 PROMOTIONS,
TOTALING   630,700 IMPRESSIONS DURING THE PAST 12 MONTHS.

NOTE - THE SYMBOL * INDICATES THAT THE BOOKING REQUEST CAME FROM THE SPONSORS ORGANIZATION.   FORM # 103

Fig. 26.1 A report on showings of a public relations motion picture.

PLANNING VISUAL AIDS

One of the great problems in the use of visual aids is lack of planning. Large sums of money are wasted because of the tendency to leap into production without due consideration of the audience to be reached, the purpose to be served, and the kind of visual aid that will be most efficient. Costly motion pictures are produced when filmstrips would do the job and, conversely, slide presentations or filmstrips are used to save money when a more expensive movie would get more results per dollar. The steps in planning are: determining the audience, determining the purpose, and determining the kind of visual aid to use.

Determining the Audience

The first question to be asked when considering visual aids is: "Who do you want to reach?" Audiences are not "found" for visual aids; visual aids are prepared for audiences. Questions that should be considered are: Is there one audience or are there a number of audiences? What kind of people are they? How interested are they? What do they know about the subject? How many people do we want to reach? Where are they? How can we get them together to see and hear the message? Where can we present the story to them?

In other words, before any other steps are taken, there must be a thorough and comprehensive study of the audience.

Determining the Purpose

This, too, requires careful consideration. Is the purpose to inform, teach, train, explain, persuade, arouse, inspire or, as occasionally happens, flatter the head of the organization? If it is the latter, the result is likely to be a motion picture of high cost and low value. (Many useless motion pictures have been produced because the president could not resist the idea of seeing himself on a screen.) Fortunately, however, there are few organizations which can afford such luxury and, in most cases, it is possible to focus on the question: "What do we want to accomplish?"

Determining the Visual Aid to Use

When the two preceding questions are answered, the next step is to consider production costs, number of possible users, and the characteristics of the visual aids. If the usage is for one or a few times, the slide presentation is logical. If the subject is "nuts and bolts" or if the audience is a "captive audience," the answer may be filmstrips. If motion is essential to the telling of the story or if it is important to arouse emotion, a motion picture may be the solution if there is an adequate budget. Not all decisions are this easy, but the right choice will be made if there is a maximum of serious thought and a minimum of emotion.

Whichever aid is chosen, it should be done well. A good filmstrip may be more effective than a sloppy motion picture.

PRODUCING VISUAL AIDS

When a decision has been reached as to the type of visual aid to use, the next step is the actual production. Since each type of visual aid involves very different production problems, they will be treated separately.

Slides

The first step is to plan the talk or speech they illustrate. It is, of course, possible that slides will be available and that a talk may be written to use existing material but, whenever possible, the slides should be used to illustrate the message rather than vice versa.

All important points in the message should be illustrated and, conversely, every slide should be explained. In this way every item will be covered both visually and vocally.

Slides should be visually excellent and uniform in appearance. That is, color slides should not be mixed with black and white, vertical framing should not be interspersed with horizontal framing, and all slides should look as if they belong together in one set or series. Horizontal color slides should always be used if possible.

Filmstrips

All that has been said about slide production applies to filmstrip production because a filmstrip is really a slide presentation on one piece of film. Filmstrips can be made from any kind of illustrative material. Occasionally existing pictures or charts can be used, but generally the requirements of uniformity necessitate producing every frame "from scratch."

The steps in producing a filmstrip are: writing the script, determining the illustrative material for each frame, taking all necessary pictures, preparing all titles and captions, preparing the master negative, and producing the necessary quantity of prints. This usually requires professional assistance. The cost of using experts is very small when consideration is given to the quality of work that will be done and the disastrous results that can occur when such a task is undertaken by amateurs.

Motion Pictures

As with other visual aids, the first step in production is the writing of a script. This script describes every scene and specifies every word or sound that will be on the sound track.

Script writing is normally a task for an expert and this creates a problem. It is desirable to have a script on which producing organizations can base their bids but most scriptwriters are employed by producing organizations. When one of them submits a script that is approved, there is an obligation to let that firm produce the film. This precludes competitive bidding. Asking several firms to submit competitive scripts is not the answer.

One solution for this problem is to prepare a very detailed description of the film in terms of content, length, sound, special effects, cost, location, etc. Then, in consultation with several producers it will be possible to clearly determine what is involved and to negotiate a price. Occasionally it is possible to retain an independent scriptwriter and, in that case, competitive bidding is no problem.

When a script has been finalized and a producer selected,* the actual production is started. Each scene is filmed and viewed. The best "takes" are selected and a "rough-cut" film is assembled. When this is corrected and approved, a master negative is made and the sound is recorded on it. From this negative, it is possible to produce prints in quantity as needed.

Suggested Readings

Audio Visual Communications, 200 Madison Ave., New York, N.Y. 10016.
Business Screen, 402 W. Liberty Drive, Wheaton, Illinois 60187.
Klein, Walter J. *The Sponsored Film.* New York: Hastings House, 1976.
McGuire, Jerry. *How to Write, Direct and Produce Effective Business Films.*
    Blue Ridge Summit, Penna. TAB Books, 1977.

*In choosing a producer be sure to (1) see samples of previous work, (2) inspect the production facilities, (3) meet the people who would do the work, and (4) determine whether they understand what you want.

AUDIENCES

Most visual aids are made for a specific audience but it is possible to reach two or even more audiences with one motion picture or filmstrip. Often collateral audiences will profit by seeing such films even though they may not be primary targets.

Direct Audiences

These audiences are the people who have a direct financial interest in the organization. The category includes employees, stockholders, dealers, distributors, and possibly, suppliers. Because of their involvement with the organization, it takes relatively little effort to get them to the film or get the film to them. In one sense they are "captive " audiences.

Indirect Audiences

These audiences include all other publics. Especially important in this category are the community, customer, government, and educator publics. Usually these people have little financial interest in the organization but they can have a major effect upon it. These audiences are not as easy to reach as those having a direct interest. They must be persuaded, rather than directed, to view the motion picture. And they must often be reached through other organizations such as business clubs, social groups, fraternal organizations, churches, schools, and colleges.

DISTRIBUTION

Distribution to direct audiences is simple and is controlled completely by the producing organization. A film for employees can be shown at an employee meeting and a substantial attendance will be automatic. A film for distributors will find a ready audience at a meeting of distributors. A film for stockholders fits ideally into the annual meeting.

For indirect audiences, the problem of distribution is a bit more difficult because these audiences are not controlled and often are quite remote. There are three suitable methods of reaching them: through the sponsor, through commercial distributors, and through libraries. An essential factor in distribution is the determination of the number and kind of people reached. For every showing, there must be a report as to where and when it was shown, how many people saw it and, if possible, what the reaction was.

Sponsor Distribution

This method involves establishment of a complete facility for receiving orders, repairing and reconditioning films, shipping them to users, and handling returns. It necessitates accurate record keeping and requires film handling equipment and storage space. Naturally, this activity requires personnel to do all the necessary work. Usually this method is most suited to a very small organization where few films are used and only a small amount of manpower is needed or to very large organizations where a complete film department is justified.

Commercial Distribution

For many organizations, this is the most efficient method of getting motion pictures and filmstrips distributed. A commercial distributor can handle every phase of the operation. All the sponsor has to do is supply the distributor with enough prints to fill the demand. The distributor takes care of shipment and recovery. He repairs or reconditions films and gives reports on usage including number of showings and number of people in attendance. Commercial distributors can be located through film producers, through visual aid trade journals, through the Yellow Pages under the classification "motion picture film distributors," or through firms which use them.

Library Distribution

Motion pictures and filmstrips are frequently presented to film libraries where they are catalogued and made available to all. Among the types of organizations that have film libraries are colleges and universities, high schools, trade associations, business firms, government agencies, churches, social service groups, service clubs, and fraternal organizations.

When films are placed in libraries, there is no control of distribution, no assurance that they will be used, and little likelihood of accurate reports of usage. Nevertheless, library placement is desirable because, in general, it automatically insures that a larger audience will be exposed to the message.

PROMOTION OF USE

A visual aid is useless in storage and it will not get out of storage unless people know it is available and are persuaded to request it. The availability and desirability of these aids can be publicized through several channels, among which the more frequently used are: direct mail, film catalogues, advertising, and distributors.

In every form of promotion, it is necessary to enable the interested recipient to order what he or she wants. Whenever possible, there should be an order form specifying the item or items desired, the date wanted, and the name and address of the person to whom shipment should be made.

Direct Mail

Leaflets or booklets describing available filmed materials are mailed to potential users such as program chairmen, instructors, audio-visual specialists, libraries, and any other individuals or organizations representing groups that are suitable audiences for the motion pictures or filmstrips.

Film Catalogues

Film catalogues listing the offerings of many sponsors are prepared and distributed to prospective users of visual aid materials. Educators' Progress Service (Randolph, Wisconsin 53956) publishes *Educators' Guide to Free Films, Educators' Guide to Free Filmstrips, and Educator's Guide to Free Tapes, Scripts and Transcriptions*. These are revised annually. Listing can be arranged by correspondence with the publisher. The U.S. government publishes a pamphlet listing film libraries offering free films.

Advertising

Advertising describing films and filmstrips are published in visual-aids trade journals and in the trade journals of those industries or fields of education most likely to be interested. In many cases, the publications provide a special order blank section to expedite handling of requests.

Distributors

Most film distributors, in addition to handling the physical shipment,

415

will also do considerable promotion. They are paid for the services they perform and the easiest way to increase their income is to perform more service. The distributor, therefore, usually makes a strong effort to promote the films he handles. This is another persuasive reason for using a film distributor.

Use in Theaters

It is possible to get PR motion pictures used in commercial theaters. Frequently an exhibitor will book a major film and need short subjects to fill out a program and provide a "cushion" of time between showings of the feature. Film distribution houses that represent major producers should be contacted to make arrangements for placing PR films.

Use on Television

Television stations will occasionally use motion pictures from a PR source. The preference is for films suitable for a half-hour slot (27 minutes approximately). Sports and travel are their favorite subjects. A small amount of sponsor identification is acceptable. The commercial distributors previously mentioned can and do handle this distribution.

VIDEOTAPE

Use of this visual aid has increased dramatically in recent years and the trend shows no sign of abating. The technology is being used in many situations where slides and motion pictures were once the favored communication device.

Videotape permits production of a moving picture or a show which appears to be live in very little time. Instant playbacks enable the producer to see the results without delay. Retakes and editing can be done on the spot. The technical quality is excellent and the speed of production can save both money and time.

In public relations, most videotape is being used for in-house or closed-circuit television. It has been especially useful in reaching employees but it has also been found useful at meetings of stockholders and other groups.

Because videotape is shown on monitors, it cannot be shipped like a motion picture with the assurance that someone will have a suitable projector and screen. However, more and more organizations are acquiring the necessary viewing facilities.

Technology in this medium is progressing steadily and the limitations of today may disappear in a short time as engineers find new ways to solve the problems.

Equipment to produce videotape is at present bulky and costly, yet many organizations are making the necessary investment because of the great advantages it has. And in a few years both the bulk and cost may be substantially reduced.

Using videotape, it is possible to produce a message with movement and color and give that message to a selected audience in a remarkably short time. Subject matter can include: policy changes, new products, dialogues between employees and management, question-and-answer sessions, explanations of organization problems, and so on. Perhaps the greatest advantage is that it can provide face-to-face communication through taped meetings. For additional ideas on this, see "In-House TV" in Chapter 29.

EXERCISES

1. Have you seen an industrial or business film that you remember as especially good? Why do you think it was good?
2. Have you seen an industrial or business film that you remember as particularly bad? Why do you think it was bad?

Case Problems

1. Select some historic old building or beautiful natural area that is, or could be, endangered by "progress."

   Plan a slide presentation (20 slides) to be used in a plea to have the building or area preserved as a "historic site" or park. Describe each slide to be used.

2. Prepare a "treatment" (brief outline) for a 25-minute motion picture to be used in "selling" the voters of Big City on a $100,000,000 bond issue for construction of a nonpolluting garbage incinerator. At present, garbage is being dumped in a nearby canyon which will soon be filled.

   Describe the principal scenes to be shown and what will be said.

Publicity | **27**

Publicity is the best known and most conspicuous tool of public relations. It is often erroneously assumed that publicity *is* public relations. Its power is frequently overrated. It is often classed as propaganda and therefore an undesirable influence on the public. On the other hand, people and organizations like publicity about themselves or their causes.

Publicity is a major activity for public relations people and, when properly handled, it can be a material aid in making a PR program effective. Essentially the public relations practitioner tries to create good publicity and to avoid bad publicity.

DEFINITION

There are many definitions of publicity. Some people see it as "advertising you don't pay for," but this is incorrect. It is not free, nor is it a substitute for advertising. Publicity has been called "the science of news management" but news management is not scientific and publicity does not manage news.

Webster* defines publicity as:

1. The quality or state of being obvious or exposed to the public view.
2. An act or device designed to attract public interest — specifically information with news value issued as a means of gaining public attention or support.

Neither of these is very satisfactory for PR purposes. The first is imprecise and the second is limited to voluntary action. It overlooks the fact that publicity can exist without effort and that it can be negative as well as positive. The following definition seems a bit more useful:

*By permission. From *Webster's Third New International Dictionary* © 1966 by G. & C. Merriam Co., Publishers of the Merriam-Webster Dictionaries.

Information that is distributed to the public through media that are not controlled by the source of the information.

A house organ is a controlled medium. It publishes exactly what the sponsor wants to say. An item in a house organ is not publicity. That same item in some other organization's house organ, or in a newspaper, is publicity because the medium is not controlled by the source of the item. An advertisement is not publicity because it is controlled by the advertiser. Newspapers, magazines, radio, and television stations publish what *they* choose to publish. They are, in theory at least, impartial. The news they publish is presumably unbiased and factual. News distributed through the general media is therefore more desirable than that which is controlled and presumably biased.

CHARACTERISTICS OF PUBLICITY

To clarify this definition, it is necessary to point out several characteristics of publicity:

It Can Be Favorable or Unfavorable

A newspaper story telling about an airline's purchase of new planes is favorable. It indicates progress and better service for its customers. A newspaper story about a plane crash is very unfavorable. It arouses fears and doubts.

It Can Be Voluntary or Involuntary

A corporation planning a new factory may voluntarily decide to make this fact known to the public through the news media. But when a factory burns down, that becomes involuntarily known to the public through the same news media.

There Can Be Too Much or Too Little

The amount of publicity has no direct relationship to the importance of the news. A small incident may get a great deal of attention and a very important event may get very little. Bad news or a currently popular subject may generate too much publicity. An unpopular topic, a poor publicity job, or a competing news story may be responsible for too little publicity.

Publicity Can be Too Early or Too Late

Timeliness is essential in publicity. A topic may interest the public on one day and be ignored another day. When the first astronaut went into orbit, almost any story relating to the subject was likely to be published. When orbital flight became more commonplace, there was a marked decline in news items about space travel. News media use many items about driving safety just before or after a three-day holiday but give it scant space at other times.

Quality Is More Important than Quantity

What is said is much more significant than how much is said. Publicity has a purpose. In pure press agentry, it may suffice to make a name or face well-known, but in public relations the objective is to create favorable public opinion and that depends very much on what is said and how it is said.

Dissemination Does Not Mean Reception

News items may be published in many media but that does not guarantee that the items will be read, seen, or heard. Nor does it assure understanding. Also, it is entirely possible for the news to be widely circulated but to reach only a few of the people who should receive it.

Reception Does Not Mean Acceptance

People may get the message but fail to believe it or refuse to agree. Some people are chronic skeptics, others are opinionated, and some are just contrary. For this and other reasons, it is wrong to assume that anything has been accomplished just because there has been some favorable publicity.

There is a Limit on Publicity

Most news media receive far more publicity items than they can use. As a result, they must be highly selective. This means that no single topic will get any more space or time than the editor feels it is worth. Many publicity people have found that a blizzard of press releases does not work. Multiplying the number of news items sent out does not necessarily multiply the number published. It is not likely that any subject will get more favorable publicity than it merits but, since bad news is exciting, it is very easy to get more unfavorable publicity than is really deserved.

GETTING FAVORABLE PUBLICITY

Favorable publicity can be obtained by supplying news media with information the editor will accept as "news." There is just one basis for that acceptance. News is what the editor thinks will interest his readers, listeners, or viewers *today* or, in the case of weeklies or monthlies, *this week* or *this month*. The key then is *interest* and *timeliness*.

Because these are highly subjective decisions, there is a very great difference in the criteria used to select or reject news items. One editor may give major coverage to a story which his competitor treats briefly or rejects completely. All editors are adept at determining whether a publicity item will interest their readers. If it will, it has a chance of being used; if it will not, it will be classed as "publicity" and ignored.

Fig. 27.1 This is one of the top five public relations photographs in a contest conducted by the *Public Relations Journal*. The objective was to dramatize the beauty of TWA stewardesses and, by implication, the high quality of service. It has appeared all over the world and is TWA's most widely published picture. The photographer was Bernard G. Vannier.

Judgment of news value is not the only criterion. Policy of the medium can be a major factor. Most media reflect in their news coverage the attitudes of the ownership or management. Consequently, they give better treatment to what they favor and worse treatment to what they oppose. Thus, a newspaper whose publisher is an advocate of publicly owned utilities will give major emphasis to stories supporting that viewpoint and ignore stories favorable to private utilities. The "image" of the medium is also important. A "crusading" editor will use material that his colleagues will refuse. A "liberal" editor will reject items that his "conservative" competitor will accept.

Personal whim, too, can be a factor. For many years a major newspaper in Kansas City refused to print the word "snake" because the publisher hated them. And for years one of the largest newspaper chains refused to print the name, even in an advertisement, of a famous movie star because she was disliked by another star who was the favorite of the chain's owner.

This problem becomes more acute with broadcast media. Sometimes only one side of a controversy gets coverage. When nurses struck all the hospitals in a major city, all the TV stations gave substantial coverage to the nurses' side of the story but none to the other side. When a controversy arose about some supposedly "wild" horses, the TV stations in an Idaho city gave considerable time to those who wanted to save the "wild" horses. The stations refused to show ranchers riding the so-called "wild" horses, which were actually domesticated horses.

In these cases, the stations felt that the items covered were news and that the "equal time" provision did not apply. In general, broadcasting stations are required to give balanced coverage to controversy, but in many cases this becomes a matter of interpretation by the stations.

On the other hand, when a station or network believes that an issue is worthy of treatment as a public controversy, it is quite likely to solicit appearances by both sides. Whenever a public relations practitioner believes that the cause or organization he or she represents is not receiving balanced treatment, an appeal to the top management of the station is in order.

WHAT NEWS IS

The word news is a derivative of "new." If a thing is not new it is not news; timeliness is vital. There is nothing deader than yesterday's newspaper, nothing surer of rejection than a tardy news item. Timeliness is not the only requirement though — the story must also be interesting, because it must convince the editor that it will interest his audience and then must live up to his expectations.

Kinds of News

From the standpoint of public relations, there are two kinds of news: voluntary and involuntary. Voluntary news is news that can be created, planned, guided, or influenced by the public relations people. The announcement of a new product, the results of a meeting, a report of earnings, a story of reorganization, plans for expansion — all are voluntary or should be. Involuntary news is unplanned and, at least in its earliest stages, unguided. A fire or flood, an accident, the death of a key officer — all can seriously affect an organization but they cannot be anticipated, although there can be standby plans for use in a crisis.

Fundamentals of News

Any news story is basically an answer to the question: "What happened?" (or "What is going to happen?"). However, to understand what happened, it is essential to answer several other questions, "Who did it happen to?" "How did it happen?" "When did it happen?" "Where did it happen?" "Why did it happen?" Without these answers, the story is not complete. This is why editors for generations have demanded that every story contain the answers to these six questions: what? who? how? when? where? why?

Elements of a News Story

Every news story contains one or more of the following elements:

1. Timeliness.
2. Novelty.
3. Well-known people.
4. Public interest.
5. Conflict.
6. Mystery.
7. Tragedy.
8. Humor.
9. Confidentiality.
10. Romance.
11. Sex.
12. Future.
13. Money.
14. Human interest.
15. Animals.

Most news items prepared for a public relations purpose will be based on timeliness, public interest, conflict, or future, but any of the others may be used.

Finding News

Newsworthy events may occur in any organization. The big stories are obvious. A major change affecting many people, a new discovery, an expansion plan, a construction project, and similar events will be recognized by all concerned as news deserving of public attention. But these are not the only newsworthy items. Many a news story has been published because a good public relations practitioner recognized its worth when no one else in the organization was aware of its interest or timeliness.

The secret is simple: the public relations practitioner must constantly look for news. He must know what is news and which editors will think it is news. He must always remember that an item may be old to the organization but new to the readers of some publication. Most publicity is of a rather predictable nature. An analysis of publicity received by major companies showed that almost all of it was in four major categories.

Of more than one million corporate news stories analyzed by its computers in a continuing study of newspaper and radio-TV publicity gained by 16 billionaire companies, PR Data Inc. (NYC) reports that 34.5% involve product publicity, 28.9% are "growth" stories (increased earnings & sales, mergers & acquisitions, expansion), 7.8% cover general marketing activity, 7.6% are about corporate social concern, and 2.8% involve negative news (sales & earnings down, wages up, employment off & such). The balance were miscellaneous.

Demonstrations

A demonstration is almost irresistible to a TV station news department. Other media may also respond. Up to now, most demonstrators have been activists who are protesting something. Generally they represent only a small number of people, but they do get a lot of publicity.

Demonstrations need not be monopolized by the activists. Any organization can utilize demonstrations to express its position. Obviously it won't work if the president and department heads are the center of attention. The Glutz Manufacturing Company can't stage a demonstration — but its employees can.

This, of course, demands that the interests of the employees be involved and that they be sufficiently concerned to stage the protest. To do this requires skillful use of the "grapevine" that is described in Chapter 29.

A successful demonstration has a grass-roots flavor. The placards are handmade. The whole atmosphere suggests a spontaneous uprising of little people who are protesting something that will injure them. Actually, most demonstrations are carefully planned. The TV stations and other media are always informed in time for them to get their reporters to the scene. Some observers have noted that sponsors of demonstrations habitually wait until the TV cameras are in place before they start the demonstration!

GETTING NEWS PUBLISHED

To get a news story published, it is necessary to know which editor or editors are likely to be interested. This requires familiarity with the kind of news they publish or broadcast. An item that is very interesting to a trade publication may be of no interest to a newspaper. A story that pleases one editor may get the cold shoulder from another. The importance of knowing the media cannot be overemphasized. This requires reading and listening and watching.

Many metropolitan dailies won't use releases. They do appreciate phone calls which give the gist of the story. Often a reporter will be sent to get details.

Never send identical feature stories or pictures to competing media. Editors are very jealous of their individuality and will be extremely upset if they find a competitor has run the same story or picture. "Exclusive to you in your circulation area" is a good practice and is frequently included in the heading of the press release or picture caption.

When a story is planned for wide distribution, as with product publicity, it is necessary to prepare several different versions and to make up noncompeting mailing lists. Under this system, Story A goes to papers on the A list, Story B goes to papers on the B list and so on. On the other hand, brief announcements, such as appointments and promotions or financial news, need not be individualized because only the bare facts will be used.

Using the same basic facts, it is possible to prepare stories that will interest several different classes of media and several different media within each class. Of course certain stories cannot be adapted to different fields, but this is not always the case. To clarify the problem of getting news published, it will be worthwile to examine each of the major media.

Daily Newspapers

Individual papers may have their own peculiarities but most of them have similar techniques for getting and publishing news. The key people are:

__The publisher__   He may be the owner or represent the owners. He is the general manager of the paper. He sets policies and supervises the production, advertising, and editorial function.

__The managing editor__   He determines the news policy of the paper and decides on a long-range basis how much time and space to devote to any topic.

__The news editor__   He gets the paper out and supervises all the personnel connected with the news-gathering function and sees to it that the stories are written and that the various special editors and feature writers are doing their jobs. He decides how much emphasis to give a story — when to use it and when not to use it.

__The city editor__   He supervises the local reporters and is responsible for the news originating in and around the city of publication.

__The Sunday editor__   He runs the Sunday paper. Sunday editions always carry much more news and features than the week-day editions and the Sunday editor is overall coordinator of the work of publishing this special edition.

__The special editors__   These are the specialists. Sports, business, real estate, food, fashion, society, science, entertainment, features, and other such subjects are usually included in this category. Each of these men or women concentrates on one subject, although in some cases, one person may have two or more specialties.

__The wire editors__   These people select, from the mass of news coming into the paper from the wire services and the out-of-town reporters, those items which appear to be most interesting to the particular paper.

__The columnists__   Whether local or syndicated, the columnists have a special status and usually a very large audience. Most of the time their material is published without editing. Columnists rely heavily on tips and contributed items. The way to contribute is to send the right item — and this requires a thorough familiarity with the column.

The reporters   The "in-town" reporters channel their news to the city editor — often through rewrite men but, occasionally, directly. Out-of-town news normally comes to the wire editors. There are two kinds of "out-of-town" reporters: the full-time reporters in Washington, D.C., or the state capital and the part-time "stringers." One "stringer" is likely to be present in every sizable town within the news area of the paper. He is often the editor of a country weekly.

General news stories for a local daily paper can reach the paper in several ways. The story may be written and mailed to the city editor. It can be telephoned to the city desk. A request for a reporter can be phoned to the city desk. This usually requires that highlights of the story be given on the phone to prove its importance. Stories may be given to reporters either verbally or as written press releases.

Stories of special interest to the feature editors go directly to the editor concerned, either by mail or phone.

On rare occasions, a press conference may be justified. Alerting reporters to a possible news "break" is always advisable.

News Magazines

The news-gathering structure of a news magazine is very much like that of a major daily newspaper. These weeklies have offices in the principal cities throughout the world. All their material is staff-written but they do appreciate tips or leads and frequently utilize help from the organization which is the subject of a story. To get an item into one of these magazines, the steps are: first, find out if there is interest; second, if there is interest, give their reporters every possible assistance.

Wire Services

Most daily papers use one or more of the wire services such as Associated Press or United Press International. The wire services collect news through their own reporters or from newspapers. This is telegraphed or teletyped to member papers and to broadcasters. The wire services provide international, national, and regional news.

Wire services have offices in many cities throughout the world. When a story is believed to be worthy of wire service attention, it is handled just like a story for a local newspaper. A telephone call to the city desk is probably the first step. A story important enough for wire service coverage is likely to be too important to be mailed.

Public Relations Wire Services

These wire services do not gather news but do, for a fee, teletype news items to newspapers, radio and television stations, trade magazines, and press association bureaus. Using their own leased wires and their own teletype printers in the newsrooms or wire rooms or in the offices of the business editors, these wire services provide a fast and economical means of distributing news to many outlets. They do not reach all news media but they do reach many of the most important.

There are seven of these services in the United States, each serving a separate region but all available on a reciprocal basis. That is, a story placed with one service can be distributed to any or all of the other services for additional fees.

The services are:

    Business Wire_____San Francisco and Los Angeles,
    PR Newswire_____New York,
    PR News Service_____Chicago,
    Press Relations Newswire_____Detroit,
    Press Relations Wire_____Washington, D.C.,
    Southwest Press Relations Newswire_____Dallas.

Weekly Newspapers

With weekly newspapers, the editor is usually also the reporter. Since these papers are so widely scattered and so numerous, news stories for their use are normally mailed to the editor.

Boilerplate

The word "boilerplate" was coined many years ago to describe material supplied to small weekly newspapers which could not find enough news in one week to fill their pages. The editorial material consisted essentially of feature articles and small novelty items covering a very broad range of interest. Orginally it was prepared solely as "filler" material but it was soon recognized as a simple and cheap way to distribute publicity items.

In a very short time the "boilerplate" producers were charging a price for inclusion of items in the material they shipped to their newspaper customers.

In the earliest days the material was distributed as metal plates which could be used in printing (hence the name "boilerplate"). Later the material was shipped in "mat form" or as newsprint paper which had one printed side and one blank side for local news and advertising.

In recent years, as local printing facilities have improved, most "boilerplate" is distributed as "mats" (which can be cast into letterpress type) or "slicks" (which can be reproduced by an "offset" process).

Boilerplate is still an efficient means of distributing publicity items, especially when the target is a large number of publications. Several firms perform this service. They are listed in *Editor & Publisher Yearbook* under the heading of "Mat Services" or "Feature Syndicates" or "News and Picture Services." Using such a service requires agreement on how many releases will be handled and to whom they will be sent. Once the scale and scope of the operation is determined, the user of the service has only to supply illustrations and copy. The service firm does all the rest of the work of preparation and distribution.

General Interest Magazines

This field includes many national and regional magazines of general interest. Their content is usually written by staff members or by skilled free-lance writers. They usually do not accept unsolicited material but do occasionally follow up suggested story ideas. Smaller regional and local magazines will however use contributed materials. (The editor is usually the prime contact.)

Special Interest Magazines

The number of publications catering to special interests has grown enormously and in the process has probably detracted from the general interest magazines. Covering such diverse subjects as needlework, travel, gardening, golf, hunting, skiing, stamp collecting, photography, and a vast number of other interests, these magazines frequently accept contributed articles and news items. The editor is the person to whom such material should be submitted.

Trade Magazines

These publications are especially receptive to news items and feature

Classification Groupings — Business Publications — Continued

CLASSIFICATION 20—Continued

Arizona Modern Business and Industry
Business Horizons
California Business
Cervi's Rocky Mountain Journal
Chief Executive, The
Columbia Journal of World Business
Commonwealth, The Magazine of Virginia
Conference Board Record, The
Executive Life
Federal Accountant, The
Florida Trend
Hawaii Business
Houston Magazine
Indiana Business and Industry
Industrial Real Estate Managers' Directory
Internal Auditor, The
Leasing World & Capital Financing
Long Island Commercial Review
Management Accounting
Michigan Challenge
Michigan Manufacturer and Financial Record
Michigan Tradesman
Missouri Business
Modern Franchising
National Public Accountant, The
National Trade and Professional Associations of the United States
New Englander, The
New Jersey Business
New York Certified Public Accountant
Pacific Business
Personnel Administrator
Personnel Journal
Plant Location
Practical Accountant, The
Site Selection Handbook
Texas Parade
Wall Street Transcript, The

21A. CAMPS & CAMPING

NON-AUDITED

(Also see Hotels, Motels, Clubs & Resorts

Camp Directors' Purchasing Guide
Camping Magazine
Camp Management
National Camp Directors Guide

25. CEMETERY & MONUMENTS

NON-AUDITED

American Art in Stone
American Cemetery
Catholic Cemetery, The
Monumental News Review
Southern Cemetery

26. CERAMICS

(Also see Brick, Tile, Building Materials, China & Dinnerware, Glass.)

AUDITED

Ceramic Age
Ceramic Data Book
Ceramic Industry

NON-AUDITED

American Ceramic Society Bulletin
Ceramic Scope

27. CHAIN STORES

AUDITED

Chain Store Age—Drug Executives Edition and Drug Store Edition Combination
Chain Store Age—Drug Store/Drug Executives Edition—Pharmacists Reference Issue
Chain Store Age—Executives Edition Combination
Chain Store Age Store Planners Annual With Directory of Sources
Chain Store Age—Supermarket Executives and Supermarket Store Managers Editions
Chain Store Age Variety Store—General Merchandise Managers Edition and Variety Store—General Merchandise Executives Edition
Drug Topics
Merchandiser/Magazine of Mass Retailing, The
Progressive Grocer
Supermarketing

Chemical Purchasing
Chemical Week
Detergents and Specialties
Hydrocarbon Processing
Journal of American Oil Chemists Society
Oil, Paint & Drug Reporter
Soap and Chemical Specialties

NON-AUDITED

Accelerator, The
Chemical Engineering Catalog
Chemical Engineering Progress
Chemical Materials Catalog
Chemist
Detergents and Emulsifiers
Electrochemical Technology
Filtration Engineering
Industrial and Engineering Chemistry
Isotopics
Journal of Biological Chemistry, The
Journal of the Electrochemical Society
Materials Protection and Performance
Modern Chemicals
Naval Stores Review International Yearbook
Naval Stores Review & Terpene Chemicals
OPD Chemical Buyers Directory
Soap Blue Book
What's New in Chemical Processing Equipment

28A. CHINA & DINNERWARE

(Also see Ceramics. Giftware. Glass. Home Furnishing.)

AUDITED

China Glass & Tablewares
China Glass & Tablewares Red Book Directory Issue

31. CLOTHING & Furnishing Goods (Men's)

(Also see Department and Specialty Stores.)

AUDITED

Daily News Record
Men's Wear

NON-AUDITED

American Needle Trades Directory
Apparel Executive
Apparel Manufacturer
California Men's Stylist
Made to Measure
MascuLines
Needle's Eye
Southern Garment Manufacturer
Teens' & Boys' Outfitter
Western Outfitter

32. CLOTHING & Furnishing Goods (Women's)

(Also see Corsets, Brassieres & Undergarments, Department and Specialty Stores. Fashion Accessories. Textiles and Knit Goods)

AUDITED

California Stylist
Texas Fashions

NON-AUDITED

Agent, The
Bobbin Magazine, The
Buyers Guide, The—Apparel
California Apparel News
Femme-Lines
Garment Manufacturer's Index
New England Apparel Retailer
Uniforms and Accessories Review
Western Apparel Industry

32A. COAL MERCHANDISING

(Also see Mining, (Coal, Metal, & Non-Metallic)

NON-AUDITED

Black Diamond
Keystone Coal Industry Manual

34. CONTROL & INSTRUMENTATION SYSTEMS

AUDITED

Control Engineering
Instrument & Apparatus News
Instrumentation Technology
Instruments and Control Systems
Measurements and Data Group

NON-AUDITED

Chilton Electronics and Instrumentation Group of Magazines, The
Electronic Systems Engineering
Experimental Mechanics
Instruments and Control Systems Buyer's Guide

34A. CORSETS, Brassieres & Undergarments

(Also see Clothing (Women's), Department and Specialty Stores.)

AUDITED

Body Fashions
Corset, Bra & Lingerie Magazine

NON-AUDITED

Body Fashions Directory
Corset, Bra & Lingerie Magazine Annual Directory

34B. COSMETICS

(Also see Drugs, Pharmaceutics.)

AUDITED

American Perfumer and Cosmetics
Beauty Fashion

NON-AUDITED

Cosmetics Fair
Drug & Cosmetic Catalog
Journal of the Society of Cosmetic Chemists

34C. DAIRY PRODUCTS (Milk, Ice Cream, Milk Products)

(Also see Food—Processing and Distribution. Produce (Fruits & Vegetables)

AUDITED

American Dairy Review
Dairy & Ice Cream Field
Dairy Record

NON-AUDITED

Cheese Reporter, The
Dairy Industries Catalog
Dairy Industry News
Journal of Dairy Science
Journal of Milk and Food Technology
Milk Hauler and Food Transporter
Southeastern Dairy Review
Southern Dairy Products Journal
Western Milk and Ice Cream News

35. DENTAL

AUDITED

Dental Management
Dental Products Report
Dental Survey

NON-AUDITED

ADA News
American Journal of Orthodontics
Anesthesia Progress
Dental Abstracts
Dental Assistant, The
Dental Digest
Dental Economics
Dental Industry News
Dental Laboratory News
Dental Laboratory Review
Dental Products Annual Report
Dental Student
Dentists Market Place, The
Illinois Dental Journal
Journal of the American Dental Association
Journal of the American Dental Hygienists' Association
Journal of Clinical Orthodontics, The
Journal of Dental Education
Journal of Dental Research
Journal of Dentistry for Children
Journal of Oral Surgery
Journal of Peridontology

Fig. 27.2 Part of an index page from the Business Publication section of Standard Rate and Data Service. This gives an idea of the great number of trade magazines.

articles concerning their special field. In many cases there are several highly competitive magazines covering the same trade. When this situation exists, it is necessary to avoid sending the same feature articles to more than one. (No editor will want to run the same story that his competitor uses.) Brief news items can be sent to all publications in a field but, for anything more extensive, the stories must be individualized. Representatives of the trade press should be invited to any event that might be of interest to the readers. (See "Why Case History Articles Get Published," *Public Relations Journal*, August 1976.)

Feature Services

Many newspapers utilize feature material prepared by the news feature syndicates. Any of these may use material sent to them, providing it is suitable. Knowing the kind of material they distribute is the only way to determine what to submit for consideration. Many are listed in *Editor & Publisher Yearbook*.

House Organs

Many house organs will accept contributed material. Often the editor badly needs articles and pictures to fill his pages with items that will add variety and scope to the news from his own organization. As with other media, the problem is to determine which publications might be interested. The *Gebbie House Magazine Directory* is very useful here. For every important house organ in the country, it lists the name, circulation, editor's name, and the kind of material he can use. (The publisher is House Magazine Publishing Company, P.O. Box 1111, Sioux City, Iowa 51102.) The directory is published every three years.

Free-Lance Writers

It is frequently possible to engage a free-lance writer of established reputation to write a story for use in a controlled publication (house organ). It is also possible to interest one of these writers in a potential story for submission to some general publication. In this case, he is paid by the publication.

Broadcast Media

Radio and television must, by their nature, keep most of their news stories brief, but both networks and individual stations do carry features that permit more thorough coverage. Typical of the latter are such programs as Meet the Press, Wall Street Week, Face the Nation, Editors Forum, and many others. As with the editors of print media, the directors of these programs will use only what they think will interest their audience. An analysis of the nature of the program is the first step in deciding whether to contact the director about a specific item.

General news coverage by broadcast media is pretty much "on the spot." If a news story seems worthy of coverage, a telephone call to the news department of the radio station, or assignment desk of the TV station is in order.

There is, in addition to this active news coverage by the broadcasters, some use of "filler" material at other than prime time or for filling out and balancing program content or supplying background for a news item. It is possible to get tapes or records used on radio stations or films or videotapes used on television stations in the same way that "boilerplate" is used by newspapers. Items that run from one to two or three minutes are often used in addition to the program features mentioned in the chapter on visual aids. Distribution to stations can be direct or through the distributors who specialize in this service.

Network News Services

All the major radio and television networks — NBC, CBS, and ABC — operate a news service similar in function to the newspaper services. That is, the network news staff covers national and world news and feeds this to central locations where it is edited. Items are then selected and assembled into a news program. The networks also pick up news from their affiliated stations. Usually, only news of national importance is likely to be covered but novelty stories do occasionally make the grade.

Non-Network News Services for Television

Both Associated Press and United Press International supply a wire news service to radio stations. In addition they supply a film news service to television stations. This is delivered by mail or messenger and so is often 24 hours late. Television News, Inc., feeds news in color over telephone lines to subscribing stations. It can be recorded on tape for use when needed.

Personal Appearances on Radio or Television

It is often possible to arrange for a personal appearance on radio or television stations. Typically this will be an interview by the person who conducts a topical program. This gives exposure to a wide audience that might not be reached through other media. Also, it is common practice to arrange these appearances in a number of different cities when added coverage is wanted and network exposure is not attainable. As with other media, the procedure is to contact the program director and determine if there is interest in what you have to offer.

Television News Film Clips

Television stations in smaller cities and towns located a short distance from a major metropolis are not always able to have news crews cover their own local events and those in the core city.

For example, a television station in Springfield or Worcester would be interested in using major news items of events happening in Boston. However, it cannot send crews to cover every major event in Boston.

If they receive news filmclips, in color and preferably sound, in time for the next newscast, then the clip will be considered for use. If the film is silent (no sound), then it should be accompanied by a script so the announcer can do a "voice over" during the newscast. (See "ABC's of TV News Film," *Public Relations Journal*, June 1977.)

Television Slides and Film Clips

If executives of an organization tend to be "in the news" a good deal of the time, it is sometimes beneficial to give area television stations color slides of the executives. Then, when the executive delivers a major address, which is subsequently picked up by a wire service and distributed to all television stations in the state, any of the stations can have the commentator do the "voice" with a picture of the executive flashed on the screen behind the commentator.

If you also distribute "canned film clips," television stations have the option of using these clips while a story concerning your company is being read.

Radio Tapes

Just as most cities have off-duty television cameramen who can shoot television news film clips on a free-lance basis, they also have off-duty radio announcers and editors available. Radio news tapes of news events have an even wider appeal than television news film clips.

Finding the Media

Local media are easy to locate. Finding the addresses of "out-of-town" media and the names of key personnel is a simple matter if the right directory is available. (See the Selected Bibliography for names and addresses.)

All these directories try to provide accurate information, but they become obsolete rapidly because of personnel shifts. For this reason every mailing list should be regularly updated. Sending a release to someone who is no longer there is not only a waste, it is an irritant to the media and it suggests that the sender is incompetent.

PREPARING NEWS STORIES

There is no guarantee that any publicity will be used, but you will have a much better chance of acceptance if certain rules are followed.

General

A news story should have a general objective. It should be prepared for a specific audience. It must be interesting and timely and it must answer the questions: what? who? how? when? where? why?

Format of a News Item

All stories should be prepared in "pyramid" form. That is, the first paragraph tells the story very briefly and succeeding paragraphs elaborate and amplify, each giving more detail and more background information. There are two reasons for this. First, people do not usually read everything in a newspaper or magazine. If they read only the first part of the item, they will still get the essentials. Those who want all the information can read the whole story. Second, editors often cut the length of items, and the cut starts at the bottom. A good article will still be understandable after one or several paragraphs have been cut, provided it is written in the proper sequence.

Essentials of a Good News Story

Every news story should answer all the reasonable questions a reader might ask. The significance should be explained in terms of the audience.

It must be newsworthy in order to withstand the competition of all the other stories clamoring for space. It should reflect the nature of the organization favorably. It should have all the facts, names, dates, and figures correct and it should be understandable.

Format of a News Picture

Editors will not use pictures that are too high or too wide. A look at any newspaper or magazine will give a general guide as to what proportions are usable. Usually the picture should be 8″ x 10″ or 4″ x 5″. Vertical photographs are preferred. For newspaper or magazine use, the picture should have a glossy finish. For television, it should be horizontal, with matte finish, and in color. The caption should be pasted to the back and at the bottom of the picture. It should indicate the source and name the people shown (from left to right) or identify the scene. There must be no writing on the picture, either front or back. Never fold or staple a picture. Color pictures can be used by magazines or Sunday supplements. Horizontal color slides can be and are used by television stations.

Essentials of a Good News Picture

To justify publication, a news picture must contain news. It must tell a story. It must contain action and not be static. It should be clean and sharp. The background should help make the subject visible. Contrast is imperative. The picture should be well-composed and it should be interesting. Usually it is advisable to employ a professional photographer.

Mechanics of Press Releases

Any item prepared for release to any news medium should be typewritten on 8½″ x 11″ paper. It should be double-spaced with wide margins and only one side of the paper should be used. One page is preferable but, if the story requires more, each page should be numbered. At the bottom center of each page except the last should be the word "more." No sentence or paragraph should be split between pages. The release should have a caption indicating its contents. This caption can greatly influence acceptance of the item. When a professor appeared on television to report his research on the dropout problem, someone captioned the press release: "Professor Appears on Television," which is a very dull title. It was rewritten to read "New Approach to Dropouts." Every press release should indicate its source, the contact person, and the time when it may be used.

John Doe Company
Public Relations Department
123 Doe Street
Doeville, N.Y. 12345

Contact Pete Ryan (123) 456-7890

For release to morning papers Aug. 19, 19xx.
or . . . . Hold for release August 25, 19xx.
or . . . . . . For immediate release.

Contact: Sue Guyette
San Mateo, CA
(415) 341-7441
Lee Stillwell
Washington, D.C.
(202) 554-9000

NFIB NEWS
NATIONAL FEDERATION OF INDEPENDENT BUSINESS
HOME OFFICE: 150 WEST 20TH AVENUE, SAN MATEO, CA. 94403
LEGISLATIVE OFFICE: 490 L ENFANT PLAZA EAST S.W., WASHINGTON, D.C. 20024

FOR IMMEDIATE RELEASE: JULY 25, 1977

                    NFIB OFFERS SOCIAL SECURITY PLAN

The National Federation of Independent Business (NFIB), largest small
business organization in the country, has proposed an alternative to the Carter
Administration's plan for bailing out the nation's troubled Social Security
program.

William J. Dennis, Jr., NFIB Research Director, outlined the NFIB proposal
in recent testimony before the Senate Finance Committee's Subcommittee on Social
Security.

The NFIB proposal would divide the current Old Age and Survivors Insurance
(OASI) program into two parts, Dennis said. Part A would resemble the existing
insurance program, but with some conceptual changes. Under Part A, each individual would receive as a benefit his or her accumulated employee-employer contribution, plus interest.

Since the Part A benefit may not be enough for some individuals or families
to exist at reasonable standards, Dennis said, there is also a need for Part B,
patterned after the existing Supplemental Security Income (SSI) program. Part
B beneficiaries would receive two checks--their Part A entitlement based on
employment contributions and their Part B benefit based on family need. Since
Part B benefits would be social subsidies and not earned entitlements, they
would be financed from the general revenues, subject to annual appropriation.

Dennis said NFIB's proposal "places rationality and equity into the benefit
structure from the beneficiaries' perspective. That is not now true. Persons
who contribute don't necessarily receive benefits; persons who don't contribute

                              more . . . .

Fig. 27.3 First page of a press release. Printed headings are frequently used when a large
number of releases are made.

Timing of Press Releases

Any item prepared for a news medium must not only be timely, it also must respect deadlines.

Afternoon papers need material by 9 a.m. Morning papers need material by 6 p.m. Sunday papers should have stories by Friday morning but can use spot news as late as 4 p.m. Saturday afternoon.

The best day for a news story is Monday. Most business and government offices are closed on Sunday so there is far less news for Monday's papers than for any other day in the week.

Weekly magazines can accept news up to about one week before publication date. Very important news may be covered on a tighter deadline — and features often require even more than a week of lead time. Monthly magazines must have material at least a month ahead of publication date; with some of the large national publications, the time can well be several months.

Clipping Bureaus

Use of a professional clipping service is necessary if there is wide distribution of press releases. It is easy to watch local newspapers and trade magazines for published material. With general magazines, the publication date of an article is normally known well in advance but, when news items are sent to media remote from the place of origin, it is nearly impossible to monitor their use. Clipping bureaus are listed in classified telephone directories of major cities. They can cover any class of media and any kind of item, depending on what the user needs.

Broadcast Monitoring

Similar to clipping bureaus are several organizations which record TV and radio news. The subscriber receives an "off-the-air" record of what was broadcast. Entire newscasts of specific subjects may be ordered.

PRESS RELATIONS

Good relations with the press — and by press we mean all media, whether print or broadcast — are very important in any public relations program. They can result in more favorable publicity and less unfavorable publicity. Accordingly, cultivation of cordial relations with the press is imperative. This requires an awareness of the possible points of conflict between the public relations people and the press — and of the things that might foster good relations between them.

Hewlett-Packard gives all its managers a booklet," *How to Deal With the Press.*"

CRITICISMS OF PUBLIC RELATIONS PEOPLE

Many people associated with the news media have no real criticisms of PR practices and probably none of them would voice all the criticisms listed below. These should be considered as the kind of things that make for poor relations and not as a broad and universally agreed-upon critique. Nevertheless, they should be kept in mind. (See "Newspapermen and Practitioners Differ Widely on PR Role," *Public Relations Journal*, August 1975.)

Coloring News

Everyone tries to present his story in the most favorable light but sometimes this is done to such an excess that the press reacts against it, and tends to disbelieve the whole thing.

Pressure

Attempts to influence acceptance of publicity items by contacts with higher management or with the advertising department are universally resented.

Ignorance

Sending out publicity items that are not really news is a common practice. It does not fool the press and they dislike having to sort through all the chaff.

Snow Jobs

A multitude of publicity items sent to any medium can result in apathy or solid resentment. Press people react against a blizzard of stories no matter how good they are individually. On one day the Chicago office of Wall Street Journal received 266 pieces of mail. Three-fourths of this went into the wastebasket.

439

Hindering Reporters

In spite of all that has been said about frankness with the press there are still solid complaints that reporters cannot get help and are often actually hampered.

Lack of Frankness

Devious and deceptive answers to reporters do not succeed in covering up the story but they do cause a lot of ill will.

CRITICISMS OF THE PRESS

Public relations people have some countercriticisms. These are not universal but they do exist and should be recognized as points of possible friction or conflict. Since the press is aware of them, there is no point in belaboring the subject.

Uninformed Reporters

Most reporters are generalists, yet they are often assigned to cover highly specialized subjects. This is particularly critical when the subject is business or economics. All too frequently, the result is an inaccurate story.

Several attempts to remedy this have been made. The Graduate School of Industrial Administration of Carnegie-Mellon University has conducted special courses in economics for business journalists. Wharton School of Finance and Commerce has for several years held seminars for business writers. Columbia, Princeton, Missouri and other universities have also conducted special courses for journalists. These are important projects and should be continued.

Inadequate Investigation

Reporters sometimes write stories based on unverified information. One of the worst examples is the "tanker myth." During the oil shortage in 1973-74, there were many stories about tankers waiting offshore for oil prices to go up. Despite denials by every credible source and exhaustive investigation which failed to turn up a shred of confirmation, the stories continued for several months. The stories were completely false, but they were believed by many people.

Distorted Coverage

Television in particular can distort news in the editing process. By selecting scenes out of context it is possible to put together a completely deceptive news story. This *is* done, and sometimes by some of the most prestigious media. In the CBS documentary "The Selling of the Pentagon," excision of a key phrase left a totally incorrect impression about a statement made by a high government official. This is not meant to imply malice. It is meant to show that errors can and do occur.

Unbalanced Coverage

As stated elsewhere, the news media give more space and time to indictments and charges than they give to dismissals and refutations. *The New York Times* gave front-page treatment to an indictment of Mobil Oil Company but didn't publish one line about dismissal of the suit. With television there is even less chance for coverage of dismissals and refutations because TV news is almost entirely headline news.

Hostile Reporters

Every public relations practitioner must recognize the fact that "adversary journalism" is here to stay. "Investigative reporting" is a popular phrase. If it were always an honest search for facts it would be beneficial, but in some cases it is a search for scandal. Some reporters simply will not believe facts which contradict their beliefs.

For further comments on the attitudes of reporters see "Our Highest Court: Public Opinion" in *Public Relations Journal*, December 1977. The author is Professor Walter Seifert, APR, of Ohio State University. In general, Professor Seifert confirms the foregoing statements and cites such prominent journalists as Howard K. Smith, Chet Huntley, and Jack Anderson, who have pointed out the dangers inherent in the attitudes of investigative reporters.

The Double Standard

There is some evidence that journalists apply a double standard to reporting news. The shortcomings of journalists and of media seem to be unmentionable by the media. UPI ran a story naming public officials who got free tickets to West Virginia University football games. When the University released a story naming publishers, editors, and reporters who got free tickets to the football games, UPI refused to run the story.

Bias Against Public Relations

Some press people have a solid prejudice against public relations people and anything they write or say. This makes the task of the PR practitioner extremely difficult if not impossible.

BUILDING GOOD PRESS RELATIONS

The key to good press relations is attitude. The organization and those who represent it (usually the public relations people) must be cordial to the press. By making a real and sincere effort to cooperate with the news media, it is possible to earn their goodwill and thus eventually increase favorable publicity and reduce or eliminate unfavorable publicity. A friendly press is a valuable asset. The first step toward that goal is to be a friend to as many representatives of the press as possible. This requires a continuing positive effort but it will be a very worthwhile investment.

A brief written policy for press relations is most desirable. Essentially, all it has to say is, "We'll cooperate with the press. We'll tell them the truth, the whole truth and nothing but the truth. We'll trust them, and we hope they'll trust us."

No two statements of policy are identical but all are similar in that they have the same objective — to assure the press that it will be treated fairly.

Dos And Don'ts Of Press Relations

There are many things that should be done in dealing with the press, and there are many that should be avoided. Here are some of the more important:

1. Do help reporters. They will be grateful.
2. Do not beg. It lowers your status.
3. Do tell the truth always. It builds trust.
4. Do not ask a reporter to kill a story. He will not.
5. Do be frank. Reporters will appreciate it.
6. Do not be evasive. It only stimulates more probing.
7. Do be available. Trying to avoid reporters never works.
8. Do not warp facts. The truth will come out eventually.
9. Do expect to be quoted. Then there will be no surprises.

10. Do not say "off the record." It is a moth-eaten phrase.
11. Do say "this is not for publication" (when it is necessary).
12. Do not be windy. Reporters dislike hot air.
13. Do protect exclusives. A man who finds a story deserves full credit.
14. Do not play favorites. It creates resentment among others.
15. Do balance the breaks (e.g., give a.m. and p.m. papers an equal chance).
16. Do not complain about minor errors. Many cannot be helped.
17. Do be careful with facts, names, and figures.
18. Do not try to mislead. It will not succeed and it creates ill will.
19. Do protect your sources of information. If you do, you will get more.
20. Do not complain if your story is not used. The next one may get there.
21. Do trust reporters. Very rarely does one abuse his trust.
22. Do not waste reporters' time. Have the facts or story ready.
23. Do be willing to give all the news — bad as well as good.
24. Do not get into a fight with a reporter or a paper. You will lose.

Suggested Readings

Gluck, Felix (Ed.). *Modern Publicity*. New York: Viking, 1972.
Klein, Ted, and Danzig, Fred. *Making the Media Work for You*. New York: Macmillan, 1976.
Lendt, David (Ed.). *The Publicity Process*. Ames, Iowa: Iowa State University Press, 1975.
O'Brien, Richard. *Publicity: How to Get It*. New York: Harper & Row, 1977.
Weiner, Richard. *Professionals' Guide to Publicity*. New York: Weiner, 1975.
Staff. *Stylebook and Libel Manual*. AP Newsfeatures, 50 Rockefeller Plaza, New York, N.Y. 10020.
Staff. *UPI Stylebook*. United Press International, 220 E. 42nd Street, New York, N.Y. 10017.

PRESS CONFERENCES

A press conference can be a valuable aid to public relations if it is justified and if it is conducted properly. Conversely, calling a press conference for no good reason will either result in a poor turnout or a large turnout of disgruntled reporters. Even if there is a good reason for a press conference, if it is handled poorly it will do more harm than good. Accordingly, it is very important to know when to call a press conference and how to conduct it.

When a Press Conference is Justified

Press conferences should be used with restraint. If they are called too frequently, their significance and importance will diminish. Do not call a press conference unless it is really necessary.

The key questions to be asked are: Is the news really important? Is equal treatment of all competing media imperative? Is it essential that all reporters get the news at the same time? Are reporters likely to ask questions? If the answer is "yes" in all cases, a press conference is very much in order.

There are no specific criteria to determine the importance of news. What is important to one medium may not be important to another. This should serve as a guide to preparing an invitation list. Thus, a given piece of news might justify a press conference of food editors or trade editors but only a press release to general newspapers. As stated before, the thing to consider is who would be interested and how much they will be interested. Some of the subjects that might justify a press conference are:

Political announcements   A decision to run or not run for public office.

Labor disputes   A statement of company policy in a strike situation.

Major construction   Announcement of plans to build an important facility.

Major policy change   A reversal of a widely-known policy or attitude.

Major product development   A revolutionary improvement or outstanding new product.

Celebrity appearance   An opportunity to meet and talk with a very well-known person.

Tragedies   Any catastrophe resulting in deaths or injuries or major property damage.

Technical developments   Any announcement that is so technical that reporters may need to ask questions for clarification.

An important meeting   Any meeting where decisions affecting the public will be discussed.

Conducting a Press Conference

A press conference should be planned thoroughly before it is called. Among the things to consider are:

Who to invite It is very important to invite everyone who could reasonably be interested and who might publish the news. It is better to invite too many than too few. In case of doubt, an invitation should be extended. Invitations should be mailed a week in advance, if possible. They should state the time and place, the subject to be covered and the names of the sponsoring organization's representatives who will attend.

Spokesman Some responsible senior executive of the organization should be present and ready to make a statement or answer questions. The spokesman must be thoroughly briefed.

Photographs It is possible that photographs will be taken. Any arrangement that will aid the photographers should be made in advance. Most helpful in this area is a location from which photographers can take pictures of the participants. Seats near the speakers' platform will be appreciated.

Television If television coverage is expected, a large amount of space will be needed and advance preparations will be extensive.

Release or press kit A complete information kit should be available for each reporter. This should include a press release containing the full story, pertinent illustrations, background information, and anything else that will help the reporter do justice to the news. For example, Commonwealth Edison Co. held a press conference on what it was doing to clean up the environment. The press kit contained:

1. the basic story,
2. statements attributed to two top officials of the company,
3. three technical papers — "Toward Clean Air," "Toward Clean Water," and "Toward Nuclear Power" — all carrying the names of technical experts in these areas,
4. a chronological history of the company's environmental control efforts,
5. four photos describing the electrostatic precipitator story, the high stack story, Dresden facilities, and the Zion facilities under construction,
6. two maps showing the company's generating stations in the Chicago area and the system,
7. two graphs describing the coal-burn reduction plan and the national sources of air pollution.

(The press conference was very successful and the publicity was extensive and highly favorable.)

THE PRESS PREVIEW

A very effective means of publicizing an event is to invite the press to a preview. Normally the preview is held at least a day before the general public is admitted, so that the reporters can get their stories published in time for the public to read about the event and thus be stimulated to attend. A press kit is commonly prepared for a preview.

Typical reasons for a preview are open houses, plant tours, and new-product announcements.

LEGAL RESTRICTIONS

Any news release can get an organization into trouble. Public relations firms have been held legally responsible for releasing false information even though the client assured them that the facts were true. The SEC has brought action against firms that issued publicity on matters that were in litigation.

Congress and various government agencies are increasingly critical about press releases and other publicity efforts. When one organization did reaserch into consumer attitudes about government regulations, it caused an uproar. One senator demanded a Federal Trade Commission investigation.

In the Imdrim case, the Federal Trade Commission charged false advertising. A federal district court denied an injunction which was appealed by the FTC and later reversed by a federal circuit court. While the appeal was pending, the company issued a news release about the case. The FTC claimed that the release contained misleading references to the original action. The FTC then brought a second case against Imdrim.

Laws of libel must also be considered. It is necessary to know what can and cannot be said. In general, it is advisable to avoid any statement that defames a private citizen. With public officials there is a bit more free-dom. Here, malicious intent must be proved. This is interpreted as reckless disregard of whether the statement is false or actual knowledge that it is false.

With "public figures" the ground is a little more vague, but it seems that they may be treated like public officials. Matters "in the public interest," that is, matters which are widely publicized, seem to bring individuals into the "public figure" category where malice is the key, but this should not be relied upon.

In determining what is safe to say it would be well to consult the *AP Stylebook and Libel Manual*, listed in the Suggested Readings. In general, any release which names an individual and which could be detrimental in any way should be checked with a lawyer who is familiar with the *latest* court decisions.

This, however, should not be interpreted as a suggestion that lawyers write the press releases. Lawyers are likely to be very cautious in matters like this and may elect to wait for a trial in court while the organization is being tried and convicted in the court of public opinion.

Keeping up with the news is particularly important in this context. Any information about court decisions concerning libel, invasion of privacy, slander or defamation of character should be noted — and clipped if possible. Lawsuits filed by individuals or organizations should also be noted.

Guidelines on distribution of information are periodically released by government agencies such as the Securities and Exchange Commission, Federal Trade Commission, Food and Drug Administration, etc. These are generally reported in the general press or trade press. These, too, should be noted and clipped.

EXERCISES

1. From a local newspaper, clip two items giving examples of:
   (a) involuntary publicity
   (b) voluntary publicity.

2. From radio or television, cite two news items giving examples of:
   (a) unfavorable publicity
   (b) favorable publicity.

Case Problem

You are public relations director of a state university. Because of budget limitations enrollment must be reduced by 20%.

How would you publicize this fact? To whom? Through what media? Would you call a press conference? If so, prepare an outline for the conference. Write a press release for all state newspapers announcing this situation.

Advertising | **28**

The Association of National Advertisers says: "Advertising is mass paid communication, the ultimate purpose of which is to impart information, develop attitudes and induce action beneficial to the advertiser" (Colley, 1961).

Obviously, then, advertising is a logical and important communications channel. It may be used by any organization but its most conspicuous users are public utilities such as gas, electric, or telephone companies, trade associations like airline, railroad, or trucking groups, public-service groups such as the Advertising Foundation, and corporations particularly sensitive to public opinion such as lumber, mining, and oil companies.

In recent years, there has been a great increase in the use of advertising for public relations purposes. There are several reasons for this upsurge.

First, both print and broadcast media receive far more news items than they can use. Yet, more and more organizations continue to send news to the media. This means that publicity is becoming a less efficient channel of communication. The competition for space and time is intense. Even if an item is used, it may be garbled or buried.

Second, public concern about various issues and the need for organizations to state their positions on these issues has made it imperative to use messages which will be widely distributed in the exact language which the organization wants to use and with all the ideas which it wants to convey to the public. Advertising isn't edited, cut, or omitted.

Third, the "fairness doctrine" and "equal time" provisions which apply to broadcasting create unusual problems for those who want to use the electronic media. In some cases, an organization can't get its story told by TV or radio, so it must rely on newspapers or magazines.

PUBLIC RELATIONS ADVERTISING

Public relations advertising has been called "institutional" advertising, but that term has fallen into disrepute because so much was wasted on institutional advertising which was merely bragging about the virtues of the sponsor without really saying anything which was of concern to the reader. At the present time, public relations advertising is largely concentrated in three major categories.

"Advocacy" or "issue" advertising is used to persuade the readers to accept a certain viewpoint on a matter which concerns the public. The American Railroads (Fig. 28.1) and General Foods (Fig. 28.7) advertisements are good examples.

"Informational" or "corporate" advertising is used to inform the readers about the policies and actions of an organization and thus build favorable opinion about the organization. The Weyerhaeuser (Fig. 28.2), American Trucking Association (Fig. 28.3), and Bethlehem Steel (Fig. 28.6) advertisements are all designed to attain this goal.

"Public Service" advertisements are designed to benefit the public and indirectly build good will for the sponsor. The Allstate (Fig. 28.4) and Pacific Gas & Electric (Fig. 28.5) advertisements are examples of this.

ADVANTAGES OF ADVERTISING

Public relations advertising has several advantages as a means of communicating with the public. The most important are its reach, its economy, and its control.

Reach

Through advertising, it is possible to reach almost any public desired. Whether it be the community, an industry, a special public, or the entire public, the message or messages can be delivered to practically everyone whose opinion is to be influenced. By selecting the right media, there can be a major concentration on those who are important and a practical elimination of those who are not. Advertising can be very helpful in getting the right message to the right people at the right time.

Regardless of the nature of the public, there are special media that are highly selective and through which almost any group can be reached. Doctors, lawyers, plumbers, apple growers, retail clerks, suburbanites, ethnic groups, Texans, Iowans, Chicagoans, Evanstonians, men, women, youngsters, oldsters, night workers, and hundreds of other groups can be efficiently reached through paid advertising in media directed especially to those groups.

Economy

Media advertising is a fairly economical channel of communication. For example, a full-page advertisement in a newspaper with 300,000 circulation might cost $6,000. This is $20 per thousand circulation. In a large national magazine with one million circulation and a cost of $7,000 per page the cost would be $7 per thousand. Costs for television and radio are competitive but vary so widely from program to program that no generalizations can be made.

By way of contrast, a direct mail campaign might cost $300 per thousand for stationery, production of the message, cost of mailing list, and postage. Because advertising and mailing rates are not stable, these examples are illlustrative only. For actual rates see the *Standard Rate and Data Service* catalogues which are available in most advertising agencies and in many libraries.

Control

With paid advertising, it is possible to say exactly what is desired and to know that the message will be delivered without change or modification. It can be published at the most beneficial time. It can be repeated as often as seems necessary. Advertising can be started or stopped on a predetermined schedule. The advertisements can be as large as the budget permits. The subject matter cannot be edited by the publishing media so long as it conforms to the requirements of legality, good taste, and, in some cases, accuracy requirements of the publisher.

ERRORS IN PUBLIC RELATIONS ADVERTISING

In spite of its advantages, the use of advertising as a communications channel carries with it some problems. These do not exist in every case, but they should be remembered.

Wrong Purpose

A considerable amount of money has been spent on PR advertising that was misdirected. One of the most common errors is the use of advertising to brag about the excellence of the organization. This never succeeds in building goodwill because it focuses on the organization rather than on the public to which the advertising is directed. Another error is to use advertising in an effort to gain sympathy. This is occasionally done in connection with disputes with either labor unions or government agencies. Advertising is used very effectively in such situations when it informs the public about the facts affecting them.

Wrong Timing

Often advertising is called upon to help overcome a crisis. But this is like trying to buy an insurance policy for a burning building. It would be far better to do the advertising before the crisis becomes acute. In some such situations it may be better to do no advertising at all than to try to rescue a lost cause.

Wrong Media

Many companies are spending large sums of money on public relations advertising in business publications. This may be beneficial, but it leads to the suspicion that these advertisers are talking to people who already agree with them. Perhaps the money would be better spent in media reaching people who are not already convinced.

There has been much issue advertising about free enterprise in the *Wall Street Journal*. The *Wall Street Journal* is a fine newspaper, but the advertising about free enterprise might do more good in *Rolling Stone*. One prominent public relations practitioner expressed the point this way: "My mission is to tackle the people who hate our guts rather than talk to the people who pat us on the back."

On the other hand, there may be benefit through advertising to people who *are* sold. It may reinforce their opinions, and if a call for help on some issue is the purpose of the ad it should be directed to friends.

Bethlehem Steel carefully researched readers of magazines in which it considered running issue advertising. Bethlehem wanted to reach opinion-leading influentials, aged 25 to 64, active in the community or politics, with incomes of $20,000 or more — the people government officials consult in taking the pulse of the nation. The study covered: *Atlantic, Harper's, New Yorker, Saturday Review, Smithsonian, Newsweek, Sports Illustrated, Time, U.S. News & World Report, Business Week, Forbes, Fortune* and *Wall Street Journal*.

Bethlehem studied the attitudes of the readers and classed them in relation to Bethlehem's position. The range was from strongly in favor, through moderately in favor, neutral, moderately opposed, to strongly opposed. Big differences were found between the readers of two business magazines. Similar differences were found between the readers of two newsweeklies and between the readers of two cultural magazines.

The cost of reaching the target audiences varied widely among the magazines, especially when weighed in terms of the attitudes. The study enabled Bethlehem to buy its advertising with the lowest cost in terms of reaching the prople who were important to its program (Latshaw, 1977).

Fig. 28.1 The Association of American Railroads used this ad (and others) to tell the public its side of a controversy with the union.

Deer crossing a tree farm area where heavy brush is being removed to make room for a new crop of trees.

We're now cultivating
the deep woods to give forests
a head start.

After a timber crop is harvested, brush and weed trees spring up fast. In some areas, they crowd the very life out of young Douglas firs. Or keep a new seed bed from ever getting a good start.

When this is likely to happen Weyerhaeuser foresters move in. They've found that uprooting the unwanted vegetation just prior to planting or seeding allows the new forest to get a jump on competition.

The new trees grow faster, straighter and produce a more bountiful crop to meet tomorrow's needs.

Advanced forestry techniques like this are now helping us get more and more yield from our tree farm timberlands. And at the same time, maintaining a forest rich in wildlife, recreation and natural beauty.

Tilling the soil is only one way we combine science, ingenuity and muscle to make sure America will always have trees. For paper, cartons, lumber, plywood and scores of other wood products you use. To learn more, write for a free booklet, "Tree Farm to You." Box A-2, Tacoma, Washington 98401. (Include *your* zip code.)

Weyerhaeuser

Fig. 28.2 Weyerhaeuser Company uses ads like this to tell how it reforests cut-over timberland.

Admit it.
The guys are good.

You've seen it dozens of times. A truck pulls to a stop near a narrow alleyway. Or in a crowded terminal.

With only a glance in the rear-view mirror, and the feel of the wheel in his hands, the driver moves quickly and confidently. He snakes 55 feet of tractor and trailer back into a spot you'd have trouble backing the family car into, and snuggles it right up to the loading dock.

Someone nearby can't resist saying, "Another coat of paint and he wouldn't have made it."

At that moment, nobody has to tell you who the best drivers on the road are. You know.

Of course, there are other reasons why the trucking industry has the best safety record on the highway, and why it gets better each year. Like better trucks, better highways, and better equipment maintenance programs. But the biggest single reason, by far, is the skill of the men behind the wheel.

Next time you see one doing his stuff in a tight spot, take a good look. You're watching the greatest highway safety device ever invented at work. The professional truck driver.

American Trucking Associations, Inc.
1616 P St., N.W., Washington, D.C. 20036

If you've got it,
a truck brought it.

Fig. 28.3 American Trucking Association builds goodwill with ads like this which point out the skill of truck drivers.

He's drunk. Here he comes, over to your side.

You've waited too long to make your move.

The time to make your move against the drunk is <u>before he gets behind the wheel</u>.

Get his license pulled and keep him off the road.

You can help get the job done by letting your governor and state legislators know where you stand—that you support the strong drunk driving laws outlined by the National Highway Safety Act.

And you can do it by supporting your judges, prosecutors, and police when they enforce the drunk driving laws fairly.

A study reported to Congress by the U.S. Department of Transportation shows that one out of every fifty drivers on the road is drunk. Not just drinking. *Drunk*. The situation is bad and will probably get worse, unless you'll help reverse the trend.

Will you help? Start by sending for the Allstate Action Booklet, "Drunk Drivers and Highway Safety." Write the Safety Director, Allstate Insurance Companies, Northbrook, Illinois 60062.

Help stop the traffic slaughter

Fig. 28.4 One of a series of Allstate Insurance Companies' anti-drunk driver ads, which won first-place public-service award for accident prevention from the National Safety Council. These ads were a major factor in many states' passage of legislation to remove drunk drivers from the road.

Homeowner's Combat Manual
How to fight this summer's PG&E electric bills.

Motivation: This summer, electric rates will be higher than ever.

Preparation: A. Get air conditioner in shape. Clean filter. Oil motor. And whatever else owner's manual recommends.

B. Weatherstrip to keep house cooler.

C. Insulate attic to keep house still cooler.

D. Keep sun out by closing shades and/or drapes.

Evaluation: If all proper steps are taken, house may be cool enough that you will not need to run that electricity-guzzling air conditioner at all.

Conclusion: A. It pays to follow the manual. It contains lots of other things to do to save electricity, and how to do them.

B. Get a copy. Free. From PG&E.

PGand**E**

Save energy-you'll save money, too.

115CGE-D677

Fig. 28.5 Pacific Gas & Electric Company uses ads like this to urge customers to save energy.

457

Waste Circulation

There are times when a general circulation medium is used to reach a group that is much smaller than the total audience of the medium. For example, a company might wish to reach its employees or a union might want to reach its members by using newspapers or broadcast media. In such a situation, there will be much waste circulation because many people will not be interested and because many in the target group may not get the message.

USE OF ADVERTISING

The decision to use or not use advertising in public relations should be made on the basis of its efficiency in communication. Having determined who must be reached and the message to be given to them, the question becomes "Which communications tools will do the job most efficiently?" The number of people to be reached, the number of times they should be reached, the cost of reaching them, the impact with which they should be reached — all these factors should be carefully considered.

MARKETING ADVERTISING

Most advertising money is spent to promote the sales of goods and services. This is a function of marketing, but the public relations people should be involved for two reasons — the nature of the advertising and the marketing concepts behind the advertising.

The Nature of the Advertising

The consumer movement is extremely critical of some advertising. Stereotypes of women and ethnics bring adverse reactions. Some advertisements are silly or inane. Network television shows periodically lampoon such commercials. Harsher criticism comes for advertising which is untrue or deceptive. Advertising aimed at children has been vigorously protested.

If these criticisms only affected sales, there could be a temptation to let the marketing people suffer the consequences. But the criticisms have a much bigger effect. They not only hamper sales, they also create hostile opinion about the organization which does the advertising.

Mrs. Conte's wash is cleaner now

you are interested in the details of Bethlehem's program to combat air and water pollution, send for our free 36-page booklet, "Keep It Clean." Write: Room 1034, Bethlehem Steel Corp., Bethlehem, PA 18016.

Mrs. Anna Conte lives in a neat white house on a hillside overlooking our steel plant in Steelton, Pennsylvania near Harrisburg, on the Susquehanna River.

Mrs. Conte has been hanging her wash outside all her married life because, as she says, "I like the clean, fresh-air smell." There was dust in the air, of course, but she didn't mind. After all, her husband worked in the steel mills for 42 years before he retired.

"But now," says Mrs. Conte, "my wash is whiter and cleaner. We just don't have that much dust in the air any more, thanks to whatever Bethlehem Steel did."

What we did, Mrs. Conte, was install new furnaces with $2 million worth of dust and fume collection equipment. It works on the same principle as your vacuum cleaner, but on a gigantic scale. This highly efficient system captures 90 per cent of the dust particles caused by steelmaking operations.

Today, in this community about *36 tons* of dust particles every day are prevented from escaping into the air—and onto Mrs. Conte's wash!

What we've done to improve the quality of the air in Steelton is typical of our efforts to improve the environment in many locations. We want to be good neighbors wherever we have operations. We will keep at it until the job is finished.

BETHLEHEM STEEL

Fig. 28.6 Bethlehem Steel Corporation spends large sums of money to reduce air pollution and it uses ads like this to inform the public.

"Dear General Foods, What happens when I eat a preservative?"

The same thing that happens when you eat any food—for example, an orange.

Once eaten, an orange is broken down into the ingredients that make it up: chemicals. (One of these chemicals is—of all things—a preservative. It's called Citric Acid, and it's put there not by man but by nature.)

This product is packed with a preservative before it leaves the plant.

The body then uses the chemicals it can, and eliminates those it can't. But the body doesn't choose between them based upon whether they have chemical-sounding or natural-sounding names. The body does care about two things: what the chemical is and how much of it is there.

How much is too much?

The U.S. Food and Drug Administration has established complex and thorough guidelines for the safe use of additives. Briefly, it determines the maximum "no-effect" level of an additive in test animals, and then prescribes an appropriate fraction of that amount (usually 1/100th) as the maximum allowed in a food for human use. And at General Foods, we use the smallest amount of any preservative that will still do the job for which it's intended.

Back to nature.

The idea of preservatives didn't originate with General Foods. It originated with nature. We simply try to use in our foods the same or similar devices nature uses to protect its foods. For example, we use Citric Acid as a preservative. It occurs naturally in such foods as oranges. We also use sodium benzoate as a preservative, and it, too, is a compound formed of naturally occurring chemicals.

For more information.

To help you better understand preservatives and other food additives, we'd like to send you our booklet, *Today's Food And Additives.* For your free copy, write to Miss Peggy Kohl, V.P., Consumer Affairs, G.F. Consumer Center, White Plains, N.Y. 10625. (One to a family, please.)

Our reasons for telling you all this are a mixture of helpfulness and pride in our products. The more you understand about food, the better off you'll be. And the more you understand about our foods, the better off we'll be.

GF GENERAL FOODS

©General Foods Corp., 1976

Fig. 28.7   One of the General Foods advertisements mentioned in Chapter 1.

Public relations people should see every ad before it runs and should vigorously oppose any which can create unfavorable public reaction.

The Marketing Concept

Marketing decisions have historically been based on estimates of potential sales. Almost anything may be offered if there is a belief that it can be sold profitably. Now consumer activists are protesting the proliferation of products, overpackaging, insignificant improvements, "gimmick" products, the annual style changes in automobiles, and a host of other things which may be saleable but which do not really offer very much to the buyer.

Some public relations practitioners have urged that potential sales should be only a part of the consideration; that public relations people should sit in on marketing decisions and even say such things as, "Sure, we can make money on this but it will have an adverse effect on public opinion. Let's drop the idea."

RESTRICTIONS ON PR ADVERTISING

Freedom of speech and of the press would seem to apply to advertising, but this is not always the case. There are limitations on the use of advertising for public relations purposes.

Some activists have protested any use of advertising by public utilities and by energy producers. On a less extreme scale, public utility commissions have ruled that issue advertising can not be classed as a cost of doing business and must therefore be paid for out of after-tax profits. Some have ruled that *any* expenditures for public relations falls under the same rule. This has been applied even when the utility proves that it has to spend large sums of money to answer questions from customers. There have also been rulings that a utility cannot insert any "controversial" material in bill envelopes even though it does not increase the cost of mailing.

The AFL-CIO has attacked corporate sponsorship of TV shows on the Public Broadcasting System. There have been protests against the Advertising Council's public-service spots in favor of free enterprise.

Insurance companies that have run advertisements urging people to realize that big awards for damages mean higher insurance costs have been sued by lawyers who claim that these advertisements indicate a conspiracy to subvert the jury system and that the advertisements are unfair, untrue, and deceptive.

Texaco ran a TV ad while Congress was considering a bill to break up the big oil companies. It showed that it took years to build the company and that the integration of the various segments of the company benefited the consumer. Nothing was said about the bill.

The Federal Communications Commission, spurred by activist complaints, ruled that the advertisement was politically biased and ordered the stations which aired the commerical to give equal time to opposing viewpoints.

Mobil Oil Company has been accused of presenting "one-sided" newspaper and magazine advertisements. The accusation was followed by demands that Mobil pay for advertisements urging that Mobil be broken up.

The equal-time provision which creates many problems for users of broadcast media does not apply to printed advertising. As a consequence, it is easier to use print media. Nevertheless it is always advisable to be sure that the advertising is not going to create new problems.

The Internal Revenue Service and the courts generally consider institutional advertising as tax-deductible. There are, however, forces which don't want any corporation to use advertising for any purpose other than sales. There may be efforts to place this restriction into law. Anyone who proposes to do any advocacy advertising should read the books by Sethi and Stridsberg which are listed in the Suggested Readings in this chapter.

THE ADVERTISING PLAN

Any activity will be more effective if it is planned, and that is especially true in the case of advertising. A PR advertising plan should be in writing, and it should include the following major points: the problem, the objective, the audience, the media, the message, and the budget. Or, in simple terms — who is to be reached, why they must be reached, how they are to be reached, what is to be said, and how much it will cost.

The Problem

The problem is defined by analysis of inbound communication. This reveals the attitudes or beliefs of the public. These may be very general or quite definite but they must be known and clearly understood. They can range from a broad general ignorance of the organization's existence to very specific complaints about its practices or policies. The entire public may be involved or, conversely, only one special public may be concerned. The important point is to know exactly *what* attitude or belief is to be improved or corrected and in *whose* minds.

The Objective

Essentially, the objective is the answer to this question: "What attitude do we want these people to have?" When this is known and understood, the advertising can be effective. If there is no objective, the advertising will be wasted. The more specific the objective, the easier it will be to measure results. It is not good to state the objective as "to improve public regard for XYZ Company." It is far better to state it as: "to increase by 50% the number of people who say 'XYZ Company is an asset to the community.' "

The Audience

This is the "who to reach" part of the plan. It is derived largely from the analysis of the problem. Knowing the audience will affect not only the selection of the media, but also the nature and content of the message. Marketing advertising is carefully aimed at the most likely prospects. The same rule should be followed in public relations advertising.

The Media

This is the "how to reach them" section. As stated before, there are many media that can be used for public relations advertising. Each has advantages and disadvantages. None is perfect, but some are better for certain situations than others. Selection of media requires analysis of both the audience and the message. It is possible that an audience can be most efficiently reached by newspapers but the message may be best delivered, in terms of impact, by television. This is not to say that a media decision is made after the "message" is completley prepared. Creative and media planning must go hand in hand (Sandage & Fryburger, 1975).

The Message

This really means the idea to be conveyed to the people in order to affect their opinion. It includes the words, the figures, and the illustrations designed to create the desired favorable attitudes and beliefs. This is the "what to say" section, the actual advertising to be used. It may be in print or in broadcast. It may be one advertisement or a continuing campaign. Sometimes this is called the "creative" section of the plan. It can also be called: "how we'll persuade them." This requires a decision as to the actual advertisements to be used. How many, how large, how long, what is said in each one, in what order they will appear, etc. (Kleppner, 1973).

The Budget

The costs of advertising are low in terms of persons reached per dollar but they can represent very large sums of money. It is important, therefore, that an advertising plan include a precise set of figures that shows how much money is required and how many people will be reached with that money.

CREATING THE ADVERTISING

With rare exceptions, public relations advertising is created by an advertising agency under the guidance of the public relations director. Titles and organization charts may vary but, regardless of these differences, there must be someone in the client organization who is the prime contact with the agency and who is responsible to management for the advertising. In some cases there may be a PR advertising manager under the director. There may also be a product advertising manager, who is likely to be in the marketing department and completely separate from the PR function.

Creating advertising is a complex process and usually requires many specialized skills. Most of these are provided by the advertising agency but some may be furnished by the client. The specific situation will dictate whose talents and skills will be used to prepare the advertisement. In one case the agency may do almost everything and in another it may do very little. But if the advertising is to be effective, it must be created in an atmosphere of mutual confidence and trust with each party cooperating wholeheartedly.

The ultimate responsibility for the advertising falls upon the PR director, but his work will be easier and more effective if his role is that of "partner" rather than "dictator."

Since this chapter is only a brief description of the advertising process, some further reading is very much in order. There are many excellent textbooks and choosing the best would be difficult indeed.

Suggested Readings

Dirksen, Charles J., and Kroeger, Arthur. *Advertising: Principles and Problems*. Homewood, Ill: Irwin, 1973.
Kleppner, Otto, and Greyser, Stephen. *Advertising Procedure*. Englewood Cliffs, N.J.: Prentice-Hall, 1973.
Sandage, Charles H., and Fryburger, Vernon. *Advertising: Theory and Practice*. Homewood, Ill.: Irwin, 1975.
Sethi, S. Prakash. *Advocacy Advertising and Large Corporations*. Lexington, Mass.: Heath, 1977.
Stridsberg, Albert. *Controversy Advertising*. New York: Hastings House, 1977.

The following description of the steps in producing advertising is grossly oversimplified. But for our purposes, it will at least serve as an introduction to the things that have to be done.

Print Advertising

Whether it is in newspapers or magazines, black and white, or full color, every print advertisement involves the following steps:

Copy   The message to be carried by the advertisement is written and submitted to the client for approval.

Layout   A drawing showing what the ad is to look like (size, style of type, size and kind of illustration, and arrangement of these elements) is made up and approved.

Production   Type is set, illustrations are prepared, and the complete advertisement is assembled in semifinal form and a printer's proof is made. When this is approved, the printing plates (or equivalent) are prepared and when final proofs are OK, this material is sent to the publication.

Orders and billing   The publication receives an order stating where and when to run the advertisement. When the advertisement is published, the publication sends a tear sheet (which proves that the advertisement did actually run) and a bill to the agency which in turn bills the client for the space plus production costs.

Radio Advertising

The steps involved in radio advertising are similar but fewer. They are:

Copy   The message to be broadcast is written and approved.

Production   The copy is prepared in script form for use by a live announcer or as a record or sound tape for use without a station announcer. When approved, the script or record or tape is sent to the station or network.

Orders and billing The station or network receives an order to run the announcement at specified times, and it submits an affidavit of performance along with its bill which goes to the agency and eventually to the client.

Television Advertising

This is a more complicated process but it still parallels the steps in other media.

Copy This is normally written in "storyboard" form, which shows the key scenes of the announcement along with the supporting copy. (In basic structure, this is somewhat like a comic-strip.) When approved, the announcement is ready for production.

Production Most television commericals or announcements are filmed or videotaped before broadcast. Essentially, this process is similar to production of a short motion picture. It is a job for experts only.

Orders and billing The procedure is the same as with radio.

EXERCISES

1. From a recent publication (newspaper or magazine), clip a PR advertisement.
   (a) What is its purpose?
   (b) Does it convince you? Why?
2. From television or radio, cite an example of a public service advertisement you have seen or heard.
   (a) What was its purpose?
   (b) How would you improve it?

Case Problem

You are public relations director of a "strip" coal mine. Management has a program of restoring the land to its original condition (as nearly as possible) by replacing the disturbed soil and by planting trees.

Write a one-page advertisement for *Readers Digest* to inform the public about this program. Include a rough layout with descriptions of any illustrative material.

29

Miscellaneous Channels

In addition to the major channels, which are treated in separate chapters, there are a number of other means of communication used in public relations. These are grouped here for convenience. Some are used regularly and others only occasionally or by just a few organizations. The following are the most common.

THE TELEPHONE

The telephone has two major roles in public relations. In the ordinary course of operating any organization there will be many telephone calls to or from members of the public. The way in which these calls are handled can have a beneficial or detrimental effect on public relations. It is therefore imperative that everyone who makes or receives telephone calls be aware of the importance of good telephone manners and expeditious handling of calls.

Regular checking of telephone procedures should be the rule in any organization, and instruction on how to use the telephone should be part of the indoctrination of every employee who may be called upon to make or receive telephone calls.

Telephone companies provide their customers with booklets that tell how to use the telephone in the most efficient and courteous manner. It can take from eight to sixteen pages to list all the suggestions for good telephone usage. But those pages are worthwhile reading for anyone who uses a telephone.

As a positive public relations tool, the telephone is often overlooked; yet, it can be very effectively used for outbound communication. Telephone calls may be more effective than letters. The cost may be quite reasonable and, in spite of the difficulties of reaching the right people, it can reach many of them in a hurry. Very few people can resist a ringing telephone and people who will not open a letter or read printed or typewritten messages may respond to the same message when it comes by telephone.

There is an urgency about a telephone message that makes it especially effective in stimulating people to action at a specific time.

When the telephone is used specifically as a PR tool, those who are to make the calls must be provided with a carefully prepared script and must be checked constantly to be sure that they are following it. And, finally, with all telephone messages the tone of voice can be a great builder of goodwill. The "voice with a smile" is more than a slogan, it is a must.

LETTERS

Letters, too, have a dual role in public relations. Those written in the regular course of business can create good or bad impressions depending on how they are written. There are many books on the art of letter writing.

If any organization has a substantial volume of correspondence with the public, its outbound letters should be constantly checked to be sure that they will create the right impression.

As a communications channel, letters provide a highly selective means of delivering messages. They can deliver messages to the exact audience desired. They can carry illustrative material, and they can be referred to and preserved by the recipient.

Letters must be carefully written and carefully produced. Whenever possible, they should be personally addressed and individually typed. These letters get far more attention than the "Occupant" mailings that fill so many mailboxes. Mass production of individually written and addressed letters is often done by direct mail firms which, through use of automatic typewriters and addressing machines, can do the job for much less than it would cost if done in the conventional way.

Suggested Readings

Blumenthal, Lassor A. *The Art of Letter Writing*. New York: Grosset & Dunlap, 1976.
Editorial Staff. *How to Write a Good Letter*. Englewood Cliffs, N.J.: Prentice-Hall, 1967.

LEAFLETS AND BOOKLETS

A leaflet is one piece of printed paper. It may be one page or it may be folded into several. It is usually designed to be read once and discarded but occasionally it may have a different future.

A booklet has several pages which may be glued or stapled together. Usually it has at least eight pages. It is normally planned for leisurely reading and retention.

Any printed matter should be produced with quality paper, good illustrations, and large readable type. One clear illustration will be more effective than two muddy, irrelevant ones. One hundred words in 12 pt will probably accomplish more than two hundred words in 6 pt. The objective is to get a message read, so everything that can help the prospective reader should be included in planning leaflets or booklets or other materials.

Printers are usually able to provide considerable help in designing printed materials and some of the large paper companies distribute booklets explaining the printing and binding processes in enough detail to enable the neophyte to understand what has to be done and to avoid gross errors.*

Printed materials are used extensively for many different purposes in public relations. Some of the most frequent uses are these:

Booklets

1. *Public relations* — to tell employees how they can aid the public relations program.
2. *Orientation* — to introduce employees to the organization.
3. *History* — to tell how the organization started and grew.
4. *Safety* — to explain safety rules and their importance.
5. *Organization* — to explain the organization — its procedures and structure.
6. *Policy* — to explain policies, rules, and procedures.
7. *Benefits* — to explain benefits available to employees.
8. *Training* — to teach employees how to do their work.
9. *Suggestions* — to explain the workings of a suggestion system.
10. *Credit union* — to familiarize employees with the credit union.
11. *Insurance* — to explain costs and insurance benefits of the organization.

*One of the best is *Pocket Pal* distributed by International Paper Co.

12. *Medical* — to clarify rules on payments to doctors and hospitals.
13. *Retirement* — to explain retirement benefits available to employees.
14. *Special purposes* — this category is practically limitless. Whenever a public relations communications task justifies a voluminous treatment, a booklet is in order.

Leaflets

1. *Activation* — to urge action on or support for something.
2. *Information* — to give accurate information in brief form.
3. *Notification* — to make an official announcement.
4. *Apology* — to express regret for error or inconvenience.
5. *Explanations* — to tell how or why something is done.
6. *Greeting* — to welcome employees or visitors or customers, etc.
7. *Progress* — to give periodic reports on progress of a long-time project.
8. *Change* — to inform about changes that will affect the recipient.
9. *Supplements* — to supplement or amend booklets.
10. *Special purposes* — to serve any other communications need requiring wide distribution of an explicitly worded message.

Information Racks

Booklets and leaflets are frequently distributed by means of information racks. Quantities of the items for distribution are placed in packets or pigeon holes at a central location where there is considerable traffic. Those who pass by are invited, by means of a sign, to help themselves. A fair evaluation of the relative interest of such items can be made by counting the number carried away.

BOOKS

Books are used chiefly to tell a very complete story about an organization. Usually they are written as histories. Sometimes these histories are biographies of the founder. This is most likely to be the case when the founder dominated the organization for many years.

Writing a book requires a great amount of research and time. Frequently this task is turned over to a free-lance writer who does most of the work but is aided and counseled by the public relations personnel of the organization.

Books are distributed mainly to employees, owners, important customers, suppliers, and individuals who may be especially interested. Distribution to the general public is not at all common.

BULLETIN BOARDS

The bulletin board is the most frequently used channel of communications. Rare indeed is the organization without one. In some cases it is the only channel used. Common as they are, bulletin boards are rarely used efficiently. Yet, when properly used, they can be invaluable. The key to successful use of a bulletin board is to keep it so interesting that it will be examined every day. Most bulletin boards are for employees, but many organizations have bulletin boards for customers or for suppliers.

General Rules

Every bulletin board should conform to these rules:

Location   It must be readily visible, not stuck in an inaccessible corner. The preferred location is one that will be passed daily by all who should see what is displayed on it.

Neatness   It must be kept clean and uncluttered. Materials should be displayed in an orderly manner with each item visible. Crowding should be avoided.

Timeliness   It must be periodically checked for timeliness. Old and out-of-date items must be eliminated and replaced. A new item every day is a good way to draw traffic.

Interest   It must be kept interesting by mixing official and personal items and by adding entertaining odds and ends.

Responsibility   Someone must be in charge so that all of the foregoing rules will be followed.

Content

Almost anything can be displayed on a bulletin board, including stray earrings, but the most logical items are things such as:

1. construction plans
2. cafeteria menus
3. shutdown notices
4. new product announcements
5. new equipment announcements
6. suggestion system notices
7. meeting announcements
8. safety notices
9. policies and rules
10. club announcements
11. posters
12. credit union notices
13. opportunity announcements
14. insurance news
15. medical announcements
16. holiday or vacation notices
17. lost and found items
18. for-sale, -rent, or -trade items
19. photographs
20. parking notices
21. cartoons
22. humorous items
23. letters
24. clippings
25. news items about individuals
26. promotions
27. transfers
28. assignments
29. recreation news
30. leaflets.

PUBLIC ADDRESS SYSTEMS

A PA system will permit instantaneous communication to all within hearing distance. It can be used effectively for important news but it should not be used to repeat the same message over and over again. Because the PA system suggests a strong atmosphere of paternalism, any usage urging people to do something should be done rarely and with great care.

Fig. 29.1 An excellent bulletin board. Anaconda American Brass Co. carried out a highly successful employee relations program by skillful use of its bulletin boards.

COMMUNICATORS

The communicator presents a prerecorded message which can be heard by dialing a certain telephone number. Somewhat like a PA system message, it has the virtue of being listened to only by those who want to hear it. Many large organizations use them regularly.

473

POSTERS

Posters are particularly useful as a means of emphasizing an idea. They are widely used to promote safety, courtesy, efficiency, quality workmanship, reduction of waste, elimination of defects, promptness, and other causes. Often posters are syndicated and thus available for very low costs. Any poster must be simple, eye-catching, limited to one idea, and contain very few words.

EXHIBITS AND DISPLAYS

Exhibits and displays can be small, simple, and inexpensive or large, complex, and fabulously expensive. They can be used in the offices or plants of the organization or in public places such as schools or conventions. The location often determines what kind of display or exhibit is used. Things like honors or history are commonly used within the organization while such subjects as products, manufacturing methods, and public benefits are often displayed in more public locations.

Suggested Readings

Carmel, J. H. *Exhibition Technique.* New York: Van Nostrand Reinhold, 1962.
Hayett, W. *Display and Exhibit Handbook.* New York: Van Nostrand Reinhold, 1967.
Mauger, E. M. *Modern Display Techniques.* New York: Fairchild, 1964.

Purposes

Exhibits can serve many different specific purposes, but nearly all have the same basic objective — to improve public opinion by providing information in graphic form. Occasionally an element of entertainment is included in order to attract a larger audience, but this is seldom the primary purpose although, in rare instances, exhibits are designed solely to please the public (e.g., the musical puppet show of Pepsi Cola at the New York World's Fair in 1964-65).

What to Tell

Exhibits can supply many different kinds of information, but usually they are most effective when they concentrate on one major topic such as:

1. past history of the organization
2. present activities of the organization

Fig. 29.2 Syndicated posters from the National Safety Council.

3. future plans of the organization
4. products of the organization
5. how products are made
6. location of plants, offices, mines, etc.
7. raw materials used
8. honors or recognition
9. how the public is, or will be, benefited by the organization.

How to Tell It

The ways in which information can be imparted by an exhibit are innumerable. Here are a few of the more frequently used devices:

1. photographs
2. paintings
3. maps
4. miniature factories
5. models
6. dioramas
7. working models
8. schematic models
9. cutaway machines
10. historic equipment
11. diagrams
12. charts
13. X-ray views
14. "exploded" models or machines
15. puppets
16. animated characters
17. motion pictures (continuous projection)
18. slides (continuous projection)
19. advertising proofs
20. sound tracks
21. special lighting effects
22. actual products
23. skits (using live action)
24. musical or dramatic presentations
25. awards (plaques, medals, etc.)
26. raw materials
27. travelling shows (like the General Motors Motorama).

Construction and Transportation

A small exhibit or display can often be created from existing materials and erected by staff personnel. Larger units normally require employment of professional display builders who participate in the planning. If a display is to be moved from place to place, there must be careful consideration of the means of transportation, the crating and uncrating, and the availability of personnel to do all the work necessary to get the exhibit shipped, delivered, uncrated, erected, manned during the showing, torn down, crated, and reshipped. Moving a large exhibit is a slow and costly job.

IN-HOUSE TELEVISION

This channel is becoming more important as a means of reaching employees. For a generation which is so thoroughly conditioned to television at home, this is a particularly effective means of distributing information.

Dow Chemical Company has a daily six-minute news show which is repeated throughout the noon hour and shown on monitors scattered through its Midland, Michigan, plants and offices. The show includes general and corporate news. In one case, it showed a videotape of a fire in progress at a Dow factory.

When a critical bill affecting Dow was before Congress, the news show explained how the proposed law would affect Dow and its employees. Without asking for letters to Congress, Dow did urge employees to be active in the political process. The employees understood — and acted.

Such companies as General Telephone, Gulf Oil, Xerox, and many others use closed circuit television for "press conferences" with top management. Numerous other kinds of programs are being used, and it appears that this relatively new channel may become one of the most effective.

THE CALL-IN

This is a relatively new channel of communication. Whirlpool has used it with great success in its customer-relations program. A nation-wide

477

toll-free telephone number is advertised widely and has generated many calls. More important, it has enabled customers to get prompt adjustment of their complaints and problems.

Other uses of the call-in which are being introduced are: free phone calls from employees to the CEO and even free calls from outsiders. Naturally, activating a call-in program requires publicity. Also, there is the danger that there may be too many calls to handle, and even crank calls. Nevertheless, this channel seems to open up new possibilities for humanizing an organization and its top executives.

DIRECT MAIL

There is much complaint about the mass of "junk mail" which clutters so many mail boxes. Nevertheless, direct mail can be a valuable channel of communication, especially if it is personalized and selective.

With direct mail, it is possible to reach the exact category of people who are most important. There is no waste circulation caused by sending messages to people who are not concerned. Of course, the recipients still must read the messages, but at least the messages are delivered to the right people.

Several organizations sell mailing lists which enable the user to reach almost any specified group. Just for example, one mailing list catalogue includes such diverse groups as acoustical consultants, clergymen (by denomination), drive-in theaters, guidance counselors, petroleum geologists, soybean processors, yacht owners, contributors (to charity), and 120 different lists in the educational field.

There are many business firms which specialize in direct mail, and they are usually listed in the Yellow Pages of the telephone book.

THE GRAPEVINE

This is an uncontrollable channel, yet it exists in every organization. It functions at the water cooler, in the rest rooms, and almost anywhere that people gather. Individuals who move around the organization are quite likely to be links in the chain. The grapevine is amazingly fast, frequently inaccurate, and often faithfully believed.

In Chapter 5, it was recommended that the public relations practitioner get out of the office and talk to people. This is a sure way to get hooked into the grapevine. People like to talk, they love to be "in on" things, and they like to display their knowledge. A competent practitioner can take advantage of this and not only learn what people are saying, but also feed information into the grapevine.

RUMORS

Rumors spread through the grapevine. They spread for two reasons. One reason is "leaks." Someone who knows something tells someone else and the story spreads. The other reason for rumors is guesses based on lack of adequate two-way communication in the organization.

Stopping "leaks" is very difficult, as every recent President of the United States has learned. Leaks can be reduced by limiting sensitive information to a few people who are urged not to talk. Sometimes this works, and sometimes it doesn't.

Preventing rumors based on guesses or untruths requires action to provide true and timely information to all who may be concerned. Whenever an organization is in trouble, whenever false information is available, whenever critical decisions are delayed, whenever the normal channels of communication fail to function or are not trusted, there will be rumors.

When a rumor spreads, it should be investigated. The first step is to find out what is being said. If unimportant it may well be ignored. If it is true, there should be confirmation and explanation. If it is untrue, it should be squelched. This requires determination of the source and the reason why the rumor started. When this is known, the rumor should be counteracted by releasing correct information. This may be done through normal channels or by feeding the information back into the grapevine.

EXERCISES

1. Look at any bulletin board accessible to you.
    (a) Is it cluttered or neat?
    (b) Is it up-to-date?
    (c) How would you improve it?
2. Find a PR leaflet or booklet.
    (a) What is its purpose?
    (b) Is it effective?

Case Problem

You are public relations counselor to an insurance company. You have persuaded the president to print an orientation booklet for new employees. He has approved and asked for an outline.

Prepare the title page, introduction, and complete outline. Include all information that you, as a new employee, would like to know.

Events 30

Public relations events generally fall into two main categories: those conducted primarily to generate publicity and those whose chief purpose is to improve public relations through personal contact. These purposes are not exclusive. An event that is planned primarily for publicity can create considerable goodwill in the community — for example, the Macy's Thanksgiving Day Parade in New York. An event created primarily to improve relations between members of an association can result in large quantities of favorable publicity — for example, the annual convention of the American Medical Association.

The Macy's parade was originally an event designed to publicize the store as a place to buy Christmas gifts, but it is now an institution in New York and it creates much goodwill for the store. The AMA convention is planned to enable doctors to exchange information and to work on problems of the profession, yet the convention always gets a very large amount of publicity in all the major news media.

Every public relations event presents at least some opportunity for publicity and every special event program should include a plan for publicity.

There are many kinds of events which can be used as tools of public relations but all of them must conform to these four requirements. An event must have a purpose, it must be planned, it must be controlled by someone, and there must be a budget if any expenditure is involved.

MEETINGS

Meetings can be large or small, they can be formal or informal, but, regardless of their nature, they must have purpose, planning, and control. There are generally two types of meetings: those in which the audience actively participates through discussion and those in which the audience listens to speakers. For easy reference, these two types of meetings will be classed as "participation" meetings and "listening" meetings. These distinctions are not rigid. It is often advisable to use speakers in a "participation" meeting, and "listening" meetings are frequently improved by providing an opportunity for discussion.

"Participation" meetings are often used for problem solving — for example, a meeting of department heads to formulate a policy or a meeting of representatives of different organizations to resolve a conflict or to formulate plans for cooperation in some joint activity.

"Listening" meetings are often used to inform people — for example, a meeting of employees at which they are informed of some policy or rule change or a meeting of some "outside" group that is to be told of the virtues of some organization or activity.

A good meeting can be a valuable aid to a public relations program. A bad meeting can do a lot of damage. Here are some of the points to consider when planning a meeting.

Purpose

Every meeting must have a purpose. It may be held to obtain information (inbound communication), to give information (outbound communication), or to exchange information (two-way communication). If there is a purpose, the meeting can accomplish something, which is its only justification. A meeting is an act of communication, not a pastime or an entertainment.

Plan

An unplanned meeting has little chance of success. With large meetings, this is obvious; but even the smallest and shortest meeting will be more effective if there is a plan. For a small, informal, "participation" meeting, the plan may be an agenda for discussion and a mental note as to the purpose. For larger and longer meetings, the planning becomes more complete and more formalized. Every plan must consider the key points: Who will attend? Who will speak? Where will the meeting be held? When will it be held? How long will it run? What topics will be covered and when? What facilities will be needed?

Control

A meeting without control is not a meeting. Someone has to start it, keep it going, keep it on the right track, keep it on schedule, and, eventually, stop it. Also, someone (not necessarily the same person) has to see to it that all the people and things necessary for the success of the meeting are available when needed.

Location

The meeting room must be large enough for the expected attendance and it must be convenient in arrangement. To determine this, it is necessary to know what will be done at the meeting.

Seating Arrangement

For a "listening" meeting, the seating may be of the "theater" type where the primary requirement is that the audience be able to see and hear what is presented.

For a "semi-listening" meeting, a schoolroom setup is in order. With tables or desks, it is possible to take notes and to look over materials distributed to those in attendance.

For a "participation" meeting, it may be best to seat the people at one or more tables where they can see the others with whom they may be talking. If people are to be assigned to certain tables, these should be conspicuously numbered and in logical order.

Invitations and Acceptances

For internal meetings (e.g., employees), a simple announcement of the meeting is normally adequate. If any noncontrolled group is involved, it will be necessary to issue invitations, check on acceptances, follow-up on promised attendance, and seek answers from those who did not reply.

Speakers

Speakers must be scheduled well in advance. There must be adequate follow-up to be sure they do not forget the meeting. With unknown speakers, it is advisable to hear them speak before issuing an invitation, or at least to obtain trusted reports on their ability from people able to render impartial judgment. With out-of-town speakers, it is usually necessary to make hotel reservations and to arrange for someone to meet them on arrival both in the city and at the meeting.

Facilities

All the physical items needed must be checked and double-checked before the meeting. Some of the more common items to be considered are:

Lighting   Can the room be darkened or lightened when necessary? Where are the switches? Where are the pull-cords on drapes? Who will handle lighting?

Charts   Are the words, figures, and lines visible throughout the room? What kind of stand or easel will be needed? Are all the necessary charts on hand and in the right order? Who will handle the charts?

Blackboard   Is it in a good location? Is it clean? Is there chalk and an eraser?

Films   Are they correctly wound on the reels? Are they properly identified? Are they ready for use when scheduled?

Film projector   Is it in the right location? Will it clear the heads in the audience? Is it threaded properly? Is it focused? Is it hooked up? Is there a spare bulb? Can anyone kick the cord and thus disconnect it? Who will run the projector? Does he know his cues?

Slides   Are they loaded in a tray that will fit the projector? Are they right side up? Are they in the right order? Is there more than one slide tray? Are they identified?

Slide projector   Is it properly located? Is it focused? Is it loaded? Is it hooked up? Will the speaker operate the projector with remote control or will someone at the projector operate it? If the latter, what are his cues?

Screen   Is a screen available? Can it be seen by the audience? If the screen is in a room with immovable seats (e.g., a theater or auditorium), what can be done to seat the audience in the areas with the best view of the screen?

Tape recorder   Is a tape recorder available? Is it loaded? With the right tape? Is it set for the right speed? Is it hooked up? Who will run it? What are his cues?

Platform or stage   Can everyone see the speaker? Is there a speaker's desk or lectern? Is it adequately lighted? Is there a PA system? Is it working? If there is to be a group or panel on stage, is there adequate seating? Table? Microphone? Lights?

Audience helps   Do the attendees have a program or agenda? Note pads? Pencils? Can they find the meeting room? Is it identified on the bulletin board? Are there directional arrows, if needed?

Identification

Unless everyone at the meeting knows everyone else, it is desirable to provide name tags. These should be hand printed in bold block capitals. Longhand or typewritten names are not legible at any distance.

Speakers should be identified with name cards visible throughout the room. These can be placed on the lectern or, if a panel is involved, the name cards should be in front of the speakers.

Program

A definite program is necessary for all but the briefest meetings. A written program enables all attendees to know just when a subject will be covered and by whom. It can be typed or mimeographed but, if the meeting is large, it will be best to have it printed.

Greeting

Whenever an "outside" group attends a meeting, they should be met and greeted by a representative of the organization sponsoring the meeting. If the meeting is very large (several hundred people), the personal greeting may be impossible and must be replaced by appropriate remarks from the chairman. A meeting will be more successful if the attendees feel that the sponsors of the meeting know they are present.

A good meeting may require more time in planning and preparation than in execution. Everything that goes into the meeting must be planned, checked, and double-checked. Rehearsals are imperative for any meeting that involves a "listening" audience. Speakers and their aides must thoroughly understand what each is going to do, so that there will be no missed cues or embarrassing pauses.

Disruptions

Some meetings may be subject to disruption. Among the most likely are: stockholder meetings of large corporations, meetings of college or university regents or trustees, meetings of public utility commissions, boards of education, foundations and charitable or health-care organizations. In addition to these, almost any meeting or an organization which is involved in a public issue may be a target.

Disruptions may range from actual or threatened violence, from noisy demonstrations or picketing to attempts to take over the meeting and dictate decisions.

Whenever there is a possibility of disruption, there should be a plan to handle the problem. This may include arrangements for police protection, procedures for controlling admission to the meeting and, above all, mental preparation of the officials conducting the meeting.

They should be briefed on questions that may be asked and demands that may be made. They must be prepared for heckling and for attempts to keep them from speaking. They should have their answers ready and must be very careful not to over- or underreact. (See "The Radicals are Coming," *Public Relations Journal*, December 1976.)

CONVENTIONS

For all practical purposes, a convention is a series of meetings, so everything that has been said about meetings applies. Most conventions are held by associations. Generally, a convention lasts for more than one day, and is usually held at a location which is "out-of-town" for a substantial percentage of the participants. Recreation is often a part of the program, and wives or husbands of members are increasingly included in convention activities.

Purpose

All conventions usually have some common purposes. These are to report to members on the accomplishments of the organization, to discuss and solve problems, to learn things of benefit to the members, to get acquainted with and to renew friendships with other people in the same line of work, and, in most cases, to have some fun. In general terms, a convention is a "member relations" activity.

Planning

Convention planning is a time-consuming activity. It often starts months before the scheduled date and, in the case of large national conventions, there may be hundreds or thousands of man-hours involved. The principal items considered in convention planning are location, program, facilities, recreation, and administration.

Location

In choosing a location, it is necessary to consider distance and travel time, accessibility to public transportation, availability of suitable meeting rooms and hotel rooms, cost of rooms, eating facilities and prices, quality of the accommodations available, and the atmosphere of the location (a glamorous spot will always get better acceptance).

Program

While a convention is a series of meetings and while it is planned to get certain work done, it will not get satisfactory attendance unless there is a strong inducement. Location and recreation are incentives, but they do not suffice. The program itself must promise meaningful sessions on important problems and speakers with a real message.

Meeting Facilities

Convention facilities are simply meeting facilities multiplied several times. For every meeting on the program, there must be an adequate room with all the properties and tools needed for the particular sessions scheduled.

Recreation

A convention should allow some specific times for recreation. These may range from organized activities such as golf tournaments or sightseeing to such a simple thing as open time. The kind of recreation offered must be based on knowledge of the interests of the group in attendance plus a consideration of available facilities. Often it is advisable to offer alternatives at any given recreation period.

Administration

The first step in running a convention is getting people to attend. This requires announcements or invitations and reply cards with which members can indicate their intention. These cards are also often used to make hotel reservations.

If the location is remote from airports, it may be necessary to arrange buses to transport the participants to their hotels.

When people arrive at convention headquarters, they must be registered and supplied with programs, name cards, and any other materials they will need.

A message center should be provided so that people in attendance can be informed about telephone calls and telegrams. A blackboard at the convention registration desk is a good way to notify people about such messages. For a large convention, a press room should be provided.

OF FOOD AND DRINK

Breakfasts, luncheons, dinners, banquets, cocktail parties, and hospitality rooms are some of the most frequently used public relations events. Such eating or drinking activities may be in connection with a meeting or convention or they may be completely independent events which perform a public relations function on their own. Practically all these events are held in hotels. Arrangements must be made well in advance. The hotel officer with whom such arrangements are made may be called the catering manager, convention manager, or maitre d'hotel. The arrangements must be very complete and should be in writing. The agreement should state exactly what food, drink, services, and tips are included, the costs involved, and gurantees that must be fulfilled.

Breakfasts

At conventions, breakfasts are often scheduled to get the attendees up and going. In nonconvention situations, breakfasts are frequently used to reach people who cannot or will not come to a luncheon or dinner. They frequently include some sort of meeting, although this does not always happen at conventions.

One of the biggest problems with a breakfast is getting the food served. With a large group, it can take a great deal of time to process the different orders, and a uniform breakfast is nearly impossible because of the wide variations in individual breakfast tastes. There is also the problem created by people arriving late. One of the best solutions is the self-service buffet breakfast. With a good selection of fruits, juices, and cereals plus a hot table offering bacon, ham, sausage, hash, scrambled eggs, rolls, and toast, it is possible to please practically everyone, to handle late arrivals, and to get the meal served in a very brief time.

Fig. 30.1 A small PR event. Breakfast for American Women in Radio and Television.

Luncheons, Dinners, and Banquets

Luncheons are usually a little more formal than breakfasts. Normally there is at least one speaker and it is possible to start at a predetermined time. It is very important that the luncheon terminate on schedule. If a convention is involved, there is usually an afternoon schedule to meet. If the luncheon is a completely separate event, it still must end promptly so people can get back to work. The latest deadline that should be tolerated is 2 p.m., and 1:30 p.m. is far better.

If the luncheon is small, there may be only one table. If there are to be more than 20 or 30 people, it will be advisable to use a number of tables seating 8 or 10.

For a large luncheon where there is a speaker (or several speakers), there should be a head table occupied by the chairman, the speakers, and other dignitaries. This requires that all people in the room be able to see and hear the speakers. (See section on meetings for facilities needed.)

If people are assigned to tables, these must be conspicuously numbered in a logical order. If table assignments are not made, it is advisable to have a last-minute count of the number of people expected so that the number of places set will not be much greater than actual attendance. A room full of half-filled tables looks bad. The same room half-full of filled tables looks good. A fixed menu is standard for luncheons. Handling individual orders is practically impossible for a group that exceeds 20 people. If any special food item is placed on the menu at the request of the sponsor, it is imperative that it be checked with the chef. The latter should know exactly what he is expected to serve and how to prepare it. Many hotels and restaurants will prepare and serve a sample meal to the person who is arranging for a large meal. This provides a certain precheck of what will be served later.

Dinners are usually more formal than luncheons and banquets are the most formal of all "eating" events. Most of what has been said about luncheons applies equally to these evening meals with the exception that "breakup" time is not as critical. The end of the meal is the end of the day in most cases, although some "night owls" may want to seek some recreation afterwards. Menus are normally predetermined, although in some cases it is possible to offer a choice of entrees. Most hotels and restaurants demand a "guarantee" for any large group meal. This simply means that the sponsors must pay for a specific number of meals. If 200 steak dinners are guaranteed and only 180 are eaten, the sponsors pay for 200. Depending on the menu, it is possible to adjust the guarantee up or down until a reasonable time before the meal. This requires a very careful count of the number of people who are going to attend and a definite understanding of the deadline after which no adjustments can be made.

Cocktail Parties

A cocktail party may be the kickoff for a luncheon or dinner or it may be a complete event in itself. It may be a small affair in a hotel suite or a large party for thousands in a grand ballroom.

The key questions are: How many people will attend? What room will be used? What beverages will be offered? What food will be served? Who will provide the service? What will it cost? When will it start? When will it end? How will it be ended?

For a very small affair in a hotel room or suite, the arrangements may be as simple as obtaining a few bottles of liquor plus mixes, ice, and glasses. Such an event can be handled by a call to room service. For a large party, there must be complete planning with the catering department.

A preluncheon cocktail party should be planned as a half-hour affair. If it's scheduled before dinner, it can last an hour or more. If no dinner is scheduled but large quantities of hors d'oeuvres or a buffet are offered, the party may stretch to several hours if the budget can stand it.

A cocktail party really starts when the first guest arrives, hopefully on time. There is only one method to end a cocktail party — stop serving drinks. For a preluncheon or predinner party, a definite time should be determined and adhered to. If no other event is to follow the party, some representative of the sponsoring organization must decide when to close the bar. It is a good idea to announce when the bar will close a few minutes prior to closing.

Hospitality Suites

Many organizations participating in large conventions establish "hospitality" rooms or suites in hotels at or near convention headquarters. These are primarily "customer or dealer relations" activities. The room or suite is manned at all times when guests are expected, beverages are available and sometimes food. Not quite a cocktail party, but more festive than a pure business contact, the hospitality room provides a means for talking to customers and friends in a semiprivate location and in a rather relaxed atmosphere. A hospitality room operates without a definite schedule, and it usually is open every day of the convention.

PARADES

Most people enjoy parades; parades are certainly attention-getters. However, with our ever-increasing traffic congestion, it is becoming more and more difficult to stage a parade. Still, while the circus parade is almost extinct, there remain many small and a few large parades every year.

Purpose

The purpose of a parade is to publicize something. When circus parades were common, the purpose was to induce people to come to the circus. Now most parades are used to publicize some other event: a convention, a grand opening, an anniversary, the visit of a celebrity, a significant date, or any other occasion or event about which the community should be informed.

Planning and Control

A parade requires careful planning and firm control to be successful.

Fig. 30.2 A large PR event. A parade publicizing the Nihonmachi Cherry Blossom Festival at San Francisco's Japan Center. Photograph supplied by San Francisco Convention & Visitors Bureau.

Any weakness in either of these areas can result in a chaotic mass of people and/or vehicles which creates a negative attitude toward the parade and its sponsor.

Planning should begin far in advance. Control begins long before the parade starts and does not end until the parade route is clear and the last element is on its way home. The major points to consider are:

Timing   The date and hour must be suitable to the event and feasible so far as street usage is concerned. A parade blocks other traffic. The less traffic it blocks, the more likely it is to create a good impression.

Route   The route must be one which will enable many people to see the parade. Usually the goal is to use the main streets of the city but this is not necessarily the best selection. Comfort of viewers, control of side streets, and assembly and dispersal must be weighed too.

Permits   Any parade using public streets will require a permit from the police department involved. This should be procured as soon as tentative route, date, and time have been selected.

Traffic control   Arrangements must be made to keep nonparade elements out of the parade. This requires blocking all access to the parade route and clearing of the route before the parade starts. Usually this is done by the police department.

Participants   It must be clearly understood who is to be in the parade. Some groups may be wanted and may require an invitation. Others may wish to be in the parade yet not be wanted by the planners. This is a sticky problem but it must be solved well in advance.

Assembly area   Provision must be made for the various units to assemble near the beginning of the parade route. Side streets are generally used for this purpose. The number and size of the units must be known in order to provide enough space. Their place in the parade (march order) must be known so that each can get onto the route at the right time.

March order   An early determination must be made as to the order in which each unit will appear. This not only prevents confusion and disorder but also makes for a better balanced parade and avoids having all the bands in one group, etc.

March control   A definite timetable should be prepared. This should specify (to the minute) exactly when each unit should move onto the parade route from the assembly area. The rate of march should be considered carefully. If there are marching units, the speed will be about three miles per hour. If only motor vehicles are included, the speed may be greater but it should still be in the five-mile an hour range so that the spectators can see each unit. Because the best laid plans can fail, it is necessary to have someone at the assembly area hold each unit off the route until there is room for it.

Disabled vehicles and people   Tow trucks should be ready to remove disabled vehicles and provision should be made for ambulance service to take care of any people needing medical attention.

Dispersal area   At the end of the parade route, there must be an area into which all units can move, thus enabling following units to continue moving. Location should be assigned to every unit so that there will be no halting on the actual route of the parade which would bring the whole thing to a standstill.

Cleanup When the parade is over, the route must be cleaned up. Usually this is arranged with the sanitation department.

SPECIAL EVENTS

This category can include almost any stationary activity designed basically as a crowd attraction. Grand openings, anniversaries, festivals, special days, and special weeks are some of the more common special events. Most of them are staged as sales stimulators. Often they are sponsored by a group of organizations such as a merchants association, chamber of commerce, or a shopping center, although a single organization can be the sponsor. Almost everything in this section is applicable to such a situation but we will deal primarily with group action.

Purpose

Since most special events are aimed at promoting sales, the prime objective is to attract a lot of people to a definite location in the hope that they will stay and buy. The objective then is to create a festive atmosphere with numerous attractions that will appeal to a large number of actual and potential customers.

Participants

Since costs are involved, it is necessary to secure the participation of all organizations which will benefit. Allocation of costs must be equitable, a budget must be established and adhered to, and a prearranged plan for collection of funds must be made and activated.

Committees

Because many different organizations may be included and many activities undertaken, it will be necessary to have committees to approve plans, to handle finances, and to act on other problems of common interest. A committee is more a legislative body than an executive one. Its members are not likely to do much of the work but its approval and backing are vital.

Planning and Control

The amount of planning necessary is directly proportional to the magnitude of the special event. A one-day event for one store is much easier to arrange than a two-week festival in a shopping center or downtown business district. With one organization, it is fairly easy to get approvals, but when there are several participants working through committees, the red tape can be burdensome. In either situation, however, the plans must be as complete as possible. The more important items to consider are:

Schedule This must include everything that is to happen and it must be precise, not only to the day and hour but to the minute, so that everyone knows exactly what is to happen at any time.

Location While this is usually obvious from the start, it should be clearly understood just where the boundaries are. Is the entire downtown area involved or just certain streets? Does it include just a specific area or can anyone get in the act?

Traffic and parking Because a special event is designed to attract people to a certain location, it will undoubtedly create problems of vehicular traffic, parking, and also pedestrian traffic. These problems must be solved before they become critical.

Police cooperation Early contact should be made with the police department. Permits may not always be required but extra policemen may be needed to handle the crowds. At the very least, the police department should know that normal traffic patterns may be disrupted.

Decorations and lighting If decorations or special lighting are desired, an early decision must be reached as to what they will be, how they will be put up, and who will pay for them. This avoids disagreements and insures they will be available on time.

Minor events There may be numerous smaller events within a large special event. These can include opening and closing ceremonies, speches, concerts, stunts, parades, choral performances, circus-type acts, skits, pageants, contests, prize drawings, etc. All must be planned and scheduled in advance.

Safety precautions A careful precheck to eliminate hazards is a must. Provisions should be made for first aid and the location of first-aid stations should be known to all participating organizations.

OPEN HOUSES AND PLANT TOURS

An open house or plant tour is a special event designed to show the facilities with which it works. Thus, a factory might show how it turns steel and wood into garden tools. A newspaper might show how it gathers news and prints the paper. A hotel might show the kitchens, dining rooms, meeting rooms, and sleeping rooms with which it serves the public.

Most open houses and plant tours are held on a specific day but many organizations operate these events every day and consider the event as a continuing activity of public relations.

Purpose

The basic purpose of an open house or plant tour is to improve relations with the community but such an event can also be of great interest to every other public, especially to employees and their families.

Principles

An open house or plant tour should give visitors a clear understanding of what they have seen and a good impression of the organization.

Clear understanding depends on a careful routing of the tour and a clear explanation of what is being seen. In general, the route should follow the normal flow of work, for example, from raw material to finished product. Explaining what goes on requires the use of signs and a carefully prepared script for the employees who serve as guides. (Many an expert cannot explain what he does.)

A good impression of the organization depends on enthusiastic efforts by all employees. It requires careful preparation, adequate rehearsal, and a large amount of checking and rechecking. The tour should not be too long because people can easily get tired. It should be lively so visitors will not get bored and it should keep moving so they will not get annoyed.

Planning and Control

As with every public relations event, planning and control are the factors that make for success. Points to be included are:

Timing The date and hour must be convenient for both the organization and for visitors.

Guests For a one-time event, invitations are sent to all whose presence is desired, usually about a month in advance. If the tour is a continuing event, the public must be notified by use of signs or inclusion of the invitation in advertising and publicity.

Traffic and parking   Arrangements must be made for handling vehicular traffic and parking and for handling pedestrians.

Reception   Guests must be met and greeted by a representative of the organization. If it is a one-time event, the top executives should be involved.

Cloakrooms and restrooms   These should be easy to reach and conspicuously identified.

Safety precautions   Great care must be taken to physically guard or barricade hazardous equipment and to be sure that walkways and stairways are safe, well-defined, and well-lighted.

First aid   Personnel and equipment must be ready in case of accident or illness of any visitor or employee.

Route marking   There must be a clearly marked route so that, even if people lose their guides, they will be able to get back on course.

Guides   To lead visitors through the tour, there should be guides who know the route and the story that the open house or tour is meant to convey. In some cases the visitors will move in groups with a guide. In others, it may be feasible to use nonmoving guides who will help keep the visitors moving along.

Explanations   Signs should be provided at all key points or departments. When anything is being done, the person doing it should explain his actions. (His explanation must be carefully prepared so that it will be understandable. If it is not written or memorized, he should be thoroughly coached and rehearsed.)

Emergencies   All employees should be informed as to what to do and whom to notify in case of an emergency.

Housekeeping   It should be obvious but no harm will be done by emphasizing that the entire premises must be in good repair and immaculate.

Dress   Employees should be as clean and as well-dressed as their duties permit. The clothing should be appropriate to the work done, clean and neat.

Handouts   A booklet or leaflet illustrating the tour is very desirable. If the tour is long, a route map will be most helpful.

Suggested Readings

Bradford, Leland P. *Making Meetings Work*. San Diego, California: University Association, 1976.

Leibert, Edwin R., and Sheldon, Bernice E. *Handbook of Special Events.* Washington, D.C.: Taft, 1977.

Maude, Barry. *Managing Meetings.* New York: Halsted, 1975.

DEMONSTRATIONS

In recent years, the word "demonstration" has come to mean a number of people carrying placards and protesting something. Sometimes the number may be only a handful; at other times scores of thousands may gather. Occasionally these demonstrations erupt into violence. Their effect on public opinion is questionable. They do often receive much publicity. Undoubtedly some of them harden public opinion and it is doubtful whether they persuade large numbers of the uncommitted.

When students at San Jose State University bought a new car and buried it as a protest against automobile-caused air pollution, they received a large amount of publicity. Yet, the most frequently heard comment was: "I'll bet most of those demonstrators arrived in an automobile carrying one passenger." When groups of demonstrators demanding concern for the environment leave their meeting place covered with paper, garbage, and bottles or cans, they destroy any possible good their demonstration might do.

On the other hand, when a girl in Florida sought to protest against pollution of the beaches, she flushed dye and identifiable pieces of paper through a hotel toilet. This "demonstration" proved that the local sewage was being dumped into the ocean.

A good public relations demonstration shows and proves something. Thus, a lumber company may have a "demonstration" tree farm to show how it replaces the trees it cuts. A coal mine may have a "demonstration" of how it restores "mined out" areas to their original condition. An oil company in Wyoming has an almost perfect demonstration — a lake teeming with fish and wildfoul and fed with carefully treated wastewaters from its refinery.

CONTESTS

Contests are common in the field of marketing where their purpose is to stimulate sales. They are also used in public relations but to a lesser extent. Here the purpose is to build favorable public opinion for the sponsoring organization or to encourage interest in a project the sponsor is supporting.

One of the best-known contests in the United States is the annual Pillsbury Bake-Off. Originated as an event to promote sales of flour, the Bake-Off has become a national institution which receives a large amount of publicity and creates much goodwill for Pillsbury in addition to stimulating sales of Pillsbury products.

Another well-known national contest is that sponsored by Freedoms Foundation of Valley Forge, Pennsylvania. It offers prizes for essays on patriotic subjects. The Sons of the American Revolution sponsor oratorical contests on patriotic subjects and similar contests are conducted by many fraternal and public service groups.

The range of subject matter for contests is limited only by the ingenuity of those who sponsor them. Here are a few examples:

automotive trouble-shooting contests sponsored by Plymouth,
4-H livestock shows sponsored by many supporters,
the Miss America and Miss Universe contests,
state and local beauty contests,
"mutt" dog contests,
"pancake" races.

The list could go on for pages, but this will give a hint as to the possibilities.

For large contests, it is possible to secure the services of professional contest-management firms. These organizations can handle all phases of the work. They can plan the contest, set up the rules, secure prizes, perform the judging, and even deliver the prizes. Smaller contests are usually handled by the organization sponsoring them. When this is done, it is important to follow these rules: (1) Every would-be contestant must understand the objective and know exactly what is to be judged, (2) eligibility and rules must be clearly understood, (3) the judges and judging procedures must be absolutely impartial.

AWARDS

Awards can be very useful in public relations. They appeal to that deep-rooted desire for recognition in everyone. Awards can result in much favorable publicity for the sponsor and, more important, they can stimulate others to try for similar recognition. Awards can be periodic or they can be made whenever recognition and reward are justified.

Kinds of Awards

An award must be appropriate to the organization and to the recipient, and it must be of respectable quality. A cheap or trivial award will do more harm than good. The company that gives a dozen roses as a 25th anniversary present to employees is not building good employee relations. The company that gave employees their choice of a can of tuna or a can of dog food for Christmas got bad publicity and bad employee reaction. (While this latter case was not truly an "award," it illustrates the point.) Appropriate awards may be:

> testimonial luncheons or dinners,
> scrolls or plaques,
> medals,
> watches,
> trophies,
> money,
> lapel buttons,
> trips,
> rings,
> scholarships,
> silverware.

Granting Awards

All who are eligible for awards must know the rules or requirements. If judging is involved, it must be as impartial as in any contest.

Presenting Awards

Any award should be presented by the highest ranking official of the organization sponsoring the award. It should be presented before as many people as possible and it should receive all the publicity possible. Half the value of any award is the recognition that goes with it.

Awards should be presented with dignity and ceremony. A horrible example of how *not* to do it is the case of a retail chain which sent an unsigned mimeographed letter to a store manager. It notified him that having completed 40 years of service, he was now entitled to a watch — or its equivalent in cash.

SPONSORED ACTIVITIES

Considerable goodwill can be earned through sponsoring activities of public interest. The sponsorship can be of an established organization or of activities created by the sponsor.

Established Organizations

This category includes such groups as Junior Achievement, 4-H clubs, Little League baseball, school bands, science clubs, and many others that perform a valuable public service but need financial or managerial support.

Created Organizations

A company baseball or bowling team is a first thought in this area but the possibilities go far beyond this narrow horizon. Worthwhile organizations that fill a public need can be created and supported by any willing organization.

STUNTS

Stunts loom large in the minds of many, who often think of them as a major part of public relations. This, of course, is an extremely erroneous impression; yet, stunts are a minor tool of PR. Their chief usage is to obtain publicity — to make a person or organization or place known. Thus, a "human fly" climbing the side of a building may result in published photos of the "human fly" *and* the building. A man searching for a needle in a haystack at a grand opening will attract additional attention and draw people to the location. A treasure hunt can produce a large amount of publicity throughout a community.

In considering stunts it is necessary to maintain perspective and to avoid placing too much value on them. In most cases the only value is public awareness of the stunt itself.

A POINT TO REMEMBER

If you worry enough before the event, you will not have to worry afterwards.

501

EXERCISES

1. What public relations events have you seen or attended?
   (a) What was the purpose?
   (b) Was it successful?
   (c) How would you have improved it?

Case Problem

Prepare a plan for the centennial celebration of a university. Include all activities, personnel to be invited, exhibits, displays, literature, publicity, and anything else that will help make the centennial a success and, by so doing, increase public support for the university.

Dialogue V

Dialogue with Mr. Jon B. Riffel, Vice-President Public Relations, Southern California Gas Company, former president of the Public Relations Society of America.

> This dialogue deals with the energy crisis. Both President Carter and Mr. Riffel believe that it will be acute in the early 1980s. Demands for energy conflict with demands for protecting the environment, and demands for jobs bear upon both of these factors. This dialogue, along with those with Mr. Henning and Mr. McCloskey, gives a preview of the climate in which public relations programs of the near future will have to operate.

Q. Why did the United States get into an energy crisis?

A. During the last decade or two the government kept natural gas prices artifically low; therefore we greatly increased our use of this energy without any public appreciation of the fact that there were limits to our supplies.

Q. Didn't anyone foresee the shortage?

A. Yes, a few people did but they weren't heeded. Even the big producers of energy were caught napping. They failed to prepare for the situation that now confronts us.

Q. How important is natural gas in the energy supply of the United States?

A. Aside from the energy used in transportation, almost half of our total energy comes from natural gas. In addition to its use as fuel, natural gas has many uses as a raw material in manufacturing.

Q. Can't we use other fossil fuels in place of natural gas — coal, for example?

A. Not very easily. In California, for example, there are few facilities for distribution or burning of coal. In many other places the situation is similar. We just can't switch from gas to coal — or even fuel oil. Think of the millions of household furnaces which would have to be replaced. Think of the problem of storing coal in a house with no basement.

Q. What about nuclear power?

A. That has been a disappointment. Many people expected that nuclear power would by now be able to provide a large part of our energy but it isn't doing so — primarily because of "activist" groups and their scare tactics. The problems have proved to be much bigger than anyone anticipated.

Q. Some people are saying that we must face a permanent reduction in energy consumption; that future generations will have a lower standard of living.

A. I don't believe that. I'll grant that we have a real problem but I am confident that American technology *can* develop enough energy if we are given a chance to do so.

Q. How can we do it?

A. We really have two energy problems — long-term and short-term. During the twenty-first century, we may exhaust a large part of the fuels on which we have traditionally relied. To replace them will require development of some revolutionary ideas. This we can do if we can squeeze through the remaining years of this century.

Q. How can we squeeze through?

A. We'll have to speed up the development of conventional energy supplies. We need to hasten the production and use of liquefied natural gas. And we will need intelligent conservation.

Q. Can't solar power fill the gap?

A. It won't be a major factor in the twentieth century. Now it is really just a supplement. It can heat houses and swimming pools, but it will not be in general use as a major energy source for a long time.

Q. How about geothermal and tidal power?

A. Again, these are esoterics with potential for the next century, not solutions for this one.

Q. Where else can be find energy in large quantities?

A. The source that is most interesting to me is the utilization of hydrogen from sea water. There has been some encouraging progress, and if it succeeds it will provide an almost perfect solution. The supply is practically infinite, and hydrogen could be distributed through existing pipelines and used in existing equipment.

Q. What are the prospects for solving both the short-term and long-term problems?
A. We can solve both if government agencies will let us, and if the no-growth partisans will ease up on their opposition to development of energy sources. If we aren't allowed to go ahead, we could have a disaster in the near future.
Q. Developing new energy sources will take enormous sums of money. Where is it coming from?
A. That is a most difficult problem. It should come from the companies which are now producing energy, but capital requirements — thanks largely to inflation — are rapidly becoming too big for individual companies to handle.
Q. The big oil companies would seem to be logical developers of new energy supplies, but there has been a lot of public outcry against their entry into new fields and even attempts to break them up into smaller units.
A. The actions of politicians in this situation have been absolutely apalling. The hostility to the oil companies is probably largely due to the increases in the price of their products, but the price of oil and gasoline is largely dictated by the Organization of Petroleum Exporting Countries. They raise the price and the public blames the U.S. companies. Politicians, who actually know better, use the oil companies as convenient whipping boys. It's a disgusting example of political charlatanism.
Q. What would be the effect of fragmenting energy producers?
A. It would greatly handicap, or even prevent, a solution to the energy problem. This is a large scale operation. It can't be solved by little organizations. We're dealing with billions of barrels of oil, billions of tons of coal, and billions of cubic feet of natural gas. We're dealing with the homes and jobs of over 200 million people. Let me give you an example of how fragmentation of resources works.

A few years ago Ecuador was the largest shipper of bananas to the United States. Now it has dropped to fifth place because the American consumer wants a different kind of banana, the kind produced in Central America. That same kind of banana will grow in Ecuador, but Ecuador isn't producing them. The reason is that a few years ago the government broke up the big banana plantations and parcelled them out to small farmers. These small farmers don't have the capital necessary to replant their groves to the preferred kind of banana so they go on with an inferior banana and a restricted market. What seemed to be a socially desirable action has turned out to be an economic disaster for the people it was intended to help.

Q. What is the role of public relations in the energy crisis?

A. Next to the development of new energy supplies, it is the key to the whole problem. We in public relations must convince the public that the problem of energy is one of the most important, if not *the* most important, problems of their lifetimes. We must make them aware of the critical time span in which solutions must be found. The early 1980s are the period during which the short-term energy crunch will be most painful. It will vary somewhat in different sections of the country, but if the public can be persuaded to take this seriously and if we can get public support for the measures necessary to get through the next few years, we should be able to develop the long-term solutions for the twenty-first century.

Q. How can we accomplish this?

A. I wish I had an easy answer. We are using every proven technique of public relations to try to convince the public that the situation is critical; that we are doing our best to provide them with the energy they need and to solicit their support as we struggle through these next few years. Practically all of our public relations activity at Southern California Gas Company is devoted to that purpose. This is a horrendous problem, but I hope and believe that we can do it — if we are permitted to.

Bibliography

Alexander, Yonah, and Finger, Seymour M. (Eds.) *Terrorism: Interdisciplinary Perspectives.* New York: John Jay Press, 1977.

Allen, Ronald B., and McKerrow, Ray. *The Pragmatics of Public Communication.* Columbus, Ohio: Merrill, 1977.

Allport, G.W., and Postman, L. *The Psychology of Rumor.* New York: Russell & Russell, 1947.

Anderson and Anderson (Eds.). *An Introduction to Projection Techniques.* Englewood Cliffs, N.J.: Prentice-Hall, 1951.

Anscher, Melvin (Ed.) *Managing the Socially Responsible Corporation.* New York: Macmillan, 1974.

Ardrey, R. *African Genesis.* New York: Atheneum, 1961.

Ardrey, R. *The Territorial Imperative.* New York: Atheneum, 1966.

Ardrey, R. *The Social Contract.* New York: Atheneum, 1970.

Asante, Malefi K., and Frye, Jerry K. *Contemporary Public Communications.* New York: Harper & Row, 1977.

Barbera, D.A. *Art of Listening.* Springfield, Ill.: C.C. Thomas, 1965.

Barnes, L.B. *Organizational Systems and Engineering Groups.* Boston, Mass.: Div. of Res. Harvard Business School, 1960.

Barrett, L. *The Treasure of Our Tongue.* New York: Alfred A. Knopf, 1962.

Bell, D. *Toward The Year 2000.* Boston, Mass.: Beacon Press, 1969.

Benje, Eugene J. *Elements of Modern Management.* New York: American Management Association, 1976.

Berlo, D.K., Lemert, J.B., and Mertz, R. "Dimensions for Evaluating the Acceptability of Message Sources," *Public Opinion Quarterly,* Winter 1969-70.

Bernays, E.L. *Public Relations.* Norman, Okla.: University of Oklahoma Press, 1952.

Blum, Milton L. *Psychology & Consumer Affairs.* New York: Harper & Row, 1977.

Blumenthal, Lassor A. *The Art of Letter Writing.* New York: Grosset & Dunlap, 1976.

Bolles, Richard H. *What Color is Your Parachute?* Berkeley, Cal.: Ten Speed Press, 1976.

Boorstin, Daniel J. *The Americans.* New York: Random House, 1974.

Booth, A. "Personal Influence Networks and Participation in Professional Association Activities," *Public Opinion Quarterly,* Winter 1969-70.

Bortner, Doyle M. *Public Relations for Schools.* Cambridge, Mass.: Schenkman, 1972.

Bradford, Leland P. *Making Meetings Work.* San Diego, Cal.: University Association, 1976.

Bradley, J.F. *Role of Trade Associations and Professional Business Societies in America.* University Park: Pennsylvania State University Press, 1965.

Burack, Elmer, and Smith, Robert D. *Personnel Management.* St. Paul, Minn.: West Publications, 1977.

Cantrill, Hadley. *Gauging Public Opinion.* Princeton, N.J.: Princeton University Press, 1972.

Carlson, Robert O. (Ed.) *Communication and Public Opinion.* New York: Praeger, 1975.

Carmel, J.H. *Exhibition Techniques.* New York: Van Nostrand Reinhold, 1962.

Carson, R. *Silent Spring.* Boston: Houghton Mifflin, 1962.

Chase, S. *American Credos.* New York: Harper & Row, 1975.

Churchman, C.W. *The Systems Approach.* New York: Delacorte, 1969.

Colley, R.H. *Defining Advertising Goals for Measured Advertising Results.* New York: Association of National Advertisers, 1961.

Commager, Henry S. et al. *American Heritage and Horizons.* Memphis, Tenn.: Memphis State University Press, 1977.

Commager, Henry S. *The Empire of Reason.* New York: Doubleday, 1977.

Costello, T., and Zalkind, S. *Psychology in Administration.* Englewood Cliffs, N.J.: Prentice-Hall, 1963.

Creel, G. *How We Advertised America.* New York: Harper & Bros., 1920.

Darrow, Ralph C. *House Journal Editing.* Danville, Ill.: Interstate, 1974.

Davidson, P.G. *Propaganda and the American Revolution.* Chapel Hill: University of North Carolina Press, 1941.

de Bell, G. (Ed.) *The Environmental Handbook.* New York: Ballantine Books, 1969.

De Lozier, M. Wayne. *The Marketing Communication Process.* New York: McGraw-Hill, 1976.

De Lozier, M. Wayne. *Consumer Behavior Dynamics.* Columbus, Ohio: Merrill, 1977.

Detwiler, R.M. "PR in the Marketing Mix," *Public Relations Journal,* October, 1970, p. 31.

Dichter, E. *Handbook of Consumer Motivation.* New York: McGraw-Hill, 1964.

Dirksen, Charles J., and Kroeger, Arthur. *Advertising: Principles and Problems.* Homewood, Ill.: Irwin, 1973.

Dolbeare, K.M., and Hammond, P.E. *"Public Opinion and the Supreme Court,"* *Public Opinion Quarterly,* Summer 1968.

Drucker, P.F. *The Age of Discontinuity.* New York: Harper & Row, 1968.

Dunstan, M.J., and Garlan, P.W. *Worlds in the Making.* Englewood Ciffs, N.J.: Prentice-Hall, 1970.

Editorial Staff: Prentice-Hall. *How to Write a Good Letter.* Englewood Cliffs, N.J.: Prentice-Hall, 1967.

Ehrlich, P.R. *The Population Bomb.* New York: Ballantine Books, 1968.

Ehrlich, Paul R., and Ehrlich, Anne H. *The End of Affluence.* New York: Ballantine, 1974.

Ember, C., and Ember, M. *Anthropology.* Englewood Cliffs, N.J.: Prentice-Hall, 1977.

Evans, Garth, and McDowell, John (Eds.) *Essays in Semantics.* Oxford: Oxford University Press, 1976.

Fabun, D. (Ed.) *The Dynamics of Change.* Englewood Cliffs, N.J.: Prentice-Hall, 1969.

Fast, J. *Body Language.* New York: Evans, 1970.

Fees, Charges and Overhead in the Practice of Public Relations. New York: Public Relations Society of America, 1972.

Feinberg, Samuel. *Management's Challenge – The People Problem.* New York: Fairchild, 1976.

Fillmore, Charles J., and Langendoen, D. *Studies in Linguistic Semantics.* New York: Irvington, 1977.

Flesch, R. *How to Write, Speak and Think More Effectively.* New York: Harper & Row, 1964.

Flesch, R. *Say What You Mean.* New York: Harper & Row, 1972.

Flesch, R. *The Art of Readable Writing.* New York: Harper & Row, 1974.

Glenn, N.D., and Simmons, J.L. "Are Regional Cultural Differences Diminishing?" *Public Opinion Quarterly,* Summer 1967.

Gluck, Felix (Ed.) *Modern Publicity.* New York: Viking, 1972.

Greenwood, Davydd, and Stini, William A. *Nature, Culture and Human History.* New York: Harper & Row, 1977.

Hammer, W. Clay, and Schmidt, Frank L. (Eds.) *Contemporary Problems in Personnel.* Chicago: St. Clair, 1977.

Hardesty, Donald L. *Ecological Anthropology.* New York: Wiley, 1977.

Harlow, R.F. *Public Relations and the Social Sciences.* New York: Harper Bros., 1957.

Harlow, R.V. *Samuel Adams, Promoter of the Revolution.* New York: Henry Holt, 1923.

Hartman, E.L.; Isaacson, H. Lawrence; and Jurgell, Cynthia M. "Public Reaction to Public Opinion Surveying," *Public Opinion Quarterly*, Summer 1968.

Hayakawa, S.I. *Through the Communication Barrier.* New York: Harper & Row, 1978.

Hayett, W. *Display and Exhibit Handbook.* New York: Van Nostrand Reinhold, 1967.

Heise, David R. (Ed.) *Sociological Methodology.* San Francisco, Cal.: Jossey-Bass, 1977.

Hennesey, B.C. *Public Opinion.* Belmont, Calif.: Wadsworth, 1965.

Hersey, Paul, and Blanchard, Ken. *Management of Organizational Behavior.* Englewood Cliffs, N.J.: Prentice-Hall, 1977.

Herzberg, F. *The Motivation to Work.* New York: Wiley, 1959.

Herzberg, F. *Work and The Nature of Man.* Cleveland, Ohio: World, 1966.

Hiebert, R.E. *Courtier To The Crowd.* Ames, Iowa: Iowa State University Press, 1966.

Hiebert, Ray Eldon; Ungarait, Donald; and Bohn, Thomas. *Mass Media – An Introduction to Modern Communications.* New York: McKay, 1974.

Hill & Knowlton Executives. *Critical Issues in Public Relations.* New York: Parker, 1976.

Hirsch, Fred. *Social Limits to Growth.* Cambridge, Mass.: Harvard University Press, 1976.

Hyman, H. *Political Socialization.* New York: Free Press of Glencoe, 1959.

Josephson, M. *The Robber Barons.* New York: Harcourt Brace, 1934.

Katz, Elihu, and Lazarsfeld, Paul F. *Personal Influence.* New York: Free Press, 1964.

Klein, Ted, and Danzig, Fred. *Making the Media Work for You.* New York: Macmillan, 1976.

Klein, Walter J. *The Sponsored Film.* New York: Hastings House, 1976.

Kleppner, Otto, and Greyser, Stephen. *Advertising Procedure.* Englewood Cliffs, N.J.: Prentice-Hall, 1973.

Kobre, Sidney. *Successful Public Relations for Colleges and Universities.* New York: Hastings, 1974.

Kornhauser, A.; Sheppard, H.; and Mayer, A. *When Labor Votes.* New York: University Press, 1956.

Kristol, Irving, and Weaver, Paul H. *Americans 1976.* Lexington, Mass.: Lexington Press, 1976.

Krock, A. *The Consent of the Governed.* Boston, Mass.: Little, Brown, 1971.

Ladd, B. *Crisis in Credibility.* New York: New American Library, 1968.

Latshaw, William A. "Target Group Research," *Public Relations Journal*, November 1977.

Lawrence, P.R., and Seiler, J.A. *Organizational Behavior and Administration.* Homewood, Ill.: Irwin, 1965.

Leibert, Edwin R., and Sheldon, Bernice E. *Handbook of Special Events.* Washington, D.C.: Taft, 1977.

Lendt, David (Ed.) *The Publicity Process.* Ames, Iowa: Iowa State University Press, 1975.

Lerbinger, Otto. *Designs for Persuasive Communication.* Englewood Cliffs, N.J.: Prentice-Hall, 1972.

Lesly, Philip. *The People Factor.* Homewood, Ill.: Dow-Jones, Irwin, 1974.

Lippman, W. *Public Opinion.* New York: Macmillan, 1965.

Mambert, W.A. *Elements of Effective Communication.* Washington, D.C.: Acropolis, 1971.

Mambert, W.A. *Effective Presentation.* Somerset, N.J.: Wiley Interscience, 1976.

Mann, Charles. *Editing for Industry.* New York: International Publication Services, 1975.

Maslow, A.H. *Motivation and Personality.* New York: Harper & Row, 1954.

Maslow, A.H. (Ed.) *New Knowledge in Human Values.* New York: Harper & Row, 1959.

Maslow, A.H. *Toward A Psychology of Being.* New York: Van Nostrand Reinhold, 1968.

Mati, Paul. *How to Manage by Objectives.* New York: Wiley, 1975.

Maude, Barry. *Managing Meetings.* New York: Halsted, 1975.

Mauger, E.M. *Modern Display Techniques.* New York: Fairchild, 1964.

McGregor, D. *The Human Side of Enterprise.* New York: McGraw-Hill, 1960.

McGuire, E. Patrick. *The Consumer Affairs Department.* New York: Conference Board, 1973.

McGuire, Jerry. *How to Write, Direct and Produce Effective Business Films.* Blue Ridge Summit, Penna.: Tab Books, 1977.

McLuhan, M. *Understanding Media: The Extension of Man.* New York: McGraw-Hill, 1965.

Meadows, Donella H. et al. *The Limits to Growth.* New York: Potomac, 1974.

Meyer, Philip. *Precision Journalism.* Bloomington, Ind.: Indiana University Press, 1975.

Miller, George A. *Communication, Language and Meaning.* New York: Basic, 1977.

Miller, J.C. *Sam Adams, Pioneer in Propaganda.* Palo Alto, Calif.: Stanford University Press, 1960.

Mock, J.R., and Larson, C. *Words That Won The War.* Princeton, N.J.: Princeton University Press, 1939.

Morgan, C.L. *Introduction to Psychology.* New York: McGraw-Hill, 1961.

Morris, D. *The Naked Ape.* New York: McGraw-Hill, 1967.

Morris, D. *The Human Zoo.* New York: McGraw-Hill, 1969.

Newman, Edwin. *Strictly Speaking.* Indianapolis, Ind.: Bobbs-Merrill, 1974.

Newman, Edwin. *A Civil Tongue.* Indianapolis, Ind.: Bobbs-Merrill, 1976.

O'Brien, Richard. *Publicity: How to Get It.* New York: Harper & Row, 1977.

Oskamp, S. *Attitudes and Opinions.* Englewood Cliffs, N.J.: Prentice-Hall, 1977.

Packard, V. *The Status Seekers.* New York: McKay, 1959.

Pei, M. *The Story of the English Language.* New York: Simon and Schuster, 1972.

Pickens, J. et al. *Without Bias – A Guidebook for Nondiscriminatory Communication.* San Francisco, Cal.: IABC, 1977.

Pigors, P., and Myers, C.A. *Personnel Administration.* New York: McGraw-Hill, 1977.

Pomper, G. "Ethnic and Group Voting in Nonpartisan Municipal Elections," *Public Opinion Quarterly,* Spring 1966.

Public Relations and Public Relations Counselling. New York: Public Relations Society of America, 1966.

Regier, C.C. *The Era of the Muckrakers.* Chapel Hill: University of North Carolina Press, 1932.

Reich, C.A. *The Greening of America.* New York: Random House, 1970.

Reynolds, Fred D., and Wells, William D. *Consumer Behavior.* New York: McGraw-Hill, 1977.

Roalman, Arthur (Ed.) *Investor Relations Handbook.* New York: Amocom, 1974.

Robinson, E.J. *Communication and Public Relations.* Columbus, Ohio: Merrill, 1966.

Robinson, E.J. *Public Relations and Survey Research.* New York: Appleton-Century-Crofts, 1969.

Robinson, J.P. "Public Reaction to Political Protest, Chicago, 1968," *Public Opinion Quarterly,* Spring 1970.

Rogers, Everett M., and Rekha, Agarwala. *Communications in Organizations.* New York: Free Press, 1976.

Russell, John M. *Give and Take.* New York: Teachers College Press, 1977.

Sandage, Charles H., and Fryburger, Vernon. *Advertising: Theory and Practice.* Homewood, Ill.: Irwin, 1975.

Schumacher, E.F. *Small Is Beautiful.* New York: Harper & Row, 1973.

Selltiz, Claire; Wrightsman, L.S.; and Cook, S.W. *Research Methods in Social Relations.* New York: Holt, Rinehart & Winston, 1976.

Sethi, S. Prakash. *Advocacy Advertising and Large Corporations.* Lexington, Mass.: Heath, 1977.

Sherif, Carolyn W. *Attitude, Ego Involvement and Change.* Westport, Conn.: Greenwood, 1976.

Sherif, C.W., and Jackman, N.R. "Judgment of Truth by Participants in Collective Controversy," *Public Opinion Quarterly,* Summer 1966.

Silberman, C.E. *Crisis in the Classroom.* New York: Random House, 1970.

Simons, Herbert W. *Persuasion, Understanding, Practice and Analysis.* Reading, Mass.: Addison-Wesley, 1976.

Sonquist, John A., and Dunkelberg, William C. *Survey and Opinion Research.* Englewood Cliffs, N.J.: Prentice-Hall, 1977.

Staff. *AP Stylebook and Libel Manual.* New York: AP Newsfeatures, 1977.

Staff. *UPI Stylebook.* New York: United Press International, 1977.

Steinbeck, J., and others. *America and Americans.* New York: Viking, 1966.

Steinberg, Charles S. *The Creation of Consent.* New York: Hastings, 1975.

Stephan, Frederick F., and McCarthy, Philip J. *Sampling Opinion.* Westport, Conn.: Greenwood, 1974.

Stenvenson, William. *A Man Called Intrepid.* New York: Harcourt, 1976.

Stridsburg, Albert. *Controversy Advertising.* New York: Hastings House, 1977.

Strumpel, Burkhard (Ed.) *Economic Means for Human Needs.* Ann Arbor, Mich.: University of Michigan Press, 1975.

Strunk, W., and White, E.B. *The Elements of Style.* New York: Macmillan, 1972.

Taft, J.R. *Understanding Foundations; Dimensions in Fund Raising.* New York: McGraw-Hill, 1967.

Toffler, A. *Future Shock.* New York: Random House, 1970.

Wagner, R.V., and Sherwood, J.J. *The Study of Attitude Change.* Belmont, Calif.: Brooks/Cole, 1969.

Wales, La Rae H. *A Practical Guide to Newsletter Editing and Design.* Ames, Iowa: Iowa State University Press, 1976.

Walker, Albert D. *Status and Trends of Public Relations Education.* College Park, Md.: Foundation for PR Research and Education, 1975.

Weiner, Richard. *Professionals' Guide to Publicity.* New York: Weiner, 1975.

White, Jan. *Editing by Design.* Ann Arbor, Mich.: Bowker, 1974.

White, T.H. *The Making of the President 1964.* New York: Atheneum, 1965.

White, W.J. "An Index for Determining The Relative Importance of Information Sources," *Public Opinion Quarterly,* Winter 1969-70.

Wiesen, Jeremy L. *Regulating Transactions in Securities.* St. Paul, Minn.: West, 1975.

Selected Bibliography

BOOKS ON PUBLIC RELATIONS

Adams, A.B. *Handbook of Practical Public Relations.* New York: Crowell, 1965.

Bernays, E.L. *Crystallizing Public Opinion.* New York: Liveright, 1961.

Bishop, Robert L. *Public Relations: A Comprehensive Bibliography.* (Published annually as a supplement of *Public Relations Review.*)

Budd, J.F. *Executives Primer on Public Relations.* Philadelphia, Penn.: Chilton, 1969.

Canfield, B.R., and Moore, H. Frazier. *Public Relations.* Homewood, Ill.: Irwin, 1977.

Center, Allen H. *Public Relations Practice-Case Studies.* Englewood Cliffs, N.J.: Prentice-Hall, 1975.

Cutlip, Scott M., and Center, Allen H. *Effective Public Relations.* Englewood Cliffs, N.J.: Prentice-Hall, 1978.

Darrow, R.W., and others. *Public Relations Handbook.* Chicago, Ill.: Dartnell, 1967.

Farley, W.E. *Practical Public Relations for the Businessman.* New York: Fell, 1968.

Lesly, P. (Ed.) *Lesly's Public Relations Handbook.* Englewood Cliffs, N.J.: Prentice-Hall, 1971.

Lesly, Philip. *The People Factor.* Homewood, Ill.: Dow-Jones, Irwin, 1974.

Newsom, Doug, and Scott, Alan. *This is PR.* Belmont, Cal.: Wadsworth, 1976.

Roalman, A.R. *Profitable Public Relations.* Homewood, Ill.: Irwin, 1968.

Ross, Robert D. *The Management of Public Relations.* Somerset, N.J.: Wiley Interscience, 1977.

Simon, M.J. *Public Relations Law.* New York: Appleton-Century-Crofts, 1969.

Simon, R. (Ed.) *Perspectives in Public Relations.* Norman, Okla.: University of Oklahoma, 1965.

Simon, Raymond. *Public Relations: Concepts and Practice.* Columbus, Ohio: Grid, 1976.

Stephenson, H. (Ed.) *Handbook of Public Relations.* New York: McGraw-Hill, 1971.

Zollo, B. *Dollars and Sense of Public Relations.* New York: McGraw-Hill, 1967.

INFORMATION SOURCE BOOKS

Ayer Directory of Publications (a listing of daily and weekly newspapers and consumer, business, technical, trade and farm magazines). Ayer Press, West Washington Square, Philadelphia, Penn., 19106.

Bacon's Publicity Checker (a listing of media and media contacts for publicity). Bacon's Publishing Co., 14 E. Jackson Blvd., Chicago, Ill. 60604.

Broadcasting Yearbook (a listing of TV and Radio stations and their key personnel). Broadcasting, 1735 De Sales Street, Washington, D.C. 20036.

Selected Bibliography

Congressional Staff Directory (a listing of personnel in offices of members of Congress). P.O. Box 62, Mount Vernon, Va. 22121.

Contacts (a newsletter listing items that editors want for publication). Larimi Communications Associates, 151 East 50th St., New York, N.Y. 10022.

Editor and Publisher International Yearbook (a listing of newspapers and their key personnel). Editor and Publisher Co., 850 Third Ave., New York, N.Y. 10022.

Educators Guide to Free Films, Educators Guide to Free Film Strips, Educators Guide to Free Tapes, and Scripts and Transcriptions (publications circulated to educators). Educators Progress Service, Randolph, Wisconsin 53956.

Gebbie House Magazine Directory (a listing of important house organs giving name, circulation, editor's name and kind of material wanted). National Research Bureau, 424 N. Third St., Burlington, Iowa 52601.

Index of Public Interest Groups (a listing of activist, special-interest and pressure groups). Foundation for Public Affairs, 1220 Sixteenth St. NW, Washington, D.C. 20036.

National Directory of Weekly Newspapers (a listing of U.S. weekly newspapers, including names of key personnel). National Newspaper Association, National Press Building, Washington, D.C. 20004.

O'Dwyer's Directory of Public Relations Firms. 271 Madison Ave., New York, N.Y. 10016.

Professionals' Guide to Public Relations Services (a listing of organizations which provide services needed by PR practitioners). Prentice-Hall, Inc. Englewood Cliffs, N.J. 07632.

P.R. Bluebook (a listing of PR firms and their clients). P.R. Publishing Co., P.O. Box 600, Exeter, N.H. 03833.

Standard Rate and Data Service Catalogues (a listing of all major advertising media with names of key personnel). Standard Rate and Data Service, 5201 Old Orchard Road, Skokie, Ill. 60076.

PERIODICALS USEFUL TO THE PUBLIC RELATIONS PRACTITIONER

Audio Visual Communications. 200 Madison Ave., New York, N.Y. 10016.

Business Screen. 402 W. Liberty Drive, Wheaton, Ill. 60187.

IABC News. 870 Market St., San Francisco, Cal. 94102.

Jack O'Dwyer's Newsletter. 271 Madison Ave., New York, N.Y. 10016.

P.R. Reporter. P.O. Box 600, Exeter, N.H. 03833.

Practical Public Relations. 31 Gibbs St., Rochester, N.Y. 14604.

Public Relations Journal. Public Relations Society of America, 845 Third Ave., New York, N.Y. 10022.

Public Relations News. 127 E. 80th St., New York, N.Y. 10021.

Public Relations Quarterly. 44 West Market St., Rhinebeck, N.Y. 12572.

Public Relations Review. College of Journalism, University of Maryland, College Park, Md. 20742.

Index

ABO 6431

Emerson College Library